VALIANT FOR TRUTH
THE LIFE OF CHESTER WILMOT, WAR CORRESPONDENT

NEIL MCDONALD is an historian and film critic. His books include *Kokoda Front Line: The amazing story of legendary Australian war cameraman Damien Parer* (1994, 2004, revised edition 2012). He is co-author with Peter Brune of *200 Shots*, an analysis of the visual evidence of Australian fighting on the Kokoda Track and Beachhead.

PETER BRUNE is bestselling author of *A Bastard of a Place: The Australians in Papua*; *Those Ragged Bloody Heroes: From the Kokoda Trail to Gona Beach 1942* and most recently *Descent into Hell: The fall of Singapore – Pudu and Changi – the Thai Burma railway*.

Chester studio portrait c. 1952 by Raymond Wilson. Courtesy Jane Wilmot Crane.

VALIANT FOR TRUTH

THE LIFE OF CHESTER WILMOT, WAR CORRESPONDENT

NEIL McDONALD
WITH PETER BRUNE

NEWSOUTH

To Phillip Knightley OA –
the first to tell the truth about war correspondents

A NewSouth book

Published by
NewSouth Publishing
University of New South Wales Press Ltd
University of New South Wales
Sydney NSW 2052
AUSTRALIA
newsouthpublishing.com

© Neil McDonald and Peter Brune 2016
First published 2016

10 9 8 7 6 5 4 3 2 1

This book is copyright. Apart from any fair dealing for the purpose of private study, research, criticism or review, as permitted under the Copyright Act, no part of this book may be reproduced by any process without written permission. Inquiries should be addressed to the publisher.

National Library of Australia
Cataloguing-in-Publication entry
Creator: McDonald, Neil, 1940– author.
Title: Valiant for truth : the life of Chester Wilmot, war correspondent / Neil McDonald, Peter Brune.
ISBN: 9781742235172 (hardback)
         9781742242583 (ebook)
         9781742248035 (epdf)
Notes: Includes bibliographical references and index.
Subjects: Wilmot, Chester, 1911–1954.
Journalists--Australia--Biography.
War correspondents--Biography.
World War, 1939–1945--Journalists--Biography.
Other Creators/Contributors:
Brune, Peter, 1951– author.
Dewey Number: 070.4092

Design Josephine Pajor-Markus
Cover design Xou Creative
Cover images FRONT With an Infantry Assault team across the canal, BBC war correspondent Chester Wilmot (left) broadcasts from an observation post on the roof of a home, The Netherlands, 1944. (Photo by George Silk/The LIFE Picture Collection/Getty Images.)
BACK Chester Wilmot in front of map of Europe c. 1952. (Courtesy Jane Wilmot Crane.)
Printed in China

All reasonable efforts were taken to obtain permission to use copyright material reproduced in this book, but in some cases copyright could not be traced. The author welcomes information in this regard.

This book is printed on paper using fibre supplied from plantation or sustainably managed forests.

CONTENTS

Abbreviations		*vii*
Preface		*1*
1	First things	*6*
2	The shop	*14*
3	Half-cocked college guys	*24*
4	Ashamed to be an Englishman	*41*
5	Two captains and a mister	*79*
6	A lot of little cuts first	*91*
7	I could 'ave been a blinkin' General	*105*
8	Caught in the open	*116*
9	A desire to seek the underlying causes	*150*
10	Sand in their shoes	*176*
11	We are slow to learn	*195*
12	Syd is coming	*224*
13	Unnecessary Australian graves	*241*
14	The freedom of the press	*265*
15	A dangerous subversive and a Communist	*290*
16	Such a complete victory	*305*

17	Broadcasting as an arm of warfare	*317*
18	Hello BBC! Hello BBC!	*340*
19	Viva BBC!	*369*
20	Unhappy phrases	*390*
21	So big was Wilmot's story	*404*
22	A rather different spectacle	*426*
23	Passing to the other side	*443*
Notes		*464*
List of maps		*475*
Bibliography		*476*
Index		*482*

ABBREVIATIONS

ADC	Aide-de-Camp
ABC	Australian Broadcasting Commission
ANGAU	Australian New Guinea Administrative Unit
AIF	Australian Imperial Force
AWM	Australian War Memorial
BBC	British Broadcasting Corporation
C-in-C	Commander-in-Chief
CO	Commanding Officer
COSSAC	Chief of Staff to Supreme Allied Commander
DOI	Department of Information
DSO	Distinguished Service Order
GHQ	General Headquarters
GOC	General Officer Commanding
LHQ	Land Forces Headquarters
MCN	Mike Charlie Nan (BBC mobile transmitter)
MCO	Maintenance Control Office
NUAUS	National Union of Australian University Students
NCO	Non-commissioned Officer
OC	Officer Commanding
OKW	Oberkommando der Wehrmacht (German Supreme Command of the Armed Forces)
RAF	Royal Air Force
SHAEF	Supreme Headquarters of the Allied Expeditionary Force

PREFACE

When a book title has the name of the author and underneath 'with', and another name following as we do here, it usually means that the second person subedited and formatted the copy, suggested cuts, acted as a sounding board and made suggestions as to structure. He might also have researched the maps and inserted the occasional explanatory paragraph. Important as this work is, it does not amount to being a co-author.

My old friend and colleague Peter Brune did all of the above. He suggested I cut back on my tendency to tell much of the early part of the narrative of Wilmot's early work as a correspondent through his dispatches. Certainly our subject wrote well and that, Peter insisted, could be seductive. Eventually I agreed.

After eight attempts to find an opening Peter came up with the idea of using the passages describing the flight of Wilmot's glider across the Channel and its landing in France from *The Struggle for Europe*.

For the chapters describing the Kokoda battles Peter Brune went even further. He became my collaborator. The command crisis in New Guinea was the only time Wilmot became involved directly in a military operation. Also, in the broadcast, 'And our troops were forced to withdraw', Wilmot left an indelible portrait of the

Australian withdrawal. Denied permission to use the troops' real names he employed their nicknames. I knew some of these men but Peter had interviewed them in depth, so he was able to use Wilmot's description to illuminate the experiences of these remarkable soldiers.

I had located General Sydney Rowell's ADC, Lieutenant Gordon Darling. He described how Wilmot wrote, at the General's request, a report on the campaign, and he (Darling) had given me a copy of his diary. Through the good offices of Stuart Braga I had also secured a copy of a fragment of the principal censor George Fenton's diary. This enabled the human, military and political story of Kokoda to be told as it has never been told before. In this context too, famed war photographer Damien Parer's intervention when he praised Rowell in his on-camera introduction to the newsreel *Kokoda Front Line!*, was especially significant, and of course, I was Damien's biographer. But Peter is an authority on the campaign itself, and if Wilmot's role was to be understood, it had to be placed in the wider political and military context. We had some great material but it could only be related by both of us. And that is what we did. Peter may not be the co-author of anything more than these chapters, but his collaboration here, together with his wise counsel throughout the writing has, I believe, enhanced *Valiant for Truth* immeasurably.

In our earlier work Peter and I have relished the challenge of using the oral history from participants in conjunction with official records, diaries, letters, stills and films. This is of course what we did when we co-wrote *200 Shots: Damien Parer, George Silk and the Australians at War in New Guinea*. Peter drew on his interviews with participants for *Those Ragged Bloody Heroes*; I used the interviews I had recorded with Parer's surviving friends and subjects for *War Cameraman: The Story of Damien Parer*, plus a lengthy interview with George Silk. And of course we both used conventional documentary sources. With Chester, however, I was too late – almost. I did meet Edith Wilmot, who first helped me long-distance from England with the Parer biography, but when she visited Australia she tactfully refused to read the passages in the manuscript alluding to Chester. Her daughter Caroline told me later that her mother was becoming confused because of the onset of Alzheimer's disease. But I was able to see what she must have been like when she met Chester. Edith's greatest contribution to *Valiant for Truth*, however, was to donate Chester's papers to the National Library of Australia, all fifty-five boxes of them. Although she alerted me to the donation, her decision came because of patient earlier negotiations by Graeme Powell, then Head of Manuscripts. This is not the first time Australian scholars have had reason to be grateful to this wise and patient man.

In spite of our very different politics I found Bob Santamaria delightful. He spoke with a clarity and objectivity that I also found in Chester's work. Santamaria gave me a participant's understanding of the debates of the period and Wilmot's role in student politics at Melbourne University in the 1930s. He was perceptive too about Ernest Scott, under whom he and Chester had studied history. 'Scott was a Whig historian who was very kind to individual Catholics', Santamaria said with a smile. I was looking forward to our next meeting when I saw the famous Catholic apologist's death notice in the *Sydney Morning Herald*.

I gained two contrasting impressions of Chester Wilmot's personality from Frank Gillard and James Aldridge. Aldridge was a war correspondent in the Middle East with Chester during 1941–42 and as well as his reports had written *Signed with Their Honour*, a fine novel about fliers in the Greek campaign. He found Wilmot always helpful but a little remote: 'I had no idea what he was like as a man'. I was able to tell him that Chester liked the book, which he thought was influenced by Hemingway. Aldridge agreed. 'Hemingway's was the only voice we had from the Great War.' Frank Gillard, whom I met in 1996 at his club in London, admired Wilmot greatly. A gracious English gentleman who had begun his life as a schoolteacher, Gillard gave me a unique insight into the establishment of 'War

Report' – the organisation that was to cover the Allied invasion of Europe. He also conveyed to me what it was like to have Chester Wilmot as a colleague. This complemented George Silk's description of how it felt to go into action with Wilmot.

On a more personal level Mary Kennehan gave me a sensitive account of her sister Therese Denny's affair with Chester and Therese's contribution to the writing of *The Struggle for Europe* when she worked as his assistant. Her son Bill Denny described his adventures with his Aunt Therese in 1970s London. JDB (Bruce) Miller told me about meeting Chester after his meeting with Prime Minister Curtin in the Great Hall of what is now the Old Parliament House. Bruce also provided a vivid description of what it was like using the equipment the ABC Broadcast Unit had brought back from the Middle East for outside broadcasts in Sydney. AGL (Alan) Shaw shared with me his memories of Chester Wilmot as Captain of Melbourne Grammar from the point of view of a boy in the junior school. Fortunately, as Wilmot was a major figure in my Parer book, I interviewed ABC General Manager Sir Charles Moses in 1983 about the feud between the broadcaster and Sir Thomas Blamey.

For all this, the two collections of Wilmot Papers are the principal sources for the life of Chester Wilmot. They are divided between the National Library of Australia in Canberra and the Liddell Hart Centre for Military Archives at King's College London. Wilmot left most of the papers connected with the writing of *The Struggle for Europe* to his friend Basil Liddell Hart. However the division is not a precise one. I found a report about British tactics in the Western Desert in Canberra that only made sense when I inspected the files in London. On the other hand, a series of delightful one- and two-line letters from Field Marshal Montgomery are to be found in Canberra. Getting the relevant material copied was enabled first by Gary Mackay, and then by my close friend Anne Dunne, who then took on the arduous task of putting the photographs on my computer.

Writing the book was an exhausting pleasure. Wilmot wrote

Preface

well but how much should you use? Are you missing something because you have not checked the context? You lived with anxiety. Then there were the other collections that had to be consulted. Most of the transcripts of Chester's ABC broadcasts are in the National Archives as is some vital correspondence. The story of the making of Wilmot's only surviving film *Sons of the Anzacs* is to be found in the Australian War Memorial. The documents relating to the setting up of 'War Report' are to be found in the BBC's Written Archives in Reading. The sound of his surviving broadcasts is in the ABC and BBC sound archives. It has been an arduous but exhilarating journey.

I must thank Jane Wilmot Crane OBE for making the stills from the family archives and Edith Wilmot's letters to Chester and her family available, and Fay Woodhouse, who shared with me her research on the University of Melbourne in the 1930s. The staffs of the National Library of Australia, The Liddell Hart Military Archive and BBC Written Records, and the Australian War Memorial were unfailingly helpful not just to me but to Peter Brune when he was with me in England, and Debra Holland when she was tracking some final pieces of the puzzle at the National Library in 2014.

It was a pleasure to have Debra Holland, who was my research assistant on the Parer biography and my good friend Clare Mok, to help with final revisions.

I am very grateful to Neil Thomas for his ongoing support and advice, but most of all, for his sensitive, professional editing, and his unerring eye for detail.

Finally, I owe much to my publisher, Phillipa McGuinness, Emily Stewart and all at NewSouth Publishing, for their faith, enthusiasm and professionalism in seeing Chester Wilmot's story into print.

Neil McDonald
Sydney

1

FIRST THINGS

There is soft rain on the perspex of the cockpit and all we can see is the guiding light of the tug, until a break in the clouds gives us a brief glimpse of the south coast from which the invasion fleet has long since sailed. Half way across the Channel it clears again, and we can see the dark, stormy water, flecked with the wake of countless ships. More cloud, and we are flying blind again at 2,500 feet. The glider begins to pitch and bucket in the gusty wind that threatens to sunder the tow-rope and leave us drifting helpless in the sky.

Does the enemy know we are coming? What will the flak be like? Are there mines and booby-traps as well as obstructions on the landing-zone? Will the paratroopers have had time to clear it? Will a battle be raging there already as we come in to land? Will the pilots ever find it in this weather?

If these thoughts are also running through the minds of the other 26 officers and men sitting in the dark fuselage of the glider, they show no sign of it. Above the steady roar of the wind beating on the glider's wooden surface, you can hear a snatch of song or a gust of laughter.

Three o'clock: half an hour to go. The clouds clear for a minute and we are warned of the closeness of the coast – and another tug and glider which has cut across our bow, perilously near.

Suddenly the darkness is stabbed with streaks of light, red and yellow tracer from the flak guns on the coast. There are four sharp flashes between us and the tug and then another that seems to be inside the glider itself. It is, but we don't realize at first that we have been hit, for the shell has burst harmlessly well aft.

Over the coast we run out of cloud and there below us is the white curving strand of France and, mirrored in the dim moonlight, the twin ribbons of water we are looking for – the Orne and the Canal. The tug has taken us right to the target.

Soon one of them [the pilot] turns and calls back to us – 'I'm letting go, hold tight.' As it leaves the tug the glider seems to stall and to hover like a hawk about to strike. The roar of the wind on the wooden skin drops to a murmur with the loss of speed and there is a strange and sudden silence. We are floating in a sky of fathomless uncertainty.

We are jerked back to reality by a sharp, banking turn and we are diving steeply, plunging down into the darkness. As the ground rises up to meet us, the pilots catch a glimpse of the pathfinders' lights and the white dusty road and the square Norman church-tower beside the landing zone. The stick comes back and we pull out of the dive with sinking stomachs and bursting ears. The glider is skimming the ground now with plenty of speed on and is about to land when out of the night another glider comes straight for us. We 'take-off' again, lift sharply and it sweeps under our nose. The soil of France rushes past beneath us and we touch-down with a jolt on a ploughed field. It is rough and soft, but the glider careers on with grinding brakes and creaking timbers, mowing down 'Rommel's asparagus' and snapping off five stout posts in its path. There is an ominous sound of splitting wood and rending fabric and we brace ourselves for the shock as the glider goes lurching and bumping until with a violent swerve to starboard it finally comes to rest scarred but intact, within a hundred yards of its intended landing place.

It is 3.32 a.m. We are two minutes late. Shouts and cheers echo down the glider, and a voice from the dark interior cries out, 'This is it, chum. I told yer we wouldn't 'av ter swim.'[1]

From midnight on 6 June 1944, three airborne divisions – two Americans and one British – were landing in France as the vanguard of the greatest amphibious invasion in human history. The British division was the 6th Airborne, and its task was the capture of bridgeheads over the river between the sea and the town of Caen. The above account was written by BBC war correspondent Chester Wilmot, in the glider, and proudly wearing his 6th Airborne Division red beret. This dramatic landing was the climax of a career that had seen Wilmot report and chronicle a significant part of the Allied experience of World War II.

Wilmot was one of the most famous broadcasters during the war. From the early 1940s, his had been an instantly recognisable voice in Australia and Europe, when radio was the most powerful mass medium in the world. As reporter and commentator his broadcasts were uniquely trusted by listeners to the ABC and BBC from the time his voice had been heard on both networks during the Siege of Tobruk. He became the star of the BBC's 'War Report', the special program set up to cover the Allied invasion of Europe.

Wilmot covered just about every kind of military confrontation: the rapid mobilised advance in the Western Desert and France; set-piece defences, notably at Tobruk (the subject of his first book); the fighting withdrawal; open and jungle fighting; and, most spectacularly, airborne assaults.

At a time when reporters were expected to be patriots and propagandists, Wilmot was unique. Although a patriot to his bootstraps, he strove to be objective, always seeking the underlying causes of the events he was reporting and always prepared, within limits, to criticise. The BBC admired his skill at analysis but he was equally adept at straight description. Above all, with one notable exception, he won the respect, then the trust, of commanders in the field and at GHQ, together with the affection of the ordinary soldiers he persuaded to tell their stories into his microphone.

Wilmot is one of the very few correspondents to have directly influenced the events he was covering, most famously in New Guinea, but also in Europe where he became a confidant of Field Marshal Montgomery. His last book, *The Struggle for Europe*, published in 1952, became the definitive statement of the British case in the Anglo-American debate over Allied strategy and diplomacy. This is his story.

* * * *

It all began on 21 June 1911 – during the coldest night his mother Jane Wilmot (known in the family as 'Janie') could ever remember. Chester was born into modest affluence. The family lived in Boort, a house named after a town twenty miles from a family property owned by Chester's grandfather. This 'new' Boort was a rambling colonial-style home with wide verandahs and long French doors, in the comfortable Melbourne suburb of Brighton. Surrounding the dwelling were orchards, a miniature fernery shaped like a gully, the plants seeming to grow wild; old trees, flowerbeds and wide lawns.

The new baby's name was to be Reginald William Winchester Wilmot, almost the same as his father's (Reginald William Edward). To avoid confusion it was quickly shortened to Chester. Later this was to give him a useful opening line as a compere of Melbourne University reviews: 'My name is Reginald William Winchester Wilmot, but you can call me Chester.' The announcement would be followed by gales of laughter.

Chester was the first boy in what had been hitherto a family of girls: his sisters, Louise, Jean and Nancy were twelve, ten and nine years old respectively.

When Chester was a boy his father, a sporting journalist nicknamed 'Bung', regularly took him to football and cricket matches. Naturally Chester wanted to play cricket, the game that had come to mean so much to his father, but while he was to become a fine test match commentator, he was only moderately talented.

The Wilmot family moved from Brighton to a two-storey house at Mont Albert when Chester was thirteen. He was given a room upstairs, with a view of the open paddocks and the orchards, and a porch was made into a sleep-out. The ground floor verandah was set aside for his sister Nancy, who was in the first stages of TB. This had been the ostensible reason for the move, to get Nan away from Brighton's damp sea air to higher ground. But there is reason to believe the family was almost as worried about Chester.

It would be called hay fever, or sometimes a cold, to make it sound innocuous, but the descriptions of Chester's symptoms as a boy and a man are those of a chronic asthmatic; tickles in the throat, fits of coughing, breathlessness, wheezing; a potentially crippling handicap for someone who expected to achieve the glittering prises in law or business that had eluded his father when he'd taken up journalism. Both as a boy and a man, he did his best to act as though the asthma was a trifle. In this he was supported by his family. This is the only explanation for an extraordinary expedition Chester undertook with another boy when he was fourteen. Somehow he persuaded his parents to let him go on a walking tour to visit some relatives in Gippsland, camping at night, living off the land and shooting rabbits and hares for food. The idea could have come straight out of a John Buchan novel; and for a boy with a possibly lethal affliction, it was highly dangerous. What's more it was a near-run thing. Chester proved to be a terrible shot and the boys nearly starved. Somehow they stumbled over a terrified hare and killed it, and that provided them with enough food, together with some supplies they were carrying, to get them to their destination. Later it all became a family legend but it was really a perilous gamble. Clearly his parents understood that Chester needed to do something like that to give him confidence and prove his independence.

He was soon to need this new confidence. The notes taken from family members in the 1950s are a little vague and Chester himself only alludes to it briefly in one of his letters, but it is clear that he missed almost a year of school. His parents had gone overseas to the USA to visit Jean, now married and living in Boston and then to England to see Janie's relatives, leaving Chester with relations in South Yarra. They returned to find Chester seriously ill with asthma. As a result he missed his Leaving Certificate exam and had to take it the following year. This long absence from school helps to explain why Chester was so widely read. His letters make no great display of erudition but the range of his knowledge and interests is extraordinary. So it is easy to imagine him reading in bed on his balcony as he gradually recovered. Perhaps he went downstairs to spend time with Nan, who was by now gravely ill with the TB that was to take her life not long after. Certainly he spent a lot of time with Nancy in her last days. She is remembered as being ethereally beautiful, gentle and uncomplaining in her last illness. When Bung told Chester she had died he said 'O Father, thank goodness I knew her.' He sat for his matriculation exam the same day. When the results were posted they read, 'RWW Wilmot – Pass'. Although Chester never wrote about his grief at Nancy's death the shock was probably worse for him than for his parents. With the optimism of youth he had expected her to recover.

Nonetheless the late 1920s and early 1930s were a happy time for Chester. He went to dancing school, where he seems to have been a great success with the girls. Being brought up with three sisters had its advantages. Janie persuaded him to cut some of his dance classes and to go to the school debating club. When Chester complained that he had no one to debate with she replied, 'Debate with me'. So mother and son went at it with gusto: the beginning of Chester's dramatic public speaking style. Before long he was the leading light of Melbourne Grammar's inter-school debating team. A childhood friend who had first met Chester during family holidays at the beach represented Scotch College against Melbourne Grammar in debating, and remembered him as 'very powerful' and wished they had someone as good on their team. The adjudicator was a certain RG Menzies whose exercise of his wit at the expense of the boys was mildly rebuked in the *Melburnian*'s report of the debate. Chester was to encounter Menzies many times in later years as prime minister and opposition leader and always found him amiable. Bung and Menzies were both members of the Savage Club while Janie's women's club hosted a luncheon for the politician when he was Victorian Attorney-General. But Chester never shared the Melbourne establishment's high opinion of Menzies's ability and seems never to have quite trusted him. Could these doubts have begun with an urbane politician making jokes at the expense of grim-faced boys tensely waiting for his decision?

There is no record of anything but the most formal relationship between Chester and the Headmaster of Melbourne Grammar, RS 'Lofty' Franklin, who can be seen towering over his prefects in the school photographs. But he was a fervent believer in the traditional classical education. Perhaps Chester's insistence as a university politician on the importance of a liberal education reflected his old headmaster's influence.

By the end of 1929 Chester had matriculated and passed the Leaving Certificate. He had also been made a prefect. Franklin then suggested an arrangement to Chester that is understandable only within the public school tradition. WAT Samball, a famous 'oar', had been offered the captaincy if he would return to school for the first term and row for the school so they could win the Head of the River. Following the anticipated victory, he would then leave, as he would have turned twenty. Chester would then take over as school captain. It was an arrangement that reflected little credit on the school or its headmaster, but Chester accepted the proposal probably because he, like Franklin, wanted Melbourne Grammar to win the boat race. By all accounts he proved to be an excellent captain. To ensure the school turned out to support the sporting teams Chester instituted roll calls on Friday afternoons when inter-school matches were played. Alan Shaw, who was in the junior school during Chester's time as captain, remembered an imposing, authoritative figure with great energy.

At the end of the year he won the RE Millear Scholarship 1931–1933 to Trinity College, Melbourne University, the same college which his father had attended and from which he had been expelled thirty years before.

2

THE SHOP

Chester was on holiday surfing on the southern coast beaches when he received a letter any son would be proud to get from his father. Written in Bung's execrable handwriting, for which the old man was endlessly apologising, it began by congratulating the young man on his success at Melbourne Grammar: 'You have done all that could be expected of you, you have been a source of pride to your family, you have done credit and brought honour to your school and you have with it a record with which any boy might well be proud.' Then after more in a similar vein, he raised the age-old parental fear that the 'new ideas' Chester might encounter at university

> will lead you towards extreme views. This is to be avoided
> for the greatest asset of the successful man is moderation ...
> The religion, the politics, the business ideas, of your predecessors
> have been well tested. If in this testing there have been faults
> then by all means remedy those faults but let the change be
> deliberate as well.[1]

By 1931 the Depression had reached Australia. For many, capitalism seemed to have failed, which was why a very conservative man like Bung Wilmot was preaching the virtues of gradual change. He was, if anything, even more worried that Chester might be turned into an atheist or agnostic by his studies of psychology or philosophy.

> The Christian religion is based on justice, love, honour, fair dealing between man and man … The student of Philosophy is apt to be led aside by new nostrums; but if these are tested and weighed in the balance by the teaching of Christ, the new knowledge will only prove more and more the truth of the original gospel.[2]

We don't know exactly Chester's response to this well-meant advice. Certainly he respected his father's sincere faith. Years later he recalled how at each of the family's birthdays Bung would read Psalm 103. 'It was never intoned, Father had a good voice and it was delivered with great sincerity.'[3] They were, of course, Anglicans and more or less regular churchgoers. Like many Protestants of the period the family was bitterly anti-Catholic. 'Oh Chester was very bigoted,' Bob Santamaria told the author. 'He would constantly assail me with stories about the Renaissance Popes, as a result I found myself defending the actions of people I'd never have supported otherwise'.[4]

Nevertheless he and the young Catholic became friends. 'Chester was never a fop – he was a bloke,' Santamaria said.[5] And while Wilmot did become a socialist he never embraced the fashionable 1930s Marxism and communism of the university Labour Club.

He did, however, embrace every aspect of undergraduate life. Not only was Chester going to get honours in history and law, he was going to be a student politician, represent the university in debating, be secretary of the Athletics Association, and become a champion hurdler. The latter was a severe trial to his new girlfriend Ann Elder, as Chester refused to go out at night, because he was in strict training. Predictably Chester proved as poor a hurdler as he was a cricketer and his and Ann's relationship returned to normal.

University life in the early 1930s at Melbourne University was at once privileged and deprived. There were only three thousand students and most came from the public schools. Activities centred on the Gothic Wilson Hall and the quadrangle where the administration and Law School were located. Nearby was the mock Tudor of the yellow sandstone Arts building, the red brick of the Medical School, and the Edwardian baroque of the Teachers' Training College. The residential colleges – Trinity, Newman, and Ormond – were set in spacious grounds. According to Chester the Warden of Trinity ended his address of welcome with 'I must warn you gentlemen, that three things are absolutely sacrosanct: the fire extinguishers, the College cows and the young ladies of Janet Clark Hall.'[6] Students dressed more formally then, sometimes in suits, more often in sports clothes. Gowns were almost invariably worn by academics when delivering lectures. 'It would have been an insult to your students not to,' one contemporary observed.[7] Students were addressed as 'Mister' and responded with 'Sir' or their lecturer's title. Still, for all this gracious formality Melbourne University was seriously flawed.

Half the books in the library were uncatalogued. These were located on the second floor and only a few students were allowed to use them. The Union dining room for male students had formerly been an old museum that had been painted with a special paint that was supposed to lower the temperature. But the paint tended to peel and fall into the soup. There were few other amenities on campus, so most student discussions took place in nearby cafes, or in coffee shops and pubs around the Victorian State Library.

Although students were constantly in and out of Melbourne, the university was separated from the life of the city, even though most leaders of the Melbourne Establishment had been educated there. Popularly known as 'The Shop', the term reflected an indifference that was reflected in miserly funding and a lack of basic amenities.

Professors were their own secretaries, did their own administration, and undertook most of the marking as well as the bulk of the teaching. For all of the leisured charm of the campus there was, Chester found, little sense of a community.

Conditions were a little better at Trinity – for one thing there was a bar – but there is reason to believe Chester found the restrictions of college life onerous. Certainly when he lost his scholarship (for failing to get honours in Latin), he worked hard the next year to regain it, but then, honour satisfied, he decided not to return.

By 1932 Chester was writing for the student newspaper *Farrago* and was secretary of the debating club. He was also writing for the *Sun*. Rather than use their own reporters the papers hired students to cover events on campus. It was at this time that Chester became involved in many of the great causes célèbres of the university. He covered political debates – and the occasional confrontations between opposing factions – and became friendly with both the Professor of History, Ernest Scott, and the newly appointed lecturer in political philosophy, Macmahon Ball.

On Monday 2 May the University Debating Society of which Chester was secretary held its regular meeting. The subject was 'That Modern Democracy is a Failure'. In the chair was Professor Kenneth Bailey from the Law Faculty. First speaker for the affirmative was Alan Nicholls and Frank Shann led for the negative. Sam White, an avowed Marxist, spoke fifth. He had just stated that 'fascism and communism were each the spearhead of their respective classes' when a series of loud explosions from some Chinese fire crackers came from the back of the hall.[8] Then a flying wedge of medical students from the front row led by 'Weary' Dunlop and Vin Youngman made for the dais. They seized White and carried him through a side door into the corridor and outside only to encounter a crowd of unemployed men armed with batons and broken bottles. 'We kept White between us and them,' Dunlop told his biographer, 'only to run into two policemen.'[9] Rather shamefacedly they explained it was just a student prank. The police told them they could go ahead after they had dispersed the crowd. But White managed to elude his captors and headed back to the lecture hall. Meanwhile Chester, Ball and Shann, had managed to restore order. A dishevelled White, by now something of a hero, finished his speech to 'sympathetic' applause.

The next day a special issue of *Farrago* appeared with descriptions of events at the debating society and an editorial denouncing the Labour Club. Soon after a mob of students 'captured' White and his friend Vellacott and forced them to 'embrace the lake'. Pitched in at the same time, probably by mistake, was Bob Santamaria. 'It wasn't the water that was the problem,' he told the author, 'it was getting the vile smell of the refuse in the lake out of your clothes.'[10] In a photograph of the incident Chester can be seen in the back row, wearing a hat, taking notes. Partly because of stories he and the other student correspondents filed with the Melbourne papers, the ducking of the radical students was fiercely debated on and off campus. Chester came to believe that the real issue was not White's opinions or his 'boorishness', or even the Labour Club's skilful exploitation of the whole affair; it was freedom of speech.

By Chester's second year at university he had fallen deeply in love with Kate Elder. They first met when Chester was captain of Melbourne Grammar, and started going out together at university. She is remembered as a fascinating girl with many admirers. But from a rather sad letter she wrote in the 1950s Chester was her favourite. An engagement was contemplated. 'You mustn't rush things' was his mother's predictable response.[11] Then it was over and Kate married another admirer. From some guarded notes in the Wilmot papers it seems Chester believed his mother intervened to break up the romance. Just how Janie managed it is not known. Certainly the arguments between mother and son at this time were beginning to worry Bung. 'Your mother is not always wrong,' he wrote to Chester from Colombo, where he was covering cricket test matches.[12] James Smibert, a close friend, remembered walking around Melbourne with a distraught Chester after the break-up. Later there was a brief affair, possibly with someone who came from the wrong side of town, or perhaps was of the wrong religion. Chester, as one would expect, was very discreet.

It was about this time that Bung covered and then wrote the history of the notorious 'Bodyline tour'. When *Defence of the Ashes* was published Chester was already what was known at the time as a 'sporting casual' filing occasional stories on university matches. Then the *Argus* decided to launch a new afternoon newspaper, the *Star*. Chester was offered the job of Melbourne University correspondent. At the same time he was to write a regular column on schools and amateur sport. With his first cheque he bought a second-hand copy of *Who's Who*, looked up the birthdays of prominent people, and wrote potted biographies – 'first edition fillers' – on the appropriate days.

Soon after Chester bought himself a second-hand car. According to George Johnston, who was then a cadet journalist on the *Argus*, 'Chester … embraced journalism with a gusty good-humoured vitality and a terrifying exuberance. Everybody liked him although there were times when his boyish enthusiasms were almost overwhelming.'[13]

Chester's contemporaries believed that the journalism and his extra-curricular activities with the SRC, debating and *Farrago* (more journalism) were the reason he failed to achieve an honours degree in history. To be sure they took up a great deal of time, but Chester worked very hard at his studies, and as is obvious from just about everything he wrote from 1937 on, he gained a great deal from his university courses. Why Chester failed to achieve the kind of academic success he had at school seems to be more complicated.

Two great figures dominated Wilmot's academic life: W Macmahon Ball and Professor Ernest Scott. Scott was coming to the end of his career when Chester encountered him; 'Mac' Ball, only nine years Chester's senior, was almost a contemporary. He was a charismatic lecturer. Although never a Marxist, Ball had a lively awareness of economic forces, and was at this time virtually a socialist. He made no secret of his distaste for fascism and Nazism but never insisted on conformity. Ball awarded a valuable prize to Bob Santamaria for an essay defending Mussolini. 'There was no two ways about yours being the best essay,' he told Santamaria years later.[14] Tall, erect and handsome, with a gentle, gracious manner and a light, pleasant voice, Ball exercised an enormous influence on his students. Chester was no exception. Soon he was spending long hours in Ball's office discussing world politics. The close analysis of factories and cooperative farms Chester undertook during his European tour in 1938, and later as a BBC reporter owes much to Ball's influence, and Ball eventually became a great admirer of *The Struggle for Europe*.

Ernest Scott was very different. If Ball was aggressively modern, 'Scotty' was emphatically a 'Whig' historian. 'Behind him I could see the shadows of Macaulay and Trevelyan,' Bob Santamaria recalled.[15] Coming as Santamaria did from the elite Catholic school St Kevin's — then only four rooms — Scott's interpretation of British history as a progress towards constitutional monarchy and the established Church of England would have been alien to the young man. Nevertheless, 'I soon found that for all his Protestant bias Scott could be immensely kind to individual Catholics,' Santamaria told the author.[16] Chester on the other hand would have found Scott's attitudes only too familiar. The aim of one textbook used at Melbourne Grammar, *History of England* by Arthur D Innes MA, was 'to enable [the student] to realize how the British Race has become the most free and most law-abiding in the world, how the British Nation achieved the greatest Empire the world has known.'[17]

Scott was never quite as crude as that, but his three books on Pacific exploration that earned him the Melbourne chair — *The Life of Captain Matthew Flinders R.N.* (1914), *Laperouse* (1912) and *Terre*

Napoléon (1910) – were fine examples of colonial and imperial history. An honours student like Chester studying under Scott

> learned the history of ancient Greece, the Roman republic and its imperial record, the political history of Britain from the Norman Conquest, the European Middle Ages, Renaissance and Enlightenment, the rise of the nation-state and the rivalry of the great powers, the expansion of Europe and the extension of its control across the rest of the world.[18]

When Scott became professor he revolutionised the methods of instruction. Previously, lectures were a dry recitation of facts, each one part of a continuing story students were expected to memorise. Every Scott lecture, however, was a public address, complete in itself, delivered with the style and panache of an experienced public speaker. Ironically, for all his apparent ease, he suffered agonies of stage fright before each of his public appearances. By the 1930s, when Chester encountered him, 'Scotty' was a character. 'Short, plump, balding, his moustache tobacco stained, but the eyes still bright and alert, he distinguished himself from his more conventional colleagues by his dapper appearance, a dark blue chalk stripe suit worn with a wing collar and a polka dot bow tie.'[19] Another distinction was the absence of an academic gown. He was the only professor without even a pass degree who had been appointed solely because of his learning. Above all he taught historical enquiry. Every student essay in the honours course had to be based on original research.

Chester revelled in such an approach to learning. As a result, for the rest of his life he was always at home with primary sources, going beyond the written and printed word to pioneer oral history. In addition, most of the Whig historians, Scott included, were masters of narrative. They tended to emphasise the drama, and often indulged their prejudices, but it did make for lively writing.

Chester proved to be an excellent narrative writer, never indulged his prejudices and, as reporter and historian, excelled at research and analysis. He would also have known that the greatest of the Whig historians, Lord Macaulay, frequently visited the sites of the battles he was going to describe in his history, a practice enthusiastically adopted by Chester as a reporter and historian.

Another area in which Chester employed the research techniques he learned from Scott was debating. One team-mate wondered why someone as clever as Chester worked so hard. But he did, and was in the Melbourne University debating teams of 1933, 1934 and 1935. It was through his debating that he met Alan Benjamin, a tall, elegant law student, who as a speaker excelled at witty repartee – but not so good at argument, Santamaria recalled.[20] They, plus Kevin Nicholls, were all trying out for the inter-university team when Nicholls made a brilliant opening speech. Chester was so impressed that he sent a note to the selectors suggesting Nicholls lead the team. The selectors took Chester's advice but also included Chester, Alan Benjamin and BA Santamaria. The final was to take place in Adelaide, and on the morning of the last debate the team was taken, perhaps with malice aforethought, to a wine tasting. The wines, Santamaria recalled, came in no particular order. 'I seem to remember the port coming first. Afterwards I had to go back to where we were staying to sleep it off.'[21] When it was time to go to the debate he found that all he had prepared was the peroration. Hoping to improvise, to his horror when he was called on to speak, all Santamaria could think of to say was this oration. He heard Chester mutter from behind him 'he's going to break down'. Then to everyone's relief he found himself expanding on the argument and triumphantly filled his time.

Among the audience in the university refectory was Edith Irwin. 'I first saw Chester speaking for the winning team during the final,' she was to write. 'I still have a clear memory of that vibrant voice and bulky figure. The rhetorical fluency of the practiced debater, the complete confidence in his ability to dominate an audience, a style where a hammer's blow was more natural than a rapier's thrust, all came easily to him.'[22]

There is another image of Chester from about the same time. Geoffrey Littleton, who lived four doors from the Wilmot house in Mont Albert and was a fellow student at Melbourne University, remembered a substantial man with flashing blue eyes and great presence, usually walking quickly and whistling to himself, who always seemed to be on his way somewhere.

But exactly where young Chester was headed in 1935 was still uncertain.

3

HALF-COCKED COLLEGE GUYS

Late in March 1935, Chester was invited to meet Raymond Priestly, the new Vice Chancellor. The University Council had at last decided to appoint a salaried administrative head and one of the first things Priestly wanted to do was to see all the university press correspondents. Wilmot was the last of the three students representing the Melbourne papers to be interviewed. After their meeting Priestly wrote in his diary: 'They all seem to be decent chaps.'[1] Chester was now enrolled for his LLB but still writing for the *Star* and was still active in university politics. Priestly's arrival was to give his last years as a student much-needed direction.

Possibly because he had a more varied background than most educational administrators, the new Vice Chancellor believed the university had to be more than a degree shop, a view reflected in an article Chester wrote for the *Star* a few days after their first meeting. Priestly had been on both the Shackleton (1907–09) and Scott (1910–13) Antarctic expeditions, and had won a Military Cross in the Great War before graduating from Christ's College Cambridge and being elected a Fellow of Clare College. From the outset he had been appalled at the conditions in which the students at Melbourne University were expected to study. The state of the buildings was bad enough, but the lavatories 'were not worthy of a third rate slum'.² The main problems were a lack of government funding and the indifference of the Melbourne business community to the needs of the university. Inevitably this was fuelled by the constant 'exposés' by papers like the *Argus* of left-wing influences on campus. Priestly, however, probably felt his main problems came from the conservatives rather than from the woolly-minded Marxists. Twice drunken mobs had broken up Labour Club, Council Against War and Fascism meetings, using tear gas obtained from the Melbourne University Rifles. Then the medical students published an outrageously offensive issue of *Speculum* full of gross anatomical jokes that were harmless enough but bound to cause offence in a Melbourne still very close to the Victorian era.

Priestly believed that freedom of speech was essential for any university worthy of the name, but scandals like this only made his position more difficult. Chester blamed the narrowness of the courses in medicine, not to mention engineering, for these problems. This was not arts student arrogance. Both medicine and engineering involved long hours of drudgery which made outbursts like the *Speculum* affair and the Sam White ducking inevitable.

Early in 1936, Priestly embarked on an overseas tour to undertake a survey of British, American, Canadian and South African universities. Meanwhile, Chester was elected President of the Students' Representative Council. He stayed clear of the increasingly bitter debate over the Spanish Civil War. He sympathised with the Republicans and almost certainly knew about the antics of some members of the Campions (the newly formed Catholic society), who at beach parties would march around chanting pro-Franco marching songs. But the pro-Republican cause in Australia had been dominated by the communists, and Chester was already well aware of Stalin's persecutions in Russia, and the excesses on both sides in the Civil War. Still, he refused to support the Nationalists in any of the intervarsity debates in which he was involved. In his diaries, Chester's main criticisms were levelled at the 'neutrality' of Britain and France, and the intervention in support of Franco by Hitler and Mussolini.

Meanwhile, he concentrated on raising money for the new Union building using his father's contacts in the city, plus, according to the 1950s biographical notes, veiled threats to publish the names of reluctant donors in the *Star*. Chester also threw himself into organising a university fete to raise money for the 'University Review' for which he was writing much of the material. Anzac Day was celebrated in fine style with a piano recital in the Wilson Hall and Chester reciting Pericles's oration at the end of the Peloponnesian War.

No sooner had Priestly returned than there was a new free speech crisis. The Reverend A Penry Evans in an address to the Congregational Union attacked the 'anti-God communist activities' at the university. 'Anti-God Communists … are concentrating on the youth at the University,' the Reverend insisted, adding darkly 'the influences sometimes come from extraordinary quarters'.[3] Always anti-university at this time, the *Argus* printed its report under the headline 'Nefarious Influences at the University'. Priestly used his welcome home reception to reply: 'A university should be a place of free thought, ready discussion and free speech. Thought in a university should be more liberal and conservative than the general thought of the community.'[4]

Four days after the original attack, Chester called an SRC meeting to debate the issue. Over eight hundred students attended. They passed a motion supporting the Vice Chancellor that was published in the *Argus* the next day. It is not hard to see Chester's hand in the drafting:

> That this SRC affirms its unqualified support of the stand taken by the Vice Chancellor … in defense [*sic*] of intellectual freedom in the University.

That the maintenance of the principle of free speech, research and expression is fundamental to any university.

That by the impartial treatment of controversial subjects in the spirit of science and not of propaganda this principle does not result in practice in the subversion of students by "nefarious influences". Such influences have no more support inside the university than outside it.[5]

The following day Chester called a further SRC meeting to counter headlines that made it appear that the university supported General Franco. A motion was passed 'to dissociate itself from any such expression of opinion'.[6] Faced with this, the other Melbourne papers rallied to support the university. All of this seemed to bring the aggrieved cleric around, and Priestly and the Reverend Evans made peace at a luncheon on 3 November. The fete and pageant that had been planned since the middle of the year were a great success, and Chester, to the great relief of his family, passed his exams and was now BA, LLB. However, Chester's involvement with Melbourne University was not over.

In October 1936, Priestly had met with his opposite number at the University of Sydney, Dr RS Wallace, to finalise the agenda for the first Australian and New Zealand Universities' Congress. They also decided to invite students from each university to send representatives and to 'collogue together by themselves'.[7] Priestly then approached Chester to develop the project. The new law graduate agreed, even though one would have expected him to be anxious to complete his articles and begin practising his profession. But it was clear Chester really did not want to become a lawyer. He was already a journalist like his father. This was something Bung dreaded even though he was proud of the new part-time job Chester had with the ABC hosting a series of actuality broadcasts from locations such as the local fire station. This prestigious assignment from the university gave Chester time to take stock. Another reason was the high regard he had for the new Vice Chancellor. 'You have no idea what a marvelous [sic] man Priestly is,' he wrote to Jean. 'He has an amazing power of inspiring those around him to work and a most prodigious capacity for work himself ... already he has worked wonders.'[8]

Nearly a year later in a family letter from Britain, Chester mentioned that he had worked with Priestly for three years, but still didn't know him. But if their relationship was a formal one there was considerable mutual respect. It probably dated from the time when an exhausted Priestly was addressing a meeting of students and found himself unable to continue and Chester stepped in and tactfully retrieved the situation.

Chester arranged the student conference almost single handed. 'I can't help feeling that the NUAUS is my creation,' he was to say later.[9] The SRCs of Melbourne, Sydney, Adelaide, Queensland and Western Australia all met for the first time at the universities conference. On the first day Wilmot presented a paper, 'The Relationship Between Students and University Authorities: A Plea for Greater Co-operation'. By all accounts Chester gave quite a speech that reflected all his ambitions since he had enrolled at 'The Shop', in Santamaria's words '[he was] still gilded with the captaincy of Melbourne Grammar'.[10]

On the last day the Australian Universities Students' Conference resolved to represent all Australian students nationally and internationally. The conference then approved a debating tour of America, England and Japan by representatives of the new NUAUS. Chester Wilmot and Alan Benjamin were chosen by both the conference and Melbourne's SRC to make up the AUS and University of Melbourne Debating team. It was exactly the opportunity Chester needed. It gave him an entrée all over the world and the chance to practise his journalism. Priestly also more than hinted that he would like Chester to become head of external studies on his return. With this in mind, Chester decided to 'investigate student affairs abroad on behalf of the Union'.[11] An official letter of introduction was secured from the Prime Minister, Joe Lyons. At the same time Chester received briefings from the Department of External Affairs for the debates. In return Lyons asked him to report back on the countries he visited. The exact status of these reports is uncertain. Certainly he and Alan were already considerably more than inter-varsity debaters.

★ ★ ★ ★

Chester and Alan were roused by 'two university fellows' back from a Japan–America conference at Stanford University and taken to lunch. The Japanese were friends of one of Chester's many overseas contacts and the meeting was part of the two Australians' plan to collect as much information about educational and political issues as possible. Over lunch Chester recorded in his diary:

Sunday, 12 September 1937: Japan.

When they found that we wanted them to speak out ... they gave us their real views ... They said frankly the rest of the world has virtually closed its doors to our manufactured goods, we find it difficult to get the necessary raw materials; we must have markets, but we have no colonies or 'economic reserves,' China is our natural market and we intend to make it our actual market ... A simple thesis ... and a realistic one – one that can only be attacked on moral grounds, or on the ground that in any case it does not pay. But Japan is as yet too young a nation to realise that. They are still living in a mental age in which WAR IS GLORIOUS.[12]

Chester's allusion to Japan's 'mental age' was anything but condescending. His diary continues:

> Are we very much older? Would we not whoop for another Imperialist war, as we did 20 years ago? Would we not clothe brutality and a battle for POWER and markets in the holy garb of a War to end War – to make the World safe for democracy – and save humanity and civilization, and then at the end make another Versailles, in which we do in the name of Justice, exactly what Japan is doing today? Reflecting on the past does not fill one with much moral complacency in criticising the Japanese today. The only thing to do is to condemn the whole lot, and if you do that it leads you perilously close to Marxian conclusions, as the only solution; and I would hate to think they are the solution![13]

The tour had begun on 10 July 1937, when Alan and Chester boarded the SS *Changte*, one of the ships sailing up the coast of Australia and on to the Philippines. Two days later they were berthed in Sydney Harbour. As well as the obligatory visit to the University of Sydney – Chester found the Sydney quadrangle far better than Melbourne's – there was also a meeting with ABC General Manager Charles Moses. 'He kept me waiting for half an hour,' Chester wrote, 'but when I did [see him] it was satisfactory.'[14]

While Moses couldn't guarantee there would be a job waiting for Chester on his return, if he did the BBC training course when he was in London, this would make him very valuable, and Moses guaranteed that if he was still general manager there would be a good job for Chester with the ABC eventually. At the time Chester thought this was 'eyewash'.[15] Five years later the ABC General Manager's support for Chester was to prove vital.

After debates in Sydney and Brisbane, the two friends sailed for the Philippines and their first international contest. The first encounter was at the Ateneo de Manila Auditorium, a huge venue that held 1500 seated. Chester and Alan were astonished to find every seat filled and three hundred standing. It was a hot and steamy night and the Australians were not at their best. The Filipinos' interpretation of the topic that democracy had failed because it was not government by the people took them by surprise, and they won the debate with a majority verdict. Nevertheless Wilmot was pronounced 'brilliant' in the local press report. 'All baloney,' Chester noted, 'we were well beaten.'[16] He delivered a gracious speech congratulating the winners: 'I had thought your boxers were good but your debaters are better.' This went down well. 'Apparently they are surprised to see good losers,' Chester thought. A day later they won convincingly against the Philippine Law College in spite of their opponents' one good speaker who 'just tripped merrily from quip to quip.'[17]

For the final debate they were up against the same team that had beaten them earlier so they were taking no chances. Chester and Alan prepared all Wednesday, 11 August and most of the following day at the Manila Club where they had been made honorary members. That evening they affirmed 'Patriotism Is Out of Date' and while their principal adversary from the earlier debate, a dapper law student named Rodrigo, spoke well, his colleague was very poor and to the Australians' relief the result was never in doubt. The trophy was presented to them by the Vice President himself. It was a very handsome silver cup that Chester and Alan in turn presented to the Australian Union of Students as the inter-varsity debating trophy. The following day they sailed on *The Empress of Asia* for Hong Kong.

They arrived to find the war news worse with reports of an aerial battle over Shanghai the night before and bombs falling on the international settlement. The Vice Chancellor of Hong Kong University, Sir William Hornell, came by and took the two Australians for a swim at Stanley Bay. 'It's amazing what the British have done,' Chester thought as they drove to Hornell's 'shack'. A network of roads had been carved out of what had been the bare rock of the hillside, which had been grassed over 'although the grass is no use for fodder', Chester discovered. Hornell told them the government had done wonders – the streets were spotlessly clean and the buildings in the city were all solid stone and, they found, 'very attractive.' 'I feel like becoming a prof,' Wilmot wrote when told about the £1300 a year wage; the rent-free house; free water, light and phone; and, incredibly, no income tax.

Back at the ship they found Hong Kong by night magical. 'It's unbelievably beautiful,' Chester wrote in his diary. 'The black rock rises up from the water and it's just a blaze of lights – house after house shines its lights from the side of the peak until it looks like an illumination show.' Chester was, however, more interested in the politics than sightseeing and the next day called on Alec Pratt, an ex-*Age* reporter who was editing Hong Kong's *Daily Press* news.

After briefing Chester about Western business interests and the internal power struggles in China, Pratt had given them an introduction to a General Morris Cohen, formerly of the British Army, and the adviser from the central government to the governor of Kwangtung Province at Canton. A colourful character with a reputation for 'slick shooting,' Cohen had been head of the personal bodyguard for Sun Yat-sen. The General made all the right anti-Japanese noises in his interview, which Chester carefully noted for the article he was writing for the Australian papers. Alan and Chester soon came to see for themselves the extent of the Chinese hatred for the Japanese. They sensed the anti-Japanese feeling at a screening of a naïve but effective propaganda film. There was a boycott on shark's fin, a great Japanese delicacy, and they heard that the 'Jap' consul and his staff had left, ostensibly recalled, but really because they could not get food or service in the restaurants. Through an interpreter Chester and Alan questioned coolies, shopkeepers, and rickshaw boys. There was no fear, 'rather an itch to get at them'.[18]

On the morning of 18 August 1937, air-raid sirens wailed over Canton. Chester and Alan were at the Governor's office with

Cohen, where they watched Japanese scouting planes being turned back at the outskirts of the city by the Chinese Air Force. They then interviewed the governor Fu-Teh-Chen at his residence outside the city – 'very modernistic ... surrounded by guards and anti-aircraft guns'. He told them, 'we may not gain a military victory but we will succeed in the end by a policy of exhaustion'.[19]

The Canton Government had ordered the evacuation of all women and children. After the air-raid scare the streets were crammed with people carting their belongings in rickshaws, cars and trolleys. Chester and Alan were to leave by the night train. They arrived at the station to find the platform – just about every square inch of it – crowded with refugees, their children, and their belongings. As soon as the 4.50 pm train left the station two hours late, 'the Chinese jumped down onto the line and hopped across the track to the other train which was waiting on the next line ... coolies bundled in everywhere ... six deep.' Chester and Alan stood on the back platform – 'it was certainly more hygienic even though uncomfortable and dirty from the smoke'. Chester felt that 'it was remarkable how philosophically they took their troubles, and even when they "mobbed" the train, they did so in an orderly manner. They were determined to get on board, but there was no pushing or shoving, and when people wanted to get out they stood back and let them'.[20]

In Hong Kong they found that the first ships were returning with refugees from Shanghai. The exhausted women and children were reluctant about being interviewed, even by the obviously sympathetic Australians, and Chester and Alan did not press them. There was time for a last swimming party as guests of Sir William Hornell during which Chester and two Chinese students had to rescue the Vice Chancellor when he was knocked out when a squall caused the so-called diving yacht to sweep over him as he was coming up after a dive. They made certain he was out of danger before sailing for Japan on *The Empress of Asia* two days later.

On the night of Tuesday, 4 August, Chester was working 'till all hours', and so he decided to stay up and see the ship come into Nagasaki. 'The harbour is ringed with tree covered hills, backed by mountains several thousand feet high,' he wrote, 'and as there was a full moon it was beautiful, as the ship stole up the harbour smooth as glass'.[21] Chester could see ashore three or four large townships ablaze with light. Later while they were still anchored there the Japanese held a military exercise. A complete blackout was ordered for a mock air-raid. The only problem was that none of the planes could find the town. These images were to haunt Chester in 1945 when the news came that Nagasaki had been one of the two targets for an atomic bomb.

Chester was very soon left in no doubt that he was in a police state, and a very puritanical one at that. After 'an orgy of argument with the university fellows' about Japan's aggression in China, the Australians went out dancing with some English and White Russian 'lasses'. Chester was always going out dancing with pretty girls – lasses – during the tour, all the while keeping up a hectic work schedule. After all he was just twenty-seven. He was walking through a park about a mile from where some troops were encamped when, as Chester described it in his diary:

> A policeman held us up and wanted to know what we were doing – Margot, a White Russian, told them we were walking home. He didn't seem satisfied, and rode off and got another policeman. Then the two of them started cross examining us – Margot having to bear the whole brunt of it, as she could speak Japanese. It appeared they wanted to take us to the police station as I had no passport with me. We protested strongly so after fifteen minutes of this one of them ... went off and returned with two more policemen. More heated altercation between the four, and they marched us off to the box nearby while they rang headquarters. Apparently headquarters thought it was alright,

and they let us go, but only after calling a taxi, and telling the driver on pain of death to take us to the respective addresses we had given ... Apparently we could have been held up ... for nice people do not walk along streets or in parks after midnight, and if I had been with a Japanese girl I would certainly have gone to the jug.[22]

They were regularly filing stories with the Melbourne papers through Chester's father. So in the next dispatch the story of the encounter with the Japanese police was included in a press release. 'It is thought he may have been arrested for flirting with his companion', it stated. An amused Bung, who knew his son only too well – 'have you a girl in every port', one of his letters asked – nevertheless excised the reference to flirting before forwarding the story to the papers.

Only one debate had been scheduled with the Japanese, plus a public discussion earlier in the day. The discussion was rather strained; the debate went much better. In the circumstances, Chester felt, '[the Japanese] did remarkably well for it was the first international debate ever held in Japan and the first time these lads had ever debated in English.'[23] At first Wilmot disliked the militarism of so much university life in Japan – the uniforms and the prison-type haircuts. They appeared to Chester as shackles on the mind as much as the body. But contacts like the Australian academic Peter Russo, then teaching at a small university outside Tokyo, introduced him to institutions and teachers who were trying to inculcate the kind of independent thought he had come to believe was essential for a university. However, Chester remained sceptical about the country's politics. He found the Foreign Minister 'smiling and smarmy' and couldn't help noticing the lack of enthusiasm of the crowds farewelling troops bound for China. Still, in the two broadcasts over Radio Tokyo to Australia, he and Alan were careful to be tactful without compromising their integrity. Chester was also not above using conditions in Japan to criticise the Victorian Government.

> We have visited a number of Universities in and around Tokyo – both privately owned and State controlled institutions. All have been exceedingly well provided ... The important point is that in spite of the heavy burden of expenditure, which the Japanese Government has had to bear in the last ten years, it has continued to give liberal support to State Universities at a level that far exceeds the government grant to any Australian University ... In these circumstances, it was disappointing for us to learn [that] the government of Victoria has again refused to grant the University of Melbourne funds adequate for even its essential teaching and research work. It was even more distressing to learn further that as a result of this niggardly policy the University of Melbourne is about to lose the services of its Vice Chancellor [Dr Priestly].[24]

There was no danger of these observations failing to reach Melbourne. When the ABC local office refused to program the broadcast, Bung found a commercial station that would. Late one night he and Janie were invited into the studios and listened to their son 'live' on the short wave as the sound was recorded. Chester also reported Japanese views about the need to find markets in China, carefully omitting his own pro-China sympathies, at least for the moment. In his notes for what seems to have been a later broadcast of a discussion with Benjamin, Wilmot stated, 'Very doubtful if British fleet will be able to leave the North Sea or Mediterranean in sufficient numbers to stop Japan [in the event of war] ... In these circumstances present Australian defense [sic] policy [of building more navy to co-operate with British] is ill advised ... will be useless without the British'.[25]

Of course the Service chiefs had been saying much the same to successive Australian governments, but this was one of the first public expressions of the advice military and public service insiders had been vainly trying to give their political masters since the early 1930s.

Clearly Chester was already moving from educator to political commentator. It must have begun in earnest when he first heard about Priestly's resignation. As he wrote later to the former Vice Chancellor, 'it knocked the bottom out of my academic plans'.[26] Nevertheless, Wilmot continued to collect information about universities, and went ahead and applied for the Head of External Studies position; but on discovering that the successful applicant would be debarred from making any kind of political comment, Chester withdrew his application.

Just before leaving Japan he was taken to see a silk factory. 'It was certainly a model factory,' Chester noted, and the girls, who worked there from the ages of fourteen to twenty-two, when they went home to get married, were well cared for.

> But here comes the evil – they have no freedom at all. They cannot leave the factory compound without permission, and that is given only on Sundays … They cannot read anything the employer does not want them to … Japan today is a remarkable example of industrial feudalism … exactly the same as that between feudal lord and his villain. There is no chance of a strike – no chance of these girls (or the men either) becoming anything more than wage slaves … No wonder the American and European capitalists envy the stranglehold the Japanese have on their workers; they criticize their low standard of living, but all but the best of them would gladly be in a similar dominant position. While there is this feudalization of labour, there is also the most modern development of finance capital organization, so far as the control of industry is concerned … That is I think one of the secrets of Japanese industrial success. Capital is unfettered but the feudal tradition still holds in position the army and the navy. They are responsible to the Emperor only.[27]

This, Chester argued, allowed the military to enforce capital levies for military war. 'Not that big business is opposed to the militaristic expansion – it never is – but it is a little embarrassed at times when the army goes too far and too fast'.[28] These observations come from Wilmot's diary letters to his family but would also have been included in his reports to Foreign Affairs. They must have made disturbing reading.

* * * *

Chester and Alan sailed for America during September 1937 as the clouds of war gathered over Europe.

In March 1936 Hitler had occupied the Rhineland; he was already planning the Anschluss: the 'incorporation' of Austria into the greater Germany. America remained strictly isolationist and President Roosevelt could do nothing about it. Even though he had won an overwhelming victory in the 1936 presidential elections, Roosevelt's administration had become embroiled in a battle with the Supreme Court, which was using every available legal pretext to strike down the New Deal legislation that had been introduced to regulate industry, and combat the Depression.

They arrived in San Francisco on 6 October, and soon met up with Dr Bill Bryden, the Warden of the University of Melbourne Union who had arrived the day before. He brought news of the debate in March on the Spanish Civil War between, among others, Nettie Palmer – wife of the writer Vance Palmer – and Chester's former team-mate Bob Santamaria. Bryden also briefed Wilmot on Priestly's resignation. It had all come down, in Chester's words, to 'the power issue'. From the beginning the University Council had been uncomfortable with the fact that Priestly was hired to be the executive head of the university. But even when he was first appointed, Priestly was advised not to mention that he was now the chief administrator 'because although true it might cause offence.'

The one most likely to be offended was Sir James Barrett, then Deputy Vice Chancellor and later Chancellor, who was reluctant to give up power to the distinguished newcomer, and continued to interfere in the administration of the university. Priestly became disillusioned, and when the State Government refused to increase the university's grant, that was the end of it. Chester felt that Melbourne had let the Vice Chancellor down. As he wrote to Priestly:

> I fear not only are we to lose you, but worse, the forces of reaction and dissention seem likely to carry the University back into the doldrums of the pre 1935 era. No one who was not a student at Melbourne both before and after 1935 can appreciate the almost complete transformation which you brought in almost two and a half years.[29]

Chester did not abandon the vision he shared with Priestly of a university community dedicated to freedom of speech and independent enquiry. Throughout the debating tour he filled his letter diaries with observations about universities in the USA, Canada and Britain. Wilmot was particularly critical of the American practice of 'spoon feeding' – teaching the facts and examining through objective tests with multiple choice questions. He found an unlikely ally in a young lecturer at the University of Minnesota, Hubert Humphrey, not surprisingly one of Chester's most accomplished debating opponents.

Nevertheless, valuable as Wilmot's descriptions of American education remain even in the twenty-first century, his portrait of America on the eve of World War II when the Roosevelt administration's New Deal was at its height is, if anything, even more fascinating. Moreover, their debates were reported in all the local newspapers and some were even broadcast. Judging from the press clippings the Australians were, for a while, minor celebrities. And, of course, the debates themselves, with topics such as 'American

Isolation Is Not Splendid', were very political. As a socialist, Chester was an admirer of President Roosevelt and the New Deal, although he was certain once the crisis was past, the controls on wages and conditions would be lifted. He even managed to include an allusion to the President's conflict with the impossibly obdurate Supreme Court during a broadcast debate with Johns Hopkins University. The Senator chairing the debate later referred to Wilmot's comment on the floor of the Senate. 'Some alleged defects of the court are so notorious that they are known to two gentlemen from the Antipodes who recently visited Washington.'[30]

The debate was going to air 'live' on a station owned by William Randolph Hearst: a bitter opponent of the President. (Hearst later became the model for Orson Welles's 1940 film *Citizen Kane*.) Knowing this, Chester went on to deliberately praise Roosevelt. At this the station manager tried to cut him off, then thought better of it. Later they heard he had demanded an advance script from the next visiting speaker nominated by Johns Hopkins. 'We've had too much trouble lately with half cocked college guys who shoot their face off about politics'.[31] The 'college guys' were delighted.

America's isolationist policies could evoke similar passions. In a debate sponsored by the Jeffersonian Club of St. Paul Minnesota, with Chester affirming 'America should abandon its isolationist policy', his opponents 'just abused the British and spat scorn at me, for advocating that America should come and help Britain play "her dirty little racketeering game" … they made no attempt to argue sensibly on the real issue whether isolation would save America anyway'.[32]

Nevertheless, Wilmot was never to lose his affection for America and the Americans. He despised the arrogant anti-Americanism he encountered in Britain, and when the time came to criticise Roosevelt's policies at Yalta in *The Struggle for Europe*, Wilmot was to do so as a friend.

4

ASHAMED TO BE AN ENGLISHMAN

Like all great reporters Chester Wilmot was often there when things happened. In February 1938 he arrived in Europe just in time for the Anschluss and was still there for the Munich crisis. Chester was not able to observe events at close quarters, but he did have an impressive range of contacts, and on the whole he got it right.

Europe in 1938 was still the creation of the Treaty of Versailles of 1919 that formally concluded the Great War. There was no shortage of clauses that specifically penalised Germany: the declaration that Germany was solely responsible for the war; the limitations on armaments; the reparations compensating France and Britain for their losses; the secession of territory; the annexation of German colonies; and the demilitarisation of the Rhineland. In addition, Germany's principal ally, the Austro-Hungarian Empire, had been dismembered. Among the countries created in its stead were Austria (which was strictly forbidden to unite with Germany) and the new state of Czechoslovakia, an amalgam of Czechs, Slovaks and Sudeten Germans.

Wilmot was far from alone in believing the Versailles treaty lacked moral validity. It was absurd to hold Germany solely responsible for the outbreak of the 1914–18 war. This appeared to be confirmed when collections of the treaties and diplomatic exchanges between the great powers were published in the 1920s and early 1930s. However the editors' choices had been highly selective. It is clear that certainly the responsibility for the outbreak of war in 1914 was not exclusively Germany's, but as Winston Churchill pointed out in *The World Crisis*, Germany certainly had been pursuing a dangerously threatening foreign policy for nearly ten years before the outbreak of World War I. This was not a popular view and a significant body of opinion inside and outside the parliament in Britain believed Germany had legitimate grievances and these should be appeased.

For Wilmot, however, his criticisms of Versailles were counterbalanced by a distrust of dictators like Hitler and Mussolini, not to mention the appeasers themselves, particularly Neville Chamberlain, the new Conservative British prime minister; his close ally, Lord Halifax; and the former's immediate predecessor as prime minister, Stanley Baldwin. And looming over this preoccupation with German grievances was the Spanish Civil War, where the rebels, led by General Franco and supported by the fascists and Nazis, were still locked in a deadly conflict with the legitimate Republican Government, while the British and French steadfastly refused to intervene. By February 1938 Wilmot was in London. A meeting with one of his contacts prompted these reflections.

Wednesday 16 February 1938:

Lunched with William Thompson Manager of the National Bank of Australia …

He took me to the Old Carlton Club … Interesting was his opinion of the Spanish Affair … Told me what I'd always suspected that the city was strongly pro-Franco … and in fact pro all the dictators … The defeat of Franco in Spain would mean the triumph of Communism and the city feared this. The City also wanted 'peace' with Hitler and Mussolini ... The bankers etc. felt that some compromise must be made. Hitler's Austrian 'putsch' has certainly made him immensely more powerful ... not only so far as Austria is concerned ... but in Czechoslovakia. It is more serious as a foreboding of what Czechoslovakia can expect before long ... and it seems to me his clamour about Colonies is just bluff and he's using it for its nuisance value ... And judging by the policy of Chamberlain, Halifax and Co ... which is completely over-riding Eden's saner policy ... Britain will give in and let him butcher Czechoslovakia as we are letting Hitler and Mussolini butcher Spain ... The whole thing is a grand racket ... The Chamberlains care little or nothing for democracy or justice ... They have only two policies ... Peace at any price, which we do not have to pay ... i.e. if we can buy peace by sacrificing someone else to the dictators alright – e.g. Spain and in future Czechoslovakia or some other East European state. Secondly they want to keep the Fascist dictators in power at almost any price ... and they are prepared to make sacrifices to see that this is so. They fear that if either Hitler or Mussolini fall that there will be social revolution and that the position of the British ruling classes will be undermined ... The present British Government has outstripped Baldwin for its hypocrisy, treachery and sheer disregard of anyone but the ruling class in Britain.[1]

Chester's bitterness about the British upper classes was fuelled by seeing the appalling slums in the industrial centres when he and Alan had debated at the so-called provincial universities. Still, they were enjoying themselves. Chester and Alan won comfortably at University College London when they affirmed 'The Empire Is an Unfair Burden on the British People'. Chester noted that:

> English students have difficulty with their convictions when they
> debate this topic for they are nearly all strongly anti-imperialist
> and realize 'defence' is largely a racket ... and when they
> find themselves on the side they don't like they preserve their
> intellectual honesty by twisting their arguments so they can work
> from a premise with which they agree ... An attitude and a sense
> of proportion which is refreshing.[2]

The resignation of the Foreign Secretary, Anthony Eden, a few days after the lunch with Thompson, confirmed Chester's low opinion of the Chamberlain Government.

> It means we have completely abandoned the collective security
> plan ... the real split seems whether we should negotiate with
> Italy for some understanding ... without getting guarantees
> about ... the withdrawal of Italian troops from Spain and the
> cessation of anti-British broadcasts in Arabic. Eden obviously
> and rightly doesn't trust Mussolini's promises.[3]

During the debate in the Commons on the resignation Chester 'stood about in the lobbies' – there was no chance of getting into the house – 'but you could sense the atmosphere of expectancy all round. In the speeches made in the house Chamberlain tried to make out that there was no difference of principle between him and Eden ... which is rot ... the main difference of course is that Eden has principles and Chamberlain has none,' Wilmot wrote.[4]

Soon after Wilmot and Benjamin took the train to Oxford for what was to be Chester's first encounter with Randolph Churchill, son of Winston Churchill, then in the political wilderness leading the fight against appeasement. The Australians were guests at the Presidential debate: the two candidates for president of the Union against two invited speakers, one of whom was Randolph Churchill. Earlier they had met the current President of the Union, Raymond

Walton. He'd been insufferably patronising. 'Just a pair of colonials don't you know … not fit to be asked to speak before the Lords and Masters of the Oxford Union,' Chester typed bitterly in his diary.[5] There was to be no debate with Oxford. Fortunately 'Walton was the only one [they] met who had a patronizing manner,' and the two 'colonials' had been invited to the Union Society's dinner as well as the debate. Randolph Churchill, Wilmot thought,

> has very much the elder statesman manner. He is the same build as his father and has a magnificent manner and a wonderful power of rejoinder if anyone interjects … but his start was very unconvincing … he made a number of personal remarks about his opponents – not very good either … He was at his best when he proceeded to attack the government for the Eden resignation … and plastered them up hill and down dale in grand style.[6]

This did not have much to do with the debate: he was supposed to be opposing socialism. But it seems Randolph was about his father's business that night.

Winston Churchill was busy forging an alliance with the more temperate Anthony Eden against the appeasers. Privately the elder Churchill thought the former foreign secretary could have managed his departure better. Eden had been driven to distraction by the seeming fact that every time he went on holiday, Halifax and Chamberlain would find new ways to appease Italy. But nothing was going to deflect Churchill from trying to recruit Eden as an ally, or from bitterly criticising the government over his resignation in the Commons, or, it appears, from getting his son to back them both up at the Oxford Union.

Chester filled his diary with notes about Oxford and the other British universities and colleges they had visited, but he and Alan were both tired of debating. Now it was time to visit the continent and do some reporting.

* * * *

On Friday, 8 April 1938, the Friday night before the plebiscite to ratify the Anschluss – the incorporation of Austria into the German Reich – Chester and Alan made their way through the cobblestoned back streets and elegant boulevards of Vienna.

> Vienna ... was gay-gay with Nazi flags on every building – with streaming banners across every street telling people to 'Thank the Fuhrer, with 'YES'; proclaiming 'One People, One State one Fuhrer'; offering 'Work and Bread Under Hitler' ... and so on in endless variations of these themes ... Day and night Neon signs flashed similar injunctions on every hand and across the Danube Canal; a news strip in lights told the story of the glories of Hitler's Reich. There were stickers on every window – photographs of Hitler in most. On the front of several public buildings were giant photos of Hitler six stories [sic] deep. The propaganda was inescapable.[7]

Chester had only to close his eyes to hear the blare of the loudspeakers continuing the assault. There would be a snatch of some Nazi 'patriotic song' – performed by a chorus from the Hitler Youth. Soldiers would shout out some pro-German ditty as they marched past. When the two Australians took refuge in a cafe a Nazi tried to sell them souvenir postcards. They politely declined only to find the matches Chester purchased to light his pipe were marked 'Vote Yes' – 'Ja'.

It was no different at the university. Official university posters advised all and sundry to vote 'yes'. The workers' flats, built by the Vienna Socialist Municipality and bombarded in 1934 by the fascist Heimwehr during murderous street fighting with the so-called 'Vienna Reds' (really the social democrats), were festooned with Nazi bunting, red and black swastika flags and photographs of

46

Hitler. The seven trainloads of propaganda materials dispatched by Dr Goebbels had been put to good use. By the time Hitler arrived on the Saturday morning most people on the streets were wearing a Nazi button or badge. Chester had to admit 'that whatever the stagecraft the finished performance was impressive'.[8] There were enthusiastic Nazi supporters all along the route Hitler travelled. Chester noticed that behind the Führer was the inevitable movie cameraman followed by a score of gleaming black cars carrying senior SS and German Army officers.

They were experiencing the final days of the Nazi takeover. Chester knew some of the history from his discussions with Macmahon Ball and they'd both been following the story in the newspapers and on the radio. Earlier the Austrian Parliament had been closed down by the previous Chancellor Dollfuss, who had banned the Austrian Nazi Party and then suppressed the social democrats and communists, only to be murdered in 1934 by Nazi thugs in an attempted coup. His successor, Kurt Schuschnigg, had put down the coup and restored order, but since then had been under relentless pressure from Hitler to include Nazis in the government and lift the bans on the party imposed after the assassination.

In February 1938, the London papers had carried stories of a meeting between Schuschnigg and Hitler after which the Austrian Chancellor had agreed to make the Nazi, Seyss-Inquart, Minister of the Interior – a key position with control of the police – and to release all the imprisoned Nazis, including those implicated in the Dollfuss murder. Desperately seeking a way out, Schuschnigg lifted the bans on the social democrats and communists, and called a referendum. The question asked was 'Are you for an independent, social, Christian, German, united Austria?' Hitler threatened that if the referendum went ahead he would invade. Schuschnigg was not willing 'to see Germans kill Germans,' and in an emotional broadcast resigned in favour of Seyss-Inquart. Hitler invaded anyway and was now holding his own plebiscite supported by all the power of

Dr Goebbels's Ministry of Propaganda and the Austrian Nazis. On Saturday, 9 April 1938, Wilmot wrote:

> A chill wind blew the light snow across the square outside the Rathaus – the old railway station converted into a great hall where Hitler was to speak later that day. The dense crowd waited patiently. They let off steam much as an Australian football crowd would, by chanting one or other of the popular slogans such as 'Ein Volk, Ein Reich, Ein Fuhrer', or singing 'Deutschland Uber Alles.'[9]

Thousands who could not get into the building flanked the route or crowded around the entrance. Hitler stood on a high pulpit inside at the far end beneath a white gold awning, designed by the Führer's favourite architect, Albert Speer, which extended along the whole length of the hall. As usual the Führer began quietly. Then time and time again the voice would rise to passionate incoherence. Or at least that is how Wilmot and Benjamin saw it. The correspondent for the pro-appeasement *Daily Mail*, G Ward Price, described Hitler's speech as 'the most eloquent and interesting [he] had ever heard him make'.[10] It was certainly one of the most autobiographical.

As a young man, Hitler said, he had no interest in politics, then for four years he had been a nameless soldier. Those were the days when Germany had been ruined. And it was the spectacle of the havoc they had wrought that decided him to take up politics. 'As I lay half blinded in hospital, I realised that those who had wrecked Germany could never restore her … I made for the first time the resolve to speak!'[11] He went on to explain how no party could unite Germany at that time, and he had worked for fifteen years to reach this position. Then came another of his 'passionately incoherent' climaxes. 'I never gave in when I was weak, when I was in prison or when I was forbidden to speak in public. And today the power is in my hands!'[12] Hitler was shouting now, and with a triumphant sweep of his hand, he sent the microphone crashing to the floor.

There was much more of the same – ninety minutes of it – concluding with the Führer rendering thanks to God for showing him the way. Nevertheless, Chester and Alan were aware of some discordant notes. To be sure thousands stayed in the streets, but there was really nothing else to do. All shops and places of amusement had been closed since 11.30 am. Cafes had been open during the Führer's speech but no meals had been served during the speech itself. 'It isn't done to have your mouth full with the Fuhrer talking!' Chester wrote on the typescript of the article he was preparing for the Melbourne papers.

On the Friday night when he and Alan had gone to see the much-publicised film, *The Greater Germany*, the theatre was not even a quarter filled. 'What audience there was looked in silence at the celluloid story of the greatness of the new Germany, and gave only two murmurs of grudging applause to the Hitler speeches … when it concluded with the silent caption "All for One – Yes for Adolph Hitler" … there was deathly silence.'[13] The silence of boredom, Chester wondered.

On the Monday night the two Australians went to the movies again. The famous 'record' of the 1934 Nuremberg Rally *Triumph of the Will*, directed by Leni Riefenstahl, was playing to less than half-empty houses. But the MGM period drama *Marie Waleweska*, a highly romanticised version of the affair between the Polish Countess Marie (Greta Garbo), and the Emperor Napoleon (Charles Boyer), was packed out. *Marie Waleweska* – better known now under its American title *Conquest* – is a fine film, and Greta Garbo was always popular in Europe, but there may have been more to its popularity at this time than Viennese indifference to Nazi propaganda. In the movie Marie first becomes involved with Napoleon to help secure Poland's independence from Russia. Were the crowds that Monday night equating nineteenth-century Poland in the film with

Austria in 1938, or were they just seeking diversion?

Chester was not certain how much popular support the Nazis really had. As he wrote in his diary:

Vienna, 11 April 1938:

Probably a majority of Austrians want the Anschluss, possibly a majority want Hitler, but whatever the latent opposition there was dared not show itself with the Germans in virtual occupation. The next day, the actual plebiscite day, Vienna was very quiet. The great demonstration was over, the streets almost deserted. A few planes droned overhead, a few troops marched in the streets, knots of voters gathered around polling booths. But the process of making sure was complete. For Hitler it was another victory.[14]

After Chester returned to Britain stories began to trickle back about the Nazis' atrocious treatment of the Austrian Jews. But the full horror was only revealed after the war: the plundering of Jewish homes and businesses, the public humiliation of men and women forced to perform menial tasks in the streets of Vienna, became the prelude to mass extermination. Some who loved the Viennese such as the *Daily Telegraph* Correspondent, GER Gedye, never quite recovered from being forced to watch the spectacles that followed the Nazi takeover. It was not so much the brutalities of the Austrian Nazis that he witnessed or verified directly from the victims that blurred the image of the Vienna Gedye thought he knew;

> it is the heartless, grinning, soberly dressed crowds … fighting one another to get closer to the elevating spectacle of an ashen faced Jewish surgeon on hands and knees and before half a dozen young hooligans with Swastika armlets and dog whips that comes to mind … And the Viennese – not uniformed Nazis

or a raging mob but the Viennese Little Man and his wife – just grinned approval at the glorious fun.[15]

But there were moments of decency. On their way home from the Max Reinhardt Drama School two girls, one tiny and slightly plump, the other slim and dark, came across just such a group. Among the middle-aged men and women being compelled to scrub the street with toothbrushes, the smaller girl recognised the doctor who'd saved her life when she had diphtheria:

'What are you doing?' she asked one of the men in uniform.
'How dare you,' one of the brownshirts shouted.
'How dare you!' she shouted back, 'this is a great physician a saver of lives!'
'Is this what you call our liberation?' called out the other girl.
Within two minutes the jeering crowd had dispersed.[16]

Chester and Alan did not stay to witness spectacles such as these. Alan was Jewish and they did not want to push their luck. There had already been a trivial incident that had brought home to them the reality of Nazi anti-Semitism. They were driving a hired Citroën with an Australian newspaperman, Frank Sullivan, when they reached the Yugoslav-Austrian border. At the checkpoint they handed their passports to a German SS guard.

'What is your religion?' he demanded through the interpreter.
'Church of England,' Wilmot replied.
'Catholic,' said Sullivan.
'Jewish,' snapped Benjamin defiantly. The SS man had got what he wanted.
'You'll have to get a special permit if you want to enter Austria.' The Australians exploded: Chester arguing furiously with the border guards.

'There is a new law. It came into effect two days ago,' they were told.[17]

The confrontation suddenly turned into comedy. They needed more petrol if they were going to make the long drive to Budapest to get the permit and there was a petrol pump ten yards over the border. So Alan got out of the car while Chester and Frank passed through the checkpoint, filled up, and then drove back across the border and on to Budapest. The British Vice-Consul had never heard of such a law; nor at first had the German Legation. It must be a mistake. Then they discovered there was a new law. The letter from the Australian Prime Minister was produced. 'There is no law by which a British Subject of non-Aryan descent can be excluded,' they were now told.[18]

Alan dispatched a letter to Stanley Melbourne Bruce – a former prime minister and Australian High Commissioner in London. Sir Neville Henderson, British Ambassador to Germany, was instructed to ask for an explanation. Finally the German Government replied that it had been 'a mistaken interpretation of a standing instruction'.[19] It was a small victory, but whether they knew it or not, Alan and Chester had forced one of the most ardent appeasers in the British Diplomatic Corps to complain to the German Foreign Minister about an affront to an Australian Jewish lawyer.

Their European adventure over, it was time for Alan to return to Australia. Chester decided to stay in England. Reporting a crisis had proved heady stuff and he was convinced that it was only a matter of time before it would be Czechoslovakia's turn. Besides, the Australians were about to play England at Lord's, and the BBC had hinted that there might be a place for him on their commentary team.

Back in London, Chester was not only describing the cricket, but interviewing former Secretary of State for Dominion Affairs, Leo Amery, for a BBC broadcast to Australia as well as a Labour MP, Hugh Dalton. In 1938, rarely did anyone go to air 'live' without a script, or a careful rehearsal. The BBC was still haunted by an incident the year before, when the announcer describing the fireworks display following the King's review of the fleet at Spithead, exclaimed, 'The whole bloody fleet's lit up.' So was he. An ex-Royal Navy officer, he had been celebrating for too long in the wardroom.[20]

So preparation for the talk on Empire defence began with a preliminary interview – taken down in shorthand. Chester had not prepared the points for the talk sufficiently, so he

> just let Amery talk, which he did at great length very conservative ... Thinks Hitler and Mussolini will get out of Spain when the war is over ... that we will be able to buy Franco off ... that Japan threatens Australia ... that Britain really tried to stop Italy with sanctions during the Abyssinian War ... The idea of collective security and organized peace was stupid from the start ... the mere idea is ridiculous.[21]

Wilmot found the former Secretary of State: 'a rather pompous little fellow ... very talkative ... but nice and restrained ... very opiniated but aren't we all.'[22] Amery was very professional when it came to the broadcast. He willingly allowed Chester to prune the script and to interject. 'We disagreed on almost every point ... it worked out better. Of course Australia wants to hear Amery not me so I didn't have much to say.'[23]

Almost certainly this talk would have been listened to closely by Charles Moses at the ABC offices in Sydney. Not long after, Leo Amery was to figure in two of the most dramatic scenes in British political history. On 2 September 1939, when Neville Chamberlain dithered over whether to declare war on Germany for having invaded Poland, Amery was furious. As the Deputy Labour Party Leader, Arthur Greenwood, rose in the House to declare that he spoke for Labour, Amery called across the floor, 'speak for England, Arthur!' clearly implying the Prime Minister was not. Even more deadly was his intervention in the House of Commons debate over the military disaster in Norway. His bitter speech attacking the Chamberlain Government famously concluded with Oliver Cromwell's 'You have sat too long here for any good you have been doing. Depart, I say, and let us have done with you. In the name of God, go.' It was one of the best received speeches Amery ever gave and helped to bring about the fall of Chamberlain and the formation of the National Government under Churchill.

Chester thought the Hugh Dalton broadcast was less effective partly because 'we agreed about almost everything'. One remark of Dalton's seemed 'a bit hot on a government station'. 'If I lived in Australia, I'd live in Queensland and vote for Forgan Smith and the fine Labour Government he leads.'[24] Chester never discovered what the very proper ABC made of that. He did find out what Moses thought about his cricket commentaries when he received a letter from the ABC General Manager full of compliments plus some suggestions as to exactly when the commentator should start to describe the movement of the ball (when it is played, not when it leaves the bowler's hand). Chester replied thanking him and continued the discussion. The exchange of letters survives in the Wilmot papers, a rare example of two great reporters exploring the art of radio description; an art that would soon be employed to convey the sights and sounds of events far more dangerous than a cricket match.

This was not the only compliment Wilmot received. The leading BBC cricket commentator, Howard Marshall, whose distinctive deep voice was famous throughout Britain, pronounced Chester's descriptions as the best he had ever heard. Marshall and Wilmot were to meet again in 1944 when they were part of the team of reporters covering D-Day.

Chester was being well paid for his work for the BBC, so between commitments, he embarked on some sightseeing in Scotland and Ireland. As usual he shared his experiences with his family and the diary letters home are filled with fine descriptive writing.

In Dublin the Australian Prime Minister's letter got him an interview with the President of Eire, Eamon de Valera, who after the Easter Rising had been sentenced to death by the British. Chester liked de Valera.

> [He] is a most interesting and convincing person ... very softly spoken ... very easy in speech and manner ... with soft eyes and a smooth voice ... "w's" his "r's" a little ... We talked casually and easily the peace of the evening seeming to draw him on. Eventually I left him ... and as I went out to the front of Leinster House ... I passed under the shadow of a statue of Queen Victoria ... looking at her most imperious, smug and domineering ... sneering at the Irish unconcerned that behind her back meets the Daill [sic] [the Irish Parliament] which has erased the name of her family from the constitution of Eire.[25]

Almost all Chester's diaries include descriptions of regular visits to movies and include capsule reviews. He also read the 'serious' film journals and was familiar with the work of the documentary movement in Britain and the USA. In February he had seen American director Robert Flaherty's *Man of Aran*. The diary entry praises the film but Chester was not so sure about the work's authenticity. Flaherty was famous for going to remote places – such as the South Seas for *Moana*, or the Arctic for *Nanook of the North* (the silent film about an Eskimo family that made the director's name) – then bringing back 'the truth' about people living close to nature. It was of course sightseeing but Wilmot was also preparing himself for when he would be making his own documentaries.

Saturday 16 July 1939:

Off to Aran in the Dun Aengus – a little chug-chug ... that goes out twice a week with stores and mails and tourists ... A lovely sunny day and smooth as can be. Flaherty made a great film on Aran, and it was supposed to be a documentary. I was keen to find out how 'documentary' it really was. He depicted life there as very grim indeed – a battle against the roaring sea and the niggardly rock ... a life primitive and rough – a life on the edge of death and starvation ... My first inkling that this was not so – today at least – came when we got talking to a man that lives on the main island ... a man who owns hundreds of acres and several hundred head of cattle ... He told us how the part about the woman and the boy going out to scrape in between the rocks to get the soil and make fields of soil and seaweed over the bare rock was possibly never true and certainly not true today ... how the shark hunt to get oil for the lamp – was also not true of today when everyone uses paraffin ... and no one on the island knew anything about hunting sharks and the man in the film who did the harpooning had to be brought from London to do the job.[27]

Wilmot is referring to one of the most celebrated sequences in the film, where fishermen hunt a basking shark three times the size of their whaleboat. His conclusions anticipated by nearly thirty years the 1977 documentary by George C Stoney, *How the Myth Was Made*.

Until then the stories Chester uncovered were known only to Flaherty's colleagues and to specialists in film history. A note in Wilmot's handwriting enclosed with the typescript of the diary reads, 'This is not the way you should make documentaries.'[28] One of Flaherty's most distinguished friends and contemporaries would have agreed. In 1981 the author asked Basil Wright, director of *Song of Ceylon* and producer of such classics of British documentary as *Night Mail* and *Diary for Timothy*, about the shark hunt in *Man of Aran*. He replied, 'It was re-enactment posing as actuality. He [Flaherty] shouldn't have done it.'[29] When Chester made *Sons of the Anzacs* in 1943, he insisted on using the film extracts with the same care and accuracy a historian would apply to written material. Except for some sequences with a sand map and a line of trumpeters on the steps of the Australian War Memorial, nothing was staged. Arguably Wilmot was the first documentary filmmaker to treat film sources as historical documents.

Throughout this time Chester was following events in Europe. Agitation by the Sudeten Germans for autonomy inside Czechoslovakia was increasing. Wilmot rightly suspected that it was being stirred up by Berlin. We know now that Hitler's instructions to Sudeten Nazi leader, Konrad Henlein, were to ask for more than the Czech Government would be prepared to grant. Then in early May rumours that German troops were massing on the Czech border provoked a partial mobilisation by Czechoslovakia. This, plus firm responses from Britain, France and Russia, seemingly forced Hitler to back down. It appeared that a determined show of force had deterred a potential aggressor. Chester wasn't so optimistic.

> Czech Scare apparently blown over for the time being at any rate … Thank heavens, France, Britain and Poland stood firm … It shows that collective action by only a few powers can really be successful … I hope this means Chamberlain will take a firm stand in future but I doubt it … Since Chamberlain's scrapping of the League and collective action we have a nice record – Hitler takes Austria … puts economic pressure and military persuasion on Czecho-Slovakia to disrupt [that] state, get control of Sudeten Germans [and force a] break [between] Czecho-Slovak [and] Russia and bring her … under the domination of Berlin; brings Europe to the brink of war to intimidate C*S [Czechoslovakia]; this averted not by appeasement, but by collective action of other powers with Great Britain … Italian troops and munitions continue to pour into Spain – Franco's attacks on British shipping become more frequent and openly deliberate and no apologies even are forthcoming … [the] English get sixpence on the income tax to provide more

protection against dangers largely created by the stupidity of the Conservatives ... but it doesn't affect the big fellows much they are making such a fortune out of re-armament that nothing worries them ... and poor Neville has gout.[30]

Wilmot was right to be sceptical about Chamberlain's willingness to take a firm stand against the dictators. Indeed, the British Prime Minister seemed terrified by his success, becoming at times almost apologetic in his statement about the crisis to the House of Commons. As Hitler screwed up the tension by encouraging the Sudeten Nazis to up their demands, Chamberlain forced the Czechs to accept Lord Runciman as an intermediary between the government and the German minority.

The war scare was probably responsible for the Air Ministry cancelling an interview with a senior RAF officer discussing air defence that Chester was preparing. 'It's most annoying I lose five quid ... too damaging to British prestige bah.'[31] After getting the news from Marjorie Wace, the Controller of Talks for the Empire, he wandered over to Westminster Abbey. Chester felt it was spoiled by the masses of ornaments to unimportant people. 'It is littered with sculptural junk which spoils the atmosphere.'[32] The tomb of the Unknown Soldier was different.

[It] brought a large lump into my throat. The feeling that we have got to go through it again is too harrowing ... especially for one who grew up in a world before 1929 ... Not that I would be afraid to die or would refuse to fight ... but what would it be for ... to make the world safe for democracy peace – peace – civilization? Britain under Chamberlain, fighting for democracy or international justice – a commerce-ridden country like England fighting for civilization. Yet we would have to fight against Fascism ... no person who valued civilization could refuse ... But after the fighting what?[33]

Chester was not optimistic about a postwar world whatever the outcome. He also believed he had a duty to try and understand the events that were unfolding almost in front of his eyes, which is why after the test matches were over and he'd completed all the work the BBC had for him, Chester decided to return to Europe.

* * * *

He left Frankfurt for Nuremberg at 6.45 am 'on a conveyance that was not so much a train as a moving crate of sweating humanity'.[34] It had come through from Ostend, picking up on the way hundreds of patriots bound for the Reich Party Day. It was of course much more than a day.

The Nuremberg Festival was a series of rituals and pageants glorifying the Führer that embodied the theme of the rebirth of Germany under the Nazis. Members of the Nazi Party organisations were each year selected to take part in the pageants and charged with the duty of taking back to their branches the Führer's message. The Nuremberg rallies had been watched closely throughout Europe ever since Hitler had employed the 1934 Festival to unite the Nazi Party after the Night of the Long Knives, when the leadership of the SA (the brown-shirted storm troopers) had been murdered by the SS. On that occasion the festival had been filmed by Leni Riefenstahl for the award-winning 'documentary' *Triumph of the Will*. The movie had been specially screened as propaganda when Chester and Alan were in Vienna during the Anschluss. In the last few years Hitler had taken to using the occasion for some of his most alarming announcements.

Chester arrived at Nuremberg station at 11.00 am, 'where the combined effect of my ten words of German … a Brownshirt's twenty-five words of English and Joe Lyon's letter was to get me accommodation with a German family … and a ticket for the first big parade'.[35] Seeing the rallies this way, Chester felt, would give him the chance to see the technique and psychology of National Socialism in action. It also gave him time to see Rothenberg, supposedly the most perfectly preserved of medieval towns in the world.

But in Rothenberg Wilmot still could not escape the trappings of the Nazi state: the Heil Hitler, the photograph of der Führer on the wall, the flags and the relentless, inescapable militarism. His description of the town is cold. It seems the Nazi propaganda made him unable to fully appreciate Rothenberg's beauty.

Back in Nuremberg Wilmot found his way to his lodgings where he was greeted by 'a most genial and motherly Frau, the wife of one Ludwig Lehmann'. An *Ober-Inspector* of high schools, Lehmann had been partly educated in the USA and spoke English well, but was a strong Nazi. It wasn't long before Chester began to draw him out.

> He is strongly anti-Semitic and told me that the Jews were a parasitic people who were responsible for most of the evil in the world ... that they had brought Germany disgrace, ruin and poverty and had a stranglehold on the nation's culture, professions and business ... and that the only thing to do was to exterminate them or drive them out of Germany ... There was no chance of distinguishing between the good and the bad ... for they were all potentially vicious ... Now that came from an otherwise natural man ... What chance have you got against such manufactured opinion.[36]

Chester didn't have to look far to see how his host's opinions had been created. 'The streets of Nuremberg are filthy with anti-Semitic propaganda ... on the main streets outside Jewish shops they have put up big yellow notices – with an accusing black finger pointing to the shop.'[37] He noticed that signs like these appeared to have been put up for the occasion. Later in the week they had been taken down. 'The same applied to other large boardings that accused the Jews of fostering war and Bolshevism.'[38] This may have been because by then there were not that many Jews left in Nuremberg. Chester noticed a number of posters designed to convince Germans that other countries were following Germany's lead. Much was made of 'alleged anti-Semitic legislation in Mexico' and there was a poster of John Bull shutting the door against hordes of refugees from Austria while the Jewish Marxist French were portrayed as welcoming them. 'Even Australia was recorded as having refused to give refuge to "this scourge that calls itself a race".' Most surprising of all, Chester thought, was a poster of 'Uncle Sam pulling off his genial mask and revealing underneath a vile Nazi conception of a Jewish face'.[39]

There was more Nazi propaganda in Chester's next 'discussion' with his host. Lehman believed that

> Hitler [has] saved Germany and Europe from Bolshevism, he has brought about economic rehabilitation and there is now no unemployment – he [Lehman] denied this had been secured by the device of forced labour camps – by the boom of rearmament – and by forcing down wages and compelling employers to take on men ... Hitler does not want war ... will not make war ... on anyone ... Of course Germany will not allow other nations to oppress her or oppress Germans ... Give Hitler his just demands and there will be no war ... The Czechs were the aggressors in the Sudeten case ... and the Czechs not satisfied with this wanted more territory and had actually threatened to attack Germany. No it would not be Germany who started another war it would be because other nations attacked Germany.[40]

Wilmot didn't want to offend someone who was otherwise likeable and hospitable. Earlier when he had stayed in because of the rain, Lehman's wife and daughter had showed him the artificial fabrics that were now being made in Germany. Erna, their daughter, was 'seventeen, bucksome, naive but certainly not shy'. So to avoid any further argument Chester 'took Erna out to dance in a café – the Wintergarden where there was a very good band and a floor show – very good too. But it was packed with Nazis in uniform ... I dare say that now when a baby is born the nurse turns it upside down and stamps a swastika on its bottom,' he wrote feelingly in his diary.[41]

The next day was the first of the big parades and Chester stood in the cold and occasional showers 'with 50,000 other mugs' at the vast Zeppelin field and watched the parade and the drill of the Arbeits Dienst – about 42 000 of them. It would have been amusing if everything had not been so full of grim foreboding. 'I'm sure [the crowds] worship it along with the power it represents,' Wilmot thought.[42] The Zeppelin field is now familiar from literally hundreds of documentaries (most using footage from *Triumph of the Will*): the giant swastika devised by Albert Speer over the rostrum where Hitler speaks, the huge bronze dish containing a flame burns throughout the ritual and there is the huge stand.

The Arbeits Dienst was really a workers' corps but everything about them was military. They might drill with spades instead of rifles, but for Chester the hour-long march and the laying of a wreath to commemorate the war dead were just a covert glorification of war. As he saw it, Hitler's speech and the crowd's reaction was 'altogether a lamentable performance'. 'Whenever the Führer referred to Germany's great power to resist aggressive neighbours the mob howled with delight.'[43]

In the afternoon Chester went to a propaganda exhibition called 'Europe's Struggle in the East-Germany the Bulwark of Europe'. It purported to show how for centuries barbarian hordes had surged across Europe always opposed by Germany. Some had seeped through in France, in Poland, and it was supposed to be the same now with Germany surrounded by Bolshevik Marxist states – all enemies. It was a chilling display of calculated paranoia.

Just as the weather began to clear Wilmot had to leave for

Prague. Hitler's main speech was due later in the festival. Everyone expected it to be important and the British Ambassador, Sir Neville Henderson, a great admirer of Nazi pageantry, was to make a point of attending. He can be seen in the official newsreel, a spotted silk scarf around his neck, doffing his homburg to the Nazi banners. But Chester did not have a ticket for the occasion and probably thought it would be more useful to observe reactions in Czechoslovakia than with the Lehmans in Nuremberg. Moreover, it is clear Chester believed this might be his last chance to see the old Europe before the outbreak of the war he was increasingly coming to believe was inevitable. Wilmot never stated this explicitly in his diary letters – they were intended for his father and mother – but it is implicit in everything he wrote.

He took the International Express to the Czech capital. His first impression of Prague itself was that it was 'a little America for the train draws into Wilsonova Nadrazi and the first thing you see is the Hotel Wilson (named after America's wartime President Woodrow Wilson) all of which testify to the gratitude of the Czechs to the Americans who did fight for national independence and democracy whatever England and France fought [for].'[44] Although he couldn't help reflecting that the names might soon be changed to 'Adolph Hitler Platz' or 'Deutscher Hof', it was a reminder that the Czechs had fought alongside the Allies in the Great War to gain their freedom from the old Austro-Hungarian Empire.

After getting a room at the Terminus Hotel – a five shillings and sixpence bed and breakfast – Chester set out to see the city. His diary entry is almost lyrical.

> Come to Prague in the evening ... and stay in the hotel until after dusk ... then walk from near the station up the hill to the museum which tops the hill in flood lit glory above Vaclavski Nameski ... which after the Champs Elyssees must be well in the running for the loveliest street in Europe standing on the

> steps [of the museum] and beneath you down the hill runs a street twice as wide as Collins Street gay with neon signs and thronged with people ... people not in uniforms ... a street that does not proclaim its gaiety in barbaric flags and symbols.[45]

Chester could not speak a word of Czech but no one minded. As one 'very attractive lass' (of course) told him later, 'no one speaks Czech so we just learn everyone else's language'; she spoke three! Like many visitors in the 1930s the Australian seems to have fallen a little in love with the country.

> The best of Prague at night is to be seen along the Moldau. Bridges seem to cross it every few hundred yards – the more beautiful of them floodlit ... on either side dotted here and there are floodlit buildings – it matters not what they are ... all that matters is that we have a people so proud of their city that they do their best to make it more beautiful at night ... The lights sparkle back on the water ... Music from a dance band ... drifts across and mingles with the noise of rushing water ... from the breakwater further down.[46]

The next day Wilmot began to follow up the contacts he had been given in London. Over lunch and dinner, Dr Vladimir Prochazka, a major figure in international affairs organisations, briefed him on the way the British Government were putting pressure on the Czechs to make even more concessions to Hitler than they had already. Behind Henlein, he said, was the threat that there would be war with Germany if the demands of the Sudeten Germans were not met. He was right. The German General Staff had already finalised Case Green, the plan for the invasion of Czechoslovakia. The deadline was 30 September.

The next day Chester saw Dr Sychrava, editor of one of the most influential papers in Prague. Sychrava was a leader of the movement for peace that wanted to compromise with the Sudeten Germans. Speaking very slowly in French, the only language he and Chester had in common, he was even more pessimistic. Hitler was unlikely to be restrained even by the threat of world war unless it was made absolutely plain. Otherwise the dictator would gamble on taking what he wanted before France and Britain could mobilise. However, a strong declaration by France, Britain and Russia, delivered directly to Hitler, might work.

Chester also had an introduction to Vilem Fried, better known as Mickey, the leader of the national union of students. They met in one of the old-style coffee houses of the old Austro-Hungarian Empire with soft easy chairs, the newspapers of every country in Europe brought to your table. With Mickey were some other Czech students and a Bob Auty from Cairns College, a lecturer in modern languages, who had been studying the problems of the ethnic minorities in Czechoslovakia. As well as collecting information about the tensions between the Slovaks, the Hungarians and the Prague government, Chester was told that the Czech President Beneš had granted all the demands of non-Nazi Sudeten parties in early 1937. Nobody knew that six days earlier on 4 September two of the leaders of the Sudeten Nazi Party, Kundt and Sebekovsky, had been summoned by Benes to the Hradschin Palace. The scene was described by that ultimate insider John Wheeler-Bennett in *Munich – Prologue to Tragedy*, pieced together from an interview Beneš gave to Eric Gedye in October 1945, and confirmed by Beneš to Wheeler-Bennett in July 1946.

> Without preliminaries [Beneš] pushed a blank sheet of paper towards them saying: 'Please write your party's full demands for the German minority. I promise you in advance to give them to you immediately.'

Kundt was thunderstruck. He stared incredulously at the President. Sebekovsky sat in angry suspicious silence.

'Go on; I mean it. Write!' said the President ...

They shifted uncomfortably in their chairs ... The President was surrendering but he was conducting the whole affair as if he, not they, was the victor.

'Very well; if you won't write it down I will,' said the President and drawing the blank sheet of paper towards him, he unscrewed his fountain pen and sat waiting. So at the dictation of the Sudeten German Party the President of the Czechoslovak Republic wrote down what came ultimately to be "Plan No 4" ...'[47]

A summary of this plan was in the Czech papers in the coffee shop where Chester, Mickey and the rest were meeting. The full story didn't come out until after the war. It was, as the two Nazis suspected, a trap. By agreeing to their demands Beneš hoped to demonstrate that the Sudeten Germans were not some oppressed minority but were trying to destroy Czechoslovakia. As Chester wrote later, 'The rights and wrongs of the Sudetens are beside the point Hitler is interested in them merely as an excuse his aim is the conquest or domination of all Central Europe'.[48]

Wilmot also discovered that Lord Runciman was regarded with 'a certain amount of suspicion ... They rather suspect that he is another form of the non intervention committee ... an English device to waste time and postpone any definite action until it is too late.'[49] The Czechs also resented the way Runciman had spent most of his time with the wealthy Sudeten German aristocracy and had made few social contacts with the Czechs. Under the old Empire, Chester was told, the Germans, Austrians and Hungarians were the aristocracy. The foundation of Czechoslovakia had meant the equalisation of nationalities and the dethroning of the former privileged class. 'In the democratic state the bourgeois Czechs became as good as the German aristocrats.'[50] From what he was hearing, Chester believed that if the Czechs had trusted the Germans and Hungarians, there would not have been the small amount of discrimination there had been. And it was this discrimination plus the Sudetens' resentment of the new Czech status that Hitler was exploiting.

Chester may have been only on the fringes but he was being well informed. The Runciman mission was an excuse for non-intervention; it had been forced on the Czechs and it got precisely nowhere. Ultimately the Runciman Report became a clumsy attempt to justify the Munich Agreement. By 11 September 1938 the German propaganda offensive was in full swing. In Nuremberg Göring was 'booming, blustering and fulminating [against the Czechs] like the barbarian bully he is, while Goebbels was "spitting like a viper".[51] Chester found it incredible that Chamberlain could talk or think of compromise with such a regime. Beneš's broadcasts, on the other hand, he found calm and restrained. They were of course trying to influence British and American opinion with the speeches almost instantly translated into English.

Everyone was waiting for Hitler's final speech at the Nuremberg Rally scheduled for the evening of 12 September, 1938. For Chester

> Any hopes that anyone had that Hitler entertained no animosity towards England and that the Nazis generally were kindly disposed towards England must have been dispelled by listening to Hitler's speech to-night. In a violent speech ... he hurled abuse and threats all ways at once ... Those that got the most cheering were ... his attacks on the effete democratic powers England and France who will not allow great nations like Germany the right to live ... and his declaration that if the

Sudetens don't get justice from the Czechs they will get it from the Germans.⁵²

Chester and his Czech friends were timing the crowd's reaction. After each of these statements the cheers and Seig Heils went on for nearly a minute and that 'is a hell of a long time'. Nevertheless, Chester found the speech 'violent in form but weak in substance'.⁵³ There was no ultimatum or even specific demands, and Hitler added, 'negotiations must go on'. Beneš's 'negotiations' with the Sudeten Nazis had given Czechoslovakia a temporary respite.

The speech was still provocative enough to bring crowds surging onto the streets of Prague in protest. But then from speakers mounted on just about every second lamp post came the calm voice of a government spokesman urging the Czech patriots to disperse and give no provocation. As a further precaution, a torchlight procession scheduled for the next evening commemorating the anniversary of the death of their first president, Masaryk, was cancelled lest it rouse Czech patriotism to dangerous heights.

Then news came of riots in the Sudeten areas. It looked as though there could be war in 48 hours. Worried about what might happen if he was trapped in Czechoslovakia by the outbreak of war, Wilmot's new friends, who by now included Beneš the President's nephew, urged him to get out while he could. Through the window of the train for Berlin Chester could see the flags of the beleaguered country at half-mast for the late President. He wondered if they were also signalling the end of the Czech Republic.

The first news Wilmot heard when he reached Berlin was that Chamberlain had flown to Berchtesgaden to meet Hitler. 'So England is sending her Prime Minister to see our Führer,' the Goebbels-controlled newspapers proclaimed, at the same time keeping up the attacks on Prague. A lunch with Herbert Foerste, an economist Chester had met in Birmingham University when the young German had been an exchange student, provided a chillingly 'realist' view of the

Czech question. Foerste didn't even bother to pretend the Sudeten Germans were a persecuted minority.

> The Sudetens may be the best treated minority in Europe – but they are still a minority, and Germans shall not tolerate that … No homogeneous Germans can remain a minority … They are Germans and we want them in the Reich … The Czechs cannot expect to keep a bit of German populated territory for defence purposes. So long as the Sudeten regions are held by a hostile power Czechoslovakia can be used as a base for oppressing Germany. It is also the outpost of the Slavs and you must not forget that the struggle between Slavs and Teutons has been going on for a thousand years.[54]

Chester found Foerste's views perfectly rational so far as power politics were concerned. He would not oppose a unification of the Sudetens with a democratic Germany if that was what they wanted.

> But to give way to Hitler now … is to make a dangerous concession to force and to destroy the balance of power when it is the only defence the democracies now have – at the same time it would cripple Prague economically … The *Times* says 'Justice does not cease to be Justice just because a dictator asks for it' … Maybe not, but in this case the dictator is asking for anything but Justice – he is demanding power.[55]

Here Chester was going beyond journalism and political commentary. He was using the language of Pitt, Castlereagh, Metternich, Palmerston, Disraeli and Talleyrand – European statesmen who sought peace through treaties and the balance of power. In 1938 there was another European statesman who thought and acted according to the same principles. His name was Winston Churchill.

In the afternoon Foerste drove Chester around Berlin. It was largely being rebuilt by Hitler and everywhere there were streets being dug up and buildings pulled down. Chester found it a bit drab

> with no gay balconies or sun-blinds as you find say in Holland ... and all grey and very heavy in architectural style ... like a very respectable ... but rather shabby, middle aged hausfraus of the time of the Kaiser ... but still far far better than the drab grimness of Paddington and Maida Vale and Bloomsbury ... horribly nineteenth century and depersonalized by the rigidity of German efficiency.[56]

Later Wilmot met up with Ewan Butler, the acting *Times* correspondent in Berlin. 'A bit of the Eton type and rather podgy and heavy but he has some shrewd ideas and a pretty penetrating mind.'[57] Butler told him that the average German had no idea the country was on the edge of a world war, but after Nuremberg were more behind a war policy, but still did not believe Hitler's policies would result in war. Nor were they aware of how weak Germany really was militarily. (Nor was Chamberlain; throughout the Munich crisis he consistently overestimated Germany's military preparedness.)

Foerste took Chester to the inevitable Wagnerian opera – the opening night of the season at the State Opera House no less. It was a superb production of *Lohengrin*, in which a nameless knight (Lohengrin, of course) rescues the falsely accused Elsa. This was not the first time this production had played in Berlin. Already famous at Bayreuth, there had been a gala performance in August for the Hungarian Regent Admiral Horthy, during his conference with Hitler to discuss Czechoslovakia. Chester found the Wagner rather heavy in his present mood. For him Elsa was Czechoslovakia but he could not see Chamberlain as Lohengrin.

They finished the night at the popular Haus Vaterland, where 'you can dance or dine or throw at coconut shies or watch a review or look at a peep show – very respectable peep shows too'.[58] As they watched the crowds dancing to the different bands playing hot jazz or Spanish, each cabaret decorated in keeping with the music, Chester recalled the grim mood of the Prague cafes. 'No war fears here.'

The next day (16 September), there was a lavish lunch with Ewan Butler at the palatial Hotel Bristol. At a nearby table Chester spotted Joseph Goebbels. There was no news from Berchtesgaden about the meeting with Chamberlain. (Even Goebbels was in the dark. He was to fly to Berchtesgaden the next day to find out what had been going on.) The German papers were full of stories of a bloody civil war in the Sudeten areas.

According to Butler, who had just been on the phone to the *Times* man in Prague, Beneš had the situation well in hand. There were vague reports that Hitler had consented to a four-power conference. If so, Chester thought, Chamberlain must have taken a very strong line; 'he's got grit in a crisis … but why wait until the crisis comes'.[59] Butler gave Wilmot a rundown on Hitler's Foreign Minister, Joachim von Ribbentrop. 'Ribbentrop has been keeping Hitler fooled about British intentions for months and has assured Hitler England will never fight. He always belittles England's warnings and is an arrogant fool'.[60] The *Times* man then gave Chester a story about a German from the South Tyrol, then ruled by Italy, who went to see Hitler and got an assurance that the Führer cared deeply for his countrymen under foreign rule. Chester wrote it up for the *Melbourne Sun* as ironic given that Hitler had absolutely no intention of doing anything about the South Tyrol Germans, and was in no position to offend Mussolini after his support during the Anschluss. The paper ran it simply as a human interest story.

By now Chester had run out of money buying books of reproductions so Foerste – a good bloke even if he was a Nazi – took him to dinner. At 9.30 pm he 'was aboard the train for Copenhagen and civilization'.[61]

He had decided to go to Denmark to study the Cooperative Farm movement. For many intellectuals in the 1930s, the Crash and the Depression that followed proved that capitalism had failed. Many embraced Marxism or communism. Chester never went that far, but he did see capitalism as exploitative, and was interested in alternatives. But one evening in his room at the Hotel Cosmopolitan in Copenhagen – four shillings a night and for the first time in Europe a shower in the bathroom down the hall – he typed out his views on economic planning and socialism.

> I find myself rapidly coming to the conclusion that it is a mistake to think of individualism and socialism as exclusive things ... I find there is a certain muddle-headedness about the plans of most so called socialists and their critics ... The businessman will not admit anything run by the state can be any good at all and socialists think the same of anything private enterprise does. I am convinced that there are some realms of activity that should never be taken out of private hands – such as some small personal services and trades; that there are certain other fields in which group co-operation rather than state socialism should be developed, and finally in the large scale businesses that lend themselves to monopoly and are not the type where private initiative and inventiveness count for much should be socialized ... in this field come all utilities. The thing you have to strive for is to keep the best features of private initiative and at the same time destroy private power – the power that is stimulated only by production for profit instead of for use – the power which causes depressions and lives by making the market fluctuate for its own ends.[62]

These ideas were similar to the policies of the British Labour Party, and somewhat to the left of the Australian Labor Party, yet in spite of the close study of the cooperatives in Denmark and socialism in Sweden, Chester seems never to have approached any political party. To be sure he often mentioned a career in politics, and one of the reasons he did not apply for the job at Melbourne University was that it would prevent him commenting on political issues. But although he came to admire John Curtin and was on good terms with Dr Evatt, Wilmot was unimpressed with most of the labour politicians he encountered in Australia and London. Moreover, in these months before the outbreak of the war, he became increasingly preoccupied with the danger of fascism and here his opinions did not follow any party line.

Tuesday 20 September 1938:

Today I am thoroughly ashamed to be an Englishman – Chamberlain has blackmailed France into agreeing to another Hoare-Laval Plan [the agreement between Britain and France that terminated any further action over Italy's invasion of Abyssinia]. Czechoslovakia is to be dismembered and the very thing for which we were prepared to stand and fight in May is to be sacrificed without a murmur. The new frontiers are to be guaranteed ... how? England and France are a thousand miles away – Czechoslovakia will have no army – how can we guarantee unfortified frontiers from that distance when we could not according to Mr. Chamberlain guarantee fully fortified frontiers for a power that could defend itself to some extent. England has now lost the first five battles of the next world war ... even though she has not fired a shot and she has nothing to show for it ... no guarantees, no increases in strength ... nothing but a higher and higher armaments bill. Burning with fury I wrote a scorching article to the *Herald* – they probably won't print it but it got a weight off my mind.[63]

Chester was able to observe at first hand the decline in British prestige as a result of Chamberlain's agreement with Hitler. Just about every Dane he spoke to said they now regarded Britain as a second-rate power. If anything, the loss of prestige was worse in Sweden. He was told that Germany was demanding that the government curb the press criticism of the Nazis, and letters from the government had gone to editors of all the newspapers, urging them to tone down the coverage of the Czech crisis. Wilmot's information was almost certainly accurate.

Germany took a close interest in 'neutral' opinion, and this was to increase. During the war showings of the brilliant anti-Nazi film *Pimpernel Smith* were, at German insistence, confined to the British Embassy and then banned even there. Once Hitler had secured Chamberlain's agreement to the first set of demands, he upped the ante and demanded consideration of the Hungarian and Polish demands, some of which had almost certainly been discussed with Admiral Horthy in August. This was too much even for Chamberlain and he walked out. The gesture was slightly ameliorated by a note the British PM sent to Hitler before his departure, but as far as everyone knew, Germany was going to war as soon as its ultimatum expired. The Czechs had mobilised and so had the British Fleet. It appeared Europe was going to be at war within a day. On Monday 26 September 1938, Wilmot wrote:

> Prague has refused, so Germany will march on Saturday if not before and we are going to have another world war … and all because through their fear of Socialism the British Conservatives have feared to do anything that would undermine Hitler's power … of course now we will be fighting for our lives and everything we hold dear … but the reason is not that these things were in danger from the start, but because in trying to defend their private property interests the conservatives have let loose a monster.[64]

Then came news of a conference at Munich to include Hitler, the French, and as some kind of intermediary, Mussolini, but not the Czechs – their representatives were left in an anteroom. Chester spent hours at the cable office watching the crisis unfold. Much later, Hugh Seton Watson, who was in the gallery, told Wilmot about the tawdry theatre of Chamberlain's departure for Munich.

At about noon Hitler's invitation reached the German Embassy in London where it was immediately decoded and dispatched to Downing Street. At the House of Commons Chamberlain was giving a dreary speech on the diplomatic situation. Usually a dispatch this important would go straight to the front bench. This was delivered to Lord Halifax, who took it down to behind the Speaker's chair where it was taken by one of the ushers to the Chancellor of the Exchequer, Sir John Simon. He read it and thrust it in front of the PM. According to Watson, the PM did not look at the paper. 'Shall I tell them now?' Chamberlain asked in a voice that could be heard throughout the chamber. When Simon smiled the PM announced 'Herr Hitler has just agreed to postpone his mobilization for twenty-four hours and to meet me in conference with Signor Mussolini and M Daladier at Munich'.[65]

For a moment the House was hushed and then there was a roar of cheering with almost everyone on their feet. Anthony Eden, however, was so disgusted that he walked out. Harold Nicholson refused to rise. Chester's new acquaintance, Leo Amery, sat in his place, his arms folded. Winston Churchill was also seated, his head sunk on his shoulders: 'his whole demeanour depicting something between anger and despair'.[66] But he did rise as Chamberlain passed to wish him 'Godspeed'. The image of Chamberlain exiting the chamber on a dramatic peace mission was undoubtedly moving and emotional but, Seton Watson insisted, absolutely phony.

Chester was in Sweden when the full details of the Munich Agreement reached him. He read the Runciman report and the account of the debate in the Commons over dinner after a magical four hours' 'drinking in the beauty' of the architecture of the Stockholm Town Hall from 'points of vantage near and far'. Chester picked almost at once the contradictions in Lord Runciman's report.

After admitting that on the whole the Czechs were in the right, he went on to say that not only should there be a cession of territory, but a realignment of Czechoslovak foreign policy to bring it into line with what Hitler wanted. We know now that Runciman's 'unctuous impartiality' as Beneš put it, was bogus. As first drafted, the report outlined arrangements by which Germans could be satisfied within Czechoslovakia. Runciman rewrote his report when he was told that Hitler was committed to self-determination for the Sudeten Germans. As Wilmot noted, when Chamberlain went to Munich there was no hope of any settlement that did not involve the cession of territory. 'It is a terrible defeat for the British and French people and a great victory for Hitler and Chamberlain', Wilmot concluded. 'There is little doubt … that Chamberlain's sole purpose was to remove from central Europe a cause of war – if that [meant] wiping out Czechoslovakia he was prepared to do it.'[67]

Chester spent his last hour in Stockholm walking by the lake and gazing at the Town Hall with Margretta, a beautiful Swedish girl with whom he had nearly 'fallen irretrievably in love'. How far the romance went he doesn't say – he was, after all, writing to his parents. Chester describes her as having 'a gaiety and repose that is quite rare, draws very well, dances better than anyone else I know; [she has] a … charm born of softness and unsophistication'.[68] As he jumped aboard the train, leaving a tearful Margretta on the station platform, Chester felt that he had never left anywhere with such reluctance.

On 21 October Wilmot 'sailed up the slime of the Tyne in smog thick as pea soup made with coal dust' and on his way to London 'passed through interminable blocks of houses in which people of the richest empire in the world were living – or existing in conditions barely fit for animals'.[69] It was bitterly depressing after the clean and prosperous cities and towns of Sweden.

Wilmot found the euphoria following Munich had quickly dissipated. When he went to see a newsreel on the crisis he found that whenever Chamberlain appeared there was an uneasy silence, whereas shots of Beneš evoked faint applause. He also heard reports, supposedly from French intelligence, that had Britain and France stood firm at Munich elements in the German Army would have overthrown Hitler. James Smibert, now a doctor, was in town and they went to see JB Priestley's comedy *When We Are Married*. Also in London was Macmahon Ball, who was doing a late night broadcast to Australia for the BBC on what he had seen in the Sudetenland during the German occupation. So after the theatre the two Australians walked over to Broadcasting House to see him. Chester was surprised at how much indirect criticism of Chamberlain's policy he was able to get across. Later Ball told them the distress in the Sudeten territories 'was unbelievable … the Sudeten people are just bewildered although he thinks the majority now want Hitler. The Germans were forcing the Czechs to send back any non-Nazis who escaped.'[70]

Chester believed that if there was to be a war the tension between the Czechs and the Sudeten Germans would be intolerable. He was right. They were both to pay a terrible price for Hitler. In 1945, when Beneš was reinstated as president, he expelled all three million of the Sudeten Germans from land they had occupied for over four hundred years.

Wilmot was to return to Australia and when he said his farewells he found just about everyone was expecting another crisis followed by war with Germany. 'Perhaps you can come back and describe the bombs falling,' Marjorie Wace said to him.[71]

Chester was not sure what sort of job he was going to take up when he got back home but he was determined to try and expose the folly of appeasement. Friends warned him that in Australia everyone probably still believed Britain supported the Munich settlement. It was good advice. Bung had been appalled at Chester's diary letters home. Well-brought-up sons of the Melbourne establishment just didn't talk about British prime ministers like that. He feared

Chester would destroy himself if he publicly attacked the policies of the British Government. The Australian Government supported the Munich Agreement. 'The Sentinel', an anonymous commentator on 3UZ, had more or less spoken for the Melbourne establishment when he praised Chamberlain's intervention and congratulated the Czechs on their restraint, but added had they 'behaved with equal wisdom over the last twenty years the German population of Bohemia would have gladly remained in the republic instead of seeking union with their fellow nationals in the German Reich'.[72] Insiders knew that 'The Sentinel' was Sir Thomas Blamey. There had also been attempts to silence dissent. When 'The Watchman', another anonymous commentator (once named in Federal Parliament as AE Mann) denounced the Munich Agreement, the cabinet tried to get him dismissed.

But there was a man whose opinion about Munich was to mean more than any Australian commentator or politician. On 5 October 1938 Winston Churchill rose to speak in the House of Commons debate on Munich.

> We are in the presence of a disaster of the first magnitude ... do not let us blind ourselves to that. It now must be accepted that all the countries of Central and Eastern Europe will make the best terms they can with the triumphant Nazi power ... There can never be friendship between the British democracy and the Nazi power; that power which spurns Christian ethics which cheers its onward course by a barbarous paganism, which vaunts the spirit of aggression and conquest, which derives strength and perverted pleasure from persecution, and uses, as we have seen, with pitiless brutality the threat of murderous force.[73]

Chester Wilmot was to meet Winston Churchill only once, but this was not to be the only time they were to share the same vision.

5

TWO CAPTAINS AND A MISTER

Late on the evening of 23 August 1940, at Spencer Street Station in Melbourne, a small group gathered on the platform to farewell Chester Wilmot – a striking figure in his new war correspondent's uniform complete with a trench coat slung over his arm. Anyone familiar with the Melbourne scene would have recognised the dignified middle-aged man as Bung Wilmot, Chester's father; the formidable lady with the obligatory hat, handbag and gloves as his mother, Janie Wilmot; and the slim, intense young man as Alan Benjamin, Chester's fellow debater on the world tour. Smiles were forced and beneath the banter there was a lot left unsaid. As the train pulled out Chester could see Alan running the length of the platform to keep him in sight for as long as possible. 'This is the first time I have travelled alone,' Wilmot thought. Late that night as the transcontinental was passing through Tarcoola, in South Australia, a guard woke Chester and handed him a telegram: 'Keep your finger on the pulse of the world STOP Australia expects etc STOP Up the Ponsonbys [two British cavalry officers at Waterloo] STOP Hitler little knows what's coming STOP Darling I think you are wonderful Love Edith.'[1]

'Edith' was Edith Irwin, a cheerful, witty 'lass,' or so she seemed at first. He'd first met her at the NUAUS (National Union of Australian University Students) conference the day after returning from Europe. As Chester told Edith later, during the afternoon's discussions he suddenly noticed the low, attractive voice of a girl and thought it the most beautiful he had ever heard. They were introduced and she said 'Oh, I've heard about you', meaning it as a compliment. She thought he seemed alarmed. However, Edith stayed in his memory. Probably nothing would have come of it if she had not been a delegate at the next NAUS conference in January 1940 in Hobart, Tasmania. Edith recalled:

> I was part of a subcommittee which [Chester had] joined at the last minute. After repeated arguments from a well meaning speaker I felt an irrepressible irritation and asked the Chairman if we could not go on to the next item. The speaker was riled.
>
> 'You don't like me, Miss Irwin?'
>
> 'You talk too much.'
>
> 'I talk too much. What about Chester?'
>
> 'He has something to say.'[2]

As Chester said, 'It would have tickled anyone's vanity.' Perhaps Edith's barbed wit, which could be at times directed at even her closest friends, was a challenge to Chester. Anyway he was soon overwhelming her with advice about a speech she was about to give, ignoring her protestations that his suggestions were not what she wanted to say. Chester soon discovered they had a lot in common. Edith had been captain of her school and loved making speeches and debating. He regarded the narrow conservatism she had inherited from her parents as a challenge, and was soon extolling for her benefit the virtues of the planned economy. On the last night of the conference he drove her back to her lodgings. Looking across the harbour they kissed gently, and then at ease in each other's company for the first time, they began to talk delightedly about: themselves! It was the beginning of their romance. Looking back many years later Edith was surprised at how little time they were able to spend in each other's company during the following months.[3]

She lived in South Australia and only made occasional visits to Victoria, and no sooner had she got a job in Melbourne than Chester was off to the Middle East. He had rung her from the station and they spoke 'brightly' without making any commitment. As she hung up Edith realised how empty Melbourne would be without him and sent the telegram. Chester was to reply the night before he left for the Middle East. 'As a concoctor of cryptograms you rank high and I liked getting it. Write to me and explain yourself sometime,' he wrote.[4]

As the train sped across the Nullarbor Plain, to help take his mind off the 'anguish of parting', Chester wrote and thought about the months following his return from Europe. He had kept faith with Raymond Priestly and their vision of university education. There had been the detailed report on his impressions of universities in Asia, the USA, Britain and Europe to the NAUS conference the day after he returned. Chester had even become secretary of the organisation at a very nominal £60 a year. Most important of all had been his attempt to make study at university a reserved occupation. A motion supporting this proposition at the NAUS conference had been lost on the casting vote of the chairman – much to Chester's disgust. Still, his broadcast on the ABC, 'Universities and the War', as well as being a fair-minded summary of the debate at the conference, left no doubt that Chester believed that, in time of war, universities should be bastions of scientific enquiry and freedom of thought. Curtin's Labor government was to agree and made study at university a reserved occupation when they introduced conscription.

Bung had desperately wanted Chester to complete his qualifications in law. Knowing how brutally the Melbourne establishment could punish dissent, he was also worried about his son's determination to oppose appeasement. Even though they were living in the same house, Bung decided to write his son a letter, outlining why he believed Chester should complete his qualifications by serving his time as an articled clerk. It was not only a mark of the great respect he always had for his son but also shrewd tactics. Although now well able to support himself as a freelance journalist, Chester agreed. Looking back Wilmot was not sure he had made the right decision.

Friday 30 August [1940]:

On January 23rd the *Oranto* brought me back to Melbourne
… I felt then that war could only be averted by a miracle;
I was certain that Munich was no settlement nor even an
effective postponement for I could not see Chamberlain and his
Government taking advantage of the respite they had gained
… but … I did not relate this impending disaster to my own
life. I remember settling down to my life as an articled clerk
and secretary of the NAUS as though I was going to be free to
make my own way uninterrupted and settle down into a nice
comfortable bourgeois niche. Of course if I had applied my
analysis of the international situation to my own life I would
never have come home at all. I would have stayed in London and
worked with the Labour Party in the fight against Chamberlain.[5]

He had only returned because new friends like Hugh Dalton – the British Labour MP who had embarrassed the ABC during his interview with Chester with his allusion to the ALP Premier of Queensland – had said 'Go back to Australia, you can do more good fighting Chamberlain there.' Consequently Bung's advice to give

Chamberlain a chance was ignored. 'I tried ... wherever I spoke, [in] whatever I wrote to expose the hollowness and treachery of the policy that led to Munich,' he wrote in his train diary.[6] Chester was taking on powerful forces.

Prime Minister Joe Lyons had become friendly with Chamberlain during the abdication crisis, and agreed with his conciliatory approach to Hitler. Lyons was friendly with Melbourne *Herald* proprietor Keith Murdoch. The *Herald* was pro-appeasement. So was Lyons's Attorney-General Robert Menzies. He had been on a fact-finding mission to Europe (where he had met briefly with Wilmot). Menzies believed Hitler could be managed and ought not to be antagonised. He was close to David Syme of the *Age*, which also supported appeasement. The only challenge came from the emphatically down-market *Truth*, edited by the flamboyant Frank McGuinness. No wonder Chester's father was worried!

Of course, Bung's fears of some kind of conservative reprisal against his son disappeared once Hitler occupied the rest of Czechoslovakia in March 1939. Even Sir Thomas Blamey, still broadcasting anonymously as 'The Sentinel', criticised Germany, an echo of Chamberlain's bitter Birmingham speech attacking Hitler, which had been followed by the Anglo-French guarantee to Poland.

Chester doubted whether the Chamberlain Government made good use of the 'respite' provided by Munich to undertake any effective rearmament. Recent research on Lord Halifax – Eden's replacement as Foreign Secretary – indicates the preparations made before the outbreak of war were largely Halifax's initiative, and were on the whole inadequate. Moreover, neither the French nor the British had made any military plans to aid Poland if Germany did attack, even though the French treaty required them to act within four weeks. When the inevitable happened and Germany invaded Poland, and Britain and France declared war, Chester remained sceptical. 'I felt all the time he [Chamberlain] would sell out underneath us just as Petain did, and I'm quite sure he would have done so when France collapsed had he been in power. The advent of Churchill and the Labour Party was a Godsend.'[7]

Chester was right. After doing nothing to aid Poland – overrun by the German Army in a few weeks using the deadly combination of mobile tank formations and air power soon to be known as Blitzkrieg – the Allies sat pat for another five months until Germany invaded France and destroyed the French Army. The defeats in France had come almost immediately after the fall of Chamberlain and the formation of a National Government in Britain. Chester was not to study the campaign in France until after the war. Nevertheless, he knew that the German victories were not the result of overwhelming might but French defeatism and strategic blunders, hence the scathing reference to Petain. Wilmot also seems to have been aware that Churchill had been able to thwart peace moves by former appeasers after the British Army escaped at Dunkirk. How Wilmot knew is a mystery. If there were letters from British contacts – perhaps Hugh Dalton, by then in the government – they have not survived. By August–September 1940 the Battle of Britain – still being fought in the skies over England as Chester made his way to Perth – put an end to any thought of a negotiated peace with Germany.

One reason for Bung and Janie Wilmot's anguish as they farewelled Chester was that until then they'd had every reason to believe their son would be able to perform honourable service during the war in safety. To be sure he had joined the Melbourne University Rifles; Chester enjoyed the experience but thought the training lacked direction. However, shortly after, Macmahon Ball had offered him an appointment to the Overseas Broadcast Unit that he was setting up for the Department of Information, the new body responsible for censorship and propaganda. Wilmot found working at the DOI disturbing:

> Writing propaganda is bad for one who also wants to retain a critical faculty ... a sense of the importance of the evidence.

It is not that you lie. Dishonesty in propaganda doesn't pay. Rather you make a case instead of considering all the evidence, considering every factor and striving for the truth.[8]

This may be why he volunteered for the Second AIF. His application was rejected because he was in a reserved occupation.

Then the DOI wanted to get the famed Antarctic and Great War photographer Frank Hurley – 'Captain Hurley' as he liked to be known – to head the Photographic Unit in the Middle East. But Hurley had already accepted an appointment as principal reporter for the ABC's Broadcast Unit, by then in Perth, waiting to join a troop convoy heading to the Middle East. The ABC was willing to release Hurley provided they could have Wilmot as the veteran photographer's replacement. The DOI agreed and Chester became an accredited war correspondent for the ABC.

Working for the ABC was at least semi-official, so Wilmot sought an interview with CEW Bean, the Official Correspondent and historian of *Australia in The War of 1914–1918*. Bean appears to have been very impressed with the young man; he stressed to Wilmot that it was sometimes a correspondent's duty to take action that was not even possible for senior officers and to raise issues at the very top that would otherwise get lost in channels. Chester did not know that some of Bean's own interventions, such as his and Keith Murdoch's attempt to thwart Sir John Monash's appointment as commander of the Australian Corps, had been, to say the least, misguided.[9]

At the time the older man's advice confirmed Wilmot's profound scepticism about what he had seen of Australia's preparations for war. The appointment of Sir Thomas Blamey to command the AIF created a crisis of confidence among Victorian units forced to serve under him, because of the general's scandalous forced resignation as Victorian police commissioner five years earlier. He had even less confidence in RG Menzies, who had succeeded Earl Page as Prime Minister following the death of Joe Lyons early in 1939.

> We can hardly hope for much social progress from a government which during a war against Fascism has people arrested and convicted for distributing anti-Fascist literature; bans the production of Clifford Odets's anti-Fascist play *Till the Day I Die*; searches the houses of the University of Western Australia's staff and carries off Left Book publications produced under the auspices of the British Labour Party which is part of Britain's National Government.[10]

Certainly Menzies proved to be a failure as a wartime prime minister, but the administrative challenges of raising the Second AIF brought out the best in Sir Thomas Blamey and laid the foundation for Australia's later victories in the Middle East and Pacific.

On Monday, 2 September 1940 Chester wrote: 'Heavy rain during the night and [a] bleak day as we ran into Perth a little late.'[11] He was met by the head of the unit, Lawrence H. Cecil. At this first meeting Chester found him 'a really delightful man with a quiet manner and a great interest in the welfare of his men'.[12] Cecil, Chester discovered, had been a captain in the King's Royal Rifles in the 'last war', and had been a producer for the NSW division of the ABC since 1933. 'He is about 45 – medium height – gray hair brushed back – a thin line of moustache. Looks quite like [the] film actor Frank Morgan.'[13]

Although he never lost his liking for the man, Chester was to find Cecil as much of a ditherer as Morgan usually played on the screen. Indeed he had been warned. When he had been in Canberra seeing CEW Bean, he'd encountered Frank Hurley, who had just returned from Perth and was making arrangements to fly to the Middle East himself. The veteran photographer took him aside and said, 'Lawrence is a very nice man but he's a terrible ditherer and if you want to get anything done you'll have to get away from him.'[14] When they met up outside Bardia in the Middle East a few months later Hurley asked Wilmot if he had been right and Chester had to admit that he was. In fact, if Chester had been more experienced he would have realised from the outset that the problems Cecil was having with the radio engineer, Reg Boyle, could have been resolved by a more decisive leader. Certainly there was the issue of divided authority. In 1940 all the ABC's technical work was the responsibility of the Postmaster-General's Department (PMG) and Boyle was making the most of it.

> Boyle as Engineer was to be responsible for all the technical side. Boyle has interpreted this to mean that he is not obliged to take any instructions from Cecil as to the use to which the gear is put – that he is to be the sole judge as to whether we use the small truck or the main recorder van – that he not Cecil is to handle the controls when we are producing shows, which is of course ridiculous because Cecil knows what effects he wants.[15]

Inevitably Boyle was personally jealous of Cecil and Wilmot. They were on higher rates of pay and of course Cecil was a captain from the last war and a reserve captain in the Australian Army. It had all been too much for Boyle when both Hurley and Cecil were 'captains'. When Movietone newsreel had been filming an item on the unit and the commentator referred to Captain Lawrence Cecil, Captain Frank Hurley and Mr Boyle, Boyle broke in, 'We're all Mr. in this unit, there are no ranks and no Captains'.[16] Earlier he had complained to TW Bearup (the ABC's Acting General Manager now that Charles Moses had joined the 8th Division where he was for the moment serving – as a captain!) that he would not go unless he was a captain the same as Captain Cecil and Captain Hurley.

It was all ridiculous and all too painfully familiar to anyone who has worked in any bureaucracy, especially the public service. Fortunately the other two technicians, who were also from the PMG, Bill MacFarlane and Leo Galloway, were both 'very good lads', good at their jobs and 'very pleasant fellows'. Chester was 'staggered' when he saw how much equipment the unit had with it. There was a mobile studio complete with recording gear and multiple turntables. The van was ten feet high and along each side of the operating table there were benches with recording units on top of them. Recordings in the 1940s in Australia, the USA and the UK were made on wax discs, the needle acting as a receiver, cutting into the surface of the disc and transferring the sound. Preservation was not a high priority. It was felt that once a recording was played once or twice the surface would be so crackly that it would be unsuitable for broadcast. In addition, there was the ABC's deplorable practice of shaving discs and reusing them. The war and the need to make retrospective programs were to play a small but significant part in creating the ABC's sound archive.

The unit also had a 1-ton utility with a canvas tray on the back. It was not fitted with any special gear but Wilmot and Cecil realised that they could put the portable recording equipment in the back. Predictably Boyle 'flatly refused to even experiment with the portable recorder'.[17] Of course this is what they had to do eventually but their engineer stayed as far away from the portable gear as he could. After some months of this, Cecil and Wilmot became convinced Boyle was in fact trying to stay as far away from any action as he could. This 'portable' equipment was still quite bulky; it was not until 1944 that the British devised a compact disc recorder.

While in Perth Cecil and Wilmot did stories on the timber industry and minesweepers. Chester also found the city 'living up to its reputation for attractive girls and reasonably bright night life'.[18] There was news of an Italian advance into Egypt. (Italy had declared war on Britain and France immediately after the French surrender.) 'Apparently we shall not attempt to resist until they get to Mersa Matruh,' Chester noted in his diary. While they were waiting for the order to move the gear – all 13 tons of it onto the troopship – Cecil and Wilmot went to see the famous British conductor, Sir Thomas Beecham, conduct Handel's *Messiah*.

Two captains and a mister

With the news of the Italian invasion of Egypt still fresh, Chester might have been less enthusiastic had he known the reason why Beecham was touring Australia. Like many of his upper-class compatriots he believed a German victory was inevitable.

Their departure from Fremantle was 'a typical army bungle'. Chester 'couldn't help pitying the troops' as they all left on the trains from the racecourse where they had been camped. '[They were] laden up with everything but the kitchen stove. On their backs – packs and tin hats on one side haversack and water bottle on the other respirator – over one shoulder a rifle and over the other two kit bags, slung together by a cord – beasts of burden if you like, but they seemed cheerful enough.'[19]

When they reached the ship, however, it was found they were 70 bunks short. It was a Dutch ship and the Javanese stewards had all walked off in Sydney refusing to go into a war zone. The Australian substitutes objected to using the Javanese quarters and had taken over the bunks reserved for the soldiers. Meanwhile the Army authorities had not told anyone about the problem. Still, Fremantle gave the troops a rousing send-off. A local military band played. 'Thousands of Diggers were cheering, thousands of fellow Australians were cheering back as the ships drew slowly out. It wasn't all cheering, there were some heartaches too but those cheers heartened us,' Chester wrote in his diary. This, he felt, gave a lift in morale that was wanting when convoys slipped away from empty wharves.

> Diggers in the last war were left with something they could remember in their very bones ... The marches through packed streets ... the stirring farewells from crowded wharves ... these gave them heart and they must have felt going out to them from everyone who cheered as they passed. But this is a different war – grimmer colder because of the need for extreme secrecy, convoys slip silently out of port uncheered.[20]

Chester thought they were fortunate to be sent off in high spirits.

Unfortunately, they headed straight into rough, choppy seas. Just about everyone was seasick in the congestion below decks caused by the overcrowding. Early in the day the lavatories were blocked and men were sick on the decks and companionways. There was no organisation of swabbing units to ensure the decks were cleaned and the lavatories cleared. Chester could see that the subalterns did the best they could and tried to look after the men but the officer commanding the ship, who, in Chester's opinion, should have taken matters in hand, was too busy having a good time. He brushed all complaints aside with 'Yes we must see to that tomorrow – we'll have a meeting [sic] a survey of the position in the morning.' Meanwhile there was chaos.

As he described this shambles for his diary letter home, Wilmot was almost certainly feeling somewhat guilty. His time on a minesweeper had given him his sea legs so he was not ill from the ship's pitching and rolling in the heavy seas. Moreover, he and Cecil had been provided with a comfortable cabin: just two bunks and plenty of space. The only problem was that the portable gear clearly labelled 'Wanted on the Voyage' had still been stowed in the hold and would have to be retrieved if they were to make any programs during the voyage. All in all, it was an ominous beginning to their great adventure.

6

A LOT OF LITTLE CUTS FIRST

Wilmot, Cecil and Bill MacFarlane soon rescued the portable recording gear from the hold and set it up in a corner of the dining salon. Then Cecil managed to get permission for microphone leads to be laid to various vantage points on the *Indra Peura* so that if they were attacked, Cecil and Wilmot could make their way to these positions, and describe the action. As it turned out, there was no dramatic recording of the ship under attack, but it was still a tense voyage.

In his broadcasts Wilmot emphasised the effectiveness of the convoy system, the thoroughness of the precautions and the 'weakness' of the enemy; all good propaganda. But he was too good a reporter to leave it at that. Here is his description of the on-board blackout.

> It's quite a job keeping watch over a ship with hundreds of portholes and dozens of doorways, for you only need to show one light to give an enemy submarine the indication it's waiting for. On all transports every porthole is blackened and before dusk they must be closed and screened. Every doorway that opens onto a deck is shielded by a wooden screen so that no light shines out to sea when it is opened … One of the hardest jobs is stopping the troops smoking on deck at night. This is taboo

because the flare of a match that lights a cigarette may be seen well away from the ship. Even pipes are barred. The troops on our ship tried hard to get round this rule by inventing all sorts of gadgets to shield the glow … But all their ingenuity was in vain – the ban stood, for it isn't the lit pipe that's dangerous, it's the lighting of it. Taking it all round, the blackout restrictions were well observed. If any lights were shown, we soon heard about it from the other ships and in addition we had our own pickets on duty all the time.[1]

In his letters home he went further, describing the oppressiveness of the stifling 'fug' below decks at night with every porthole more or less sealed. Early in the voyage a man was lost overboard – Wilmot was told he had drunk too much celebrating a financial windfall and fallen into the sea. A destroyer circled for several hours but lost sight of him. There was a brief service the following day. Night and day anti-aircraft gunners watched the skies for enemy planes. The ship's real protection was expected to come from the naval escorts. The gunners' task was to tackle any enemy plane that managed to break through the naval barrage and try to bomb the ship from a low altitude. From early in the voyage there were sub spotters out all day long.

Boyle was enlisted to set up an auxiliary warning system. It took up much of the unit's precious wire and Chester wondered why no one in the army or navy had thought something like this might be needed before. The convoy regularly zigzagged to avoid attack by the U-boats. As Chester explained to his listeners: 'a submarine submerged can only make eight or ten knots, a convoy might easily travel twice as fast … if a submarine is to have any chance it must lie in wait along the course the ship is taking. But if the ship is zig-zagging the submarine commander doesn't know where to wait …'[2] Clearly Wilmot was making good use of the naval officers he was encountering in the mess.

A lot of little cuts first

As they moved through the so-called 'danger area', the Axis propaganda they heard on the short wave boasted the convoy had been bombed on three consecutive days, and one ship had been hit. In fact, they had not seen even a single enemy reconnaissance plane. 'Apparently their propaganda machine is better oiled than their planes,' Chester noted. 'It was', he thought, 'a good example of lying enemy propaganda and a clear indication of the British control of the sea and air',[3] a point he made in one of the scripts he was preparing for broadcast on their arrival. Wilmot also wrote this description of life on the troopship. It begins with a direction to the sound engineer to play reveille and the bagpipes.

> Those were the strains which turned us out of our bunks every morning – the blast of the bugle and the wail of the bagpipes penetrated to the farthest corners of the ship. The only people who seemed really pleased were Scotchmen [sic] and the ship's dog, who used to march round the deck at the head of the pipers, doing a goosestep that even a dachshund would have been proud of. But whether we liked it or not – round and round the promenade deck the pipers went, until even the most stubborn sleeper was awake. Hard on the heels of the pipers came the ship's crew to swill down the decks.
>
> Then hundreds of men who'd been sleeping on deck had to make a quick getaway with bedding, lifebelts, hats, water bottles and haversacks, which we had to have with us if we wanted to sleep on deck in the so-called dangerous waters.
>
> There's not much training you can do on a troopship – especially when you have on board more than twice as many men as the usual number of passengers. For the most part our troops' work consisted of physical training and preparations to meet emergencies that might arise at sea. In addition, there were

instruction classes in [procedures] signalling, anti-gas and the specialised work of the various units on board. Even so, the men had a fairly easy time and most of them regard it as almost a holiday cruise – with a few fatigues chucked in just to remind them that they were in the army.[4]

Wilmot confided these observations to his letter diary:

The Brigadier had … some terse words to say about discipline on this ship. It certainly is bad for the railway unit is composed of some tough nuts and many of them went through the last war. They are an undisciplined mob – and I don't know what would happen if there were an alarm. They are quartered well down in the ship – whenever they have money they get on the booze and on pay nights their end of the ship is a shambles – I doubt if twenty five would get out if we were torpedoed on pay night. The main trouble is that their CO will not take stern action against them when they kick over.[5]

There are a few hints of ugly behaviour in Chester's description of shore leave in Colombo, but the tone is, on the whole, benign.

The troops had their day ashore, and had a wonderful time. As we were returning to the ship about eight in the evening, just ahead of us was a Digger who'd had a very good day … He'd just bought a paper but was having some difficulty in reading it by the light of the street lamp. So he walked out into the middle of the road – held up his hand and stopped the first car that came by and then proceeded to sit down in front of it and read his paper by the light of its headlamps. He'd bought his paper and he was going to read it but unfortunately for him he was removed by the Provost before he had digested more than the headlines.

There was one Digger whom I'd have liked to follow ashore. The Sunday before this leave the Padre on our ship spoke to the troops very forthrightly about their responsibility for Australia's good name while they were on leave. He was direct and blunt and he made an impression … especially on one Digger, for as I left the service I heard this fellow say, 'Oh well, he's mucked up my day ashore now – I'll have a conscience' … But whether or not he had a conscience when he got ashore I don't know. Anyway his comment was rather a compliment.[6]

The padre was a friend of Edith's father. Cecil and Chester had arranged for him to bunk with Boyle, hoping it would 'calm down' their difficult colleague; and indeed the clergyman's Christian forbearance did seem to make the technician more amenable, at least during the voyage. The Colombo stop also enabled them to get some of their stories back to Australia. The discs went by mail, posted at a very expensive £4 a package.

Perhaps to help improve discipline on-board by providing some entertainment, Wilmot, Cecil and MacFarlane used the portable equipment to make programs with the troops. These were at first 'very messy' as the movement of the ship prevented the needle from cutting properly. They recorded a quiz, with Chester as quizmaster. It went well; not far removed from a university review, but Wilmot was relieved when the sound quality was not good enough for broadcast, as he did not want to get a reputation for 'that sort of stuff'. Throughout his career Chester was careful only to work at what were known at the time as A-class (non commercial) stations.

Even though they were in uniform, the war correspondents were civilians. 'The correct title is "Mr"', Chester wrote to the family later. But as a courtesy to Cecil, who as a reserve officer was entitled to call himself 'captain', and had won a Military Cross in the last war, both he and Wilmot were invited to mess with the officers.

Chester felt this was a great honour but it provided Boyle with yet another grievance.

The ship's first port of call in the Middle East was at Suez. Cecil disembarked at El Kantara while Chester, Boyle, MacFarlane and Galloway continued by ship to Haifa. There Chester supervised the unloading of the equipment and typed up a portrait of the town for broadcast once their gear had been set up. Cecil meanwhile was having extensive negotiations with General Sir Thomas Blamey. The AIF commander made him write out 'detailed particulars' of the aims and objectives of the unit before allotting them a house in Gaza where Boyle could undertake what he insisted was his main task: the setting up of a mast to receive transmissions from Australia that would be broadcast to the troops through public address systems set up in the camps.

At the request of the Egyptian Government, who still vividly recalled 'incidents' from the Great War such as the so-called first battle of 'Wozzer' (really Wazzir) in 1915 – when Australian soldiers made a bonfire of bedding and blankets from a brothel where the whores had infected their mates with VD; cut the hoses of the fire brigade trying to put out the blaze; then beat up the British military police sent to restore order – the AIF camps had been set up in Palestine. These had been semi-permanent, but by the time the Broadcast Unit had reached the Middle East, it was clear that the men would soon be leaving these camps to go into action. It was therefore decided that once the mast was operational, the news broadcasts from Australia would be taken down in shorthand, and sent to the camps.

In these circumstances Cecil and Wilmot believed the unit's primary duty was to report the war. Boyle emphatically disagreed. He recognised Cecil as the leader of the unit but would not take orders from him. 'I am a civilian responsible to the Chief Engineer of the PMG and I will not submit to the jurisdiction of any person from the ABC,' Boyle proclaimed repeatedly.

A lot of little cuts first

It is easy to see how a technician who had just acquired some hard-earned status would resent Wilmot with his public school manners, 'British' voice – admired and hated in equal measure by Australians in the 1940s – and ready acceptance among senior and junior officers. Even more offensive to Boyle must have been that Wilmot and Cecil saw his stubborn refusal to go anywhere near the front line as cowardice. Never stated explicitly, it was implied in Cecil's reports and in just about all of Chester's private letters, and clearly influenced their treatment of him.

Making Boyle's behaviour worse in their eyes was that by 1940 civilians in Britain were taking pride in sharing the dangers of men and women in uniform. Only a few weeks before the BBC in London had been bombed during the evening news. After being showered with debris the famous announcer Bruce Belfrage brushed the dust off his script and continued broadcasting. Boyle's intransigence continued to divide the Broadcast Unit.

****

Wilmot must have soon come to realise that Middle East Command was a snake pit of rivalries and jealousy. From the outset of the war the regular soldiers, or the Staff Corps, resented the way most of the commands in the 6th Division had gone to citizen soldiers. Brigadier AS 'Tubby' Allen commanding the 16th Brigade was an accountant; Brigadier Stan Savige commanding the 17th Brigade was a company director; Brigadier Leslie Morshead in command of the 18th Brigade had been the director of the Orient Line; and Brigadier Edmund Herring (Royal Artillery) was a barrister.

Colonel Berryman, a member of the Staff Corps – who was to be Chief of Staff to the commander of 6th Division Major-General Iven Mackay (a school headmaster) – saw these appointments as 'a damned insult to the professional soldier, calculated to split the army down the centre. We were to be the hewers of wood and drawers of water. We, the only people who knew the job, were to assist these militia fellows'.[7]

Sir Thomas Blamey's appointment to head the AIF was different. He had been a regular soldier but, as many Victorian diggers confided to Chester, Blamey was tainted by the fact that he had been found to have lied to a Royal Commission and had been forced to resign as police commissioner. His defiantly sleazy private life on display in the Middle East was also a problem. According to Wilmot's sister Louise, Blamey had 'left a trail of slime' as he journeyed by flying boat to the Middle East. Soon after his arrival, the chief medical officer warned Blamey that if he continued the way he was going, he'd be invalided home within a month.

Still, Blamey had not been Sir John Monash's Chief of Staff for nothing and, Berryman's complaints notwithstanding, his raising of the Second AIF and choice of its senior commanders had been, on the whole, sound. In addition, he had made certain that his charter from the Australian Government prevented the splitting up of Australian formations by the British, a practice he and Monash had fought against during the Great War.

The relative independence of the Australian troops had been resented by the British from the outset. The first thing Brigadier Allen of the 16th Brigade — in temporary command of the 6th Division — heard from a British officer on his arrival in the Middle East was concern that the Australians would behave as badly as they were reported to have done in 1914. Allen promptly sent for Sir Archibald Wavell's ADC, and told him in no uncertain terms that 'if your general doesn't want us I have only to speak to my Prime Minister'.[8]

Unfortunately Wavell didn't take the hint, beginning his speech of welcome with 'I'm glad to have Australian troops under MY command and I'm sure MY orders will be obeyed', continuing with 'the Egyptians have lively apprehensions of what Australians might do in Cairo and elsewhere in Egypt' and adding 'I look to you to show them that their notions of Australians as rough, wild, undisciplined people given to strong drink are incorrect.'⁹ As even the very proper Australian Official Historian, Gavin Long, then a war correspondent, put it in *To Benghazi*, 'these were not the happiest words with which to welcome a force of British volunteer citizen soldiers'.¹⁰

Wavell soon was to discover that not all of his orders were going to be necessarily obeyed by the Australians. Within a few weeks of his arrival in Palestine, Blamey blocked Wavell's attempt to set up a mixed force of Indian, New Zealand and Australian troops. Lieutenant-General Maitland Wilson, GOC British Forces in Egypt, ordered the 16th Brigade AIF to Amiriya on the eastern rim of the Western Desert near Alexandria. This violated the conditions Blamey had laid down for their use and he forbad the move.

Wilson appealed to Wavell, who put the matter to Churchill. The British PM 'insisted' the brigade should go to Amiriya. It was a bluff – something Churchill was to try again on John Curtin over troops returning from the Middle East two years later.

Blamey promptly sent his Chief of Staff, Colonel Sydney Rowell, with a copy of his charter to Wilson's headquarters in Egypt. There followed a 'stormy interview' with Wilson's Chief of Staff, Brigadier Galloway. The formidable Rowell held his ground. He insisted Galloway get Wilson to read the charter then, and before the dispute became too bitter, broke off the interview. He returned to be greeted by Wilson himself. 'I've been a naughty boy,'¹¹ the general conceded.

In a way they were family squabbles and Wilmot, although fully aware of how arrogant the British could be on occasions, was careful not to let conflicts like these affect his coverage. As Chester would explain in his book *Tobruk*, the fact that he referred to particular forces of Australian and United Kingdom troops as British 'does not imply that Australians regard themselves as any less British than the people of the British Isles'.¹²

He also knew that the 6th Division had a dark side that went beyond harmless pranks such as directing traffic in Jerusalem or pulling garrys through the streets. Shortly after the Broadcast Unit's arrival in the Middle East he wrote in his diary:

> I don't wonder the Arabs feel sore about the way the Diggers behave. There have been some ugly incidents ... One evening a leave party was returning from Tel-Aviv ... Passing through a village their bus ran close to an old Arab a shotgun over his shoulder ... A Digger picked the gun off his shoulder as the bus crawled passed ... and turning fired out of the back of the bus ... His target was a small child running across the road fortunately the child wasn't killed but that doesn't lessen the wanton inhumanity of the action. On another occasion after a bus full of Diggers had passed through an Arab village a man was found shot with an officer's revolver. There is no doubt that the bullet was fired from one of the Australian buses but they never found the culprit. And we talk of Nazi brutality.[13]

Wilmot would never have been able to include descriptions of incidents such as these in his broadcasts. Indeed, a later script including very mild criticisms of some new arrivals' lack of proper training was censored by Blamey's headquarters. But the main reason Chester did not even try to use these stories would have been his concern for the reputation of the AIF. Moreover, he knew commanders like Allen and Mackay were determined to establish firm discipline and certainly did not tolerate this sort of conduct.

Wilmot must also have known of the many visits the troops had made to the graves in Palestine of family and friends in the First AIF and the men's determination to live up to the Australians' achievements in the Great War. Indeed, as background for the unit's coverage, Chester had arranged for the ABC to buy the expensive Middle East volume of the *Official History* written by a family friend, the cabinet minister Henry Gullet, who had been killed in a plane crash at Canberra airport. Bung Wilmot and Chester had been at a dinner with him at the Savage Club in Melbourne only two days before the disaster.

Wilmot and Cecil were soon plunged into making their Christmas documentary in Bethlehem. Unlike the BBC's Richard Dimbleby, who transmitted his dispatches to London from studios in the Middle East, from the outset, the Australian unit produced programs in the field. In fairness, Dimbleby, a pioneer of actuality broadcasting before the war, was at that time the sole representative of the corporation in the area and had no portable recording equipment.

By modern standards working in the field was impossibly cumbersome. As Chester explained:

> We have been recording solidly for the last two days … working on the Bethlehem Christmas programmes … It's a long and difficult job making these feature recordings … You have to make a lot of little cuts first … [These would be on individual discs. During the war the Germans developed sound tape but all Australian, British and American programs were on disc] then try and piece them together and put in a linking commentary. The commentary in the religious programme was all done from the Church as it had to be played several times in rehearsal. You'll notice that there seems to be a lot of background noise. This is due to the fact that each time you play these recordings they get more noisy and when you make a feature you have to play them three times … We have one turntable used as a cutting table on which we have the record which is actually being cut. Beside it is an amplifier which maintains a constant level of sound to the recording cutter. From the amplifier a lead goes to the recording van mixing panel which is a kind of box with a number of dials on it – each dial controls the sound coming from a microphone or another turntable.[14]

These Bethlehem stories were the first Chester had ever designed, and he pushed the unit's resources to the limit using all three turntables to mix together commentary recorded in the church with prerecorded material running on another turntable. He even insisted on his links being backed by recorded street noises. This meant that they had to cross from table one to table three, hold it while Chester spoke, fade three and bring in table two – all in ten seconds. A few years later this would have been child's play, but in 1940 it was cutting edge. Indeed Chester was trying to create in the field the kinds of effects usually found at the time in studio radio drama. Unfortunately, the sound of the Christmas program does not survive, although it was well received at the time. Ever the perfectionist, Chester was dissatisfied with some of the transitions. The script displays an impressive command of the Biblical narrative plus some guarded reservations about the Church of the Grotto itself. As he confided to his parents, Chester found the Roman Catholic church's elaborate trappings distasteful, but felt he could not spoil his listeners' illusions by commenting further.

Soon the unit was based in a stone house at Ikingi Maryut, a small town about 120 miles outside Cairo, that provided comfortable sleeping quarters and space for the portable equipment and room for a makeshift studio, where individual recordings could be edited into features. By now the unit had expanded to include five privates as drivers and batmen. For all his ruthless perfectionism when working, Chester was far more tolerant of the occasional escapades of the soldiers attached to the unit than was the more military-minded Cecil, who invariably referred to himself as the OC (Officer Commanding).

For all his shortcomings as 'OC', Cecil's establishment of the ABC unit was an impressive achievement. They were in the field for all the major engagements of the AIF, and when they went to Greece, Cecil was able to proudly proclaim that with Boyle working on the mast in Gaza the ABC's Field Unit was operating on three continents.

A lot of little cuts first

Above all they resisted being drawn into the dangerous ambience of life in Cairo. The place was of course fascinating. Wartime Cairo, with its spies, the leisured life of the British GHQ – not to mention the regular visits by celebrities from all over the world – has proved irresistible to writers and novelists ever since. But this was not the story the Australians were there to cover. To be sure, Wilmot and Cecil experienced the abrupt and very enjoyable transition from battle conditions to the baths, clean sheets and parties of Cairo. But Wilmot came to believe these interludes broke his concentration and while he went there to make contacts and transmit their stories to Australia via the BBC in London, Chester never forgot that, in the words of his friend Alan Moorehead, 'by instinct the lady [Cairo] is a prostitute'.[15]

Six weeks after their arrival a sound was heard in the Western Desert that few expected to be heard again: the opening salvos of a British offensive!

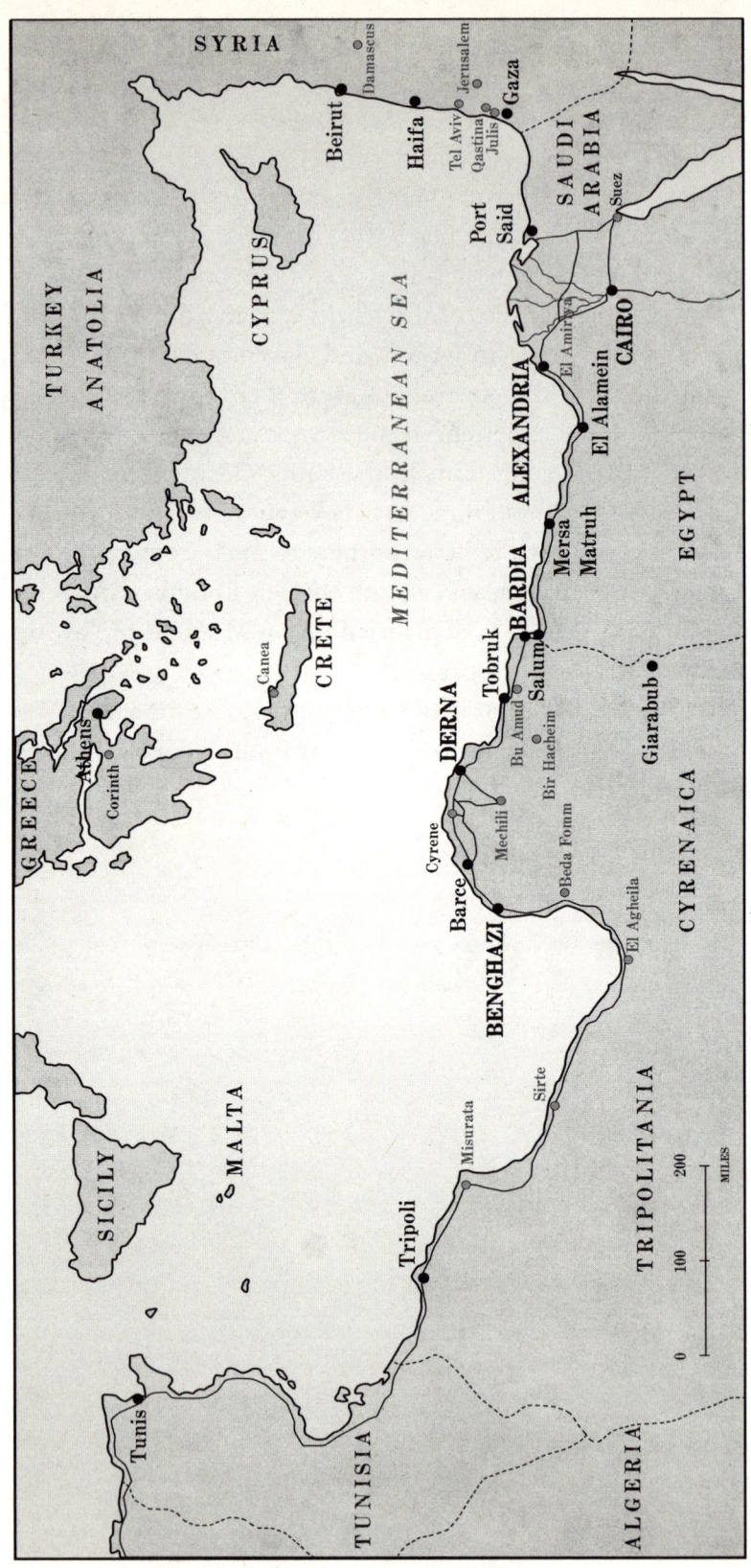

The North African Coast

7

I COULD 'AVE BEEN A BLINKIN' GENERAL

Early on the morning of 9 December 1940, Sir Archibald Wavell summoned the 'seven or eight' correspondents in Cairo to his office at the end of a long corridor in the big block of flats where the steadily expanding British GHQ was now located. Wavell was at his desk in his shirt sleeves, the wall behind him covered with maps.

> Gentlemen, I have asked you to come here this morning to let you know we have attacked in the Western Desert. This is not an offensive and I do not think you should describe it as an offensive as yet. You might call it an important raid. The attack was made early this morning and I had word an hour ago that one of the camps has fallen. I cannot tell you this morning how far we are going to go – it depends on what supplies we capture and what petrol we are able to find.[1]

Daily Express correspondent Alan Moorehead asked if the weather was favourable. Wavell answered yes, then smiling said: 'Now I should like you to tell me honestly whether any of you knew of this attack beforehand.'[2]

No one had. This of course meant that if the reporters had not heard anything then no one other than the 'authorised few' had either, quite an achievement in a city filled with spies. Wavell was later congratulated by the Egyptian Prime Minister on being the first man to keep a secret in Cairo. 'Press arrangements had always been sketchy,' Moorehead was to write later, 'In the face of a British victory they broke down almost entirely ... it was days before we reached the front.'[3]

Chester had not been at the conference but was on one of his many visits to Cairo to get stories censored when he got the tip off. He did have one advantage: the unit's utility. As soon as he found out about the offensive he headed off along the straight, double-tracked road that led to Abu Mena, past the great pyramid of Cheops, and out of the luxuriant Nile Valley and into the desert.

In the six weeks he had been in the Middle East Wilmot had used his contacts to find out as much as he could about the first moves in the campaign. One of the best had been Melbourne Grammar old boy Brigadier Edmund 'Ned' Herring. He told Chester that when the Italians had declared war on 10 June:

> Before [they] made their advance we were holding the Libyan Frontier with one infantry company and one armoured division. We had them well spread about and succeeded in giving the Italians the impression that we had at least three divisions there ... the armoured division was everywhere – day and night they worried the Italians driving across the frontier and attacking them from the rear and front simultaneously. We could do this because there is no regular consistent line [just] a series of posts – our people would drive between two posts and just at dusk would start blazing away from both sides at a place like Capuzzo.[4]

Herring added that the British forces had some difficulties with the dive-bombers, but they soon learned how to counter them.

they would shoot off in all directions then start driving round in circles which made it very difficult for the bomber to pick where to dive, then when he did start to dive they would shoot off in a straight line at an angle [away] from his line of dive.[5]

They had even captured Fort Capuzzo, but as it was of no use, they withdrew. When the Italians returned, however, the British 'blasted the hell out of them.'

Then at dawn on 13 September 1940, the Italians opened up with a spectacular, but not very effective, artillery bombardment directed at the old Egyptian Army barracks at Musaid at the edge of the escarpment, but they were empty. Once the Italians had occupied the barracks, the artillery was deployed nearby and a further barrage was opened up on the old barracks at Sollum, and the landing grounds below. As the dust cleared, observers from a platoon of the 3rd Coldstream Guards – the only British troops in the area – could see the head of the main coastal thrust. There were lines of motorcycle troops in front, followed by light tanks, staff cars and lines of lorries, stretching back in the distance.

The guards heard a roar of engines starting as they moved to the winding pass that led to Sollum; at the same time the troops who had occupied Musaid pushed eastwards to the top of the Halfaya Pass. As the Italian columns descended both passes, British 25-pounder shells fired by the Royal Horse Artillery exploded among them, RAF Blenheims dropped fragmentation bombs, and Gladiators strafed the marching troops. In the sky above them the few Hurricanes in Egypt outfought the Fiats and Macchis of the Italian Air Force.

All this was very satisfying for the British, but all they had were three battalions of infantry, which had little hope of holding against an Italian force of five divisions. Then, as the 7th Armoured Division was moving into position to try to counter any further Italian advance, a sergeant from the 11th Hussars, scouting an outlying enemy post, saw an Italian officer talking to a civilian dressed in a suit and trilby hat. Both were poring over a civil engineering blueprint. Behind them were a gang of labourers carrying picks and shovels. Soon aerial reconnaissance reported the Italians were doing what they did best, building roads and armed camps at Nibiewa, Tummar East and Tummar West. There they stayed.

The correspondents' vehicles clung close to the tracks which the heavy 'I' (infantry) tanks had made as they drove into Nibiewa – the first camp that had fallen to the British forces. Near the breaches in the walls there was a body spread-eagled on the ground and another collapsed grotesquely at the mouth of his dugout. Sixty or seventy donkeys were nosing around in the debris in a futile search for water; finding none they brayed sadly in the dust-laden air. Italian light tanks were grouped at the western wall where they had made their last stand before surrendering. General Maletti, the commander of the garrison, had sprung from his bed at the first sounds of the British attack. He had been shot down as he fired a machine gun from the opening of his tent. Maletti's pyjama-clad body, partly covered by a beribboned tunic, his face and beard stained with sweat and sand, was still lying there when the correspondents arrived.

The correspondents found Parmesan cheeses as big as small cart wheels lying in neat piles, 10-pound tins of *Estrato di Pomidoro* – the tomato extract that is still the basis of so many Italian dishes – and tins of stew, tongue, fish and beef as well as potatoes and onions. There was a spacious, tented hospital where Italian and British doctors worked side by side treating the wounded. Dugouts sometimes linked by underground passages had been planned with care and precision. As they moved around in the sand the reporters stumbled on cartridge clips, rifles, machine guns, swords and hand grenades, all seemingly flung aside in despair as the Italians had been overrun. Everywhere there was the pathetic debris of defeat: paper, orders and memos, and letters – some impossibly fascist in sentiment, others despairing.

For all the lavish food and trappings, the troops found that much of the Italian equipment needed servicing. Still, throughout the desert battles that followed, captured lorries provided much-needed transportation.

Wilmot was less interested in painting the scene than in taking notes from servicemen about the British tactics. He began his dispatch by describing how the Italian commander had built a semi-circle of armed camps to protect Sidi Barrani, pointing out that

> he had never been able to complete his system of camps. British armoured units kept open one gap through which they made a lightning drive to the coast behind Sidi Barrani. [The plan was] to make a lightning attack on each camp in turn by artillery, tanks and infantry – a thrust by an armoured Brigade through the gap in the line of camps direct for the coast west of Sidi Barrani – and a covering movement by another armoured Brigade to prevent the camps on the plateau coming to the aid of the rest – and after this an attack on Sidi Barrani on three sides. This meant an initial attack from the south – from the desert.[6]

To distract attention from this, a force had been sent along the coast road on Saturday, 8 December, two days before the main attack, Chester was told. The next day the navy had shelled the Tummar East camp.

Chester followed in the tracks of the troops, tanks and armoured fighting vehicles, which on the Saturday night had moved across the desert to an assembly area south of Nibiewa. The desert's surface consists of fine sand and sharp stones on a solid limestone base. No vehicle can drive over this without raising a cloud of dust. Chester thought it was extraordinary that five thousand British vehicles laden with troops, supplies and ammunition, had been able to drive seventy miles in broad daylight without being spotted. Even an

Italian reconnaissance plane that had flown over at 10 000 feet had not seen them. Certainly the British advance had been partly covered by a sandstorm 'but still they should have been seen', Chester concluded, as he began his chronicle of Italian ineptitude.

> When the first camp at Nibiewa was attacked, it started with an artillery barrage from the south-east – as this ended the tanks came in from the north west, thundering down in a cloud of dust and smoke. The Italians had no time to man their own tanks before ours crashed through the stone walls as though they were paper. The Italian gunners who had been firing south-east against our artillery turned their guns around and tried to stem the advance with almost point blank salvos. But their shells did no more than the hand grenades which the desperate Libyans threw at the tanks. They rolled on. Hard behind [the tanks] came the infantry [which] swept up to within a few yards of the camp in motor lorries. They came in with fixed bayonets – and they were met with raised hands.[7]

Similar tactics, Chester discovered, had been used against the other armed camps with only one giving serious resistance. Tummar East had held out for only ten minutes. The white flag 'still fluttered forlornly over it' when Chester arrived. There hadn't been much of a battle:

> There were boxes of unopened ammunition for rifles, light automatics and field guns – drums of petrol and casks of wine, boxes of hand grenades and cases of the Italian equivalent of bully beef – meat and macaroni in a thick jelly and very appetizing too. Abandoned tanks, field guns, rifles and Breda guns – the Italian Bren – lay scattered about.[8]

Chester noticed that even though the Italians had occupied these camps for ten weeks 'they had no tank traps, no barbed wire entanglements, no pill boxes, no deep trenches – merely stone walls two or three feet high with shallow trenches behind them'.[9] He could see that some of the field guns had been dug in but others were exposed to machine gun fire.

Even confronted with this overwhelming evidence of an Italian debacle, Wilmot still was among the first to report on the courage of the Italian gunners, and also to draw attention to the ancient rifles of the Libyan conscripts. They 'looked like antiquated sporting rifles and were made in 1892'.[10] He also pointed out that the Italians had no weapons to counter the British tanks, the soon-to-be-famous 'I' tanks or Matildas. 'In these circumstances,' he concluded, 'the appearance of our tanks must have been demoralizing and even the onrush of infantry … hard to face. Following the tanks they charged the camps in motor lorries enveloped in clouds of dust.'[11]

Heading north to Sidi Barrani Wilmot encountered a raging sandstorm 'so thick that we had to steer our way by compass – wondering all the time whether … we might strike a mine'.[12] He discovered that well before the British attack, the division of Blackshirts occupying the town had been isolated by an armoured brigade dispatched before the assault on Nibiewa to block the Sidi Barrani–Sollum road. It was a trap and the Italians knew it, so when the inevitable British attack came they had surrendered. As a result Chester could see little signs of the fighting when he drove into the town. There was, however, plenty of evidence of the naval bombardment. The roofs had been blown off all the buildings and the old square fort was a ruin. Ironically, the only things that seemed unscathed were the piles of weapons, the munitions dumps, the stores, the trucks and the tanks that had been surrendered.

On their way out of Sidi Barrani they passed dozens of abandoned lorries that clearly had been heading west.

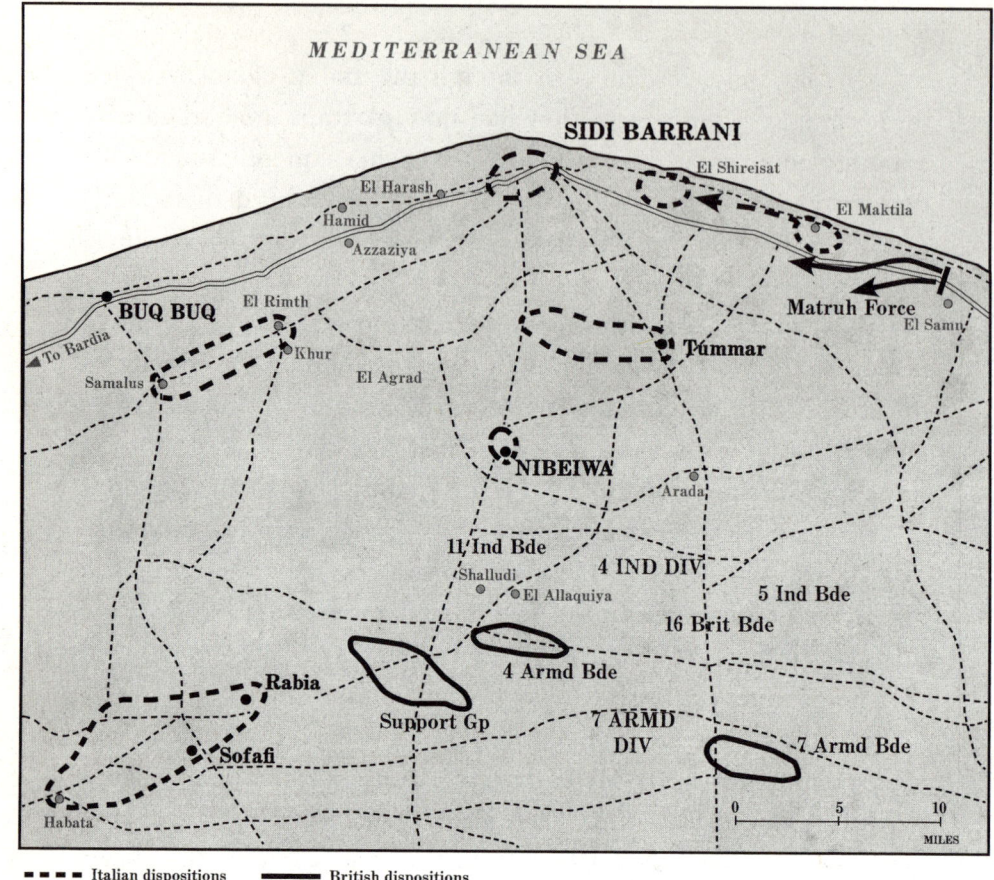

Sidi Barrani – 9 December 1940

They had borne Italians fleeing from the British attack on Sidi Barrani ... but they were soon halted by the armoured brigade. In its drive to the coast the brigade took completely by surprise the troops who were working on the road. There we saw lorries [with] stones half unloaded – picks sticking up in the road – shovels half filled with sand dropped by hands that had seized rifles. They hadn't even heard of the attack which had been launched three hours before against a camp only 25 miles away ... they were still working away on the Via Vittorio.[13]

I could 'ave been a blinkin' general

Translated, *Via Vittorio* means 'the way to victory', evidence of the fool's paradise in which the Italians had been living. This was no emergency road; Chester could see it was intended to be permanent 'with solid foundations raised above the sand drift level – banked and well drained'.[14] Now, he reflected, it would soon be carrying British troops into battle. Near Buq Buq they passed two batches of Italian prisoners trudging disconsolately into captivity, shuffling along at two miles an hour. Wilmot was told that earlier a prisoners' train had stopped at an AIF camp.

> The Diggers had given the Italians food and had swapped cigarettes for officers' pips and badges. One Digger came back with a set of Lieutenants' insignia. His CO asked him where he got them … 'I got 'em from an Iti officer, sir,' he said. 'Swapped 'em for a couple of fags … gee, for half a packet I could 'ave been a blinkin' general.'[15]

From Buq Buq Chester drove inland towards the escarpment. Here the Italians had built the camps at Sofalia and Rabia that had been intended to protect their line of retreat towards the coast. These had been abandoned before they were attacked. Chester examined the solid stone walls the Italians had built, and while acknowledging their excellent stonework, knew they would have been useless against the British tanks.

On the ground this had been a victory for the British and the 4th Indian Division, but in the air Chester was told the RAAF had given the Italians 'a hell of a time'. The dust storms and bitter cold of the desert winter had given Wilmot what he insisted on calling 'a heavy cold'. He recorded his dispatch sitting in bed with a microphone in one hand and a glass of water and a eucalyptus-soaked handkerchief in the other.

Chester probably did not know it until later that the manoeuvers he was describing were known in advanced military circles as the 'strategy of the indirect approach'. The concept had been developed by the military theorist Captain Basil Liddell Hart in the 1920s. These ideas were a passionate reaction against the slaughter of the Great War with its futile frontal assaults and seemingly endless casualty lists. 'No general is justified in launching his troops to a direct attack to an enemy firmly in position.'[16] After all, Liddell Hart had been gassed at Mametz Wood on the Somme, and throughout his life was haunted by the memory of being shelled while lying wounded and afraid on a stretcher.

Brigadier Eric Dorman-Smith, the planner of this first offensive in the Western Desert, was a disciple. He described the events of late 1940 to Liddell Hart a few months later: in November he had made two visits to General O'Connor's Western Desert headquarters; first to study the possibilities of an offensive stroke against Marshal Graziani's numerically superior Italian forces; then to plan the first moves of what came to be known as Operation Compass.

Dorman-Smith found that the original plan was 'entirely frontal' and along 'the line of most expectation', which was 'straight over a minefield which at that time we had no means of lifting.'[17] Even worse he told Liddell Hart: 'It was timed so that our artillery could have four hours after daylight for registration [of the Italian positions] which was dangerous for during that pause our troops would have lain under the menace of the enemy's very superior air force.'[18]

After taking these plans apart, Dorman-Smith persuaded O'Connor to substitute a directive that applied Liddell Hart's principle of the 'indirect approach' 'in direction, in timing and psychologically'.[19] Hence the lightning attacks on the armed camps from the rear and the sudden charges of tanks and lorries that were described in Chester's broadcast. Almost certainly Wilmot did not recognise the full implications of the strategic thinking behind Operation Compass until Dorman-Smith's letter to Liddell Hart was published as a foreword to the 1946 edition of *The Strategy of the Indirect Approach*. By then Chester had begun to write *The Great*

Crusade, the book that was to become *The Struggle for Europe*, and was a member of Liddell Hart's circle of military intellectuals. The concept of the indirect approach would become a vital tool in Wilmot's analysis of Allied strategy in 1944–45.

Wilmot returned to find Operation Compass 'paused', because the 4th Indian Division was needed in Somalia. General Iven Mackay, who had replaced Blamey as GOC 6th Division AIF when the latter had been given the I Australian Corps command, was ordered to move his division to relieve the 4th Indian Division and assume the right flank of the British advance. The offensive was about to become an Australian story.

8

CAUGHT IN THE OPEN

The next objective was the coastal town and port of Bardia. Brigadier Allen's 16th Brigade moved out along the desert road on 12 December 1940, followed by divisional HQ, and Brigadier Savige's 17th Brigade on 22 December. Brigadier Robertson's 19th Brigade was to follow later. Robertson was to move his brigade by sea from Alexandria to occupy Bardia should the Italians decide to evacuate that position. But the Italians had decided to stay and fight.

To defend Cyrenaica from British invasion, the Italians fortified the two easternmost coastal towns of Bardia and Tobruk. Bardia was about 15 miles across the Egyptian border while Tobruk was located about a further 60 miles west. Part of the town of Bardia lay on the top of a cliff overlooking the northern part of the bay below, and the remainder of the town sat below the cliff on the harbour. British and Australian intelligence estimated that the Italian fortress contained about 25 000 soldiers.

Throughout the Christmas week of 1940 a vast column of 6th Division troops, some marching, others in trucks and buses, snaked along the desert road from the Nile Delta to the outskirts of Bardia. It was a well-kept secret that the withdrawal of the 4th Indian Division and the substitution of the Australians had weakened the momentum of O'Connor's assault on the Italians. 'I was appalled

Caught in the open

at the delay of three weeks before they [the Australians] were fit to take the field', the general later wrote.[1] O'Connor wasn't blaming the Australians. Indeed, he praised the 6th Division's commander, Major-General Iven Mackay, for helping him regain the initiative after the departure of the Indians. If O'Connor was criticising anyone it was Wavell, who seems to have really meant it when he described the initial attacks as 'a five day raid'.[2]

When he heard about the new offensive, Chester was recording Sir Thomas Blamey's Christmas message, and couldn't get away to the front. Still, he did manage to attach himself to a brigade staff party when they made a tour of the Sidi Barrani battlefield, while Cecil recorded Christmas messages home from the troops. Wilmot typed up some brief impressions for the BBC, almost certainly describing the burnt-out tanks and trucks, the Italian rifles, the trail of empty petrol cans, kegs and flagons, and the huge tins of ravioli the Australian troops had ploughed through as they headed towards Bardia. The scripts haven't survived. Chester wasn't able to get back to Cairo so Cecil read the talks. To Wilmot's annoyance his boss was given the credit for the reports by the BBC. After he returned to the house in Ikingi Maryut Chester had a day in bed with a 'cold' – at least that is what he told his family. In fact the bitter cold and dust of the desert winter had triggered his asthma.

The Saturday before Christmas Wilmot and Cecil set out for the front in the ABC's 15 hundredweight utility. It was laden with turntables, inverters, batteries, discs, three weeks' supply of food and water, blankets, a pick and a shovel together with Chester, Bill MacFarlane, Cecil, and a certain Private Jack Kelly as driver. It had rained all the day before, turning the fine dust of the desert into a quagmire. The truck slid and skidded out of control as they headed for the road. Then they became bogged and had to be dragged out. They finally reached the road and were picking up speed when smoke started pouring out from behind the driver's seat. Frantically they unpacked the truck, expecting an explosion at any moment from the 48 gallons of petrol they were carrying. Finally they located the fire at the front of the truck. One of the batteries had short-circuited and burnt the outer cover of the amplifier. After extinguishing the fire they spent the night at one of the Australian camps. The next day they had a clear run to Buq Buq, 30 miles from the Libyan border. As they drove they could hear the distant sounds of the bombardment of Bardia. The following morning they drove towards Sollum through areas surrendered by the Italians. Their arms and equipment had been left on the roadside. The Australian troops had been looting there for days but 'we managed to pick up a few things we wanted'.[3]

Three shells whizzed over their heads as they reached Sollum. The Italian gunners were targeting the road but fortunately hadn't yet found the range. In the 'very battered town' they encountered Frank Hurley, who was now ensconced as head of the Photographic Unit. He told them he had found a first-rate place for a camp – a cave hollowed from the hillside just behind Sollum – and invited them to join him. The unit established themselves in another cave nearby. It was to be their base for the next two weeks. 'It was a grand place,' Chester wrote to the family: 'and by a little ingenuity we managed to make it fairly light proof ... at least enough for me to work by torch light in one corner. You'd have laughed to see me sitting on a camp stool typewriter on knee – torch hanging from the cave roof just six inches above my head.'[4]

The valley was reasonably safe from the Italian gunners and bombers. The caves were 50 feet from the bottom of the valley with the entrances covered by piles of stone. Chester calculated that they were safe from anything but a direct hit. In his first script he described the unit's first sight of the 6th Division outside Bardia:

> From Capuzzo we took the road which leads to Bardia ... till eventually we found the Australians ... They didn't look like the popular idea of a frontline ... Whichever way you looked the broad face of the plateau was broken here and there by the

blurred bulk of a camouflaged truck or by a little heap of earth which marked a dugout ... Here and there were tents and huts which the Italians had left behind them – all of them extremely well camouflaged ... not only by green and brown and yellow paint, but also by pieces of scrubby saltbush which had been fastened onto them ... But most of the troops are living in shallow dugouts scooped out of the face of the plateau ... [They are] about seven feet long and five feet wide with a bank of earth and stones around them ... and they are protected from the wind which is unpleasant by day and bitterly cold by night. If you can get down below ground level, you can keep fairly warm, but on the flat it cuts through greatcoat and balaclava like a rapier. Fortunately the troops have plenty of blankets on issue – and the comforts fund has supplied them well, with balaclava helmets, mufflers and mittens.[5]

Wilmot soon found that the Australians were adopting the same kind of aggressive patrolling the First AIF had employed on the Western Front in the Great War. He interviewed the company commander who had taken out one of the first patrols as they breakfasted with his men, huddled around their fires blazing in old kerosene tins, after they'd returned to their lines on Boxing Day. The captain told Chester that the patrol had been so uneventful that they had tried to stir things up by making a bit of a racket, but there had been no response from the Italians.

Patrols like this, however, were soon gathering valuable information, some of which the men appear to have shared with Wilmot – more than perhaps they should have. A script for the BBC that was in part based on this information was censored outright. Some pencil markings on Chester's copy indicate the military censor's concerns. Underscored is 'They [the Italians] are believed to have huge supplies of food and ammunition', 'The defences of Bardia aren't as strong as those we had around Matruh' and 'We haven't begun the intensive bombardment of Bardia but have managed to locate most of their gun positions'.[6] Chester was to encounter a great deal of idiotic censorship in the Middle East and New Guinea, but on this occasion the military censor was clearly justified. If the Italians had heard this sort of information on the BBC they could have taken countermeasures. Chester was to have many other disputes with censors – in which he was often right – but he was never to be this indiscreet again.

Christmas Day in the front lines was quiet. Cecil and Wilmot had spent the night in a dugout on a plateau between Sollum and Bardia hoping to make a sound recording of a night bombardment. There had been no action and after a sleepless night they packed up and drove into Sollum for a Boxing Day lunch. Then Bardia Bill and his flying circus came over. 'Bardia Bill' was a regular bombing raid by the Italians – ideal for a live description but the recording gear was packed in the truck.

Of course by modern standards 1940s broadcasting was impossibly cumbersome. If there was a 'fluff' they would have to use a new disc. In the surviving sound of these broadcasts, Chester can be heard struggling with his wheeze, or a tickle in his throat. On one occasion Wilmot appears to have turned off his microphone and let the disc run while he coughed between paragraphs of his script. Editing was from disc to disc mounted on different turntables. This could become even more difficult if, as sometimes occurred, the original recordings had been made at different speeds.

Everyone was terrified of live broadcasting where speakers were improvising. A description of an air-raid or a battle was fine, so were sporting events. Interviews, however, were almost invariably scripted. They would be discussed beforehand then typed out and delivered as in a radio play. Chester was very good at making these seem natural, but never completely succeeded, even with a friend like Damien Parer. He would, however, try to get improvised comments from participants during live discriptions.

These recordings in the field were taken back to Ikingi Maryut and then to Cairo, where they were radio-telephoned to the BBC in London, which then radioed them to the ABC in Australia. In spite of this roundabout method, the Broadcast Unit's dispatches were often to be broadcast ahead of the print journalists' stories even though all they had to do was telegraph their copy. At Bardia, according to Alan Moorehead, the newspapermen simply drove to Mersa Matruh to transmit their dispatches. Wilmot had taken a pile of discs back and was in Alexandria about to return to Bardia when he was ordered by Captain George Fenton (one the principal censors) to go to Palestine to record speeches by General Blamey and the Minister for the Army, Percy Spender. Chester protested that it was his duty to report the first time the Australians went into battle in World War II. Fenton, soon to become one of Wilmot and the Broadcast Unit's staunchest supporters, referred the matter to the Australian headquarters in Gaza. Chester was told these were General Blamey's orders and he had no right to query them, and so he drove to Palestine, made the recordings and missed covering the first days of the assault on Bardia, which began on 13 January. He then headed back to Bardia, as Chester put it, 'driving a thousand miles in three days'.[7]

There may have been more to Blamey's actions than the need to please a visiting politician and to exercise his authority. He had been a broadcaster himself and knew how important it was for Wilmot to cover Australia's entry into the war. Did Sir Thomas resent the young, slightly left-wing broadcaster who had been right about the menace of Nazism, when he (Blamey), as an anonymous commentator on Melbourne radio known as 'The Sentinel', had defended the Munich Agreement? Or was there an even more sinister reason? According to Rowell, with the 6th Division temporarily under O'Connor's command, Blamey didn't want Prime Minister Menzies to read about the Australian exploits in the newspapers before he had been briefed. The problem was that if you were not on the distribution list of Mackay's Chief of Staff, Colonel Frank Berryman, you could not find out anything about the impending attack. Blamey had been so concerned about the situation that he had sent Rowell to the 6th Division headquarters to see what he could find out. He even contemplated setting up a high-powered radio transmitter there so that he could be kept informed. Perhaps Blamey felt that handicapping the ABC coverage might help ensure that he knew the war news before it was broadcast in Australia. Wilmot's only comment was that he had fallen victim to politics. He did, however, take slight revenge on Spender. In *Tobruk*, Chester's bestselling book on the desert siege, he pointedly lists the Australians' deficiencies in equipment and then adds, 'Consequentially the troops were bitterly scornful of the Army Minister Spender's reported statement that they were "the best equipped in the world".'[8]

When Chester got back to Bardia he was exasperated to find that Cecil had visited some of the forward units but had not collected any reports on the fighting. Wilmot quickly started to report the remaining action. He heard that two battalions had been sent to force their way through the Bardia–Tobruk road so they could attack from the west, while another battalion tackled the fort. As he wrote later:

> They expected the fort to be a tough proposition but the infantry went in with heavy tanks blazing away and the advance company took the fort before the other companies could catch up with it. This opened the way for the advance down the road by the other battalions. They came headed by a squadron of Australian cavalry … and by 4 o'clock they were crunching down Bardia's Main Street … The town was ours.[9]

By the next morning everything seemed quiet:

Suddenly the bark of machine guns from the bottom of the cliff below the town told the troops in the town that they hadn't finished their job. Four Italian machine guns were firing across the harbour apparently at troops on the opposite escarpment. An officer from Maitland, NSW [Australian correspondents were banned from naming individual servicemen], took three men and a few hand grenades – scaled down the almost precipitous cliff, took the Italians by surprise and came back with 30 Italians and four German machine guns. Bardia was quiet again except for the shouts of Australians celebrating victory.[10]

Wilmot and Cecil drove into Bardia early the next morning to be: 'greeted by three Diggers racing triumphantly down the main street on captured Italian horses. One of them looked magnificent on a huge white charger and wearing a general's cap and uniform and a pair of terrific silver spurs. Every man we saw had his share of souvenirs, and they'd earned them.'[11] This skylarking became famous, or perhaps notorious, when it was covered in film and stills by Frank Hurley. General Mackay was furious and insisted Blamey's headquarters investigate these 'untoward photographs' taken by the Photographic Unit. Just about everyone, Chester included, thought the old man had overreacted.

In spite of his late arrival, Wilmot was still able to write an effective summary of the last stages of the battle.

On Saturday night the officer in command of the northern sector sent an envoy to the Australians offering to surrender with 7000 men. They hadn't been attacked directly though they had been shelled, but they realised their hopeless position. On Sunday morning we passed them streaming up the road from Bardia – they had surrendered without a fight … and they seemed to be glad of it.

It wasn't so easy in the southern sector ... all Saturday the Italians held out in strongly fortified positions and we didn't press home the attack. They were well dug in and they had a tremendous amount of artillery. The guns had been put in well protected emplacements, but they were placed to fire south ... and their rear was unprotected. Similarly many of their machinegun posts and pill boxes had been built to fire on the southern front ... thanks to the breakthrough in the west, our troops were able to attack from the northwest and the Italian positions weren't nearly so strongly placed to meet such an attack. On Sunday morning an intensive barrage prepared the way for an advance by the heavy tanks followed by fresh infantry. The barrage went on from nine till ten and by noon our troops had driven through the Italian positions for five miles and the last post had fallen. A Divisional headquarters and two generals had been taken in the action and thousands of prisoners as well. The strength of the barrage broke the back of the resistance, but nevertheless a squadron of our cavalry using Bren carriers shot 22,000 rounds in the two-hour engagement. Once again the infantry did a marvellous job and maintained a cracking pace in keeping up with the heavy tanks.[12]

Chester's principal sources for the main attack on Bardia earlier on 3 January 1941 were Brigadier Arthur 'Tubby' Allen and officers of the 2/1st Battalion. Allen came from Sydney and was the son of a railwayman. His father was promoted to engine driver on the same day Tubby's DSO from the Great War appeared in *Debrett's Peerage*. Allen had a well-deserved reputation for irascibility and could be very difficult after a few scotches, but he was known as a straight shooter. One retired brigadier told me that as a young officer he was fiercely rebuked by Tubby only to find himself aggressively supported by the brigadier at a conference a few days later. Chester saw another side. In his letters he describes Allen and his wife as 'the dears'. To Chester Tubby was a gentle, compassionate man, intent on getting as many of his men back home as possible. One of the first things Allen said to Chester was 'Would you ring Mrs Allen and tell her I'm all right. I've had no chance to write.'[13] Wilmot wrote the number in his notebook: Cairo 48731. As soon as he returned he rang Mrs Allen undoubtedly amplifying what he had written in his notes: 'Allen – marvelous – couldn't have done any better not reckless just determined to win.'[14] Mrs Allen was delighted to receive this call from 'a general' and by the time that misunderstanding had been cleared up they were all friends. Later that year Chester was the Allens' guest for Christmas dinner.

Almost certainly Wilmot knew that at Bardia Allen had been close up behind the front-line troops with his own staff, and the HQ of his 2/2nd Battalion, directing operations and sometimes grabbing and firing a rifle himself. The sound survives of a brilliant broadcast by Chester that was probably improvised from his notes – there is no typescript in the archives – evoking the experience of the advance of the 2/1st on a perilously narrow front. Without pretending to be an eyewitness he synthesised the various accounts he had recorded in shorthand of his own devising in one of the tiny notebooks he kept for that purpose. Wilmot described the men assembling at the start lines in dead silence and how the men advanced shouting to each other over the roar of the artillery; he recounted the desperate duels between the infantry and the Italian gunners – all in a subjective style that never becomes false or sensational.

He then recorded a further dispatch explaining the tactics. Chester's next recording described the fighting in the south and the famous assault on Post 11 in the southern sector. It was to become a minor classic of Australian war reporting.

> One strong-post held out from first to last – and we couldn't take it by direct attack. It fought back until it was completely surrounded and until all other Italian resistance had been

crushed. This was Post 11 – the most strongly fortified of all the 84 strong-posts which held the perimeter of Bardia ... it seemed almost impregnable and it was held by some of the best regular troops which Bergonzoli had. But even though the direct attack on Post 11 did fail, it still contributed largely to our ultimate victory. Let me tell you the full story ...

On the Bardia side of the main wadi the Italians had built concrete fortifications commanding the two branches [as they expected to be attacked from this quarter]. In [the] little wadis the attackers were under cover until they took a sharp turn to the left about 400 yards from the forts. But from then on they ran straight into the guns firing from underground positions in the case of Post 7, and from positions almost flush with the ground above concrete catacombs at Post 11.

The task of taking these posts was given to a Victorian battalion. The difficulties of the terrain were well enough known but the strength of Post 11 was not. It was well underground and the gun positions were so well camouflaged that it was thought that it was held by about 30 men with two machine guns and a number of Breda light automatics. The task of making the initial assault was allotted to one company and a machine gun platoon. But Post 11 turned out to be a fortress with guns in hidden positions so placed that the whole hillside could spit fire at the rate of 6000 rounds a minute of small arms ammunition alone. There were four heavy machineguns – ten medium and 22 light machineguns ... five anti-tank rifles, one anti-tank gun and three three-inch mortars intended to dump such concentrated fire into the protected part of the small valley that no reinforcements could move in it. Onto this approach too a large part of the Italian artillery was ranged ready for the attack. The CO of one battalion, and the lieutenant who took command of the attacking company, took us over the ground and told us this amazing story ...

In pitch darkness on Friday morning two platoons sneaked up the branch valley opposite Post 11 and cut their way through the enemy's wire ... crept up the slope of the hill on each side of Post 11 carrying rifles with fixed bayonets and as many hand grenades as they could. Their plan was to storm the fort – pitch their grenades in through the open entrances to the concrete trenches and dugouts and follow in with their bayonets. They very nearly succeeded. On the right the whole platoon got through the wire and up the slope before they ran into the enemy's fire. But they went on and 16 reached the outer concrete trench in which the Italians had their first line of guns. They delivered their load of grenades and some of the Italians put up their hands in surrender ... but by this time our men were right under the Italian machine guns only 15 yards away. Nine were killed – and the rest were taken prisoner ... most of them wounded.

Meanwhile on the left the other platoon found their way to the outer trench, stopped by a machine gun in a sanger outside the post. Half the platoon charged it with fixed bayonets while the other went for the trench. They didn't reach it, but they delivered their load of grenades. The men who charged the machine gun took it, but by this time they were isolated as no force could move up the valley to relieve them. One platoon did try, but met such shattering fire that it was pinned down half way up the valley. They managed to make for a small sanger, and established themselves there building up the sanger's wall stone by stone all day long. It gave them some protection and they kept up steady fire on the Italian gun positions until their ammunition ran out.

The frontal attack had failed, but the men who tried it did a wonderful job ... by their very daring they confirmed the Italian belief that the main attack would come from this quarter and so for the rest of the day the Italian gunners poured shells into the valley often at the rate of 20 a minute ...

On the Friday we fired everything we could at that fort ... but our three-inch mortar shells and 25-pounders bounced off the rock-top of the post like water from a hot stove. It was quite clear that we couldn't succeed with a frontal attack and so all day Saturday we lay more or less doggo while our troops in the north worked round behind Post 11. But the Italians kept up a steady bombardment on the approach to the fort so that little or nothing could move in the valley. To make matters worse their machine guns firing on fixed lines sent thousands of rounds into the valley and onto the solid rock-face of the side just where the valley turned. From this rock the bullets ricocheted almost at right-angles up the valley so that in effect the Italians were firing round the corner ... All day long the valley sang with the whine of ricocheting bullets. Our troops were wonderful under this heavy fire – especially when you consider that this was their first action. I had one fellow with me who kept on pulling out a mirror every time a shell burst near him. Then he'd look in the mirror to see if he had turned white. After a while we were all so covered with dust from the explosions that he couldn't tell whether he was white or brown.

In the meantime early on the Friday morning an amazingly daring and successful attack had been made by two other companies on the next two posts down the main valley – numbers 9 and 7. Under cover of darkness one company moved down the branch wadi opposite Post 7. Our barrage had just started and they met hot fire from machine guns tucked away in the hillside in a pillbox, protected from the shells by eight feet of stone and concrete. This fire forced the company back but it took another route … and came over the hilltop and slid down the almost precipitous face of the ravine, while the enemy searched for them with machine guns. How they got down that hillside I don't know … the valley here is about 300 feet deep and the sides rise at an angle of about 60 degrees. In spite of all this the company reached the bottom and set out to storm the fort half way up the other side. First they had to take a small post a little higher up the valley on the plateau. A lieutenant and one platoon scrambled up the rocky cliff below it – reached the top, rushed the post and wrecked it with hand grenades. They killed 25 Italians and took 47 prisoner. They established themselves in this post and gave covering fire, while the rest of the company tackled Post 7. Under the cover of Bren guns firing from the opposite hill straight into the Italian gun positions our men were able to swarm the post on all sides – scrambling over rocks as they scaled the cliff. They closed on it and got near enough to pitch their hand grenades in through the machinegun slits and the open entrances to the concrete pillbox. The Italians were surprised and bewildered, and they surrendered.

Our troops then established themselves in the captured positions east of Post 11 and though they couldn't attack it they managed to maintain fairly strong fire against it. During the day they had to endure a terrific bombardment and four times the Italians counterattacked … This was the Italians' final kick … next morning our forces in the north were in a position to attack the Italians from the rear. An intensive barrage silenced battery after battery and slowly the ring of infantry and tanks closed round the garrison at Post 11. Our artillery plastered the hillside with a barrage which reduced the top of the post to powder and chips of stone … and when our heavy tanks appeared the Italians had no answer to them. Their own flag went down and the white flag went up and out came the commander and 360 of the 400 Italian regulars who had started the battle. Post 11 was ours as it might have been 55 hours earlier if the bravery of the initial attackers had had its proper reward. The Italians marvelled at their courage and when the fight was over the commander asked permission for himself and his officers to salute the men whose bravery had carried them so near to victory. In Australia's military history these men deserve the greatest recognition.[15]

And that is exactly what they were to get. There was to be Ivor Hele's heroic painting that still dominates the Middle East Gallery of the Australian War Memorial and Chester's broadcast anthologised in Norman Bartlett's semi-official *Australia at Arms* (AWM 1955). If he had been a little more experienced and less delighted by the help he was being given by the Colonel of the Victorian Battalion – Lieutenant-Colonel Arthur Godfrey of the 2/6th – Chester would have been asking some awkward questions such as 'Why so little artillery support?' or 'If the main attack was not going to be in this sector why such an all out assault?' Indeed these questions were being raised at GHQ. As Mackay's Chief of Staff, Colonel Frank Berryman, told Ivan Chapman '[Godfrey] wasn't asked to. It wasn't part of his attack, but he was allowed to test the defences in front of him. The Old Man, I think, got a bit annoyed over the best part of a platoon being wiped out while testing a flank over open ground in broad daylight.'[16] After Wilmot's broadcast, however, there were no reprimands; only a DSO awarded to Godfrey for 'leadership'. It wasn't until Joe Gullett – a sergeant in the platoon that made the initial attack – wrote *Not as a Duty Only* in 1976 that the full story was finally told, not just about Godfrey, but also about Brigadier Savige, commanding the 17th Brigade.

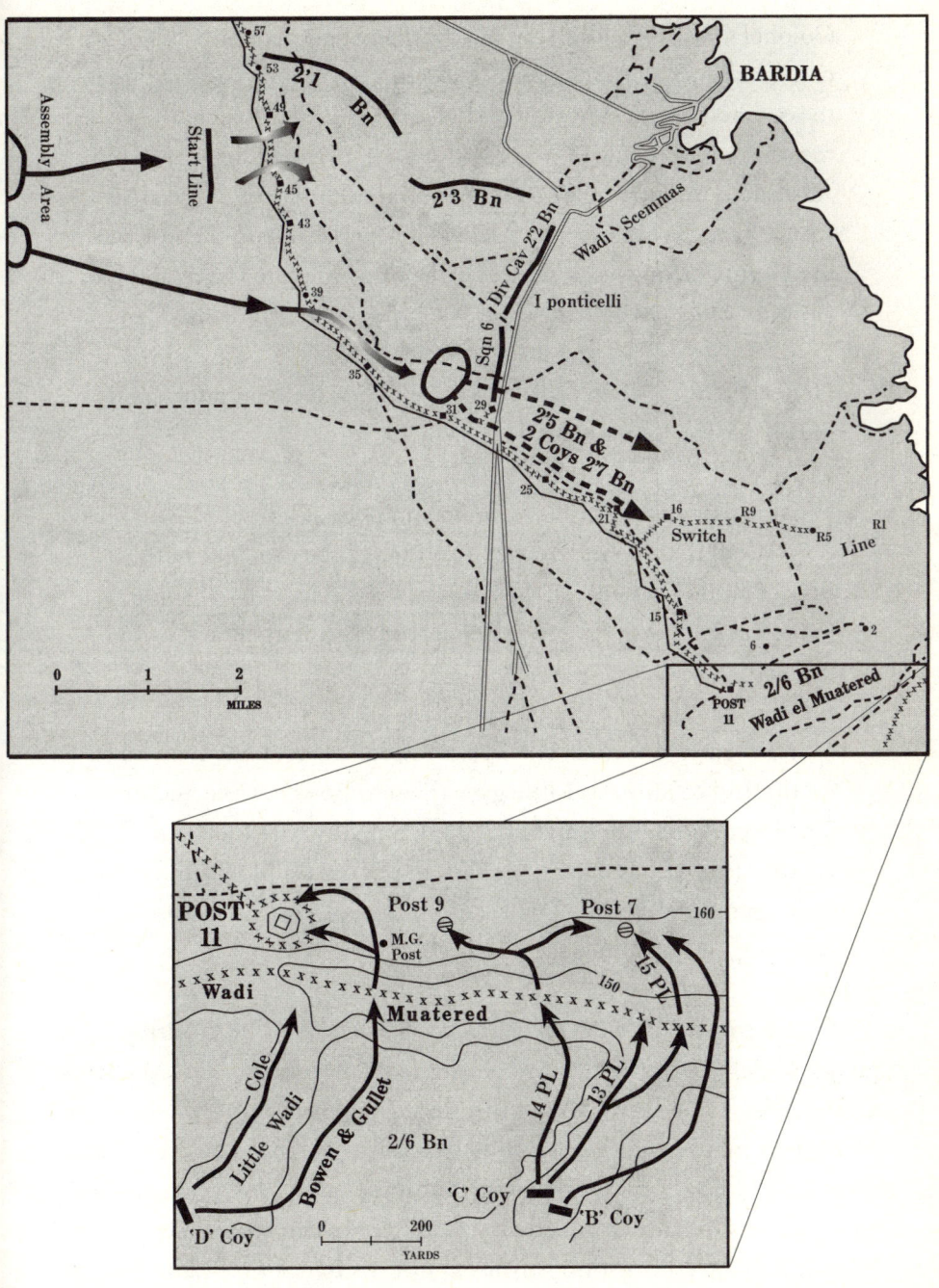

Bardia – The Plan

Colonel Godfrey, addressing his company and platoon commanders before the battle had said, 'No matter what happens to us, when we go forward we shall give the enemy such a thrashing that they will never willingly stand up to an assault by Australian infantry again.' He looked at each one of us from his square face. 'Whenever the AIF went into the line in the last war the Germans knew that whatever the outcome, they were going to get hurt. We shall give these birds to understand the same.'

General Mackay then ordered Savige to make a feint attack and Savige passed it on to Godfrey.

What is a feint attack? How far do you press it home? When do you call it a day and how can you judge the moment in the fury of battle – a battle in darkness at that? The two old soldiers looked at each other ... and they agreed ... A feint attack would not do.

Godfrey gave his orders to Captain Little and at about 1900 hours on the 2nd of January, Little gave them to Bowen, Cole and me. They were quite unequivocal. '"D" Company will attack and capture Post 11,' and later, perhaps to put the last doubt from his own mind, he said, 'I will see you then in Post 11 tomorrow morning, or I shall not see you at all.'[17]

There can be little doubt that Chester was used by Godfrey and Savige to deflect the criticism coming from Berryman and Mackay. And so Post 11 became part of the Anzac legend. Some weeks later Wilmot wrote to his father proudly describing the help he'd received from this 'Colonel of a Victorian Battalion' and how pleased he'd been when Godfrey stopped his staff car in the town square at Tobruk and gave him some stories about his battalion's activities. It was well for Chester's peace of mind that he did not realise one of the reasons for the colonel's warm greeting was that the ABC broadcast had helped ensure there weren't going to be any repercussions over the men who had died unnecessarily at Post 11.

Just before Bardia the BBC had offered to take two short talks a week from the Australians. Cecil had proposed that he do them one week and Chester the other. 'Of course,' Cecil added, 'you'll have to write my scripts.' Chester made it plain that, while he had no objection to his boss reading one of his scripts if he was not there, he 'did not think a commentary written by me should go over as ... "here is a talk by Lawrence H Cecil."'[18] Cecil did not press the matter.

* * * *

Soon after, Chester and the Broadcast Unit made for Tobruk. As they did, they were caught in the swirling dust of a blinding sandstorm on the Sidi Barrani–Tobruk road. 'Worse than a London fog,' Chester thought. Even the sun was browned out. The sandstorm died at dusk and the next morning was bright and clear. On the shell-torn road between Sollum and Bardia the ABC truck overtook a convoy of Italian Diesels driven by 'dusty, unshaven Diggers'. Wilmot was to describe the scene in *Tobruk*:

> A motley collection of British and captured vehicles streamed westward. Ten ton Italian Diesels ground laboriously on under 12 and 15 ton loads; staff cars, light trucks and empty ambulances sped past; dust laden dispatch riders on Italian motor-bikes wove their way in and out of the traffic ... overtaking everything ... a few Matildas and some reconditioned Italian tanks rolled slowly towards Tobruk husbanding their tanks and engines.[19]

Then they came to a barricade across the road and a sign: 'If you lika da spaghetti – KEEP GOING. Next stop TOBRUCH'.[20]

After a lot of driving around – mainly by Chester – the unit found a base about four miles from the front. The routine they adopted was that Chester would be up about 7 am or earlier, make a recording, and then take it to a rendezvous with the British or Australian press who had a car going to the nearest aerodrome each morning. He would then have breakfast and drive around the various battalions looking for stories.

It seems he was given at least a rough idea of the plan of attack on Tobruk from his contacts. He was probably not told that Mackay was going to try and deceive the Italians by reversing some of the tactics employed at Bardia and that the break-in point was to be on the divisional front, not outside it; the Australians were to attack at a point where the Italian artillery was strong, not, as before, where it had been weak. (It was of course vital that Brigadier Herring's gunners knock out as many of the Italian guns as possible if the infantry was not to be slaughtered.) But Chester must have known that the infantry with tank support were going to try and capture a succession of enemy posts and advance three miles within the perimeter. The night before the attack he decided it was his duty to go in with the troops. He wrote a rather awkward 'just in case' letter to his parents explaining that he wouldn't be able to live with himself after the war if he didn't share the experiences of the fighting soldier.

Lawrence H Cecil decided he wanted to capture the sound of an actual barrage. So they took all their recording gear into a valley that was surrounded by Australian artillery and a few machine guns. Chester abandoned any idea he might have had of going in on foot and decided to use the unit's truck. He described his adventures in *What I Saw at Tobruk*:

> As soon as the moon rose about 1.30 on the night of the attack, I set out by car to drive round the Australian lines on the southeastern front. At most of the units the men were still sleeping in their shallow trenches, but the cooks were already busy preparing a hot meal for them. They had dug small trenches to hide their

fires and stews simmered in huge dixies at every camp. The first units I saw were mostly Australian and British artillery batteries. They had moved to their battle positions earlier in the night, and in their command posts officers were busy studying maps and working out ranges. There was no sleep for the officers this night, but the men were apparently sleeping as peacefully as though the war were thousands of miles away. I was amazed at the calm way the men in the lines faced the start of the offensive … they might have been more worked up just before a football grand final.

The night was amazingly still and clear – occasionally a short burst of machine gun fire or the roar of an odd gun reminded me that I was at the front and from time to time I could hear the rumble of motor-lorries and tanks which were moving up to the assembly areas behind the start line. There [then] was a doomsday thunder and lightning as the whole rim of the horizon flashed as guns roared, and then came the explosions in Tobruk … They rumbled across the plain and were amplified by the hills south of the town until even the ground around us seemed to shake. In a few minutes Italian guns and shells, RAF bombs and huge naval guns of the Mediterranean Fleet added to the din. When the barrage started I was standing near a British medium battery and they fully expected to draw heavy counter battery fire from the Italian coastal defence guns. The British guns thundered out shell after shell for 25 minutes but nothing came back from Tobruk – the Italians hadn't found the battery's new position. And they didn't seem to have found the new positions of a number of other batteries either. Between six and seven I drove back just behind our artillery positions – our guns were firing, but I didn't see an Italian shell burst within half a mile of them.

As dawn broke I had reached our troops in the eastern sector. They were still putting up strong fire with mortars and machine guns to keep the Italians occupied in this sector while our main forces moved up from the south where a gap had already been made in the perimeter defences. By their intense fire these troops had foiled the Italians into thinking our main attack was coming from this direction and shells were bursting all round them … great clouds of dust like huge waterspouts marked each explosion, and in the still morning air these took some time to drift away, so that for a few minutes they looked like silver poplars.

I went to Australian Headquarters a mile behind the line to hear the latest news from all sectors. It was just seven o'clock – three quarters of an hour earlier the infantry were due to have gone through the gap in the wire … They had … In fact everything had gone like clockwork …

With an Intelligence Officer I followed through the planned timetable, and as messages came in we saw the plan working out to the minute. We checked the times as the messages came in … At 0605 the barrage lifted from the wire; the wire was blown at 0610; the first posts were attacked at 0615; they were taken by 0630; at 0645 the tanks crossed the anti-tank ditch; and so it went on as punctual as the surprise. In forty minutes five battalions had made their way through five gaps in the wire and the defences had been smashed wide open.

More troops were coming up through the wire and I went with them in their transport column … But so much traffic was trying to come through this gap that it was as bad as Swanston Street at five o'clock. The long line of vehicles crept forward – tailboard to radiator – in a cloud of dust and Military Police shouted themselves hoarse trying to keep the traffic moving.[21]

Caught in the open

It was in this traffic jam that Chester first met Department of Information cameraman Damien Parer. He was filming the cars, trucks and ambulances as they drove past. Neither man said much about this first meeting. Parer mentioned it in passing during an ABC interview with Wilmot in late 1943 and there is a brief anecdote in *Tobruk*. 'The sight of the trucks of the photographic and broadcast units parked together prompted one policeman to comment to another, "Blimey Bert, propaganda goes to war."'[22]

They probably just got on with their jobs because Chester continued in his dispatch:

> A few yards further in I took a road to the left, for I wanted to see where the first breakthrough had been made. But before I got there I found myself at a Post which was only just surrendering. It had offered stubborn resistance to the first battalion which had gone through this area and had left the post to be cleaned up by a reserve battalion. This wasn't easy … the Italians fought well and gave some trouble by sniping and throwing hand grenades. They were well underground in concrete dugouts and it was hard to get at them with grenades. The only thing to do was to smoke them out. I arrived just as this was being done and in a few minutes four officers and 34 other ranks came out. One of them explained to us that the men wanted to surrender but the commander refused to allow them to do so until the very last. As I left the officers were seeking permission to go back and get their blankets and some personal belongings … the men had brought theirs out with them all ready packed![23]

Wilmot's new friend from Bardia, Brigadier Tubby Allen, then gave him a briefing.

> He took me over the ground which his men had traversed that morning. On either side of the antitank trench we saw a line of

antitank mines as close as stepping stones … they had all been dug up and deloused – as the sappers say – by engineers who had scooped them from the soft earth with their hands. The antitank trench was only about two feet deep – the Italians had been working on it with hydraulic drills and here and there were holes already drilled to receive a plug of dynamite … 'When it's all boiled down,' he said, 'they [the engineers and pioneers] made the attack possible' …

About noon I caught up with the brigade which was driving northwards. The Brigadier [Horace 'Red Robbie' Robertson] outlined his plans for the afternoon to a party of British and Australian war correspondents. He told us that he intended to press on northwest in the hope of reaching the town that night – two battalions would close on Tobruk while a third went north to stem a possible counter attack. The brigadier's plan succeeded admirably – even though he didn't try to enter the town that night. In the afternoon we stood on a hill looking towards Tobruk and watched Australian infantry attacking two enemy positions west and south of the town. First of all our artillery shelled them heavily until they were enveloped in dense clouds of dust and then the infantry moved in … and they did move too … they advanced over this open country at parade ground pace – at 100 yards a minute … the enemy fire didn't worry them – they just pushed on and in one case as soon as the Italians saw that their fire could not check the advance they came out and surrendered. In these two brief actions we had splendid evidence of the accuracy of our artillery and the imperturbability of the men under fire.

With the capture of these two positions the road into Tobruk was open, but the Brigadier decided to postpone his entry till the following morning.

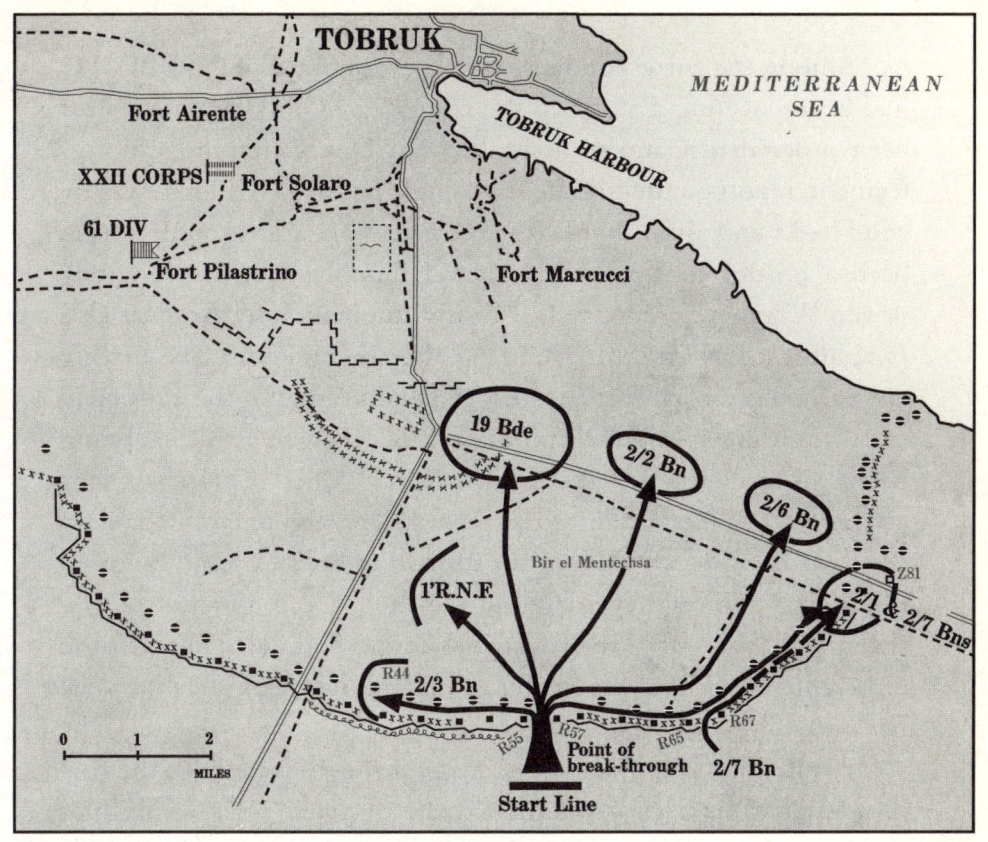

Tobruk – The Plan

Behind us from the forces in the west we could hear a solid bombardment coming. We drove out to the old Roman Fort Solara which we had seen our troops take earlier in the afternoon. There the shells were falling thick and fast near a battalion which was busy digging in for the night ... but it was a barrage of despair ... Already the Italians were burning their petrol dumps and blowing up their ammunition and all night long fires blazed and the flash and roar of explosions told of more sabotage. The battle for Tobruk was as good as over and as we went back to our dugout we had to edge our way past thousands of prisoners who seemed to be pleased that it was.[24]

Among the correspondents was Edward Ward of the BBC. He had been covering a story on the convoys to Gibraltar, when he'd been ordered to Cairo to assist Richard Dimbleby, who was still trying to report on the Middle East single handed. With his swarthy good looks and air of sophisticated dissipation, Ward couldn't have been a greater contrast to the genial Dimbleby, or the intensely driven Wilmot. As Ward tells it in his autobiography, *Number One Boy*, almost the first thing Chester did for him was save his life 'by pulling me back just before I stepped on one of the extremely unpleasant anti-personnel mines, which, when stepped on sprang in the air and exploded about waist high.'[25] Chester proposed they go back to the Australian camp, record their dispatches, then send the discs by dispatch rider to the airfield at Sollum some hundred miles away. When they arrived at the camp Cecil announced that the attempt to capture the barrage in sound had failed but that the recordings would be very useful in his radio dramas after the war! For once Chester was speechless.

By the time Bill MacFarlane had cut the discs for both the correspondents' stories, they'd missed the dispatch rider, so Wilmot and Ward drove the discs to Sollum themselves. They spent the following day driving from airfield to airfield trying to find a plane to take the recordings to Cairo. Finally a pilot agreed to deliver them to the studios. He was as good as his word. Cecil discovered later they had arrived at 7 pm that night. When they returned Ward was anxious to get into the town. They had missed the formal surrender and he wanted to see what he could find out. Chester felt he should get back to camp so he left Ward on the road into Tobruk. Within minutes the Englishman had been arrested by two Australian provosts who accused him of being a spy. Ward was more amused than alarmed, telling them it would make a good story. But after he'd established his identity and filed the story it was banned by the censor in Cairo on the grounds that it ridiculed the Military Police (MPs) who had made an 'honest mistake'. Later Chester asked the

MPs what their idea was in arresting a perfectly good BBC correspondent. They replied they knew he was on the level but they wanted an excuse to get into the town. 'As an excuse he was pretty good.'[26]

* * * *

A roughly typed diary letter to Edith Irwin describes Chester's adventures on the way to Derna, the next town to be attacked by the Australian forces. After doing his best to extract supplies from the canteen and headquarters, the Broadcast Unit packed its car and was on the road by 2 pm. Traffic moved slowly and by dark they were 85 miles from Tobruk. They stayed at a deserted inn 'now being used as a hospital'. The next day they were arranging interviews at Australian and, a few hours later, British headquarters. They recorded 'the General' (probably Mackay), then drove to Martuba where they spent the night in a mosque with some of the engineers and dined on some captured spaghetti. 'I then covered the front seat with blankets and by hurricane light's glow typed two pieces for the BBC until 2.30.'[27] The following day they were told the Italians had pulled out of Derna and the unit was able to drive into the town 24 hours ahead of the Australians. In his dispatch he made a point of mentioning that it was only after the Australians were in command of the heights that the Italian defence 'collapsed like a pricked balloon'. By a strange coincidence the highlight of the talk was this anonymous first-person account of the attack on the Derna aerodrome.

> About 16 kilo[metre]s out of the town we were advancing across the plateau towards an aerodrome. We'd gone about 1000 yards when the Italians opened fire on us with heavy machineguns and artillery. We had no supporting artillery or tanks then … it took us hours to make 4000 yards by leaps and bounds. Luckily

> RAF bombers came over once – and landed a few sticks right among the Iti's ... this raised a lot of dust and we advanced a lot before that cleared. About dusk we got within range and we let them have everything we could – from our Brens, anti-tank rifles and ordinary .303s ... and our trench mortar plastered their machine-gunners. Under cover of this we got up to within 200 yards of the Italians and then we saw they were packing up – putting their guns on lorries and driving away. We tried to get at them with our bayonets but they cleared off. That night we held the aerodrome, and the Italian artillery hit back ... and when we woke next morning they counterattacked ... Four tanks led the attack but when we set one on fire and an anti-tank gun came up the tanks turned back and the infantry withdrew.[28]

Almost certainly the source for this account was Captain Ralph Honner of C Company, 2/11th Battalion, who led the attack. However, when I questioned him about meeting Chester he had no recollection of the conversation. What is more the attack on the airstrip was the first time Damien Parer filmed troops in action. Wilmot, Parer and Honner were to be together again the following year on the Kokoda Track.

By now the unit was established in a spotlessly clean house in the town. Then Chester got a tip there was fighting outside Derna and they set off to follow the action. He described what followed in his next broadcast.

> After the fall of Derna, the Italians retreated to the rough hilly country west of the town and tried to delay our advance by harassing fire and by blowing up the roads which led up the escarpment from the coastal plain. Marching along with one platoon I saw Edward Ward of the BBC and I stopped to ask him what was ahead of these troops ... 'I don't really know,' he said, 'but if you'll give me a lift we'll go and see.' We didn't need to

> ... at that moment the bark of 75mm guns on the plateau and the whine of shells sent the troops and us flat on our faces. After about half a minute it eased a bit and an Australian Lieutenant called out to me, 'You'd better get that car off the road or it'll draw all the crabs in the world' ... Over they came again just as I stopped the car and I joined the troops on the ground ... the shells were falling thick and fast now but fortunately they were mostly going over our heads.[29]

As he and Ward took cover Chester was given a unique perspective on Australian industrial relations.

> The Digger with me had been a Wonthaggi miner before he joined the AIF ... He didn't think much of the mining game ... and he said, 'The Italians have ruined it for ordinary Australians. They don't mind what conditions they work under and we do ... that's one reason why I don't mind having a crack at them out here.'[30]

Returning to Derna with his story was going to be difficult for Chester as there were reports there were Italian stragglers on the road behind them. But the troops seem to have been as keen for the broadcaster to get his story as he was. The dispatch concludes:

> This was rather difficult as I wanted to get back to Derna that night so that I could record this talk. An Australian Cavalry major offered to escort me and the unit's engineer, Bill MacFarlane, down the main road till we met our own people or something else ... And so we set off in the dark with two men and a Bren gun in the back of our utility truck and the rest of us in the front. It was a ticklish business ... we didn't know whether the road was mined or not, so we had to have our lights on and risk drawing fire from possibly remaining Italians ... and

there was of course always the risk of being fired on by our own advanced troops. Luckily we didn't – we found one spot where a bridge had been blown away but fortunately our own troops had already made a bypass round this. We got through all right but it was a strange feeling driving up from the enemy's side towards our own frontline with our lights on ... but if we hadn't done that I wouldn't have been sitting in a garden in Derna making this recording this morning.[31]

Such was the speed of the Australian advance that the unit was soon on the road to Benghazi. Then the truck broke a spring. While they were waiting in Barce for it to be repaired by an obliging Italian mechanic Wilmot heard that the British armour were in pursuit of the fleeing Italian tanks. Chester was about to get his first scoop.

★ ★ ★ ★

The pursuit by the 7th Armoured Division took the form of a 200-mile left hook behind the Jebel Akhdar – the Green Mountains – to intercept the Italian tanks on the coast road south of Benghazi at the hamlet of Beda Fomm. Battling rain and sandstorms, and with the tanks frequently shedding their tracks, they were barely able to average 10 miles an hour. Following the advance in a staff car, and with an armoured car and another car as escort, General O'Connor and his planner Brigadier Eric Dorman-Smith were having similar problems. First, one of the cars broke down; then so did the armoured car. O'Connor and Dorman-Smith drove on in the remaining car, alone and out of contact with the army, until they reached the headquarters of the 7th Armoured Division at Wadi Azzin.

Chester left no record of his journey in the wake of the British forces. He was by now ill with flu and asthma, but for a reporter there is nothing like scooping just about everyone to keep you going, and Wilmot must have been certain that he had the story to himself – if only he could get to the battlefield in time. In fact the Australians arrived only hours after the battle ended. Chester was soon jotting down an account of the battle by 'a senior British commander'.

> At five in the afternoon we had covered 170 miles since leaving Mechili and our advanced units reported that they had intercepted the enemy on the road 65 miles south of Bengasi [sic] … the actual message from one tank said … 'The Road in front of me is packed with Italian lorries and troops' … Our tanks went in at once and even though the Italians opened up with anti-tank guns firing from lorries we managed to bite a section from the middle of the column and break through that evening so that our tanks could operate from both sides of the road. In the darkness a lot of the Italians managed to break away from the column and they took refuge in the sand-hills near the coast. But they had no chance of escape as we had sent ahead from Mechili an advanced force of armoured cars, motorised infantry and anti-tank guns to form a block across the road further south.
>
> Still … even though we surprised them, they fought well – better in fact than any Italian troops we've met in this campaign. During Wednesday night they established several batteries of field-guns around a knoll on the east side of the road and the lorries on which their anti-tank guns were mounted swung off the road into action positions. These guns started firing on Wednesday night and they kept at us all through the next day.
>
> By noon we had knocked out 46 of them, and we didn't think there would be many more. But after lunch reports came in which we could hardly believe. One spoke of 15 medium tanks leading a long transport column … the next reported 25 medium tanks at the rear … and a third said there were

30 medium tanks interspersed through the column. By fast manoeuvring we were able to take these on piecemeal but it was a really hard job ... We fought them all the afternoon and by dark there couldn't have been more than about 30 left. This was the finishing touch and during the night the remnants of the tanks made a dash south in the hope of breaking through our roadblock. Fortunately during Thursday afternoon we had sent 300 mines down to this blocking force and during the night 20 of our Cruisers pursued the 30 Italian medium tanks. An hour or two after dawn they ran into our minefield and when they found our anti-tank guns firing at them from in front and the cruisers coming up behind them, they abandoned their tanks and surrendered ... That was the end of their real resistance.[32]

Chester clearly didn't have the whole story. The description by 'a senior British commander' was of the battle in the late afternoon and evening. It ignored the experience of the British advance guard. As the Armoured Division had moved to intercept the Italians it became obvious the tanks were going to need time for maintenance before going into action. So it was decided to form a fast-moving group of wheeled vehicles – armoured cars, trucks and lorries – and, coming up in the rear, the guns. According to Kenneth Macksey's classic account of the battle it was 'just 2000 men, a few armoured cars armed with nothing better than anti tank rifles and machine guns backed by ... fifteen assorted guns of the Royal Horse Artillery – escorted by infantry, whose one hope of survival was defeat of Italian tanks by the guns'.[33] The road was empty when the British arrived and the infantry dug in among some shallow ridges. Anti-tank guns nestled among the infantry; behind them was the field artillery. At 2.30 pm 'the first vehicles of a seemingly endless column appeared over the horizon travelling in solid convoy down the road – straight into the ambush.'[34]

The Italians launched a series of attacks on the British forces, each probe a little stronger. Then in the late afternoon all three of the British armoured regiments saw ahead the long convoy of Italian vehicles. 'Engines racing, tracks slapping and roaring at full speed with turrets traversing on target, they charged home turning to left and right to run the length of the column to rake every vehicle in sight.'[35] The trap had been sprung.

By now Chester's flu and asthma were so bad that for most of the return drive to Cairo he lay in the back of the truck while Bill MacFarlane took the wheel. His next letter home was from a convalescent houseboat on the Nile located near the famous Gezira Sporting Club 'where they have dinner dances every week'.[36] To ease his parents' minds he mentions he is playing tennis that afternoon with Alan Moorehead of the *Daily Express* whose 'sensational' stories frequently appeared in *The Argus*. Then for his father's benefit Chester describes the methods of some of the other correspondents.

> I am amazed at the ethics of British journalists – in fact all the Australians are amazed … they do not hesitate to give eye witness accounts of incidents they did not see e.g. on the first day of Bardia the British correspondents found themselves at Matruh with a broken down car – into Matruh that night came an RAF senior officer who gave them a garbled account of the battle – it wouldn't have been so bad if they had just reported what the RAF man had said … but they did better – they turned his story around and made it their own eye witness account – they had the tanks leading the attack and smashing through the wire – they had the town taken on the first night … and the dateline was Bardia.[37]

Some of this is newspaperman's gossip and doubtless provided Bung with a ready fund of anecdotes for when he went to the club back in Melbourne. But there is no reason to doubt Wilmot's accuracy. Fascinatingly, he says the censors would not allow much of this through as 'they knew their stories were all wrong'.[38] Wilmot adds that 'one of the correspondents that filed these wildly inaccurate stories was from THE TIMES'. As for the 'BIG TANK BATTLE' (Beda Fomm):'the Australians were the only correspondents who saw the battlefield; the only correspondents who interviewed the men who actually took part and led the British. But the *Daily Express* and other papers had graphic stories that had little or no relation to the facts.'[39]

Chester also suspected there was another motive for the British newspapermen's repeated misreporting of the attacks on Tobruk and Bardia. Both times the Australian troops had gone in first followed by the British tanks and both times the British reporters had the tanks leading. 'They must have, they must have – they should have,' one Reuters man replied when Chester mentioned this to him, 'they always do.'[40] Wilmot concluded that: 'I am certain there was a reluctance to admit that the Australians had done the tough job'.[41] Wilmot also found he did much better on his own keeping away from even the Australian pressmen. As a result, he told his father proudly, he had managed to scoop the Australian correspondents by 24 hours on 'quite important' stories.

It is easy to see why back in Australia Edith heard how disliked Wilmot was in the Middle East. After listening to a number of Melbourne University acquaintances disparage him one night, without thinking, she wrote him a bitter letter reproaching him for his 'bumptiousness' and arrogance. Always self-critical, Chester wrote an apologetic letter back. (He was after all rather smitten by the very charming Edith.) It doesn't seem to have occurred to either of them that the main reason behind this disparagement was jealousy. Certainly with men, Chester argued to win, each point rammed home with a stab of his pipe stem, but while he was often infuriatingly dogmatic he was never personal, and as one friend remarked ruefully, usually right. With women it was different. Chester was gentle, witty, and attentive. Being brought up with two older sisters had its advantages. Edith should have realised that, human nature being what it is, turning in a string of successful stories while remaining aloof from the other correspondents was bound to get him disliked.

Of course, Chester was fiercely competitive even though he had been quite generous about sharing his Beda Fomm scoop. Another reason for the sometimes intimidating front he adopted at times was the asthma. He must have known that it could jeopardise his career. Yet there is no record of him ever confiding his fears to anyone. There are allusions to colds and flu, references to frequent visits to convalescent hospitals after bursts of intensive work – that is all. Chester seems to have lived in a constant state of denial about anything to do with his health.

As he relaxed in the houseboat, Wilmot was unaware that everything achieved in the campaign he had just reported was about to be thrown away. Beda Fomm had been fought in the shadow of plans to aid Greece against an imminent German invasion through Yugoslavia. After signalling GHQ Cairo 'Fox caught in the open' after Beda Fomm, O'Connor hoped that he could persuade Wavell and London to approve a further advance into Tripolitania. Dorman-Smith was sent to get approval for a further advance.

At 10 am on 12 February 1941 he was ushered into Wavell's map room. 'To my dismay,' Dorman-Smith was to tell British historian Correlli Barnett, 'I saw all the desert maps had gone, replaced by maps of Greece. Wavell swept an arm sardonically at the new maps: "You see, Eric, I am starting my spring campaign."'[42]

Having just reported a famous victory Wilmot was about to chronicle a military disaster.

9

A DESIRE TO SEEK THE UNDERLYING CAUSES

When the Australian Official Correspondent Kenneth Slessor returned to Cairo after the Greek disaster, he wrote in his diary 'The main and vital point ... is that either the British or Australian Government, or both, was prepared callously and cynically to sacrifice a comparatively small force for the sake of a political gesture'.[1] In questions prepared for the AIF commander, Slessor asked whether Blamey or Wavell had advised sending troops to Greece; what were the estimates of the German forces; and how the Australian and New Zealand divisions were 'best suited' for Greece as Churchill had stated? Almost certainly some of the details for these queries were suggested by Chester, as Slessor mentioned that Wilmot supplied him with his statistics. Even though at that time he had nothing like Wilmot's experience as a war correspondent — as Official Correspondent he had accompanied the Australian troops to Britain before coming to the Middle East — Slessor was asking the right questions.

In fact the situation was worse than he had imagined. Churchill and Eden's attempts to create a Balkan front of Greece, Turkey and Yugoslavia had provoked the German intervention. Australia had been poorly served by its political and military leaders. Blamey, as

Slessor sensed at the time, had been opposed to the Greek adventure. But after having fought tenaciously to secure a charter that gave him control over Australian forces, his first reaction on being told about the Greek Campaign was to try to get command of the force himself on the grounds that most of troops were Australian. Prime Minister Menzies knew about the possibility of a Greek intervention before he came to the Middle East but did not mention it to Blamey. Then Wavell told Menzies that the Australians were to go to Greece just before he (Menzies) was to leave for Britain. Inexplicably, the Prime Minister didn't delay his departure to get a briefing from Blamey and his staff. Wavell then told the Australian commander that Menzies had agreed to the expedition.

After much agonising, Blamey finally communicated his doubts to the Australian Government, but his letter arrived in Canberra as the first Australian formations arrived in Greece. His criticisms of the British policies were of course justified and should have been presented sooner. Lustre Force – made up of the New Zealand Division, the Australian 6th and 7th Divisions, I Australian Corps HQ and a Polish brigade – was no match for the seven German divisions that were poised to invade Greece. The German Air Force outnumbered the RAF 490 planes to 80. The Greek Army may have defeated the Italians, and was recklessly courageous, but it had outdated equipment and primitive transport.

Above all, it should have been obvious from the outset that if the Germans overran Yugoslavia quickly, advanced from Monastir through Florina to the Aliakmon Valley then thrust towards the River Pinios and the Plain of Thessaly, they could drive a wedge between Lustre Force and the Greek Army. So bad was the strategic position that on arriving in Greece Blamey marked suitable evacuation beaches on a road map. Consequentially, as well as reporting the campaign, Wilmot was to investigate what went wrong, not just in Greece, but later on the island of Crete after the withdrawal.

Cecil 'by persistent representations' was able to take most of the

Broadcast Unit to Greece. The party included Wilmot, MacFarlane, two drivers, the utility truck and the portable recording equipment. Compared with the other correspondents, the Broadcast Unit had considerable freedom of movement that Chester used to great effect to keep abreast of developments, and find his stories. This is why in the diaries Kenneth Slessor kept during the war Wilmot is frequently described as arriving with some vital news about the situation. Except for the major moves, such as the one to Greece, the unit controlled its own movements, reporting to individual formations or any division in whose area they were operating. 'We were never conducted in a formal sense,' Chester was to write later, 'and no AIF officer was attached to the unit in the field as a conducting officer.'[2]

The Department of Information's Photographic Unit was much the same. After the first offensive in the Western Desert there had been some tension between Hurley and the younger men in the unit. Wisely the veteran photographer had allowed Chester's new friend Damien Parer and their 'producer', Ron Maslyn Williams, to find their own stories. They had visited the dusty correspondents' camp at Ikingi Maryut, but had found themselves mired in red tape, so Williams and Parer booked passage on a small Greek freighter and arrived in time to film the rapturous reception the Australian troops received in Athens. Another member of the Photographic Unit, the still photographer George Silk, had been on HMAS *Perth* when he found out about the Greek expedition. As soon as he got back to the Middle East he picked up more film stock and crossed with the other correspondents on HMS *Breckonshire*.

Wilmot had thought the voyage was going to be difficult but all they saw were two drifting mines that were sunk by gunfire. When he arrived just about everyone was overwhelmed by the contrast between Greece and the Middle East. Chester wrote:

> Australians are in Greece and you could hardly find a place where the troops would rather be fighting, unless it's Britain

itself. After months in the dead flat, dull desert or in the fetid Nile Valley it's a relief to find yourself in a country with trees and grass; mountains and streams. It's a relief to be in a country without dust and smells. We're in a country where you can walk round the streets for hours without being besieged by touts or by seedy youths selling dirty postcards. Coming to Greece is like coming to a new world where people wave to you as you go by and old men and young kids come to the roadside and give you the 'thumbs-up' sign of confidence and victory ... a country where the people round you are also with you and are fighting for the same cause.[3]

As a university student and schoolboy at Melbourne Grammar Chester had been a rather romantic classical scholar and ancient history student. He idolised the Roman senators and the creators of Greek democracy. All of this welled to the surface when he arrived in Greece. At Piraeus, where they first landed, he looked over the countryside and the 'powder blue sea' in the distance and realised that he was probably at the place where the Persian emperor Xerxes had set up his throne to watch the Battle of Salamis when the Greek general Themistocles routed the emperor's fleet. This beautiful land, he felt, was the cradle of the democracy created in Pericles's Athens. As he wrote to Edith while being driven up to join the troops,

> I can understand now why Athens produced such intellectual and creative activity in the 5th Century BC. The mountains around it gave a certain degree of security – the port the rich land around it gave it prosperity and between the two the Athenians found leisure to think to argue and reason and to contemplate the things that were beautiful and good.[4]

Coincidentally, the Australians were later forced to defend the famous Hot Gates of Thermopylae, where Leonidas and his legendary 400 Spartans defended the pass and died to a man when a traitor revealed a secret path, enabling the Persians to get behind the Greek positions – stories Wilmot had read studying ancient history at Melbourne Grammar.

Wilmot could read classical Greek but not the modern language, so he and Cecil decided they had better do something about it. His description of their adventures, based on notes taken at the time, was the highlight of 'A Letter from the Front'.

> We went to the best bookshop in Athens and asked for a book on Greek. A girl brought us a rather formidable looking grammar, which seemed to have started life in a 19th century schoolroom. When we opened it we were sure it had. It has always puzzled me why the publishers of textbooks in French are invariably preoccupied with Auntie's farmyard or a visit to the zoo. The author of this Greek grammar was clearly brought up in the same tradition. We opened the book at random and read: 'Man is a reasonable animal … he has intellect … The rhinoceros has no intellect, because he is not a reasonable animal.' Huh … I began to wonder whether the author himself was man or rhinoceros. I was still in doubt when we read on … 'My little sister has a horn-gilded lamb … This merchant is a solvent one … In my uncle's garden there is a fine big cherry tree.'

However, as they were searching for coffee the two bewildered war correspondents stopped 'to buy a little primer entitled Greek For a Shilling (Specially prepared for His Britannic Majesty's Forces) … the author had the right idea … She had concentrated on fundamentals – and armed with this a Digger can master essential phrases like: 'That is too dear … Can I have a warm bath? … I want a packet of 20 … Bring me a bottle of beer … May I see you home'.'[5]

A desire to seek the underlying causes

* * * *

The unit left for the front at 4 am on 1 April 1941. The early start was because they had to go from the house at Kifissia, fifteen miles outside Athens where Cecil had based the unit to Glyphada, on the other side of the city, to join the Corps HQ. The Broadcast Unit arrived on time but the 'press boys' were an hour late. Chester understood the contempt of the 'press blokes' for army inefficiency and humbug but felt 'their disregard for orders doesn't do them or us any good'.[6]

Soon after when they got under way, there was 'a fine demonstration of Corps inefficiency' with the convoy going so fast that the rest could not follow and they were lost en route. 'No one knew just what the right way was and we had the humiliating scene of about thirty cars stopping in the middle of one of Athens' main streets … the lot turning round and then having to turn again and go off in the original direction.'[7]

As they drove into Eleusis, where many of the Greek destroyers were anchored in the harbour, the scene reminded Chester of the lochs he had seen on the road west from Glasgow to Loch Lomond: 'The water was dead still – a kind of polished steel grey. Half a dozen sloops and destroyers lay at anchor. Behind them rose blue hills several thousand feet high, their sharp tops cloaked in soft blue mist.' The road then ran inland to Thebes.[8]

Thebes was a disappointment. They were unable to see any of the ancient ruins. As they drove on the sun broke through the clouds and they saw landscapes that reminded Chester of the Cézannes he had seen during the debating tour three years before, 'soft pastel shades of brown and green on the mountain sides with the huge grey bulk of the … peaks beyond'.[9] One mountain seemed to Chester like an elephant lying on its side. Beyond Thebes they ran along the shadow of a mountain range which rose to 7500 feet. They stopped for lunch at a little town. As they went into the restaurant a small boy of about ten came running up to Chester. 'Please Mister do you have any English stamps?' He didn't but found an American stamp, which thrilled the lad even more. As Wilmot left the cafe later the boy came running up to him. 'Greek stamp for you thank you, Mister.'[10] A nice gesture, Chester thought. As they drove through the countryside they saw

> the amount of work that the Greek womenfolk are doing to make up for the absence of their men at the front. Wherever you go there are very few men of military age about and in the country particularly the women are doing a lot of the heavy work. I'm told that usually the women work in the fields only in the busiest times – like harvest – but I've seen them now doing all kinds of jobs … digging and ploughing and cutting and gathering the prickly gorse that they use as firewood. They're also working on the roads with their children helping them. Time and again we drove through long lines of women and children throwing the gravel back onto the roads after the trucks had swept it off … and they were doing this for no pay at all … This was their war contribution.[11]

It had become a people's war.

* * * *

The Australian troops lost no time in getting into their new positions. Chester saw one field regiment 'arrive at the top of the pass about ten o'clock one morning … By noon they had their gun pits dug … their guns were in position and camouflaged and they were unloading a fresh load of ammunition'.[12] The infantry had a harder and slower job. He saw one company 'digging in on top of a ridge … Everything had to be carried by men or mules up a narrow slippery track which seemed to go up at an angle of about 30 degrees

A desire to seek the underlying causes

most of the way.' The Greeks they were relieving lent the troops their mules, but it was still a long climb. When they reached the top they had to dig trenches and cut tracks. There was no opportunity to construct dugouts which might have given some protection from the showers which swept the pass every few hours. 'For days the troops had their heads in the clouds and their feet in mud,' Wilmot noted. 'Even with leather jackets and balaclavas and greatcoats on it was still cold, because there was no chance of getting properly dry ... even blankets got wet and the nights were miserable.'[13]

Cecil then brought up the truck and, as he later wrote, they

> spent one glorious day recording messages from the troops to their people in Australia. During the day [we] managed to put 120 Diggers on the air and [there was] a potential queue leading right back to Athens as soon as the news got round ... Unhappily a number of the Diggers who sat on a green bank that day and told their mothers or wives or children that they'd be home for Christmas won't ever be coming home.[14]

The sound of these messages does not survive, although there is film by Hurley of Cecil recording an earlier program of 'Voices from Overseas'.

When the German attack began and Tubby Allen's 16th Brigade moved forwards into new positions, Wilmot and MacFarlane followed with the portable recording gear. They waited all one day with engineers who were to blow up the road through one of the mountain passes to block the German advance. The engineers had to let through thousands of troops and dozens of tanks and lorries which were withdrawing after meeting the Germans on the plain. The sound of the recording survives. First you hear Chester setting the scene – his voice competing with traffic noises in the background. Obviously expecting the road to be blown any second he begins to ad lib. There is a pause, followed by Chester stating it is now midnight, then follows a thunder of rocks crashing into the valley. He returns out of breath to explain that the explosion was so violent that it had blown the stylus cutting the disc off the turntable. This hadn't been their only problem. Bill MacFarlane had found that the soft acetate discs on which the recordings were made became so hard in the cold that the cutter wouldn't cut properly. He could only record after he had hugged the discs to his chest for fifteen minutes or more to warm and soften them.

The following morning they learnt that the Germans were about to attack from the north behind the Australian and New Zealand positions through the Monastir Gap that led from Yugoslavia into Greece. They moved round there hoping to get sound pictures of the actual fighting. But a snowstorm froze the gear, making it unworkable, so Chester went forwards alone to observe the action, while Cecil and MacFarlane took the gear back to Athens for servicing. Wilmot reached an observation post on a hill in the Monastir Valley:

> At first the Germans were driven back [by the Australians], but then under cover of a blinding snowstorm they attacked once more and kept attacking in such numbers that even though they were repulsed time and again, eventually the Allied troops had to withdraw. The first contact was made early one morning when some British sappers were overtaken by the enemy as they were about to blow up a bridge near the Yugoslav frontier. They had gone forward under cover of darkness in an armoured scout carrier, but when daylight came they found themselves behind the advanced German infantry. The Tommies were surprised by other Germans and in the face of heavy machine gun fire they had to withdraw. They threw their explosives into the water and ran for their carrier. They found it was bogged, but while one drove the others lay flat on their stomachs and pushed the wheels till it got out. They still had to get past the advanced German troops and so the driver said, 'I'll open the throttle and you open

A desire to seek the underlying causes

that Bren gun and we'll make a dash for it.' They did and ran the gauntlet to safety.

Just after noon that day the real clash started. German motorised infantry and tanks came within range of our medium guns and we let them have it. With a ranging round one tank was put out of action and the rounds that followed were so accurate that a number of tanks and vehicles were moved out of range.[15]

Chester then went forward to an observation post on a hill just behind the front line. Below him stretched a broad plain and through a light haze he could see German vehicles dispersed on green fields.

The gunners were still harassing them and spouts of smoke and earth shot upwards as shells burst in the middle of the vehicles. The artillery pounding continued all the afternoon and the RAF joined in [when] a wave of RAF bombers escorted by fighters flew over. The German ack-ack guns put up a fierce barrage but the planes went on, and judging from the tremendous crumps and columns of smoke, the Germans must have been a little disturbed.[16]

Later in the afternoon – after he had returned to the Australian gun positions – the bombers went over singly and 'repeated the dose' and at sunset British fighters roared low over the Australians' heads 'just by way of encouragement' and went on to strafe the German troops.

Shortly before midnight Wilmot climbed to another Australian observation post and waited for the gunners to begin another shoot:

At 14 minutes to twelve there was dead silence … there wasn't even a whisper from the dead leaves on the oak trees round the post ... At 13 minutes to, the sky behind us flashed and the hills thundered with a long rolling rumble that seemed to run through them for miles. Dozens of shells whistled and whined over our heads and at half a dozen points on the plain sudden vivid flashes told us where shells were bursting. There was still no reply from the German guns, but their machine guns spat back just in case we should be intending to attack. There was sporadic firing throughout the night, but we snatched a few hours sleep. It was only a few hours, for we expected them to attack at dawn and when we woke about five we could hear the ominous rumble of tanks and vehicles moving across the plain. We were holding a line of low hills that ran from some rugged mountains on the left to a lake on our right, but it was a long line and the hills were no real obstacle to tanks. And so as we heard this rumbling we had rather mixed feelings ... Would our minefield stop them effectively? How many infantry would they be able to throw in? Might they even be able to break through?

There was silence for a while – the moon set and we couldn't make out even the main feature on the plain. The minutes dragged by and the rumbling of tanks began again ... Then away on our right there was heavy machine gun fire and right along the front machine guns here and there opened up. Almost immediately at our feet our anti-tank guns started and tracer shells laid a trail of fire through the blackness. The attack was on. Then the hills seemed to shudder with a huge explosion as a German tank ran into our minefield ... then a second explosion and a third ... They were into the minefield all right, but after these three explosions there were no more ... the Germans thought better of it ... they didn't press their tank attack and after a few minutes the machine guns fell silent also. But it was quite clear that the machine guns were firing from positions much nearer our line than they had the previous night. It was still dark then, but just at dawn our bombers paid the Germans an alarm clock call and the echoes of bursting bombs had hardly died away when our long-range guns joined in. By six-thirty it was light enough to see Veve – the town in front of our lines at the foot of the hills. We learnt the Germans had entered it during the night. As it got lighter we studied the plain through telescope and field-glasses, but we could see little or no sign of German movement. We could see right up the main road to the town where the Germans had been masking the day before, but they'd moved either forward or back. The firing died down for a while and we could hear sheep bells tinkling and oxen lowing in the valley nearly a mile away. The world was waking up … just behind our lines a shepherd was letting his flock out of their night corral … two oxen were hauling a wagon up a hill and the war seemed a hundred miles away.[17]

Chester discovered the snow had been a godsend to the enemy. Under cover of the storm the Germans had been able to get within bayonet range. One soldier (not identified in Chester's notes) told the broadcaster:

Suddenly you'd see figures appearing out of the wall of snow in front of you … we'd give them all we had and then the snow would close over them again. I thought they'd never stop coming … after a while they did, but all through the night they kept their machine guns on us. Next morning they attacked again, but they didn't get through. Later in the day we moved back – it was still snowing but we managed to get out.[18]

This story was confirmed by all the other troops he talked with. The Germans concentrated their attack on the right flank and got round behind the main body of Australian and British troops. Chester believed the Germans had been able to keep up the pace and the pressure because they went into action carrying as little as possible.

> They had no packs – no gas masks – no rations … just automatic rifles and ammunition. In spite of their superiority in numbers, the Germans didn't succeed in forcing our troops back until the second afternoon. Then during that night we withdrew out of touch and on the following morning the Germans found their advance held up by British tanks and artillery, who did their job so well that the rest of the force got back safely into their new positions without any interference from the enemy.[19]

Wilmot 'froze' for several hours in a dugout so he could observe the Divisional Artillery under the overall command of Brigadier Herring. Arguably Greece was the veteran artilleryman's finest achievement. The gunners were able to hold off infantry and panzers as the Australians withdrew. As he drove back with some of the troops and saw the hills where the troops were now entrenched, bristling with weapons, Chester reflected that 'the Australians had proved that with courage and resource even handpicked Nazi troops could be checked.'[20] It made a good last line for his broadcast.

Covering the story was one thing; getting it to air was another. One of Wilmot and Cecil's greatest problems was dealing with the Greek censorship. Wilmot quipped 'it seems that the man who thought up the censorship system there had a corner in typewriting paper. One talk [for] London had to be submitted to no fewer than six censors – our own Navy, Air Force and Army plus Greek military, civil and radio censorship.'[21] Chester conceded that it usually wasn't as bad as this, but as there were at least three censors to be satisfied each time – and as each had to have a copy to file – it meant that any decent-sized script consumed up to fifty pages of fine paper. To make matters worse, the Greek censors worked in different offices in different parts of Athens and worked different hours. Then there was transmitting the stories back. The immediate news from Greece

A desire to seek the underlying causes

was sent to London by the Athens radio. This wasn't very satisfactory. Cecil would later write that:

> You didn't have a two-way link and you had no idea whether London was really listening or not ... The BBC were supposed to listen at a set time and on a particular wavelength each day. But Athens Radio was a little uncertain. They'd change the time at the last minute when it was too late to get a cable to London warning the BBC, or else they'd give you the wrong wavelength.[22]

The result was that Chester would sit in the studio five minutes before he was due to read his dispatch and 'chatter idly away into the blue wondering if London was listening – or only Berlin – and find [himself] saying, "Hello, London, Hello BBC, this is Athens calling ... this is Athens calling London on a wavelength of ..." And so on for five minutes without knowing whether London was there at all.'[23]

Later they discovered that no more than 60 per cent of the messages which Chester and Edward Ward sent to London were ever picked up.

Making this even more frustrating was that Wilmot had excellent sources that were providing first-rate material. The most important became Brigadier Sydney Rowell, Blamey's brilliant Chief of Staff. Rowell was a regular officer who in 1911 had been a student in the first class at Duntroon. A rather old-fashioned Australian gentleman – his daughter told the author he could never understand women going out to work – he evoked great loyalty from his subordinates and was respected at all levels of the Australian Army. That Wilmot was able to win this formal, and always conservative, soldier's professional trust during the Greek campaign, and eventually become his trusted confidant by the time the New Guinea fighting began, was no small accomplishment. As our story unfolds, both will confront a common adversary: General Sir Thomas Blamey. But at the time, Wilmot did not require a source for one of Blamey's first lapses in judgement.

At Elasson Blamey insisted on establishing his headquarters in the village in spite of the protests of the headman, who was afraid their presence would attract the German bombers. He also dismissed the protests of Brigadiers Rowell and Bridgeford as well as his GOC Operations, Major Charles Spry (later head of ASIO).

When Damien Parer, Ron Williams and George Silk arrived at the correspondents' camp in the village and discovered where Blamey had located his headquarters, Williams turned to Parer and said, 'Listen I think we are going to get bombed around here if we stay a couple of days.' 'Oh, good-oh we're going to photograph it,' responded Parer.[24] The next day the photographers set themselves up on a hill overlooking the village and settled down to wait. The German planes arrived in the late afternoon. The bombers came in big lazy circles, escorted by fifty fighters. As the bombs were released they fanned out over the village. Parer started filming. Over the whistling scream of the bombs' descent Williams heard Parer muttering, 'God save those poor buggers down there. God save them'.[25] When they went down to the village the next morning they were appalled. It was their first encounter with civilian casualties and the villagers sitting in front of their ruined houses were the same kinds of people who had welcomed them in their homes as they had driven up the mountain roads to the front line.

Blamey, in Rowell's opinion, really lost his grip during the retreat from the Thermopylae Line when Tubby Allen was withdrawing his three battalions of the 16th Brigade from the mountains east of Servia and there was an unexpected threat to the Australian right flank. Rowell was becoming increasingly concerned by a series of panicky messages he was receiving from the New Zealand 21st Battalion. They had only recently come under Australian command and were on Allen's right. According to Rowell:

A desire to seek the underlying causes

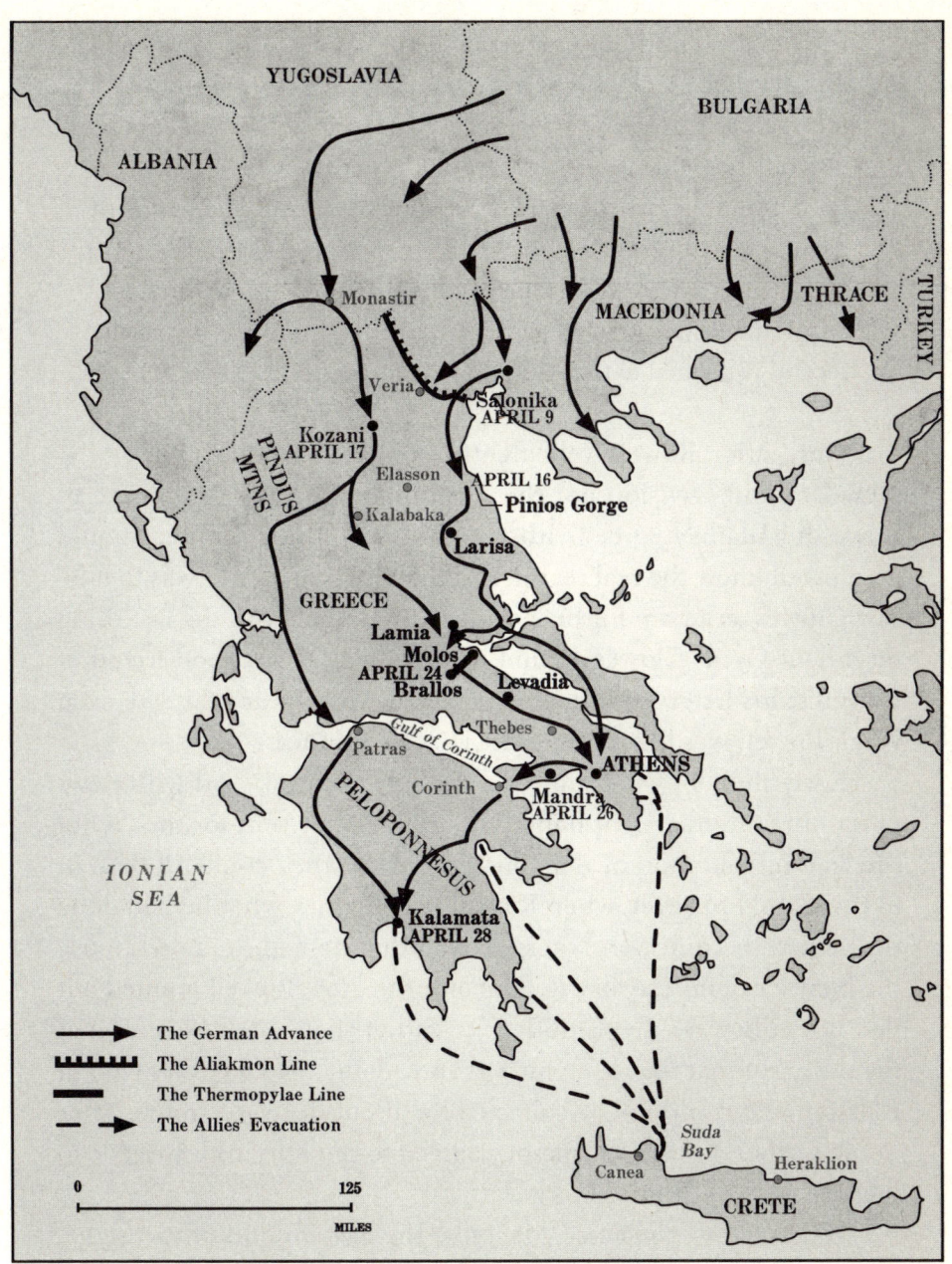

Greece – The Withdrawal

> I went across from my tent to the Corps Commander [Blamey] and discussed the position with him. It was clear from [the messages] that the CO [Colonel Neil Macky of the 21st Battalion] was in a blue funk ... and we would have to take strong action to bolster him up and if we didn't act quickly we would all go in the bag. As a first proposal I suggested we should send Brigadier Cyril Clowes ... to take hold of the situation. Blamey wanted to send a Colonel Rowe of the New Zealand Staff Corps who had been recently attached to the Australian headquarters.[26]

Only after Rowell vehemently pointed out that neither the New Zealand Division nor the Australians had any confidence in Rowe did Blamey agree 'with very ill grace'[27] that Clowes should go. Rowell knew the real reason for Blamey's reluctance was that he saw Clowes as a rival for his position. In fact this was the last thing on 'Silent Cyril' Clowes's mind. Clowes was also a good friend of Rowell's; his letters to him always began with 'Dear Old Syd' even when Rowell was his commander in New Guinea.

Early the following morning Rowell was awakened with news of the threat to the right flank. He immediately sent for the CO of the leading battalion of the 16th Brigade so they could all be sent to the right. However, when Rowell told Blamey what he had done the general became very angry, saying that he had intended to use the New Zealand Cavalry Regiment for the job. Rowell pointed out that not only were they an offensive rather than a defensive unit at the time, but that the regiment was spread out 25 to 30 miles west of Elasson, and could not be collected for about thirty-six hours. After 'some further discussion' Blamey agreed to send the 16th Brigade to the right flank at Pinios Gorge.

When Clowes reached Macky at the eastern end of the gorge, German tanks and troops on motorcycles were heading to the Pinios River. Macky was told by the Australian brigadier that 'it was essential to deny the gorge to the enemy till 19 April even if it meant extinction'[28] and that support would arrive in twenty-four hours. It soon became clear that Macky had little stomach for this task. Nevertheless, Rowell always insisted Clowes's intervention saved the day by preventing the New Zealanders from withdrawing southward and leaving the flank undefended.

Allen and his brigade major Dick Hammer finally arrived at GHQ to get their orders. (Allen had been in the mountains trying to find the 2/1st Battalion and organise its withdrawal.) Rowell's tent had been struck in preparation for a move further back to Soumpasi and he was sleeping under a tree in the rain. 'I gave him what I knew, which was precious little,' Rowell wrote later.[29] As they walked away Hammer said, 'Is that all the orders we are going to get?'[30] 'What more did you expect the poor bastard to be able to tell you,' Allen replied. Allen had been given two of his own battalions plus the New Zealand 21st Battalion, two New Zealand artillery units, a field regiment, and an anti-tank regiment to counter the German advance. There followed on 18 and 19 April 1941 some of the fiercest fighting of the Greek Campaign from which Allen and his men emerged with great credit. However, at midday on 18 April, a phone call from Mackay's Headquarters came to Allen's Brigade Headquarters informing them the 2/2nd was withdrawing. Allen said later, 'the receiver was clamped down before my HQ could discuss the matter with him.'[31] Chester seems to have been told about this almost immediately. 'New Zealanders got rather panicky,'[32] he wrote in a note dated 18 April.

The same day there was a German air attack on the Pharsala Bridge. The bombs missed the bridge and hit a truck full of explosives and blew an enormous hole in the road north of the bridge. All the traffic slowed down, started to bank up, then stopped in a solid jam. Rowell was concerned that the continued delay could put back the withdrawal by twenty-four hours. As he wrote in a letter to Gavin Long in 1947:

> I spoke to Blamey about this ... and said I thought that either he or I should go forward and see from Mackay and Freyberg (the New Zealand commander) on the spot just how things were. He said he wouldn't go himself and wouldn't let me go. I repeated my request at lunch and got no further. After lunch I told him that, if he wouldn't go, I insisted on going. To my surprise he agreed.[33]

According to Charles Spry, what Blamey actually said was 'Well go your bloody self!'[34] Rowell drove back to Larissa along the congested roads and found Mackay – always good in a crisis – keeping the convoys moving; and Rowell saw that a bypass had been cut. When he heard about the pressure on Allen at Pinios Gorge, Rowell decided that if they didn't get out on 18 or 19 April they never would and there was no question of any postponement to the 24th. When the time came to give the orders for the evacuation to Mackay and the 6th Division, Rowell observed:

> It is difficult to realize that the Blamey we saw there and the Blamey who subsequently ruled the Australian Army were and are the same man. On this occasion he was physically and mentally broken. He gave Mackay who was always a model of calm, such a garbled order that I was forced to tactfully intervene and set him straight.[35]

Rowell was so distressed that when he got back to Palestine, he wrote to the Chief of the General Staff and told him that after his experiences in Greece, he considered Blamey unfit to command troops in the field and that he was not prepared to serve him in the field again. This was all Rowell was prepared to put in writing to Gavin Long.

However, there was more. It is clear Rowell believed that Blamey was no field commander. In 1942 Rowell described to Chester how Blamey was never in the front line in Greece and rather than go forwards he insisted on his commanders coming back to his headquarters to get their orders. This often involved hazardous 60-mile journeys. When interviewed by Ivan Chapman in the 1960s Rowell described Blamey as 'scared out of his bloody mind'[36] in Greece.

There is also the question of Blamey's drinking. Brigadier William Bridgeford, the senior administrative officer, described him as dining sumptuously on champagne during the campaign. David Horner, Blamey's most recent biographer, believes Bridgeford might have been referring to a party Blamey threw at Australian Headquarters just before the withdrawal, where staff drank up all the champagne. Rowell was not amused. He came in after the festivities were well under way and barked 'I thought there was a war on.'[37] The question remains as to why there was so much champagne in the first place. In addition, Lieutenant 'Jika' Travers, Mackay's ADC, is alleged to have told the military historian the late Peter Charlton that he, together with Rowell and Mackay, found Blamey passed out under a table, an empty brandy bottle beside him.[38]

Several days before the decision to withdraw the force was made, Cecil decided to get the utility truck, Bill MacFarlane and the equipment out. It was a wise decision. The portable recording gear had given the unit an edge over the BBC throughout the battles in the Middle East. Cecil was only given two hours' notice that shipping space was available but they managed to assemble the equipment, drive to Piraeus and get onto the ship.

They lay in the harbour all that night. Next morning there was a heavy German air-raid. No bombs hit the ship but they were strafed and Cecil was hit by a small splinter from an explosive bullet that became embedded in his wrist. The ship put back to the wharf to disembark the serious casualties before getting under way. It took them five days to reach Egypt. There were three air attacks on the ship but no further casualties.

Chester described his own escape from Greece in a letter to Edith Irwin:

On Monday April 21st we set off back for the front. I started off in Ken Slessor's car. Ten miles out of Athens we broke a spring and it was late in the afternoon before we managed to get another truck. There was Ken, Ron Monson of the *Daily Telegraph*, Silk and Parer – the photographers – and I … Ken and Ron rode in the back and we had the hood off so that we could spot for aircraft. But luckily all the way up that evening we saw nothing of enemy planes on the road, though there was plenty of evidence of their bombing on the previous day … There were craters here and there on the road and dozens along the sides of the road.

We reached Corps Headquarters near Mt Parnassus about dark, and that night saw the Intelligence Officer and got a pretty pessimistic review of the situation. We slept at Corps that night well hidden in olive groves in a gully and the Hun, for the first time for a week, didn't machine gun Corps Headquarters at Reveille. The boys had learnt the art of camouflage by this time and you couldn't pick out a truck from more than 100 yards away.

Early on Tuesday morning we set off for Divisional Headquarters about 20 miles further north near Thermopylae … When we got there we talked with a few of the Divy staff about the show and got a few stories, and from the side of a hill had a grandstand view of German fighters machine-gunning the road half a mile away. All through the morning there were German planes about – we must have seen about 60 or 70 all told – but these fighters were the only ones that came near us.

After lunch we went back to Corps, much against my will and Silk's and Parer's as we wanted to go forward; but Slessor had commissioned the truck and after a rather terse argument we agreed to go back with him. When we got back to Corps we were told of the decision to withdraw from Greece and we were also told that provision had been made to evacuate the press, film and broadcasting units with the Athens Headquarters personnel from Piraeus that night, on a Greek tub which was carrying the British Embassy staff. Silk, Parer and I asked if we could stay up at the front and come out with the troops. We were told that we would not be able to do any good, and that the best thing we could do was to go while the going was good. The colonel who told us that apparently did not expect many people to get out … in fact his words to me were, 'You can help the AIF best by getting out now and trying to write the truth about what has happened over here.'

It was about 4.30 by this time and Corps was pulling out then, and it was to move back to the coast at another point that night and get away the following night – Wednesday. So off we went … We had a hectic drive to Athens … the road was packed with retreating troops … most of them Greeks in the most tumbledown lorries you ever saw … and they simply wouldn't get off the road … We wanted to get back to Athens before dark because it was a devil of a place to find your way round in. On the way down we were lucky again … we were not machine-gunned from the air once, though we did pass a car that had been set on fire only five minutes before and from the top of our truck I got quite a good photo of it …

When we got to the outskirts of Athens we were met by the Press Officer of the AIF, who had made arrangements for the evacuation of us all on the Greek tub … In the dead blackout it was a hell of a job finding our way through the twisted streets of Piraeus to the wharf, especially as a number of streets were barricaded off because of bomb damage. The port had been wrecked by the explosion of an ammunition ship on the first night of the war and by subsequent furious raids. Still, we managed to get to the docks all right. There, by the light of shaded hurricane lamps, men were toiling to coal the ship – a little 150-ton tub built about 1900 … We picked our way on board over a plank that bounced as you stepped on it and then into the bowels of the ship, already hot and fetid with the smell of crowded humanity … It was the strangest human smell I've ever smelt … not just the ordinary dank yet humid atmosphere that you get between decks when a ship is battened down, but an indescribable feverish smell, as though human beings when in fear give off some peculiar odour.

The hold and the only intermediate deck were absolutely packed. In the hold were 156 German prisoners, sullen and seething … on the half-deck above were some Diggers and Tommies guarding them … rifles with bayonets fixed and a Bren gun ready mounted. On the next deck were hundreds of civilians … Greeks, Jews, Americans, British, all sorts of people … and their dogs, their cats, their pet birds, their bedding, their suitcases and all sorts of odds and ends. A seething humid mass … all battling for the best positions, all trying to get more on than the limit, which was one suitcase and a bedroll each. On the top deck it was the same … but right forrard we got a space to put the whole Press Unit – about 23 of us with batmen, cooks and hangers on. There we spread our things out and managed to get just enough room to stretch out sardine tight on the deck.

At 12.30 we slipped out of the black harbour, threaded our way through the anti-submarine boom and out into the Gulf of Aegina. At 12.55 Piraeus had its fiercest air-raid of the war … what was left of the port was ruined, and the only remaining ships in the harbour were sunk. We woke at about six, steaming due south on an oily sea … About 9 o'clock, two Sunderland flying boats skimmed past … about 10, over came three Blenheims but never a German plane.

The passengers had settled down by this time, but they were still trying to work points. They all had to stay down below deck unless they could get in the covered space under the bridge, and we were put on the hatches to stop them coming up … but they thought of every possible ruse. They had to come up to see their wives or children or husbands or a man about a dog or something. There was only one lavatory on board, for 750 people and there was an endless queue that stretched from the afterhatch up to the bridge leading to it … No one knew whether we were going to Crete or Egypt, though we knew we were calling at Crete … We saw the mountains of Crete snow-capped about noon … and about 2.30 we slipped inside the boom. About 4.30 we had an air-raid: five Italian planes came over and dropped mines (magnetic) and bombs … but they dropped them so inaccurately and from such a height that they did no damage and most of them fell on shore, well away in the hills. The rest of the afternoon was quiet, but towards dusk the senior Australian officer on board called us all together and told us that the Greek crew had refused to go on to Egypt, had refused to leave Greek waters. They had only been asked to come to Crete and they couldn't be made to go further. There was serious danger of them mutinying and joining forces with the German prisoners and seizing the ship. All the passengers were being shifted well down aft … out of the way … Bren guns would be mounted over the German prisoners and covering the hatches, and sentries would be put on the crew's quarters, and a man with a Bren gun on the ship's armament store … Every man who had arms was to carry them at all times.

The atmosphere down in the hold was tense; all day long the Germans had been restive ... the night before and in the morning they had been singing German folk songs as only the Germans can sing, but in the afternoon the air down there was sullen and heavy ... there were whisperings among the prisoners and their officers ... But the senior German officer was called up by the senior Australian officer and told quite plainly what to expect ... He was told that men with Bren guns mounted would be covering every hatch and every corner of the hold ... that at the top of the hold would be other men with bags of Mills bombs and that at the slightest sign of trouble these men would drop their Mills bombs down in the hold regardless of the presence there of our sentries. The crew was told the same. We had no trouble ...

Next morning we were raided again ... this time by medium level bombers ... they dropped about a dozen bombs about 400 yards to our stern, apparently going for a naval supply ship and some destroyers, Greek, which were lying near the boom. As soon as the officers on one Greek destroyer saw the enemy planes, they hopped in a motor boat and scooted for shore ... leaving their ratings to look after the ship and man the ack-ack guns. One tub was sunk in this raid, but we were OK.

After lunch they started taking us off our ship, the *Elsie* ... told us we'd have to wait on Crete till we got a ship to Alexandria ... A minesweeper took us off in relays ... We were in the last party, and just as we lay alongside the jetty unloading, zoom – out of the blue came ten dive bombers roaring down in steep dives, right for the shipping round the jetty ... The ack-ack gunners hadn't realised they were there. The first thing I saw was one diving at about 500 feet, straight for us it seemed. It was going for a naval oiling ship 400 yards to our stern ... The bomb landed about halfway between us ... For some unknown reason I wasn't

A desire to seek the underlying causes

nearly as scared then as I have been on other occasions. As the planes roared down and 1000 lb. bombs sent huge waterspouts 100 feet in the air ... I crouched down beside the gunwale and took photos ... unfortunately two I took were on the same plate and the other two were taken by the censor and I've never seen them ... It was a terrific sight ... ten 1000 lb. bombs fell within half a mile of the jetty. One hit a small Greek ship which sank in 3 minutes, two missed the half-sunken cruiser *York* by about 50 feet, but covered her with spray ... and four landed in the town right at the end of the jetty and wrecked some old houses. Otherwise no damage, but a lot of fun and fury for two minutes.

We got on shore and stayed the night in an olive grove with an Australian ack-ack battery which had a number of friends of mine in it ... Next day Ron Williams of the photographic unit and I tried to get back to Greece on one of the evacuation ships but couldn't get permission to go ... Then we tried the RAF to see if a Sunderland could take us ... it could take us but it couldn't bring us back ... no good. So we spent the morning seeing General Mackay and getting his story ... And then in the afternoon our most inefficient Press Officer, having failed to get us a passage out of Crete, managed to persuade the captain of the naval oiling ship to take us back ... We left at dusk and had a quiet peaceful two-day run to Alexandria.[39]

Chester Wilmot, ABC reporter, had now recorded the fluid offensive across North Africa, and had, first hand, both experienced and documented the agonising withdrawal from Greece. As a reporter, he had shown an uncompromising drive to report with both immediacy and accuracy – but to Chester, this was not enough. The Greek campaign awakened in him a desire to seek the underlying causes of both success and failure in war. The Wilmot journey from reporter to historian was now well under way.

10

SAND IN THEIR SHOES

At 8.05 pm on 30 April 1941, the correspondents crowded into the living room of Blamey's apartment in a large modern building in the so-called luxury flat area of Cairo. Wilmot had been phoning the general's ADC, Captain Norman Carlyon, for the previous two days, to set up an interview with the general, only to be told Blamey was 'indisposed'. Now he was late. Lady Blamey dispensed cigarettes and invited the reporters to sit down and wait.

Blamey arrived at 9 pm, apologised and explained he'd been at a meeting with Wavell. He was accompanied by one of his liaison officers, his son, Major Tom Blamey, who had been at Melbourne Grammar when Chester had been school captain. Kenneth Slessor, who took his position as official correspondent very seriously, began, as he recorded in his diary, 'by asking him a string of questions about Greece'. They included: 'Would you have advised or did you advise the entering of British troops into Greece? Did General Wavell? Our estimated losses men and material? Estimate of German forces …? Were the British troops "half the force" as Churchill said? How were the Australian and New Zealand divisions "best suited", as Churchill said?'[1]

Blamey seems to have dodged all the questions. He said that he deplored any adverse criticism of the campaign as it would assist German propaganda to drive a wedge between Britain and Australia. Therefore, any criticism of the campaign or the general plan behind it would endanger British and Australian relations. 'Moreover you will never get an article containing such criticism past the censor.'[2] Blamey insisted they went in with their eyes open, adding they were told that if they hadn't come to the aid of Greece, the Lend Lease Act would never have been passed. He dropped his guard towards the end, saying bitterly, 'The politicians with encouraging words contrive fine arguments, but I am thinking of the men I sent on the mountains of Greece. What is a gesture to the politicians is death to us, as the frogs said to Aesop in these very hills. This must not happen again.'[3] Slessor managed to put one last question: 'General, you realize that when the news of the Australian casualties reaches Australia, the people will be greatly disturbed – they look to someone – a man of your position, sir – to give them his advice. Would you be prepared to tell the people of Australia that these lives were not lost in vain?'

Blamey remained silent for several minutes, then said: 'That is a difficult question and I'm afraid I can't answer it.'[4]

Blamey's anguish about Greece stayed with him. According to the war artist Ivor Hele the general 'had a thing about Greece'.[5] It was Blamey who got the artist to paint the magnificent canvas depicting the troops who had just returned from Greece on the quayside after disembarking from one of the troopships.

Whatever Wilmot thought privately about Blamey, he seems to have taken the general's warning about the danger of driving a wedge between Britain and Australia very seriously, and in his broadcasts, he walked a fine line between exposing the foul-ups and defending the enterprise itself. Within days Wilmot had prepared a script, 'Air Power and the Greek Campaign', that went beyond describing events to analysing what had gone wrong using the techniques of a historian. His original sources were the experiences of the servicemen he interviewed together with his own observations.

Understandably enough, the censors were very dubious about what Wilmot was saying. But he took the script to Air Chief Marshal Longmore, Commander-in-Chief, Air Forces in the Middle East, who gave his approval plus, it seems, an off-the-record briefing. Longmore had good reason to welcome an objective account like Wilmot's. RAF servicemen were being confronted in bars by soldiers who had come back from Greece, many of whom had seen only German planes overhead. Ivan Chapman, who served in the 2nd Machine Gun Battalion, kept score of the numbers of German dive-bombers attacking the Servia Pass positions during one day: '6.30 am: sixteen; 9.10 am: eighteen; 1.40 pm: thirty; 2.15 pm: twenty; 3.30 pm: thirty; 5 pm: twenty one; 7.30 pm: eighty.'[6] He would not have been the only one to have made this sort of calculation. Wilmot believed the record had to be set straight.

> For six months before the Anzac and British Expeditionary Forces went to Greece, the RAF had been carrying on a magnificent fight against the Italians in Albania. They had been outnumbered but never outfought … The exploits of the handful of RAF men in Albania deserve to rank with those of the men who saved Britain last year. But when the Imperial Expeditionary Force was sent to Greece the RAF wasn't proportionately reinforced and at no time did the Anzac force have more than a third of the aircraft which its command considered the essential minimum. The men that were there did all they could – they flew their machines day and night but there weren't enough machines even to do part of the job effectively. They might have given protection to the forward troops – or to the roads – or to the ports – but they couldn't cover all three.[7]

Wilmot then went on to discuss the logistics:

There were very few airbases in Greece and new ones take time to prepare in rough country. In the early part of the campaign – while the Aliakmon line still held – the RAF had a number of good bases in the plain of Thessaly and they were in a better position to support the troops. But when they had to withdraw from these bases they had only a few dromes round Athens and these were well-known to the Germans. The result was that these – and the bases south of Corinth which were later used – were made untenable by frequent German attacks and a large number of planes were destroyed on the ground.

Chester now described the war in the air as he 'and thousands of other Australians saw it.'

In the first few days of the German offensive, German aircraft weren't very active. Heavy rains in Bulgaria and Yugoslavia made many aerodromes unusable and in the few days they kept fighting the Yugoslav Air Force destroyed a large number of German planes on the ground. During these days the Germans concentrated on long-range bombing raids on key ports – Piraeus, Volos and Salonika – the three main ports through which we were still bringing in the Expeditionary Force. In these ports they caused considerable damage – especially to Piraeus. There a raid almost as furious as the one on Coventry caused such serious damage that the disembarkation of troops and supplies was disorganised and delayed through lack of wharves. The Germans were assisted by an extraordinary stroke of luck … they hit a tanker which set fire to a ship carrying TNT, which had several truckloads of TNT alongside it. The explosion was heard thirty and forty miles away – houses 15 miles away shuddered – pieces of metal were hurled four and five miles – houses across the harbour were wrecked – there was nothing left of the main massive concrete wharf where the TNT ship has been lying. It was a tragedy of the first order – for the Greeks and ourselves, and it affected the whole campaign.

In the meantime the RAF got some revenge when they found a long column of German tanks and vehicles bogged in a valley in Yugoslavia ... For several days they bombed and bombed and bombed and by doing so gave our troops time to swing round to meet the threat to the left flank of the Greek and Anzac line which this column was making. The RAF was on the offensive and during this first week we hardly saw a German plane where I was with our most advanced troops. When the Germans launched their first attack on our positions in the Monastir Gap, they hardly used aircraft at all. I saw an occasional reconnaissance plane and a few Messerschmidts, but there was no dive-bombing of the forward troops. The RAF on the other hand attacked the Germans continually. From an observation post one afternoon I saw eight Blenheims escorted by three Hurricanes bomb the German troops' concentrations as they were trying to develop an attack. This, by the way, was the largest flight of British planes that I or any other Australian I've talked with, saw at one time – eleven; so that gives you an idea of what the RAF were up against. All that afternoon there were either bombers or fighters attacking the German troops – giving them a bit of the medicine we were to taste rather too often later ... and not much later either.[8]

The dispatch described how at this time the Germans continued their raids on the towns before the dive-bombing and strafing of the roads began.

At the front they used dive-bombers in the role of artillery supporting infantry attacks, but they were remarkably ineffective. I saw the first dive-bombing attack on our troops when dozens of bombers came over in two waves and did their best to smash up a road junction at a point that was difficult to bypass. But no one bomb hit the road though several burst within three yards of it. This was in the Servia Pass and two days later when they launched their first serious attack on the New Zealanders who were holding it nearly a hundred dive-bombers came in flights of three every few minutes for a couple of hours. There wasn't a plane of ours to challenge either them or the Messerschmidts which made machine gun attacks from time to time. But the infantry attack launched under cover of this air onslaught was repulsed by the New Zealanders who held their fire until the Germans had advanced up the slope against them to within suicidal range. The dive-bombing of forward troops did little material damage – there were extraordinarily few casualties; very few guns were even touched … and these air attacks never forced our men back a yard. But they did entail a very serious nervous strain. You can stand a bombardment if you can hit back – you can stand a enemy shelling if you hear the music of your own guns answering them … but when day after day you are attacked by dozens of dive-bombers and they aren't even challenged by your own fighters, it gets pretty grim. And that's not just my opinion – I've [heard] it in rather stronger terms from dozens of diggers who've been right through it … and I don't think anyone will suggest that the men of Bardia and Tobruk can't take it. They had the satisfaction of bringing down quite a few enemy planes with their Bren guns, but this didn't do much to stop the flow.[9]

Chester believed it was worse for the men on the roads:

In the frontline they were dug in – they could see them coming – and they had some ack-ack protection. But on the roads the drivers and the troops were sitting shots, and in the second week of the campaign the Germans concentrated on them. The 260-mile road from Athens to the front became a Nazi shooting gallery and by the end of the week the Nazis ruled the roads so completely that they were machine-gunning them to within 25 miles of Athens. The lines of communications just couldn't be maintained in the face of this constant bombing and machine-gunning. If we had had the aircraft our superiority plane for plane would have enabled us to do to the German communications what they did to ours.[10]

Chester then linked deficiencies in the air with the numerical superiority of the German forces. As he put it in one of his notes, 'We needed at least two armies'.

We had few enough troops in any case; the Germans had almost unlimited reserves … The only way we could have hoped to check their numerical superiority would have been by strafing their supply lines as they strafed ours … but we just didn't have the planes to do it. Our lack of air power accentuated our lack of manpower and enabled the Germans to bring up reinforcements at will.[11]

Chester turned his attention to the supply lines which by then 'had slowed to a crawl' with the Germans 'machine gunning and bombing the roads from morning to night'.[12] He also incorporated the experiences of his friend BBC correspondent Edward Ward.

Edward Ward of the BBC did a trip from Athens to the front during the worst days and he told me that their car had to stop every 10 or 15 minutes while they raced for cover in the fields. One Sunday after they had had between forty or fifty stops like this and had averaged less than 10 miles-an-hour, they gave it up for the day and took refuge in the hills until dark. 'During the whole two days on the road,' said Edward Ward, 'I saw only one Hurricane and heard of one other which had been seen bringing a Dornier down over near the coast.' I travelled down the same road two days later and though we saw the road being machine-gunned a couple of times and though there were dozens of enemy planes about, the truck I was in was never attacked; but I've talked with dozens of drivers who went through Edward Ward's experiences day after day. They were magnificent ... they were handling great lumbering three, five and ten-ton lorries – usually they were driving alone and they had no one to keep a lookout for them. Often the first they knew of an air attack was when they heard the bombs burst or the machine guns open fire.[13]

One devastating observation was cut by the censors. They passed Chester's statement that on one day late in the campaign he had counted well over a hundred German planes in the air but he saw only four Hurricanes – but the following passage was too much.

The trouble at this stage was that the German air attacks on our bases had been so intensive and so successful that a very large part of the aircraft we had in Greece had been destroyed on the ground. We didn't have enough planes in the air to protect those on the ground, but there was one extraordinary occasion when 17 Hurricanes were destroyed on the ground in one terrific raid. After that the position became almost hopeless.[14]

If the censor's blue pencil had gone through the above, the following passage, transcribed from Chester's notebook, had absolutely no chance.

One night during the second week I counted 37 RAF men in one restaurant – most of them pilots and I asked a squadron leader [if he] knew why there were so many. And he said, 'We haven't anything to fly. Here in Athens tonight there are thirty or forty of the world's best fighter-pilots and they haven't a machine to fly.'[15]

There was nothing in either passage the enemy didn't know already. The RAF losses on the ground would have been in the Luftwaffe after-action reports while the description of the fighter pilots in the cafes would have been included in reports from German spies in Athens. It was the old story of suppressing anything that might embarrass the High Command. It is a tribute to Chester's considerable powers of persuasion that he got as much through as he did. The broadcast's conclusion, however, that more planes were needed in the Middle East and that the British troops were at a serious disadvantage on account of the German numerical superiority in the air would have been exactly the message GHQ Cairo would have wanted conveyed to London. A later broadcast concentrated on German tactics as they were being explained to Chester by many of the senior officers who were only too ready to respond to his searching questions. An interview with Herring that was supposed to be for an hour went far into the night. A lunch with Tubby Allen went on all afternoon as he took Wilmot through the whole campaign. There must also have been at least one meeting with Rowell. From these discussions he distilled passages like this:

Before we can outfight Hitler we must out-think him. We must realize the speed at which his war machine is tuned to move. No one has ever seen anything like the speed of the German drives in this war. In Greece they advanced 500 miles from the Bulgarian frontier to the southern port of Kalamata in under three weeks. To move an army this distance in this time wouldn't have been easy as a mere manoeuvre. But the Germans did it in the face of strenuous opposition on the ground – they had to fight their way south and they had to advance over blown roads, round demolished bridges and through minefields. They were able to do it because they were organised for SPEED. The roads were blown – and there were only two good roads south anyway, so they brought up their supplies by air and they improvised landing grounds as they went. An Australian colonel, who was in German-occupied Greece for a fortnight before he escaped, told me, 'The 25-mile stretch of plain between Larissa and Pharsala became one great landing ground after the Germans passed Larissa. They were landing supplies – men, guns, petrol – everything they needed for the advance was coming down by air. No wonder our blowing of the roads didn't worry them – they weren't using the roads.'[16]

Chester was also getting extensive briefings from servicemen returning from Crete, where after a close-fought battle the New Zealand and Australian forces had been forced to evacuate. Now he incorporated their experiences into his discussion of German strategy.

The RAF was in Greece for six months before the German invasion. They built several new dromes and improved others, but when the expeditionary force was sent there, the RAF had nothing like enough dromes for the planes that were needed to support the force. This was one of the strongest points the RAF spokesmen made in explanation of the position in Greece. Against Crete the Germans used probably ten times as many aircraft as the RAF ever had in Greece. They operated them from Greece and the islands from dromes which they extended or constructed in the three weeks between the evacuation of Greece and the invasion of Crete. When they got a foothold in Crete, they made a landing ground in four days near Perivolio. Many of the first planes that came down there were crash-landed, but eventually they made it good enough for planes to land and get away. The Germans got their dromes built in Greece and the islands by conscripting Greek labour for the job. We were not in a position to do that admittedly, but when you are fighting an enemy who works this way, you must take strenuous steps to keep up with him.

Because of the speed with which he was able to consolidate his position in Greece, Hitler was able to strike at Crete much sooner than had been expected. But in future this is just what we must expect – we must realize that the German supply column no longer threads its laborious way across the ground – it is in the air. In Libya the bulk of the German supplies are being brought up by plane; in Greece they brought guns right to the frontline by plane too; and we all know what they did in Crete. And knowing this we must gear our war-machine to move at the same speed.

In another broadcast on German tactics in an airborne invasion I have spoken fairly fully of the amazing organisation of their attack, but here are a couple of small points which show you what we're up against. While our men were fighting in Crete on hard rations – cold bully and biscuits, the Germans got hot meals dropped from the air. Some of this parachute food fell near our positions. The food was in hot boxes – hot stew, hot coffee and fresh bread … all prepared in Greece – flown over and parachuted down. In other parts where they held larger areas, live steers were dropped from the air to keep the cookhouses going.

This takes organisation and until we organise ourselves to compete with them we are going to have a very hard fight. But organisation means work … They have such a start that we can only win if we are prepared to work harder than the Germans.

Just as important as hard work is clear, original thinking. We can't afford to be surprised anymore. We have been thinking in terms of the last war too long, but now we must think not in terms of 1940 … but of 1942 … or even 1945. If we do we shall start thinking almost entirely in terms of aircraft … aircraft not only in their original roles of fighting in the air and bombing enemy bases, factories and supply lines, but of aircraft as the main means of bringing up urgent supplies or getting reinforcements to a hard pressed force. The main thing that the Greek and Cretan campaigns teach us is that troops on the ground cannot hold positions in the face of continuous strafing from the air … the only effective answer to low-flying aircraft – when they come in waves as the Germans did – is fighter aircraft.[17]

The material Wilmot was collecting was so devastating that he threw caution to the winds and prepared a full critique on Crete and submitted it to the censor. In it he pointed out that many of the Australian troops were unarmed because their rifles had been taken from them and given to Greek soldiers. The ordnance store worked peacetime hours. It was closed when troops came to get weapons. They were told to come back later. No obstacles were placed on the airfields or on Maleme beach to counter possible landings. Even though the British held the island for seven months before it was attacked, no adequate measures were taken for its defence, such as the building of anti-aircraft emplacements on the airfields. Unloading of ships only took place in daylight hours. Night unloading in Suda Bay only started when Australian engineers took over the job. It was promptly banned. Following the advice he had been given by CEW Bean that if he had a serious issue he should bypass normal channels, Chester went to see a Brigadier Clayton, an officer on Wavell's staff. He described what followed in a letter to his parents:

At my request he took what I had written to Wavell, and after a few minutes the C-in-C sent for me. I was very disappointed in him ... He talked in a very matter-of-fact way with a clipped accent but not quite the incisive tone I had expected. As he talked he walked up and down, his hands behind his back, and every now and again he would walk right up to me and look me straight in the eye – from about two feet away. Very disconcerting, and I'm afraid that all told he rather mopped me up. I realise now that I should have argued back more – should have argued in favour of what I had written being released – but somehow it isn't easy to argue with a C-in-C, especially when that C-in-C is Wavell, and particularly when he admits right from the start that almost everything you've written is true, the criticism is fair and proceeds to admit that a large part of the blame comes right down on his shoulders ...

We then got around to talking about the lack of drive in the Middle East. He suggested that if my piece were published we would just stir up trouble between the Dominions and Britain. To this I said that there was already bad feeling, and that feeling wasn't going to be helped by not allowing legitimate criticism, and that more ill feeling will grow as a result of the inefficiencies. Wavell then asked me why there was this ill feeling, and I said: 'The general opinion among Australian and New Zealand officers and men who come into contact with GHQ is that the British in Cairo are not taking the War seriously; are not working all-out, are not working as hard as the men in the frontline ... It is amazing and appalling to Australians that this GHQ can close down completely from 1.30 to 5.30 every afternoon; that the average working day for Middle East officers is not much over 7 hours.'[18]

It was Chester's first encounter with Wavell – he had not been at the meeting when the Commander-in-Chief had announced

Operation Compass – and he was disappointed in the man. Chester wrote to his father that:

> He was obviously very much under strain, the toll of the war was telling on him and he seemed to be rather bowed down with worry; rather apologetic for his failure to foresee that the Germans could attack so soon and so furiously, for not having seen that more had been done in the 7 months [before the German attack on Crete]. But the most disturbing thing of all was that he seemed still to think in last-War terms.[19]

Still he was very flattered that Wavell was going to take up what he had said about the short working hours of staff in Cairo. One thing Wilmot did respect about Wavell was that he made no attempt to cover up his mistakes. The correspondent was of course being skilfully handled. We know now that Churchill, in one of the many cables with which he bombarded the Commander-in-Chief, had emphasised the importance of fortifying Crete. Wavell, as he admitted later, decided which of the Prime Minister's orders he would carry out and ignored the rest; and that had included fully fortifying Crete. Churchill could be quite unrealistic, but this time he was right, and if Wilmot's criticisms had got out it would have been very embarrassing to Wavell.

Despite Wavell having just reaffirmed the ban on his critique, when Chester returned to see Brigadier Clayton he asked for a copy of what he had written so he could circulate it privately among certain officers in the Middle East. Clayton was sympathetic, assuring Wilmot that his criticisms had impressed the Commander-in-Chief, adding, 'There'll be some blues as a result.' Wavell would have been wise to have treated Chester's criticisms about the slackness of Middle East Command more seriously. He made a note to take it up with Blamey but that was all. There was a dangerous amateurism throughout Wavell's forces. The Hussars used to have crushed ice sent up to them in thermos flasks to make their cocktails. Headquarters staff kept up a full round of social engagements in Cairo. Sir Henry Maitland Wilson set up his GHQ for the Syrian campaign in a luxury hotel in Palestine. When up against tough professionals like the Germans in Greece, or the Afrika Korps who had attacked in the Western Desert in the first days of the Greek Campaign, this casualness was very dangerous. This was recognised by later commanders like Auchinleck, who made GHQ Cairo more austere, and Montgomery, who took his headquarters out of Cairo altogether. Chester, on the other hand, as well as writing prescient military analysis, was now becoming an activist. This was very dangerous. It was not long before Wilmot heard that his intervention with Wavell had enraged Blamey.

The fighting along the North African coast and in Greece and Crete during the period January–April 1941 had been a searching test for the Second AIF and its commanders, from which they had learned much. These campaigns were also of critical importance to Chester Wilmot.

His dispatches and broadcasts during the North African Campaign show a determination to seek out and then describe the battles, and an increasing ability to develop relationships with soldiers of all ranks, particularly a number of the commanders. Many reporters thrive on dramatic moments. And if the search for such 'action' proves fruitless, then they use their imagination. We have already seen Wilmot's contempt for a number of British correspondents who were cavalier about the truth. Not Wilmot. He was in the best sense a reporter who wanted to get it right and who checked and rechecked. Chester tended to avoid the other correspondents. Although he liked and trusted Gavin Long – later to be appointed the Australian Official Historian – Kenneth Slessor, Edward Ward, Richard Dimbleby and especially Damien Parer, in many ways Wilmot was professionally a loner.

His growing relationship with the ordinary Australian soldier was remarkable. The Australians who fought during World War II were fiercely egalitarian, forthright, individualistic, and did not suffer fools gladly. That Wilmot won them over, and could then elicit honest and frank accounts of their fighting experiences was no mean feat. Perhaps they saw him forward with them, sharing their dangers and experiences, and came to trust him. Wilmot's dispatches are unique: they have a quality of immediacy and provide sharp, dramatic vignettes of war. He believed 'If you are to describe accurately and graphically the actions in which the troops take part, you must see the ground over which they have to fight, and you must see the positions from which they are fighting. Otherwise you have no idea what really happens.'[20] But Wilmot was going further, trying to understand the underlying command decisions, and even, when necessary, the politico-military context in which the commanders had to make those decisions.

If the ordinary digger was a hard enough subject to win over and to interview, then surely his commanders would have been harder still. It is extraordinary to contemplate the growing trust, the detail, and the amount of time taken, by a number of Australian commanders in not only briefing Wilmot, but taking him into their confidence to the point where he was allowed to interpret campaigns, not merely recount facets of the fighting. An obvious question arises with regard to these relationships. To what extent was Wilmot being used or perhaps cultivated by the commanders? While the Australian senior officers would certainly have been keen to see the exploits of their troops receive recognition after the highly successful North African Campaign, relating reasons for failure in Greece and Crete constituted far more uncertain ground.

There were a number of Australian senior officers who placed trust in Chester Wilmot, for they all 'had sand in their shoes'. They were the men of the Australian Army who had endured the campaigns in North Africa, Greece and Crete – and later Tobruk. The senior officers knew each other, their strengths and weaknesses, and it was from among this group that most of the very senior appointments came for positions that would stretch throughout the remainder of the war. Chief among them was Rowell. David Horner has described Rowell as 'proud, very austere and sensitive, he was high principled to the degree that one senior officer remarked "the trouble with Syd is that he expects everyone to act like a saint"'.[21] Rowell and Wilmot's relationship had begun prior to the battles along the North African coast, but developed strongly during the fighting in Greece. Brigadier Tubby Allen was probably a far more down-to-earth, approachable man. Allen developed a strong relationship with Chester, continually briefed him and took him into his trust. Herring was another who assisted Wilmot.

But from Chester Wilmot's perspective, the fighting in Greece went further than a reporter establishing contacts. The Greek campaign drove a wedge between Blamey and Rowell. Amidst accusations by the likes of Rowell, Allen, Bridgeford, Herring and Vasey, Blamey's suitability to command the AIF in the field was brought into question. These officers maintained that in Greece Blamey had lost his nerve, his 'grip' of the situation, and that others (chiefly Rowell and Clowes) had had to react to the pressure that Blamey had been duty bound to accommodate.

In his biography of Blamey, David Horner points out that on Anzac Day 1941 General Lavarack, Major-General Burston, Brigadiers Rowell and Andrew and Lieutenant-Colonel Elliott dined at the Union Club in Alexandria. The dinner conversation was dominated by a discussion of Blamey's command performance in Greece. 'As Lavarack noted in his diary, Andrew stated "that Blamey did not control operations in Greece as he should have and that at a critical stage effective command was passed to Rowell." Andrew accused Blamey of cowardice.'[22] Horner also records that Lavarack recounted the dinner conversation to his ADC the next day, who wrote in his diary:

Senior officers are back from the Greek debacle. Brigadier Rowell said he wanted to resign because of events in Greece. Said Blamey showed white feather, ran out of the country in a plane with his son. The whole Australian headquarters staff is seething with more than dissatisfaction. Brig Andrews [sic], who says he can see Gen. Blamey for only an hour a week, wants an enquiry into the conduct in Greece.[23]

Brigadier Andrew, apparently the most bitter of the group, died of a heart attack only three days after the Union Club dinner. According to Horner, 'The revolt fizzled'.[24] When Brigadiers Allen and Bridgeford returned from Greece their anger at Blamey's conduct in that theatre was also considerable.

The fact that Blamey was at all times a calculating and shrewd man – and, it seems, readily prepared at times to bend the truth – is best demonstrated by his letter to the Chief of the General Staff, Lieutenant-General Sturdee, of 26 June 1941:

Rowell has very great ability; is quick in decision and sound in judgement. There can be no question of his personal courage, but he lacks the reserves of nervous energy over a period of long strain. I found him difficult in the last few days in Greece and, as a commander, had to exercise considerable tact. Rather a reverse of what it should be.

I was a little disappointed both in him and Bridgeford over their attitude in one or two matters. They were over-impressed with the danger of the dive-bomber and talked a little too freely about its effect on the men. However, a short rest fixed them both up and they are doing a great job in Syria. Bridgeford was tireless.[25]

Blamey, Rowell, Allen, Herring, Clowes and Vasey were to later become involved in Australia's most critical test: the fighting in Papua New Guinea. This campaign will vividly demonstrate how pressure increases dramatically when an army, for the first time in its brief but proud history, fights on its own soil. The stakes are incredibly high, and there is the added pressure of establishing a working relationship with a new and more powerful ally who is not part of the old imperial – and largely redundant – order. As a result the pressures, friction and controversy already identified in Greece will multiply drastically in Papua for these officers. And Chester Wilmot will assume a role far more crucial than in Greece: he will become a participant as well as an observer. If Blamey and Rowell – and others – had unfinished business after Greece, it would be the same for Wilmot. But Chester had another major assignment before Papua. He was about to report on the Siege of Tobruk.

11

WE ARE SLOW TO LEARN

During the first three months of 1941, the Second AIF's baptism of fire along the North African coast had seen stunning success against the Italians: Bardia fell on 5 January; Tobruk on 22 January; Derna on 30 January; Benghazi on 6 February; and on 21 March Giarabub fell. Much of this fighting had been recorded by Chester Wilmot. But when Hitler decided to assist his Italian allies, and the British determined that his likely advance into Greece must be contested, the crushing victories of early 1941 were quickly succeeded by crushing defeats.

Chester had arrived in Greece when the Germans struck. Rommel – soon to earn the title 'Desert Fox' – counterattacked on 31 March 1941. On 3 April the British evacuated Benghazi; three days later, the Germans invaded Greece and Yugoslavia; and on 7 April Generals O'Connor and Neame were captured by the Germans.

At a conference in Cairo on 6 April, General Wavell decided that a stand would be made at Tobruk, and that this coastal town must hold out for two months to enable sufficient forces to be built up pending a British counteroffensive. Wavell had earmarked the as yet uncommitted 7th Australian Division for the Greek Campaign, but now decided that the Australian 9th Division – currently withdrawing towards Tobruk – and one brigade of the 7th Division (the 18th) should form the basis of the Tobruk defence.

Therefore, as four Australian brigades would form the core of the Tobruk force, and the remaining two 7th Division brigades were to constitute a significant part of the defence of Eygpt, Wavell decided that an Australian commander should take over command of all forces in Cyrenaica. The GOC 7th Division, Major-General Lavarack, was chosen.

Lavarack spent the next few days gathering his 9th Division into the Tobruk perimeter and assessing the best means of defending the fortress. While he understood that his preliminary orders were to hold Tobruk for two months, he knew he had enough supplies and ammunition for four.

It was decided to use three lines of defence for Tobruk: the 28-mile-long former Italian Red Line was the outer defensive perimeter; the Blue Line was the second; and the Green Line the third. Although Wavell and the GOC 9th Australian Division, Major-General Leslie Morshead, wanted to use only the Blue and Green Lines, Lavarack insisted on the use of all three lines, mainly to allow greater depth to the defences, but also to keep the harbour and base installations out of German artillery range. The other defensive strategy employed for the defence of Tobruk was 'an active defence', that is, aggressive operations were to be conducted forwards of the perimeter.

Lavarack, a professional soldier, had been a former chief of the Australian General Staff, and he had had an impeccable military education and record, but he suffered from one enormous handicap: Blamey didn't like him. Like a number of other senior officers in the Australian Army, Blamey saw him as a threat to his position. The Australians had long resented the splitting of their forces by the British; there was a resentment by both the Australians and New Zealanders of Dominion commanders being, at times, overlooked for command appointments that they felt entitled to; and there was

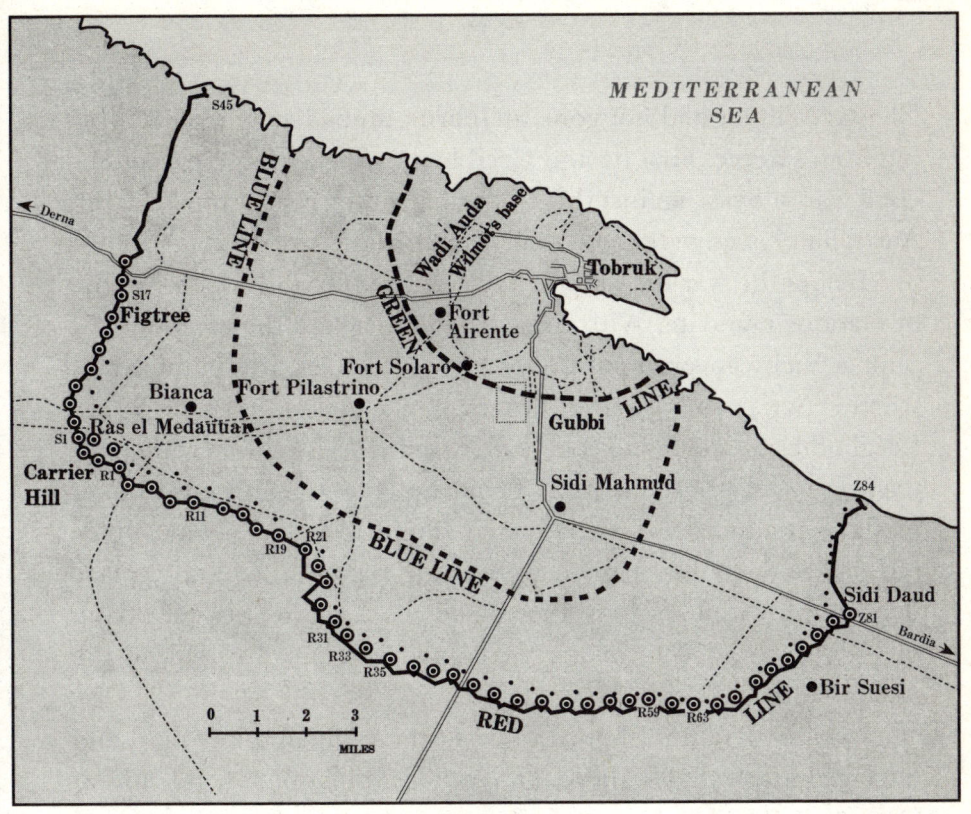

The Seige of Tobruk

a feeling at times that the British appointments to these posts were sub-standard – General 'Jumbo' Wilson was seen as an example. Blamey had been given a charter from the Australian Government to, in part, protect Australian interests.

As soon as Lavarack had been accorded a role to which the Australians had aspired, Blamey undid him. In consultation with Wavell, Lavarack was replaced as the commander of Western Desert Force and Tobruk, and sent back to his former command as GOC 7th Division. General Leslie Morshead now assumed command of all forces in the Tobruk fortress.

* * * *

Chester Wilmot had not gone to Tobruk immediately after returning from Greece. First he and Cecil had covered a largely unpublicised war in Syria against their former ally the French, in which the Australian losses were more than Greece and Crete combined.

Before the war the French had governed Syria under a League of Nations mandate. With the fall of France and the creation of a puppet Vichy government under Marshal Pétain, it was uncertain whether Syria would support Britain or take their orders from Vichy. Local officials decided to cooperate with the Axis powers while pretending to be strictly neutral. Then the Free French Government in Exile produced evidence – later found to be somewhat dubious – that the Vichy French were going to withdraw and replace their troops with Germans. Fearing an attack on their eastern flank the British decided to invade Syria and once again called on the Australians.

Cecil and Wilmot hoped to cover the campaign in sound and managed a reasonably thorough coverage, plus some good stories. One was when they 'accepted' the surrender of Sidon. Wilmot and Cecil were waiting with the forward infantry companies to enter the town when they decided to go in with the sappers who were to clear the mines and booby traps. One was a dour Scot, the other a stocky Westralian. The Scot – a veteran of the Great War – probed carefully with his bayonet for booby traps. However, soon the locals were coming forward to tell them where each mine was. After a while they lost the sappers in the general hospitality. Then the crowd started clapping and a policeman on point duty saluted. As Chester wrote in his dispatch:

> They obviously thought that we were the vanguard of the official party come to receive the surrender of the town. To the crowd, Lawrence, with his silver hair curling up round his cap, was at

least a brigadier and I presume I was taken for his ADC ... at any rate they thought we were something pretty important and all the way down the street policemen battled to keep back the surging crowd.

    Lawrence was an officer in the King's Royal Rifle Corps during the last war and it's famous for its extra-short snappy step. I learnt a swinging 30-inch step with the Melbourne University Rifles and somehow we never can keep in step. But we were never less in step than on this auspicious afternoon ... Marching in a procession with hundreds of others through packed streets is all right, but when there are just two lone people on whom the whole crowd is concentrating its gaze and its greetings, it becomes rather a trial. Still we survived it – the crowd kept back until we got to within about 50 yards of the end of the street, where the Chief of Police was waiting to receive us. When we got there the crowd surged round and swept us almost into the arms of the gendarmerie. The Chief came forward, saluted, and all his minions did the same – as they had done all down the street. In studied English he said, 'We are pleased to see you ... everything is in order in the town and we are here to do anything you wish, you can be sure of our cooperation.' Then he started to explain that the local councilors [sic] were waiting at the Mairie to make formal surrender of the town. This was too much and Lawrence hastened to explain that we were not the official party at all ... in desperation he kept repeating, 'The General will be here in one hour' ... and eventually it seemed to sink in. But that made no difference to the welcome.[1]

When Chester described the entry of the Australians into Sidon for the BBC, he felt he could not tell the story as he did for his listeners at home. His Australian broadcast concluded apologetically:

In this war certain correspondents have been vying with each other in claiming towns have surrendered to them, so much so that in the Middle East it's almost a distinction not to have had a town surrender to you. That was one reason for drawing the veil ... but the other was the feeling that after the troops have been fighting their way in, it's hardly fair for a couple of correspondents to flaunt the fact that they got the welcome that the troops deserved. But I hope that in this case the troops won't feel we were stealing their show.[2]

Cecil and Wilmot also recorded a 'live' description of the attack on Damour. The sound survives and shows Chester at his best. It was also an impressive technical achievement. Cecil then left for Cairo and Wilmot continued alone. Then he came down with a severe case of dysentery followed by an attack of asthma. Soon he was in hospital in Gaza and then was transferred to the convalescent houseboat in Cairo. He was still recovering when Cecil sent him a message ordering him to go to Tobruk. This was followed by a further message stating that if he was too ill he (Cecil) would go himself. The thought of his boss making endless recordings of battle sounds as he had at Bardia or even more 'Voices from Overseas' must have been too much for Wilmot, so even though he was still very ill he booked his passage.

Early in August 1941 Wilmot sailed from Alexandria for Tobruk on the destroyer HMS *Decoy*; the ship's departure was barely noticed in a harbour packed with merchantmen and warships. (In his book *Tobruk*, on which this account is based, Wilmot has 'July', but his letters to Cecil indicate he left for Tobruk in August.) There were two other destroyers making the run, HMS *Havock* and HMS *Kingston*, each carrying 50 tons of freight – mainly cigarettes, mail and ammunition. The passage had become increasingly hazardous. A few weeks before HMAS *Waterhen* and HMS *Defender* had been sunk while making the same run. At first the Stukas could not dive-bomb at night. By July, however, the Germans had found they could pick out the destroyers in moonlight from the foam of their wakes while the ships' gunners often could not spot the planes in the dark until it was too late.

Chester would later write:

> We were on the first run of the month and there would be the waning moon to guide the bombers to us as we got near Tobruk, but the crew hoped it would not be bright enough. [The] main worry was the last half hour before dark, when the escorting fighters had left. In this deadly thirty minute period the Stukas had tried to stop the destroyer ferry so consistently that the run from Sidi Barrani onwards was known as 'Bomb Alley'.[3]

For the time being Wilmot and his fellow passengers lay in the sun, 'the Med bluer, the ship's wash whiter, than ever before'.[4] At 3.30 pm *Decoy* was headed towards Bomb Alley. Chester spotted their air cover of eight Hurricanes with a further eight trailing behind to relieve them. These stayed until half an hour before dark then withdrew to avoid cracking up on landing with empty tanks. Then came the deadly sunset run.

> The next four hours drag slowly through as the setting moon silhouettes us on a silver sea, turning our wake into a phosphorescent trail. On the deck we wait – salt spray spattering faces and knees as the destroyer plunges into the night. Waiting – waiting – waiting – ears straining for the drone of bombers.
>
> Then above the roar of engines, wind and sea, from the rear gun-platform an officer shouts through a megaphone: 'Stand by. Action stations.' We wait again. Then, 'Stand by. Enemy aircraft.' … Above the turmoil that voice again, 'Stand by. Blitz barrage.' Behind us a great white swath of wash is even more tell-tale

than before, but they'll have seen us now and the only way to trick them is to zigzag. I look across at *Havock* – a great stream of black smoke is pouring from her funnels. Then we hear the bomber's drone and *Havock*'s guns stab the darkness with red flashes. She rolls over in a 90-degree turn and a hundred yards or so ahead of her a great white water-spout tells us that the Stuka has missed its mark.

Out of the darkness ahead we see two pin-points of light, the harbour lights of Tobruk, shielded from the air but visible to us. We slacken speed. There is no wash now, and a welcome cloud cloaks the moon and other bombers cannot see us. But they are over Tobruk and are going for the harbour. We can hear the muffled crack of the ack-ack guns and see the flashes of bursting shells high in the sky; only the 'heavies' are firing, so apparently the bombers are well up.

We slip in between the lights, past the black ghosts of wrecks, under the lee of the white sepulchre of a town. The ack-ack is still speeding the raider home, but another is coming in – lower. The Bofors are firing too, so it must be well under 10,000 feet. But we have no time to think of the fireworks display above us. As *Decoy* stops moving two barges and two launches come alongside. Troops clamber over the side, pitching their kitbags ahead of them. Unloading parties swarm aboard and slide ammunition down wooden chutes into one barge, while the rest of the cargo is dumped anyhow into the other. As soon as the troops are off, the crew start bringing wounded aboard in stretchers.

They are getting a warm farewell. One stick of bombs screams down on the south shore of the harbour; the next is closer – in the water 500 yards away. The old hands continue working, unworried, but some of the new ones, like us, pause momentarily, shrinking down behind the destroyer's after-screen. From the man with the megaphone comes a sharp rebuke – 'What are you stopping for? Those bloody bombs are nothing to do with you' …

The guns were going again as we left the jetty and went bumping out of the town in a 3-tonner. For the next hour, they were coming over in ones and twos every ten minutes or so. As the drone of one died away, we could hear the next coming in, the greeting of the guns, the rumble of bursting bombs and then the ack-ack's spasmodic farewell fire. We thought it was a fairly warm welcome but for Tobruk it was just an ordinary night.[5]

After a brief time in a staging camp where Chester was forced to stay in bed for a few days, the correspondents decided to base themselves at Wadi Audi. There were prickly pears, palms and a clump of fig trees in marshy ground near a wall. Their tents were dug in 3 feet deep and with the protection of the stone walls were safe against anything but a direct hit. As he and Bill MacFarlane planned to stay for a few weeks, Chester scrounged a table and chairs and an old Italian bedstead that would, he hoped, be beyond the leap of the fleas infesting the sand. Chester was wrong. They got into everything. Fortunately the sea was only 300 yards away and the correspondents could swim every morning.

He decided not just to cover the siege as he observed it, but to tell for the first time the story of the early battles when the Tobruk garrison gave Rommel his first bloody nose of the desert war. Initially one of his principal sources was Tobruk commander Major-General Lesley Morshead. This had its disadvantages as Morshead insisted on correcting the correspondent's every dispatch. He also made himself principal censor. 'I can see him now,' Chester was to write in *Tobruk*, 'coming out of his office with a script of mine in one hand, pencil in the other, glasses on the bridge of his nose and saying to me "Just a moment Mr Wilmot, there's something not quite right"'.[6] On onc occasion Morshead took two of Wilmot's scripts submitted to him for censorship to Alexandria when he reported to Sir Thomas Blamey (Blamey never visited Tobruk himself).

For all his pedantry and officiousness, Morshead could be surprisingly self-critical. 'You're letting me off too lightly', he said. 'I didn't handle my tanks well in the May battle. You must say that.'[7] Judging from surviving scripts, Wilmot didn't go quite that far but included the exchange in *Tobruk*.

One of his early broadcasts from Tobruk was a portrait of life in the desert fortress.

A Letter from the Front – No. 11:

So much has been said about Tobruk and yet so much remains to be said that it's a little hard to know just where to begin. But I think I'd better start with a warning – it's almost impossible to generalise about Tobruk so far as the conditions of living are concerned. What's true of one unit or one part of the defences may not be true of other units or other parts.

But there are a few conditions about which you can generalise, because they apply to pretty well everyone. Too much dust and too much bully [beef]; far too little bar and far too infrequent baths. As for the dust, I suppose every man in Tobruk is now lined with a chocolate coloured film … he's been breathing dust and eating dust for months. I've spent six of the last nine months in the desert and I've got used to grinding up dust and sand with my food. I've got used to squinting through eyes three parts closed in the face of a driving dust-storm. But I've never had to tackle the problem of trying to find and fight an enemy attacking under cover of a dust cloud; but the troops have to. They have to man their posts, and drive their vehicles without windscreens, and continue working on improving the defences, sandstorm or no sandstorm. And when their throats get parched with the dust they can wash it away only with a limited quantity of water – water that's a little brackish and more than a little chlorinated … The other night a new arrival brought up with him a tin full of Alexandria water, and in the mess a precious jug-full was passed around. We drank it neat and smacked our lips like connoisseurs tasting a new wine …

On the matter of bully, perhaps the less said the better. In any case I'll have some more to say about rations a little later on, but I should say now that bully is a great leveler … it is no distinguisher of persons. Bully and bread and margarine are the basic ration, and whether you eat in the General's mess or in a frontline post you'll get bully in one or other of the many disguises that the ingenuity of army cooks has invented.

Now the question of beer – and here we're on very dangerous ground so I'd better start by saying that on 99 days out of 100, there is no beer to be had in Tobruk. But it seems that someone has put about the story that beer is a regular issue in Tobruk, and this seems to me to have annoyed the troops far more than dust-storms or dive-bombers have … Everyone I've asked says if he were given the choice of a beer or a bath he'd choose the bath. With tea and water you can shake your thirst, but unless you can deal with the daily accumulations of dirt, you haven't much chance of holding at bay the army of fleas that the Italians left behind them as a powerful and persistent fifth column.

These then are the things about which you can generalize – dust, bully, beer and baths – but about the different conditions in different parts of Tobruk I'll have something to say later. Oh, there's one thing – one common condition – that I'd almost forgotten. Anywhere inside the Tobruk perimeter men live close to danger. It is often less dangerous to be in the front line than it is to be working near the harbour or one or other of the enemy's favourite bombing targets behind the lines. But the troops have learnt to endure discomfort and hardship, and to scorn danger, for they're determined that neither living conditions nor the enemy shall get the better of them.[8]

Unfortunately, the relationship with Morshead became increasingly difficult. Wilmot never lost his liking or respect for the man but still found his interference infuriating. As Chester pointed out to George Fenton it wasn't that he was giving away information to the enemy. On one occasion Morshead complained that Wilmot was using material no other correspondent had seen and that he as CO could be accused of favouritism. Then when Chester submitted a 300-word commentary Morshead criticised him for not giving enough attention to the air battles.

Part of the problem was the conduct of the other correspondents. Ian Fitchett, Kenneth Slessor's offsider, never went beyond Divisional Headquarters and based his stories on the intelligence summaries the general told Chester. Wilmot's friend Frank Hurley was criticised for having staged action scenes with soldiers from the garrison. However, when Wilmot went out into the Salient and attempted a realistic description, the script was banned because it was too sordid.

The Salient was the indentation made in the line when Rommel made his second attack on Tobruk. Chester's script, however, was about the men themselves. It was the kind of journalism that was to be practised by Ernie Pyle in Italy and France later in the war, but Chester's copy is less sanitised. Fenton thought it was one of the best things Chester ever did but even after the war it was never published even though there are a few excerpts in *Tobruk*. Here are a few samples:

We are slow to learn

All day we lay in a dug-out just big enough for three Diggers and me stretched out. Four feet above us was a roof of corrugated iron resting on sleepers and on top of that sandbags, earth and bits of camel bush, which made the top of the dug-out look like any other bit of desert to German snipers scanning the level plain from 500 yards away. The late afternoon sun beat down on the sandbags and we were clammy with sweat. The wind had dropped and it didn't even blow dust in through the small air vent or the narrow low door way that led to the crawl trench outside. The air was heavy with dust, cigarette smoke and the general fug we'd been breathing in and out for the past thirteen hours. We waited for darkness to give us a chance to stretch our legs and fill our lungs with fresh cool air, a chance too to have a crack at the Hun who'd been skulking in his dugouts all day.

Every so often we'd hear the rumble of guns and shells would whistle high over our heads. Our gunners and theirs were showing their first signs of activity for the day, but the enemy shells were landing well back. His machine-guns had been silent since dawn and even his mortars hadn't been landing with their usual unheralded crump around our forward posts. It had been a very quiet day – like so many days since the hard battles in the Salient in May …

Usually from dark till about midnight is the time you can safely move around the salient posts – after midnight the fun starts. By day you can't move at all … in the dead flat desert the machine-gunners and snipers on both sides can see every move. And so for 16 hours of daylight you can't do anything but lie in your dug-out and fight fleas and boredom. In most parts you can't even stand up, for the unyielding Libyan rock has made the digging of deep trenches impossible …

Once it's light, if anyone happens to be wounded or ill, he can't be moved back till after dark. He has to lie in the dug-out all day, while his mates give him what attention they can. It's not altogether a sweet job in the salient posts. Quite apart from discomforts … the fleas and flies … the lack of tea … the fuggy atmosphere … the lack of exercise and the dull rations … quite apart from the nervous strain of holding the most vital part of the perimeter, where the pressure's greatest; quite apart from all this, there's the constant fight against boredom. What can you do in the 16 hours of daylight in a muggy-dusty-cramped dug-out. You can try to make up for lost sleep; you may write a few letters, but there's not much to talk about; you may read the few well-thumbed magazines or books that are kicking round the dug-out, but you've probably read them all before you can smoke cigarette after cigarette, if you've got enough …

In spite of everything they're irrespressible … the fellows fought boredom by joking about it and by talking away about all sorts of things … from the Russian war to beer and Test cricket …

It was just dark now and a Digger came up from another post … his face was set and glue … 'They got Pete last night,' he said, 'How …?' 'Oh, he was out in front in the listening post and he copped a stray burst from Spandau Joe just as he was coming in.'

The air in the dug-out was heavy with silence for a minute or two and then Ernie said … 'so they got Pete eh … in a listenin' post … wouldn't it? … we *were* mates when we joined up … a bloke doesn't mind so much if he's knocked in a stunt … he more or less expects that … but to cop it just lyin' out there in a listenin' post. Gawd … I don't want to go that way … umm … that makes his section pretty weak … only five blokes now instead of … I wish those "reos" would come from Aussie a bit quicker … we could do with 'em'.

'Couldn't we,' said Mick. 'That's one reason why I'd like to go home for a bit … there's lots of chaps I know there, who were cobbers of mine once … they aren't married … they're not keeping their Mothers or anyone except themselves in cushy jobs, that we left. I'd like to go back and tell 'em what I think of them. One of my pals over here wrote a poem about "Those Friends who Stayed at Home" … he was killed a few days later, and we've added a couple of verses as an epitaph … would you like to hear it.' … I said I would … and he read them with a feeling that I've sensed a lot among the men who've fought so gallantly – so stubbornly and so cheerfully for months to hold Tobruk. This feeling isn't so much one of resentment as of disappointment. It's always seemed to me that the inspiring, the binding force in Australian life is not tradition or nationalism or the cohesion of a nation working for some great cultural ideal like the ancient Greeks, or for some great social experiment like the Russians … it's been quite a simple thing … Henry Lawson called it 'Mateship' … the spirit that makes men stick together in the face of common dangers … and difficulties. The strength of the AIF is this spirit of mateship … no man, no platoon, company or battalion will let their cobbers *down*. They made a name as great fighters, because they were great cobbers. I can't believe that this spirit of mateship is any weaker now than it was when the great Trade Unions were being formed in the '90s or when we sent … men away with the AIF last war.[9]

The lines about mateship are crossed out in Chester's copy but this was for emphasis. Damien Parer had arrived at Tobruk and wanted to incorporate them in his film. Like Chester he had spent time in the Salient shooting powerful sequences that more or less paralleled Wilmot's dispatch.

Their time in Tobruk marks the beginning of the close friendship between Damien and Chester. Here they began to collaborate and not just about mateship, important as this Australian myth was to both of them. Damien went down regularly to the harbour to film the Stuka Parade: the regular attacks by the Germans. Wilmot and MacFarlane spent two weeks living in a trench with some Scottish gunners not only to interview them but to record 'live' descriptions of the raids. Parer seems to have photographed Chester in action recording one of his descriptions. He was stripped to the waist, a tin hat on his head, microphone to his lips; an almost Hollywood portrait of an intrepid broadcaster. But there was more to their friendship than this. Parer watched with fascination Wilmot's close questioning of soldiers trying to work out how he could get it on film. He went out with Chester when he was trying to get the story of the Easter Battle.

Chester wanted to record the participants telling their stories in their own words. Initially just getting them to speak to him was difficult. It wasn't that they were unwilling to broadcast, but that everything a soldier said had to be vetted. Chester's diary records a frustrating day trying to get Major Balfe's account of the Easter Battle.

> Just before I left the Colonel rang the Major and told him the battle report was not available and the Major said 'Oh well, that doesn't matter because I have my own notes and I remember the whole thing perfectly. I'll write up my story and send it up to you and you might get Brigade to look over it and check it and they'll put a chit on it and send it back I suppose. It's all right for me to go ahead and broadcast it.' And the Colonel said 'Yes, that should be all right but of course I'll have to vet it too and then I can let Mr Wilmot know.' Then he turned back to me and said,

'I suppose you think this is a lot of red tape but you know, we fellows who are brought up in the army are tied up in red tape and we can't get along without it. If you don't follow the old routine, you're likely to get a rocket ...' Red tape, hell – I nearly passed out at this stage because I really couldn't say anything that wasn't rude.[10]

Just as Chester secured his clearances for the Easter Battle story the recorder broke down. Bill MacFarlane was forced to take it back to Alexandria to be serviced. While he was away Chester worked on the scripts and wondered darkly if Bill was using this as an excuse to keep away from the action. As he conceded in a later entry, this was unfair. After all the journey to Alexandria and back was extremely dangerous. When MacFarlane returned it became clear that Boyle hadn't been servicing the equipment properly. Finally in their makeshift studio in a small wadi, with the sound of artillery in the background, Wilmot made his programs. The surviving program is not the same as the scripts preserved in Australian Archives. Did Wilmot cut it in the 'studio' or was it edited in Cairo or back in Australia? Anyway it is an extraordinary achievement by two of Australia's great radio pioneers. Even though the participants are reading from scripts their laboured diction is very moving. The sound of the account by Lieutenant Mackell of the terrible night when Jack Edmondson won his VC has not survived but Chester was to include a transcript of Mackell's interview in *Tobruk*:

About a quarter to twelve we set out, Corporal Jack Edmondson, five men and myself – with fixed bayonets and two grenades apiece. The Germans were dug in about a hundred yards to the east of our post, but we headed northwards away from it, and swung round in a three-quarter circle so as to take them in the flank.

As we left the post there was spasmodic fire. Then they saw us running and seemed to turn all the guns on us. We didn't waste any time. After a 200-yard sprint we went to ground for breath; got up again, running till we were about fifty yards from them. Then we went to ground for another breather, and as we lay there, pulled the pins out of our grenades. Apparently the Germans had been able to see us all the way, and they kept up their fire. But it had been reduced a lot because the men we'd left in the post had been firing to cover us. They did a grand job, for they drew much of the enemy fire on themselves. We'd arranged with them that, as we got up for the final charge, we'd shout and they would stop firing and start shouting, too. The plan worked. We charged and yelled, but for a moment or two the Germans turned everything onto us. It's amazing that we weren't all hit. As we ran we threw our grenades and when they burst the German fire stopped. But already Jack Edmondson had been seriously wounded by a burst from a machine-gun that had got him in the stomach, and he'd also been hit in the neck. Still he ran on, and before the Germans could open up again we were into them.

They left their guns and scattered. In their panic some actually ran slap into the barbed wire behind them and another party that was coming through the gap turned and fled. We went for them with the bayonet. In spite of his wounds Edmondson was magnificent. As the Germans scattered, he chased them and killed at least two. By this time I was in difficulties wrestling with one German on the ground while another was coming straight for me with a pistol. I called out – 'Jack' – and from about fifteen yards away Edmondson ran to help me and bayoneted both Germans. He then went on and bayoneted at least one more.[11]

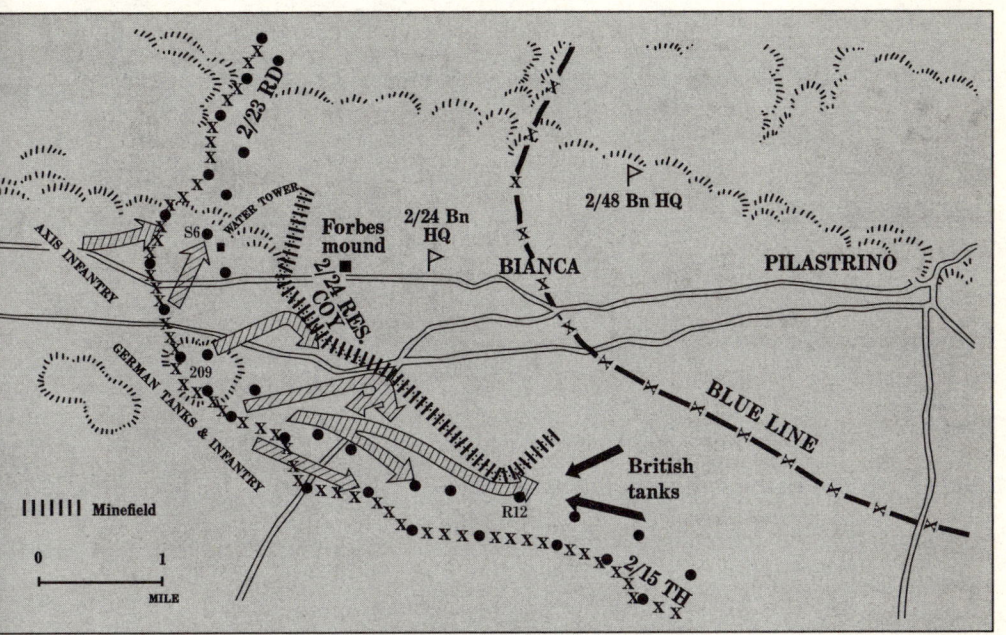

The Tobruk Salient

Chester must have thought Mackell's story was so moving that he needed to conclude his account as quickly as possible:

> After seeing his men safely back to his own post, Mackell reported the result of the attack to Balfe's H.Q ... Speaking from there to his CO (Lieutenant-Colonel JW Crawford) he said with expressive brevity – 'We've been into 'em, and they're running like – '[fucking bunnies].[12]

* * * *

Chester's 'old pal' from the first desert offensive, Edward Ward, arrived in Tobruk. Soon they were out together exploring the Salient, where, as Chester put it, 'the Germans managed to bite a small mouthful of desert from the semi-circle of perimeter posts which we were holding'. For the first time there were German and Australian troops facing each other across 'no man's land'. Wilmot described his and Ward's adventures in a broadcast entitled 'Into the Salient':

> The other night I went up to a sector of the salient with Edward Ward of the BBC and some British and Australian officers. It was a very quiet night, but we followed the ration truck forward and gained some idea of the problems of supply and movement in this area.
>
> We picked up a guide at a brigade headquarters just before dark, and in the half-light followed the dust trail of a truck loaded with mail and rations which was making for a battalion headquarters. We found it tucked away in a rough twisted wadi … We crowded into the dugout and from maps spread out on the wall the CO told us how the salient was held; how we managed to keep the upper hand by maintaining superior fire power and by constant patrols. It was quite dark when we continued our journey forward, but you could still make out the track from the line of churned up dust. Hanging on the step was a Digger to guide us through the minefields. We were glad he knew his way …
>
> After about half an hour's bumping along we got to a bit of a hollow – the furthest forward the vehicles go. A chink of light from a hole in the ground beckoned us to company headquarters. We lifted a ground sheet and dropped down a man-hole that led into an old water-cistern – roughly pear-shaped and about 30 feet long. Through a fug of cigarette smoke and dust the light of hurricane lamps lit the cistern. Fellows were sitting round eating and talking. Their evening meal had just arrived and they were busy making the most of it … It was the same meal we'd had earlier … bully-beef stew with potatoes and onions; boiled rice and tinned apricots; tea … a pretty good

feed … in the circumstances. It was pretty warm in the cistern – but at least you could have a light there. There were sticky fly catchers hanging from the roof, but they hadn't been able to do much about the fleas. I realised that after I'd been there a few minutes.³

Under pressure from General Sir Thomas Blamey and the Australian Government, the British grudgingly consented to the relief of Tobruk. At the time it was feared that a relief on the scale demanded would be extremely difficult. Before the Australians left there was to be the dedication of the Tobruk War Cemetery, which was to be recorded by the unit. The day of the ceremony there was 'a nice pickle'. Bill MacFarlane had been on the rum the night before and had an appalling hangover. Chester spent most of the morning and early afternoon looking after his technician, bathing his head, getting him drinks. Finally, by about 3 pm, Chester was able to get him to take a swim and together they set up the gear. Then as the ceremony was getting under way one of the two transformers blew. The crisis brought out the best in MacFarlane. Swiftly he ran all the equipment off the remaining transformer.

****

Chester's three months in Tobruk proved to be a triumph. He broadcast regularly for the BBC who, perhaps unfairly, regarded Mr Wilmot more highly than their own Richard Dimbleby. His collection of information, investigation and reconstruction of recent events was the work of an accomplished historian as well as a broadcaster. Chester didn't just make radio documentaries. One night he and Bill MacFarlane recorded a concert then went back at 11 pm to a dugout at Tobruk harbour to wait for the Stuka Parade.

Whenever he could, Wilmot described the experiences of ordinary soldiers and put them on the air. Chester was becoming an expert in military strategy but he was still a social historian. When Wilmot combined these vignettes of life in the desert fortress with military analysis for *Tobruk* three years later, the book became an Australian classic.

If there had been any problem with Chester's reporting, apart from Boyle's irresponsible failure to service the recording equipment, it was the censorship. Later it became even more difficult for other correspondents than for Wilmot. Was Morshead what we would call today 'a control freak'? His achievements at El Alamein and later in New Guinea indicate he was nothing of the sort. But when they were setting up the Tobruk defences the key decisions had been Lavarack's. Moreover, Lavarack had left Morshead, the citizen soldier, in no doubt that he – the Staff Corps officer – was in command. Only when Morshead was indisputably in command of Tobruk did he become a part-time editor to ensure that the coverage of his men's achievements was the best it could be. In Chester's case it most certainly was. But of course Morshead's 'editing' had nothing to do with it.

★ ★ ★ ★

Wilmot's return from Tobruk coincided with the build-up for the Crusader Offensive. The road from Alexandria to Cairo was jammed with traffic. There were heavy lorries and 25-pounder guns. Beside the road were squadrons of new aircraft, petrol dumps, spare parts, food and general stores. On 16 November 1941, the correspondents were briefed by the Field Commander, General Sir Alan Cunningham (brother of the famous admiral). His intention was to seek out and destroy the enemy armour. The relief of Tobruk was expected to follow. XIII Corps was supposed to pin down the infantry on the frontier while XXX Corps swept round the flank to attack the German armour and then link up with a break-out by the Tobruk garrison. The RAF was to blitz the enemy airfields to ground the German fighters so that the British squadrons could give the ground troops direct support. As Chester described it in *Tobruk*:

> By the evening of November 17th the attacking divisions were at their battle stations ready to move at dawn, after intensive bombing of Axis dromes. But that night thunder and lightning split the Libyan skies and the heaviest downpour in memory flooded the desert. Not one British aircraft left the ground and next morning the RAF could not immediately swing its full strength into action. But the enemy suffered far more seriously. His airfields were in the coastal belt, where the rain was heaviest and the soil like glue; for two days almost every Axis aircraft was grounded.[14]

Consequently, the first attacks plunged deep into German territory with at first no reaction from Rommel. (After the war it was discovered that he had refused to be distracted from his plans to attack Tobruk.) To the British, it seemed they were winning a series of famous victories. All of this was relayed to the correspondents by the exuberant Major Randolph Churchill, son of the British PM, and head of the news propaganda branch at GHQ. When the massive and extremely skilful German counterattacks occurred, unwarranted optimism turned to unjustified pessimism.

In Wilmot's opinion, the younger Churchill was not to blame. 'He did little more than pass on what headquarters had told him and when correspondents tried to warn the British people of the real position they were stopped by GHQ. 'The worst offenders,' Chester believed, 'were the "string men" known as the "2nd eleven", who were relying on the communiqués and the embellishments of the "Military Spokesman". He was probably the greatest optimist of all, and he was not Major Randolph Churchill, as was suggested in the House of Commons.'[15]

When the truth started to come out and searching questions

were asked in the House, the Cairo Military Spokesman left his deputy to carry on. 'The deputy immediately warned correspondents that what he said could be used, but not quoted as coming from any Military Spokesman.' This drew from an American correspondent, Sam Brewer, the drawled enquiry: 'Well, Colonel, that may be okay for you, but our papers won't take it on our say so. We've got to quote some source. What would you rather be – a military spokesman or an authoritative source?'[16]

Covering such a confused battle was difficult and dangerous for Wilmot and his friend Damien Parer. After the counterattacks came – conducted, unknown to the correspondents, by Rommel's subordinates – the German commander decided to leave the Afrika Korps in a daring 'dash for the wire'. It was a gamble but as Chester's friend Basil Liddell Hart was to point out, the attack was a shrewd thrust at Cunningham's morale. Indeed only the last-minute takeover of field command by British C-in-C, Sir Claude Auchinleck, prevented a German victory.

Wilmot described some of his own and Parer's adventures in *Tobruk*:

> Shooting up everything in sight, the column outflanked the 7th Armoured Division, scattered its transport and over-ran its supply dumps; put 30th Corps HQ to flight and generally herded across the frontier all the administrative and supply vehicles on which the forward troops depended. On the way it was severely bombed and strafed by the RAF, which hindered but could not stop its advance. On the afternoon of the 24th thousands of British vehicles were streaming eastwards across the frontier as hard as they could go. A 'flap' was on and once a flap starts in the desert it is difficult to stop, but fortunately the boundary fence provided a place at which to rally the disorganized troops. Even so the Germans' use of many captured British and South African trucks made reorganization difficult. No one could tell friend

from foe, as Damien Parer and I found that afternoon, when we drove our truck straight towards a column, which we did not realize was German until an anti-tank gun opened fire on us. We got away in time, in spite of Parer's immediate reaction which was to stall the truck, switch off the engine and step furiously on the starter. Suddenly the truck roared into action again and shot off across the desert spurred on by several shells which were no match for Parer's speed.[17]

By 26 November the head of the Allied column had established itself on the frontier wire about 15 miles south of Sidi Omar. Chester and Damien went out with the Indian cavalry to the west of the wire. They were in a kind of saddle between two low hills. The Indians had a few guns, anti-tank ack-ack, about half-a-dozen tanks and armoured cars and a lot of transport. Wilmot and Parer were told the attack was to take place early afternoon. The tanks were to attack south of the wire on the western side. From behind the correspondents' position to the east the guns were to fire on the Germans. It was intended that another tank column would sweep west to cut off the retreat, but first the RAF was going to turn on a bombing raid. All this was absolutely ideal for the correspondents: Chester could get Bill MacFarlane to record the sound; Damien would have a tank attack to film.

At midday the British guns opened up, their shells falling on the enemy positions on the other side of the wire. Then the shells started to fall short. The party, who by now had been joined by Randolph Churchill, thought they must be new guns finding the range. Finally one landed 20 yards from the sound truck. The equipment had been set up and there was no time to pack it into the truck, so they all piled into Damien's panel van and drove to a position further back. Chester and Bill MacFarlane watched helplessly as shells fell around the precious sound equipment. Where they were was reasonably safe so they began to cook some stew for lunch. Then shells began to fall only 50 yards away. Bill MacFarlane and Randolph Churchill jumped into the back of Parer's van; Chester was climbing in when he was knocked over by a heavy blow to the back. Thinking Wilmot was aboard, Parer let out the clutch and sped off. Then, realising Chester was missing, he slapped on the brakes and jumped out to see the stunned Wilmot pick himself up, stumble across to a carrier and climb in the back as it drove off.

Chester had been wounded by flying shrapnel. He'd only avoided serious injury, as he explained to the family with diagrams, because the door of Parer's van was open behind him and had absorbed most of the impact. Chester's wounds were in the groin, 'just missing [his] manhood'. At first he'd passed it off but soon realised the wounds were more serious than he had thought. As a result, December found Chester in a convalescent houseboat on the Nile again, tended by a medical colonel who was later to be accused by a court of inquiry of taking kickbacks. (Blamey cancelled the impending court martial – after all, the doctor was a friend.)

Chester was disappointed to have missed the rest of Crusader, which turned out to be a close-fought victory for the British even though yet another downpour prevented any real exploitation of their advantage. He felt even worse on learning that his friend Edward Ward had been captured during the running tank battle at Sidi Rezegh.

The bungling that Wilmot had observed at all levels made a deep impression on him that was expressed in a script, written back in Australia in June 1942, after yet another British reverse in the Western Desert. Based on confidential briefings at all levels, Wilmot dealt authoritatively with tank tactics, and especially the German's use of 88-millimetre guns:

> The most disturbing thing about the fighting in the Desert is that after two years of war we still haven't learnt enough to match the Germans in tactics or equipment. We are still being

surprised. In the early days of the war our failing phrase was 'Too little; too late' … now it seems to be 'Who'd have thought it?' Reports from the front suggest that we were surprised that Rommel dared attack in mid-summer; surprised that he used his 88 mm AA guns as anti-tank weapons; surprised that our tanks were ambushed. If we were surprised, it is only because we are slow to learn.

Our experience with anti-tank weapons is a good example of this. We hear that the 88 mm gun is something new, but I happen to know something about this. In May 1941 the British captured Halfaya Pass from the Germans, but in doing so they lost a number of heavy 'I' tanks. I was there that day and saw the German anti-tank guns which had made clean holes straight through the 5" armour of the supposedly impenetrable Matildas. They'd been made by the new 50 mm anti-tank gun firing a 4½ lb shell. This new German gun had more range and punch than our 2-pounder and this discovery naturally caused some concern in British tank circles. At once the plea went out to British manufacturers for a gun that would out-match the German 50 mm. And so the 6-pounder was planned.

But a month later when we made another move in the desert, our tank offensive was stopped short when our tanks were led into an ambush in which 88 mm guns were reported to have caused great casualties. Anyway we lost about 100 tanks and some of the tank crews blamed the 88 mm gun, but Western Desert Force command wouldn't believe that the Germans were using these anti-aircraft guns as anti-tank weapons.[18]

Even though Wilmot had revealed nothing the Germans didn't already know, his pointed criticisms resulted in protests, ostensibly from the Postmaster-General's Department, and he was ordered not to broadcast on the desert war again. The publication of the dispatch in the *ABC Weekly* was banned — an ominous preview of the clashes two months later in New Guinea.

While Chester was recovering in hospital he had been brooding about the breakdowns in equipment, Cecil's failure to control Boyle, and that he and MacFarlane had been sent out in a truck during Crusader that had been so badly serviced that it could easily have broken down. In a fast-moving desert battle this could be lethal. Earlier he had composed a carefully reasoned letter to Cecil outlining in no uncertain terms his boss's responsibility for these failings. Now he decided to send it. Like many debaters, Wilmot was under the illusion that a well-argued case would carry the day. With men of the calibre of Charles Moses or even TW Bearup and later senior BBC officers, he was right. With Cecil out of his depth and trying to cope with a brilliant subordinate such a letter was unbelievably hurtful. The dispute was soon patched up but Cecil made the mistake of sending the correspondence to the ABC Head Office in Sydney where, by then, Wilmot's credibility was far higher than his own.

After leaving hospital Wilmot did two stories on the training methods of Brigadier Robertson, pointing out among other things that recent arrivals from Australia were dangerously unfit. Both scripts were banned. This time Chester took the matter to Blamey himself. Wilmot described what followed in a report to the ABC.

> I saw the General about this and he said that it was not a correspondent's job to be critical at all and that any criticism of Australia coming from the Middle East would be taken in Australia as inspired or at least approved by him, therefore no criticism. No praise either for General Robertson so I offered to delete his name but this script was killed on the general ground that it told the enemy too much about our training methods. However, a few months later the same material appeared in

Australian papers in an article by Captain Macartney, General Blamey's press officer, with credit for the Depot's success given to the General himself.[19]

Blamey might have got the better of this first exchange but was soon on the defensive as he parried searching questions by Wilmot about his personal involvement in a contract to show films to the troops in the Middle East. Chester had been investigating why the films shown to the troops had been of such poor quality and the prints in such a damaged condition. When he had questioned the amenities officer the man's reaction had been so defensive that Wilmot became even more suspicious. At this time Wilmot probably did not think the story was all that important. There were rumours of Blamey accepting bribes from Albert Shafto, the major film distributor in the Middle East, but what did Blamey have to offer that was worth these supposedly vast sums of money? Anyway the unit was soon to return to Australia and for the moment Blamey was to remain in the Middle East.

12

SYD IS COMING

Before leaving for Australia Chester wrote a companion piece to 'When Will We Learn Enough to Win?' As he explained in a covering letter to the ABC's Acting General Manager, TW Bearup, the script had been recorded for him by the BBC on four 10-inch discs because he had no recording gear available.

In the dispatch Wilmot reiterated the criticisms he had made to Wavell seven months before. He pointed out that, 'when we had a force on Crete, for six months before the German invasion ... they did ... very little to prepare the defences of the island'. He added that, 'when the local command was formed in Cyrenaica after General Wavell's successful offensive, officers took their tennis rackets [sic] along and almost at once adopted the Cairo working day'. As for the so-called 'Cairo working day' Wilmot included the story of his encounter – confrontation really – with a British brigadier, who held an important position at GHQ Cairo at a time when the headquarters was working a seven-hour day, broken by a seven-hour siesta in the afternoon. Wilmot said to him that surely these were hardly adequate working hours in wartime. The brigadier's reply was:

> I think officers would be prepared to work longer hours, but you know it would be rather hard on the other ranks clerks orderlies

etc, [sic] they'd get rather bored.' I couldn't help asking what boredom had to do with it … and didn't he think the men in Tobruk – manning the perimeter 24 hours a day – might be bored too … and what about the men and women working 12-hour shifts a day in factories in bombed Britain. The Brigadier said he hadn't thought of it that way, and I suggested that there were far too many people in the Middle East who haven't thought of it that way either.

Chester turned to the issue of class, arguing that the war effort in the Middle East 'is hampered by restraints of the old school tie and the old regiment' and that 'there should be only one test for the fitness for a position and that is capacity to do the job. But far too much inefficiency is covered up because of the old loyalties which should mean nothing in wartime.' He argued that the 'section of the community represented by British officers in the Middle East' was one that was 'on the whole prepared to compromise with Hitler at Munich'. In addition many of these same officers 'only reluctantly accepted Russia as an ally last June. The class these officers represent can never prosecute the war with the same whole-heartedness as the mass of the British people, because they are not opposed to Fascism as a code of political life … In fact they are now caught in two minds for they see happening in Britain radical changes, which they fear almost as much as they fear Fascism.'[1] Here Chester was alluding to some of the attitudes already appearing in the mass observation surveys. Eventually they were to bring about the victory of the British Labour Party in 1945.

The dispatch has a curious history. The script was passed by the censor but on the top of the copy preserved in the Australian Archives is pencilled, 'Not to be broadcast'. Still, the piece shows that Chester Wilmot the socialist and anti-fascist was very much alive.

* * * *

While Chester had been reporting on the arrival and subsequent campaigning of the Second AIF in the Middle East and Greece, immense political and military changes had occurred in Australia as both the government and the army were forced to ponder the Japanese potential to bring them to war in the Pacific. In February 1941, the Chiefs of Staff provided the Curtin Government with an appreciation of possible Japanese ambitions and military options, and how Australia might best react to the apprehended threats.

First, it was perceived that an invading force would be likely to attack an area essential to Australia's economic ability to wage war: the region of Newcastle, Sydney and Port Kembla. Second, Melbourne, Brisbane, Fremantle, Albany and Adelaide were identified as additional defensive focal points. The Northern Territory and Papua and New Guinea, although strategically important, were seen as areas that could deplete and therefore dilute the army's ability to protect the more important centres. It was believed that the Japanese would be forced to conquer the Malay Peninsula and the Dutch East Indies as a prelude to an invasion of Australia.

To react to these needs of a South-East Asian and home defence, the forces in Australia at this time consisted of the AIF 8th Division and the militia: the 1st and 2nd Cavalry Divisions, four infantry divisions and components of a fifth division and corps troops. On paper, this seemed a formidable force; however, severe deficiencies in strength, training, equipment and, above all, leadership, due to the priority given the AIF 6th, 7th and 9th Divisions in the Middle East, caused this paper assessment to be almost totally unrealistic.

To compound an already disastrous state of affairs, the newly raised 8th Division, AIF, was dispersed in token gestures to the threatened north: a battalion to Rabaul to hold forward airfields; another portion of the division to Timor and Ambon; and the remainder to participate in the not-too-distant disaster at Singapore.

As a result of this preliminary appreciation, it was decided to raise a militia battalion to garrison Port Moresby. The role was

Syd is coming

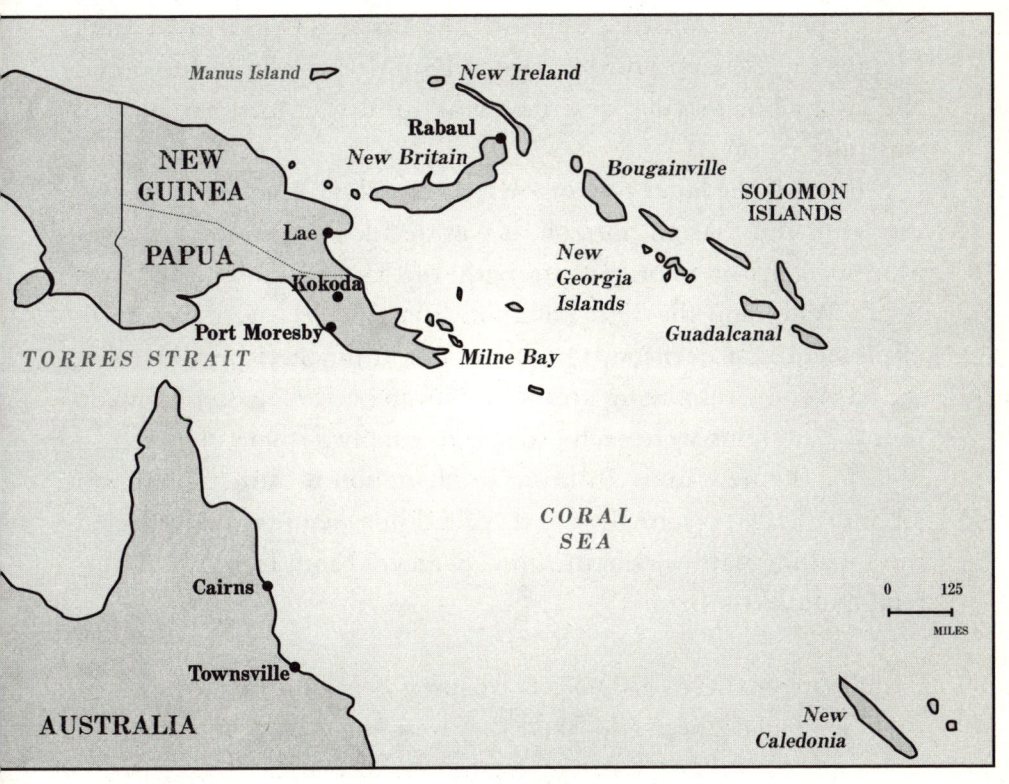

Papua, New Guinea

allotted to the 49th Battalion from Queensland. The 49th sailed for Port Moresby on 15 March 1941. The staff work, dealing with the logistics for the arrival and care of this battalion, was abysmal. It might be argued that such a state of affairs would never have been tolerated had an AIF battalion been involved. The 49th spent its time in Port Moresby building roads, unloading ships and constructing buildings, as well as the expected duties of siting and preparing defensive positions. The Chief of the General Staff, Lieutenant-General Sturdee, visited Port Moresby on 11 July 1941, and after an inspection, described it as 'quite the worst battalion in Australia'.[2]

Towards the latter part of 1941, as war clouds loomed larger on the South-East Asian horizon, it was decided to increase the Port Moresby garrison to brigade strength; the 53rd Battalion from New South Wales and the 39th Battalion from Victoria were chosen to implement that decision. Originally raised for service in Darwin, the 53rd came into being around 1 November 1941, after eighteen militia battalions were each ordered to supply a quota of sixty-two men for the new unit. To bring the battalion to full strength, an additional 100 personnel were recruited in a manner that reflected the appalling staff work at the time. Sergeant Keith Irwin, 53rd Battalion, told Peter Brune:

> These poor devils had no idea what was happening to them. They had not been told where they were going, what unit they were destined for, or any information at all. They had received no final leave, were given no chance to let their families know what was happening to them ... most of them had never seen or handled a rifle.[3]

This battalion had no chance to build an esprit de corps, so vital to any unit's morale and pride; in addition, because of the circumstances of its formation, there was to develop an anger and bitterness within its ranks that would work directly against the very qualities needed for success.

The 39th Battalion was raised in Victoria from elements of the 3rd and 4th Divisions and the 2nd Cavalry Division. The battalion's recruits were all volunteers for tropical service and were, on the whole, led by enthusiastic officers. In early April 1942, Major-General Vasey wrote to subordinate army commanders requesting monthly reports concerning the combat efficiency of brigades in the Australian Army. There were six guidelines, or ratings, from 'A': 'Efficient and experienced for mobile operations' through to 'F': 'Unit training is not yet complete'. The 30th Brigade in Port Moresby was graded 'F'.[4]

In addition to the 49th, 53rd and 39th Battalions of the 30th Militia Brigade, the Port Moresby garrison also comprised the 13th Field Regiment, the 23rd Heavy Anti-Aircraft Battery, the Papuan Infantry Battalion — consisting of Papuan natives who were led by Australian officers and NCOs — and the New Guinea Rifles, which was a unit consisting of returned soldiers and some of their neighbours who had settled in New Guinea. These were the untrained and unblooded troops who were destined to take the brunt of the early Japanese onslaught in Papua — along the Kokoda Track.

If all this was not poor enough, on 26 May 1941 Brigadier (later Major-General) Basil Morris had assumed command of the 8th Military District (Papua and New Guinea). Morris hardly had an impressive World War II record. When Blamey had first arrived in the Middle East, he had discovered that the Australian Overseas Base, commanded by Morris, was 'living in Jerusalem largely by taking in its own washing',[5] and that he was reluctant to use Morris further because he didn't 'get down deep enough into things'.[6] In other words, Morris was lazy and ineffectual. Blamey later transferred Morris to Bombay as the Australian liaison officer. His appointment to Port Moresby therefore reflects the fact that in mid-1941 it was considered nothing more than a backwater garrison.

* * * *

Chester's voyage back from the Middle East was, he wrote in his letters to his parents, quite pleasant. The only problem was that he was sharing a cabin with three soldiers, one of whom, to his and the others' disgust, was averse to bathing. Another problem was that no one was quite sure where the convoy in which they were travelling was going. We know now that the destination was the subject of a fierce exchange of cables between Winston Churchill and Australia's new Labor Prime Minister, John Curtin. Churchill wanted to use the 7th Division in Burma and had actually diverted the convoy to Rangoon. Finally, after Curtin emphatically asserted his rights as a Dominion prime minister, the convoy was redirected home.

Chester meanwhile was planning to marry Edith Irwin, the girl who had sent the unforgettable telegram to the transcontinental express as he headed to Perth. She had accepted Chester's invitation – a challenge almost – to 'explain herself' and had been ardently courted by mail ever since. Edith believed that expressing his deepest feelings towards her on paper came easily to Chester, particularly when his emotions were under pressure. He certainly had a sense of the dramatic. One letter came from a foxhole in Syria; another was written in the early hours of the morning just after he had completed an important dispatch.

Still, Chester was capable of arousing her to fury with a description of his plans to work for a new, more equal world with a fairer distribution of wealth. This was socialism – anathema to a well-brought-up girl of the Adelaide establishment. Edith told him she couldn't look at his letter for a day as it made her so angry. However, she finally agreed to make an unbiased study of the subject.

Edith was doing a diploma in social work in Melbourne so was able to visit Wilmot's parents. One can infer she had reservations about his family and they with her. The Wilmots and Miss Irwin were, it seems, excruciatingly polite to each other when she was invited to afternoon tea, but Chester had to write a rather forced letter assuring Edith how much they liked her. He then wrote to his parents emphasising what a nice girl Edith Irwin was. It seems then she was more or less accepted. Clearly Chester was not going to tolerate any repetition of the way his mother had broken up his romance with Ann Elder.

Edith was staying in a rooming house while she was studying for her diploma. There were, she recalled, 'sherry parties and much fun and gaiety'; then she got a cable to say that Chester was on his way home. In a panic she rushed into a friend's room saying, 'That man's back in Australia. And all those things I said in my letters!'

'Serves you right,' her friend said. After all, as they used to say in the 1940s, Chester Wilmot was quite a catch.

Meanwhile, Chester had stopped off in Adelaide and met her parents, who were, of course, charmed to meet him.

Bung and Janie met their son's train at Spencer Street Station. Edith was late but they waited for her. As she rushed up to the group on the platform, Edith noticed Chester seemed more mature – his face lined, his hair thinner. After an awkward first greeting, Edith felt his parents would like Chester to themselves, and she did have to complete the slum visits for the day that were part of her social work course, so she said awkwardly, 'I'm so sorry I have to go – I must get my work finished.' However, Bung and Janie sensed her embarrassment and invited her home that evening. After dinner they left the young people alone. Chester was to prove even more ardent and persuasive in person than he was in writing. Edith 'wanted to enjoy [their] happiness without intrusion; he wanted to tell the world and did'.[7] When the ABC granted him some unexpected leave and Chester wanted to use it to get married at once, Edith cheerfully agreed but with unspoken reservations.

They were married on Anzac Day 1942 in Adelaide at the St Peter's College Chapel, by Edith's father, who was one of the school chaplains. The photographs show Chester very dashing and handsome in his war correspondent's uniform with Edith radiant and elegant in a tailored suit and hat – very few white weddings took place in the early 1940s because of wartime austerity. There was a brief honeymoon in the Adelaide Hills, then a round of parties in Melbourne. Edith was left to continue working for her diploma while Chester returned to his new assignment with the ABC in Sydney.[8]

When Chester had first gone into the ABC after returning from the Middle East he'd prepared a carefully reasoned argument for an increase in pay – compared with other Middle East correspondents his pay had been scandalously low. He needn't have bothered. Wilmot was informed that as his work had been superior to that of many other senior ABC officers, there would be a substantial increase in salary. This was in marked contrast to how Chester's friend Damien Parer was treated by the Department of Information. Promises were made for improved organisation and higher salaries for the cameraman, but nothing was done.

Soon Chester was writing a report on how coverage of the Pacific War should be organised. Among his proposals was the appointment of a war news editor to whom all the recordings from all the units would go. Knowing the general picture, he could incorporate the individual stories into the day's general story. Chester suggested setting up two field units. One was to operate in the 'central zone' with Darwin as its headquarters, while the other was to be attached to the US Army. These field units should include reporters developing scripts for immediate broadcast and others to investigate the wider picture. Wilmot's proposals make good sense even now. They were designed to educate citizens of a democracy at war. They did not, of course, take into account a High Command intent on concealing its actions from politicians and people, and which was more interested in propaganda and self-promotion than news. Soon Chester came to realise his ideas were impossibly idealistic. Still, the ABC was very impressed.

Left Chester and RWE 'Bung' Wilmot with three sisters, seated L to R: Nancy, Jean and Louise taken between 1922 and 1925.
COURTESY JANE WILMOT CRANE.

Below left Bung and Janie on sofa with Arthur Streeton still life in background. Photo taken at Shipley House, South Yarra, Melbourne late 1940s. COURTESY JANE WILMOT CRANE.

Below Bung reporting public school sports. The author imagines him looking much like this when he wandered the streets of Sydney with Chester discussing the Blamey feud in late 1942.
COURTESY JANE WILMOT CRANE.

A very young looking Chester (centre) as School Captain of Melbourne Grammar.
COURTESY JANE WILMOT CRANE.

Above Chester with Melbourne University debating team, 1935. Included in picture are Bob Santamaria (mid-right) and Alan Benjamin (far-right). COURTESY JANE WILMOT CRANE.

Left Chester and Alan Benjamin in the USA. COURTESY JANE WILMOT CRANE.

Chester in full battledress, wide-brimmed hat and binoculars, at about the time he first met Frank Gillard. GETTY IMAGES LEONARD McCOMBE / STRINGER. PICTURE POST COLLECTION 652081249.

Above Chester broadcasting during raid on Tobruk, September 1941, taken by Bill MacFarlane. Chester's caption on the back of the photo reads 'Bill MacFarlane leaves the recorder to snap me during a raid.' COURTESY JANE WILMOT CRANE.

Right Richard Dimbleby at the time Chester knew him. GETTY IMAGES LEONARD McCOMBE / STRINGER. PICTURE POST COLLECTION 94253338.

Right Chester Wilmot, well known Australian writer and author and former BBC war correspondent, who has taken part in many BBC programs, January 1952. BBC 33751311.

Below right Chester posed against a display of many of the books he had to take into account while writing *The Struggle for Europe*. COURTESY JANE WILMOT CRANE.

Chester and Damien Parer. According to Chester's caption on the back of the photo 'Damien Parer makes a point – apparently my mouth is full of coffee – his truck in background was the one I was beside when I was hit. Fort Maddalena Libya, Nov. 1941.'
COURTESY JANE WILMOT CRANE.

1942 Chester with CEW Bean taken together because, according to family notes, Bean said 'I regard you as my successor.' This is the only photograph of them known to exist.
COURTESY JANE WILMOT CRANE.

Above Luneburg surrender, Chester in background. Caption reads: 'British official war office photo BU 5208. Germans surrender to Montgomery at 21 Army Group HQ at Lunberg Heath at 6.25 pm, May 4. Montgomery reads terms to German delegates. Chester is standing at the back by the tent pole.
COURTESY JANE WILMOT CRANE.

Right Chester with Ectors's children in Brussels. Thierry (aged 5) and Viviane, 1944. Courtesy Jane Wilmot Crane.

Opposite above Brigadier AS 'Tubby' Allen (left) with Major-General Iven Mackay. PHOTOGRAPHER DAMIEN PARER. AWM 005626.

Opposite below 'Syd'. Lt General Sydney Rowell when commanding in New Guinea. AWM 026299.

Above Chester broadcasting in Syria. The microphone is protected by a hood. Photographer George Silk. AWM 008619.

Opposite above Eora Creek village, Kokoda track. Frame enlargement from Parer's film. AWM 013257.

Opposite below Members of the 39th Batallion filmed by Damien Parer outside Menari. Parer's shot gives a vivid impression of the condition of the track. AWM 013288.

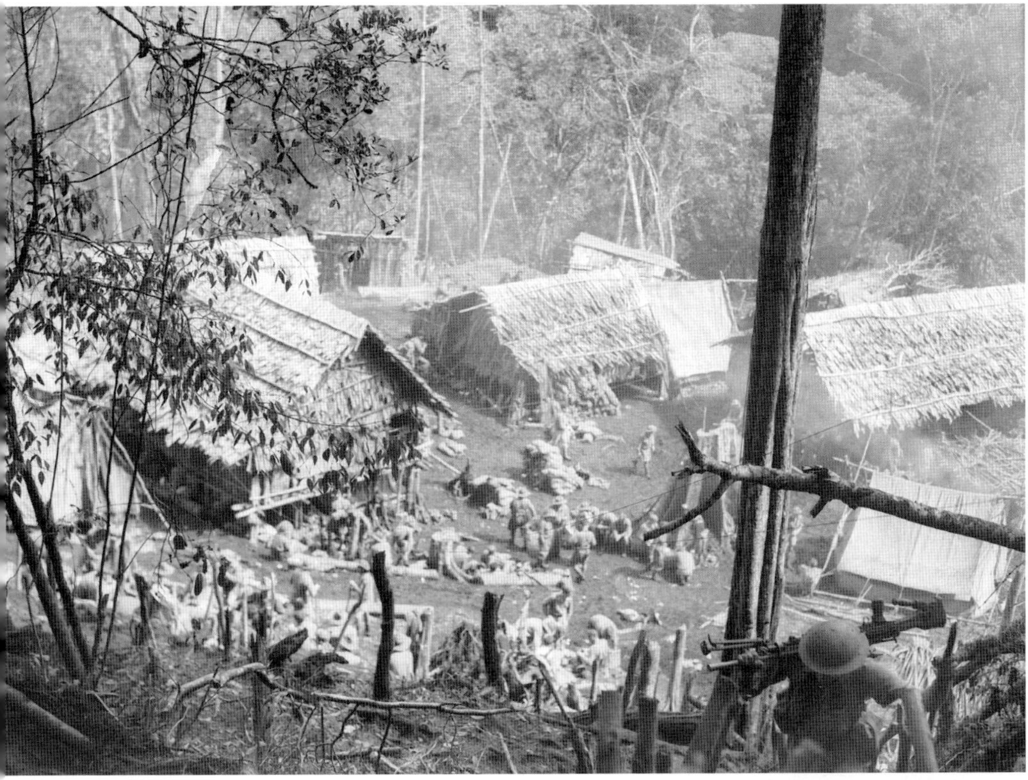

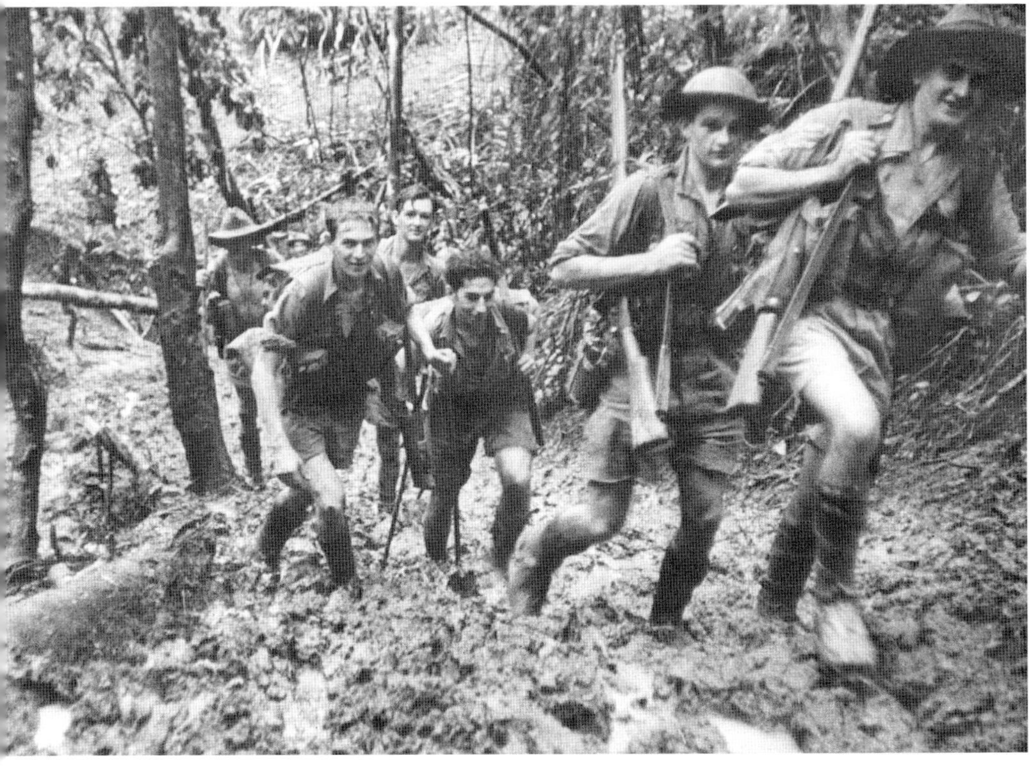

Above Osmar White (left) and Chester Wilmot on the Kokoda Track, taken by Damien Parer with the Graflex still camera he later had to abandon. AWM 013472.

Opposite top Edith and Chester on their honeymoon at Mt Lofty. According to Edith, Chester set the camera, then leaped over the gate and got into the picture just in time. COURTESY JANE WILMOT CRANE.

Opposite below Chester, Edith and family taken shortly before his last journey. Jane is left, Caroline is right and Geoffrey is in Edith's arms. COURTESY JANE WILMOT CRANE.

Chester in New Guinea with Sir Thomas Blamey. The only photograph of Blamey with Wilmot known to exist. Note Chester's cool stare and that Blamey is turned away. COURTESY JANE WILMOT CRANE.

Chester wearing earphones with a recording device. His caption on the back of the photo reads 'Me at the recorder in Tobruk. Posed to annoy Boyle.' COURTESY JANE WILMOT CRANE.

One of the few shots of Chester Wilmot with one of his most important colleagues, Frank Gillard (far-right). COURTESY JANE WILMOT CRANE.

Therese Denny and Chester Wilmot taken during the writing of *The Struggle for Europe* probably when he was a guest on her radio program. Their mutual affection is obvious. AUSTRALIAN BROADCASTING CORPORATION LIBRARY SALES.

Top Basil Liddell Hart at the time Chester knew him. Photographer Howard Coster. NATIONAL PORTRAIT GALLERY LONDON NPG X25402.

Below Charles Moses, General Manager of the ABC and a staunch supporter of Wilmot during the Blamey feud. In the 1980s Edith Wilmot asked the author to convey to, by then Sir Charles Moses, her gratitude for his support at that time. AUSTRALIAN BROADCASTING CORPORATION LIBRARY SALES.

The commission had come to believe it had to tactfully divest itself of Lawrence H Cecil. He had written a report in which he suggested that many of Wilmot's achievements were because of his guidance. But the ABC was telling Chester that it had been a mistake to send Cecil at all. This view was expressed to the author years later when he interviewed Sir Charles Moses, the ABC General Manager in the early 1940s. There had been a rather sad interview with Bearup, Cecil and Wilmot, in which it became embarrassingly clear there was no role for Cecil in the new set-up. They were all rather gentle with him. Chester pressed for a plan, and eventually accepted that he and an assistant commentator should operate in the forward areas and that Cecil would operate with the big truck in the Australian and US camps interviewing servicemen. Wilmot thought that Cecil would not want to continue with this operation for long and this proved to be the case. 'He [Cecil] was,' Chester wrote to his parents, 'all for going on a grand tour around the country visiting camps with me doing all the work. In spite of all this we are still quite friendly. I don't think anyone in the meeting thought LHC had any case at all.'[9]

After a 'useful trip' between Sydney and Brisbane, during which Wilmot and his colleague Dudley Leggett called at all the important headquarters en route, the Broadcast Unit was set up in Townsville.

Initially, they were banned from interviewing any member of the US Air Corps or the RAAF. This was soon lifted for US aircrew, but correspondents were still forbidden to talk to RAAF personnel. As well, reporters were forbidden to go beyond the communiqué. This was part of the attempt to control information by General MacArthur's headquarters, an issue that was to bedevil war correspondents for the rest of the war. Conditions in Port Moresby were, if anything, worse. There, Melbourne *Sun* correspondent Osmar White and George Johnston of the *Argus* found the situation so confused that they virtually went on strike and went south to Townsville and Brisbane – hence by-lines like 'Somewhere in Australia'. After a detailed report to Public Relations head Errol Knox, White was promised there would be improvements. In all this, Wilmot, White and others were insiders. They simply wanted to cover the war as accurately as possible and certainly didn't wish to endanger servicemen. When there were blunders – and Wilmot, White and Damien Parer were to find plenty as the New Guinea Campaign unfolded – they reserved the right to criticise, but only to remedy the situation.

Meanwhile Chester was concerned that in following the communiqués ABC 'News' could itself be discredited. 'I notice,' he wrote to Head of Talks, BH Molesworth, 'that we are frequently telling about "smashing blows" and "examples of the policy of hitting hard as possible". This is definitely not so. We are deliberately confining our activities to the minimum so as to conserve aircraft and also because there's nothing much to bomb.'[10] Chester wrote this while in bed recovering from a bout of dengue fever (Bill MacFarlane had been similarly afflicted). Then the asthma returned and he was forced to return to Melbourne for a course of injections, followed by a treatment called 'zinc ionisation'. This enabled him to cover General MacArthur's first press conference in Australia. Chester was not impressed. MacArthur used the occasion to denounce the Allied' 'Hitler First' strategy. In Wilmot's opinion, the general's 'ambition and egotism prevented him seeing any theatre of war but his own'. The description comes from *Struggle for Europe* but it reflects Chester's attitudes in 1942. Wilmot was always an internationalist.

Just after the press conference Wilmot was more or less summoned to a meeting by Frank Krcrouse, the senior partner of the firm where he had served his articles in 1939. Chester had been very happy there and thought they might have a wedding present for the newly married couple, so he brought Edith with him. When he was ushered in Edith waited outside. Chester came out angry and shaken. 'I can't talk here,' he said, and took her to a quiet restaurant in Collins Street. 'I've been warned off,' Wilmot told her, and then quickly explained his suspicions about the picture contract in the

Middle East. Through Krcrouse, Blamey had told him that it would be 'improper and unwise for him to continue his investigations'.[11] The solicitor had shown Chester a letter from 'an unnamed writer' addressed to the general stating that he'd heard Wilmot talking with several AIF officers about the contract and saying that Blamey had benefited financially from the contract and 'it stinks'. Wilmot's investigations were not complete so he apparently politely thanked his former boss and left it at that. He was of course disgusted to see Krcrouse representing someone like Blamey and almost certainly even more suspicious. Soon after, on his way back to Townsville, the ABC was to record Blamey at a parade, so Chester went along to see what his reception would be. Not only was the general quite affable but it turned out he was inspecting the appallingly trained 14th Militia Brigade. 'Do you think they'll fight?' Chester asked Blamey.

'I hope so,' he replied.[12]

* * * *

Wilmot's return to Townsville coincided with the first major attack by the Japanese in Papua. On 21 July 1942 the Japanese landed near Gona. The GOC New Guinea Force, Major-General Basil Morris, was ordered to concentrate one battalion over the Owen Stanley Range at the village of Kokoda – he chose the 39th Militia Battalion. The 39th already had one company in the process of trekking to Dobodura to occupy the ground for a proposed airstrip. The Japanese landing near Gona was, in fact, a reconnaisance in force. Fifteen hundred troops were landed with the purpose of pushing on to Kokoda, to ascertain whether the Kokoda Track was a viable route for a landward assault upon Port Moresby. If this proved to be so, the main invasion force of a further 12 000 troops of Major-General Horii's South Seas Force was to be landed for the campaign. The Kokoda Track was about to become a battlefield of grotesque proportions.

Valiant for Truth

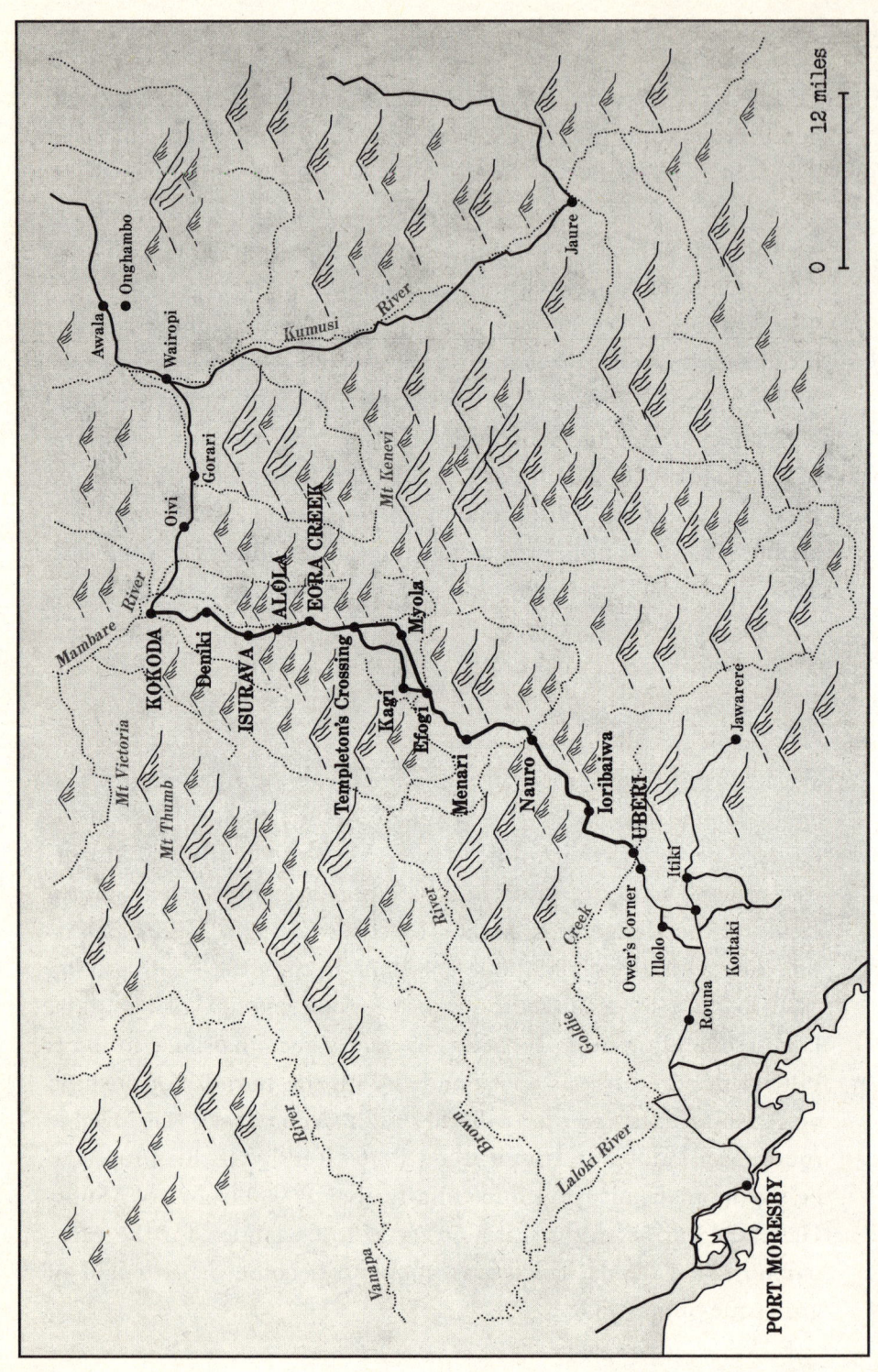

The Kokoda Track

Prior to the outbreak of hostilities in New Guinea in 1942, travellers from Port Moresby to the area beyond the Owen Stanley Range could either sail to the northern coast or fly to an inland outpost 1200 feet up in the northern foothills of the mountains. This was Kokoda, a Papuan administration post with officers' houses, a police house, native hospital, station garden, rubber plantation and the only landing strip in the region. The natives had their own routes including the hazardous one over the Owen Stanley Range: a primitive track, often only about a yard wide, restricting movement in most places to single file. Only scant knowledge of that track had reached the outside world through occasional reports of patrol officers, plantation owners and missionaries.

Neither the Japanese nor the Australians had reconnoitred the track. Maps did not exist; the problem of supplying a force over it, and then at any battleground on it, had not been examined; the problems of evacuating the wounded had not been studied; and the additional problems of support and communication were not realised.

One of the great characters of the Kokoda campaign was to be Lieutenant Bert Kienzle, a plantation owner from Yodda, just outside Kokoda. Kienzle was a member of ANGAU (Australian New Guinea Administrative Unit). This unit consisted of white planters, miners, district magistrates, police and the odd missionary. They were responsible for the administration of Papua New Guinea and its natives.

In late June Kienzle was ordered to report to Port Moresby HQ. His task was to take one of the 39th Battalion's companies over the Kokoda Track to Dobodura. One of the additional orders given to him amply explains the complete ignorance of the Kokoda Track at the time. Bert Kienzle: 'CO Angau to make arrangements to fulfil requirements up to maximum of one thousand labourers. Construction of road to Kokoda to commence not later than 29th June. Road to be completed by 26th August [1942].'[13] The Kokoda Track to this day remains one of the most challenging treks in the world – and there is still no road.

Kienzle quickly decided that native porterage alone could not supply an ever-growing infantry force fighting in that environment. Kienzle wrote:

> A carrier carrying foodstuffs consumes his load in thirteen days and if he carries food supplies for a soldier, it means six and a half days supply for both soldier and carrier. This does not allow for the porterage of arms, ammunition, equipment, medical stores, ordnance, mail and dozens of other items needed to wage war, on the backs of men. The track takes eight days, so the maintenance of supplies is a physical impossibility without large-scale co-operation of plane droppings.[14]

By 4 August 1942, Kienzle had found and recced two volcanic lake beds near the Kokoda Track and blazed a track from them to the track, which was known as Templeton's Crossing. This was to be the main drop zone for aircraft supply during the campaign. Chester was destined to fly over it and examine the supply process within about two weeks of Kienzle's discovery of Myola. Further, Wilmot would use detailed interviews with Kienzle as the basis of his later knowledge and dispatches of the Kokoda Track fighting.

One of the toughest military campaigns in Australian history was about to escalate.

* * * *

Around midnight on 27–28 July 1942, Chester was at his colleague Dudley Leggett's hotel when a US transport officer came to tell him that he had to be on a flying boat for Port Moresby at 9 am. The alert was sounded and Townsville had its third air-raid of the war.

Wilmot and MacFarlane rushed up to the top of the hill and Chester recorded a description of the raid. 'It wasn't much,' Chester wrote to the family. 'The bombs fell in the sea and there was little ack-ack fire. But there were a couple of dramatic moments when our fighters intercepted the plane and we could see the burst of tracer which was held in the searchlights.'[15]

During the flight to Port Moresby there was a drifting mist and occasional cloudbanks down to 1000 feet, even though in Townsville and Moresby it was a clear, sunny day. 'This is why it is so difficult for our planes to pick out shipping,' Chester reflected.

The correspondents had been assigned a little cottage 'a few miles out of town, that was just big enough for a man, his wife and a daughter', but now it had to accommodate nine reporters. 'When we have to work at night,' Chester wrote, 'it's a battle for the lamps as we only have four hurricanes. But we get along – people type sitting on their beds with typewriter on knee and a lamp on a side table, and manage to get their messages away.'[16]

A week after Chester's arrival Bill MacFarlane arrived with the sound gear and the truck. Bill found the heat created even more difficulties than the cold in Greece and the sand in the desert. At the back of the correspondents' house was a small shed where they stored the discs and equipment. The only problem was that the temperature inside the shed was 140 degrees Fahrenheit. This would usually melt the discs so the recording needle would not cut. The only time a recording could be made was in the cool of the late afternoon. The acoustics of the buildings were hopeless, so the broadcasts had to be recorded in a jungle clearing, about 80 yards from Bill's tin shed. When cutting a disc, Chester would sit on one ration box with the microphone set up on another, his script held at eye level. As he spoke, half-naked Papuans would emerge from the foliage to watch this strange man talking to himself.

At first Chester was impressed by the New Guinea Force Commander, Major-General Basil Morris. Mrs Morris was Edith's aunt, and Chester felt guilty at not having been able to bring the general a letter from his wife.

Morris gave Chester a confidential briefing that played down the significance of the Japanese landings at Gona and Chester drafted a script, putting the Japanese incursion 'in the right context'. Soon after, Chester was to find Morris and GHQ's failure to realise the significance of the enemy's moves unforgivable. It seemed bad enough to him in 1942, but we know now that MacArthur and Blamey were in possession of intelligence predicting the distinct possibility of a major overland attack on Port Moresby two months before.

Seven days later New Guinea Force HQ received a three-word signal: 'Syd is coming.' 'Syd' was Lieutenant-General Sydney Rowell, who to many people's relief was to take over command of all forces in Papua and New Guinea. It hadn't taken long for Chester and the other correspondents to become extremely suspicious of Morris's abilities. Arriving shortly after was the 7th Division's commander Major-General Tubby Allen; and Major-General Cyril Clowes, sent to command the forces at Milne Bay – the commanders who had played decisive roles with Lustre Force in Greece. Then there was Brigadier Arnold Potts, commander of the 21st Brigade, 7th Division, who had acquired a formidable reputation in Syria. All these men had implicit confidence in Chester Wilmot – and that trust and confidence was reciprocated. Chester was about to report on one of the greatest stories of his career.

13

UNNECESSARY AUSTRALIAN GRAVES

In 2003 Lieutenant-General Sydney Rowell's ADC, Lieutenant Gordon Darling, recalled:

> The seasoned experienced commanders who arrived in Papua New Guinea in August 1942 had absolute trust in 'Syd'; they'd been blooded fighting in the Middle East; not just in the desert but had got out of Greece. Unlike me they were very mature. They knew how to handle themselves and knew how to handle troops in war. He [Rowell] was not a look-at-me general like George Vasey … but wherever I went in the Australian Army I could see Syd was greatly respected by just about everyone. I knew I would have gladly laid down my life for him, and a lot of other men felt the same.[1]

Darling was also aware that this Middle East club included Chester Wilmot and Damien Parer. Parer had just arrived back from a journey to Kanga Force commandos operating near Salamaua. 'I could see the General had a very high regard for both men,' said Darling.

Another correspondent Rowell would quickly grow to trust

was the representative of the *Melbourne Sun*, Osmar White. He had spent the 1930s as a short story and feature writer. White's work was sold not only in Australia but in British and American magazines and journals. A few years earlier he had financed a three-year tour around South-East Asia and the islands. This had included an eight-month stay in New Guinea. Slim, lantern-jawed and fit with muscles hardened by years of rock climbing, it was he who had organised the journey to Kanga Force. Wilmot had quickly begun to quiz him about jungle conditions and was very impressed by the great care he took of himself in the tropics. Rowell, it seems, was devastatingly frank about the prospects of a campaign across the Owen Stanley Range. He told White that:

> As far as I am concerned, I'm willing to fall back and let the enemy have the rough stuff if he wants it. I'm willing to present the Jap with the supply headaches I've got. But there are those who think otherwise. We need a victory in the Pacific and a lot of poor bastards have got to get killed to provide it.[2]

Lieutenant Bert Kienzle of ANGAU had reasoned that the best way of overcoming at least some of the supply problems was by aerial dropping. He had recced Myola as that drop zone. Wilmot and White decided to see for themselves and volunteered to act as 'unloaders' on one of the 'biscuit bombers' – the Douglas Dakota planes. In a dispatch entitled 'Air Power and the New Guinea War', Chester described the mission:

> It wasn't a pleasant flight ... there were too many mountain spurs about for my liking ... too many air currents which occasionally bucketed us around as they swirled down between the spurs ... too many clouds blanketing the heads of the valleys we had to negotiate ...

At last we were flying over the dropping ground … a broad marshy space a couple of miles in diameter … One run over … round behind a hill … and then a long slow glide down with the motors throttled back … down … down … down … The treetops were flying past so quickly they were blurred …

Piled at the open doorway was a huge stack of bags of rice … Poised behind them like a cat ready to spring was the chief 'pusher-out' … with a rope lashed round his waist to stop him following the supplies through the open doorway. In the belly of the plane we had other piles ready to feed to him …

As the plane roars down almost to the edge of the clearing, the co-pilot waves his hand and with one heave the huge pile goes out the door as the plane races along less than 300 feet above the ground … Then another wave from the co-pilot and we stop pushing … The engines roar even louder and the plane climbs steeply to clear the timbered hill at the far end of the clearing … We bank … turn … and down we come for another run …
It takes us five runs before all the cargo has been shovelled out … and then comes the long gliding descent back. We take one last look at the dropping ground … already troops and natives are swarming over it gathering what we've dropped.[3]

When Parer heard about his friends' adventures he decided to go himself. An early morning flight was arranged in a Lockheed Lodestar carrying 2500 pounds of cargo to be dropped on the village of Kagi (near Myola). When they reached Myola Damien filmed the unloaders pushing out the cargo. Parer then leant out of another doorway to get shots of the supply bags falling away from the aircraft. When the plane returned to the 7-mile aerodrome at Port Moresby, Damien noted in his diary that the planes were parked wingtip to wingtip.

On his return Parer may have gone directly to Rowell, or may have passed on the information through Chester. Certainly, after checking for himself, Rowell contacted General Whitehead, the American air commander, and 'suggested' that the planes be dispersed. Whitehead promised to get onto it the next day. On the morning of Monday, 17 August 1942, Rowell and Darling drove out to the 7-mile aerodrome. They noticed the red flag was up, indicating a raid was expected. Then their driver shouted, 'They're right above us!' Darling sprang out of the car and hit the ground, only to look up and see Rowell standing there smoking his pipe and looking at the Japanese bombers plastering the US 'biscuit bombers' that were still parked wingtip to wingtip. As for the American lookout who should have turned Rowell's car back long before it reached the field, 'he was in deep, deep cover', the general acidly observed later.

Wilmot, Parer and White were just behind Rowell. Osmar White was to write later:

> The wrecked aircraft burnt fiercely. Grass fires had broken out in a dozen places. Drums of petrol kept popping ... the entire runway was ankle deep in debris – fragments of blackened and twisted duralumin, shattered motors, parachute packs ripped open and silk blasted into pieces the size of a pocket handkerchief.[4]

Parer had started filming immediately after he saw the smoke from the burning planes. As soon as he reached the field he highlighted the American blunder by panning from the planes parked in line to the burning aircraft. The footage was suppressed until 1943 but the pan was not shown until 2001.

By this time, the 39th Militia Battalion had lost Kokoda, briefly retaken it, lost it again, and had now withdrawn through Deniki to Isurava. There would be a pause while the Japanese concentrated their force outside Isurava.

Unnecessary Australian graves

The day before the Japanese bombing of the 7-mile aerodrome, the 21st Brigade had begun their trek over the Kokoda Track. Brigadier Potts's orders were simple: retake Kokoda. The codename for his force – his 21st Brigade, the 39th and 53rd Militia Battalions and ancillary personnel – was Maroubra Force.

From beneath the jungle canopy Potts heard the explosions from the Japanese bombing but didn't realise their significance. Two Dakota transports and three Flying Fortresses had been completely destroyed. A further five transports and five Fortresses were damaged. The most serious loss for the troops was the Dakotas or 'biscuit bombers' that were used to drop the supplies. Not even Rowell yet realised how the bombing of the 7-mile aerodrome would affect the campaign.

It was at this time that Rowell recruited Wilmot and Parer as unofficial liaison officers. According to Gordon Darling:

> The problem was that we didn't have a full corps headquarters and only one liaison officer. He was ex–World War One. We sent him to Milne Bay. It took him three days to get there, three days to get back, he lost five stone and by the time he returned his information was completely out of date. [Wilmot and Parer] were so much more alert and fit, and had some military nous.[5]

Neither Parer nor Wilmot appear to have been concerned about any conflict of interest. They trusted Rowell, he needed their help, and that seems to have been all there was to it.

Just before they were about to leave, the Department of Information cabled Parer, ordering him to fly to North Queensland as there was 'important work for him there'. Damien wired back asking for an extra month to complete 'some work' – a hint that a story was about to break. The department cabled back, 'Regret impossible. Proceed south.' Parer felt he had no choice but to obey. That is until

Chester found out and dragged Damien into see Rowell. 'Don't you worry, Damien,' Rowell said, 'I'll deal with the Department.' Muttering that 'we've got to keep him here somehow', he drafted a signal stating that Parer had 'gone bush'. Technically this was correct, as Port Moresby was classified as 'bush'.[6] Parer always said that but for Wilmot and Rowell, there would not have been *Kokoda Front Line*.

Bill MacFarlane drove the three correspondents the first fifteen miles in the radio sound truck. They covered more ground in three hours than they were to travel during the next three days on foot. They were going armed with grenades and rifles in violation of the Geneva Convention. As Chester put it, in the jungle you could run into anything.

If the first day's march was hard enough, the second day presented the troops and the correspondents with a nightmare: the Golden Stairs. The Golden Stairs consisted of several thousand logs of wood pushed into the ascent and held in place by wooden pegs. Putrid mud made up the rest of each 'stair'. Some of the steps were made up of exposed tree roots, irregular in distance and shape and often harder to climb. The stairs became permanently sodden and slippery due to the almost daily rain. Men fell, banged knees, shins and ankles on the exposed log steps, and struggled gamely on. The three correspondents were no different.

Parer's shirt was wet through with perspiration. Afraid that the moisture would reach the precious film in his backpack, he took off his hat, flattened it out and put it between his shirt and pack. White and Parer were probably fitter than Wilmot after their time with Kanga Force. Chester marched in a sea of perspiration. White recalled that:

> You'd get a shower bath if you went near him ... Downhill he took terrific two yard strides ... he went like a whirlwind outstripping the rest by miles. But when we struck the next hill we drew even.

Half way up we would pass him hoisting one leg after another with agonised slowness. Three hundred yards away his grunts, groans, whistlings and profane cries were audible … he was still grunting, cursing and whistling at the end of the day … and still travelling.[7]

White may have been a little more sympathetic towards Wilmot had he known that Chester had recently been undergoing treatment for his asthma. Still, it is an affectionate portrait.

While the correspondents were finding the going hard, the soldiers of the 21st Brigade were also suffering greatly. Laden with packs of anywhere between 50 and 70 pounds – plus the rotation Bren gun and ammunition – the Golden Stairs took a terrible toll. Sergeant R Clemens, 2/14th Battalion, wondered, 'How can one describe fully the monotony of following a trail over mountains, and climbing endless steps … and then finishing the day's march physically exhausted, and then after a respite, move out at first light for a repetition.'[8]

Captain RN Thompson, 2/14th Battalion, remembered 'I was one of the fittest members, but on the second day, climbing the Golden Stairs I was extremely fatigued. A small dixie of tea caused me to vomit and I could not eat. Next morning I and most others had a great craving for salt.'[9]

These experiences were continually repeated from the Golden Stairs through Uberi, Ioribaiwa, Nauro, Menari, Efogi and finally on to Myola.

During the trek to Myola, Parer, who had been ill the night before they left Port Moresby, started shaking and sweating with malaria. Wilmot and White insisted on carrying his cameras and tripod. Then White too succumbed. After stopping for a day to let the quinine take effect, they decided to undertake a non-stop forced march to Myola. Out of the shadows a sentry wrapped in a ground sheet plastered with mud challenged them. The correspondents quickly identified themselves, torch lights flashed over them, and they were passed through; they had reached Myola. At the command post they were given a meal of lukewarm stew and rice.

The following morning they discovered that the 2/14th and 2/16th Battalions at Myola were waiting for supplies. Even after the raid on the 7-mile aerodrome, Rowell had assumed the Americans had already dropped sufficient rations for twenty-five days in action – in fact they only had rations for five. Potts and his brigade were unable to fulfil their mission until the supplies arrived. The fate of the missing supplies remains a mystery.

Once he received further supplies, Potts assumed command of Maroubra Force at Alola on 23 August.

After having concentrated their force north of Isurava, the Japanese struck on 26 August 1942. In unison with the assault on Isurava, the Japanese also landed at Milne Bay. Captain Max Bidstrup, 39th Battalion: 'The 2/14th and 2/16th came up the track just as we were on our last bloody legs. We couldn't have lasted another day. We were gone for all money. Despite the fact that the blokes were down to the last human resource, they were prepared to fight, to carry on.'[10]

From the time of the complete arrival of the 2/14th Battalion at Isurava on 28 August 1942, command of the area fell to its CO, Lieutenant-Colonel Arthur Key. The 39th was supposed to have been relieved that day, but its CO, Lieutenant-Colonel Ralph Honner – and his men – would not leave the 2/14th in the lurch. Using the diminished and exhausted 39th to thicken its perimeter, the 2/14th put forth one of the most dogged and desperate defences of a seemingly hopeless position in the annals of Australian military history.

When the two battalions finally withdrew from the Isurava Rest House late on the afternoon of 30 August they had cost the Japanese four crucial, debilitating days on the northern end of the track – and very heavy casualties – when the enemy had allowed but ten days for their proposed victorious entry into Port Moresby. But the cost was heavy. The 2/14th had arrived at Isurava with 542 troops. After 'stand-to' on the morning of the 31st, it numbered 160 – little more than a company at full strength. Included in its losses were forty-four men cut off and the loss of its CO, adjutant, intelligence officer and nearly half of A Company. Lieutenant-Colonel Key was destined to be captured and later executed at Gona. Some of the soldiers who had been cut off regained their lines, while others faced a foodless, gruelling trek to regain their base area near distant Port Moresby.

From 31 August until 5 September 1942, Maroubra Force fought a series of desperate delaying actions between Isurava and two defendable localities to the south of Efogi, the first to become known as 'Mission Ridge' and the second as 'Brigade Hill'.

Chester Wilmot was to report on the nature of the fighting at Isurava and its right flank at Abuari, but the resulting Maroubra Force fighting withdrawal was captured by him with a clarity and coherence that is extraordinary. His ability to coax his information from his sources as they were enacting the history is remarkable. It was as if the Isurava–Abuari battleground comprised the top of a funnel, and, as the fighting withdrawal began, the soldiers were forced to extricate themselves through the narrow tube of that funnel: the Kokoda Track. That 'tube' was narrow but terribly fortuitous for Wilmot: his story was forced to physically pass in front of him, and his energy, guile and ability to observe and win instant trust resulted in not only first-class pieces of journalism, but the basis for hard historical analysis and writing.

After having left Myola, the correspondents stayed the night at Templeton's Crossing and pushed on early the next morning. Halfway down a ridge, they heard the thundering roar of Eora Creek and the village came into sight. White later wrote:

> I will never forget the scene, hundreds of men were standing about in mud that came up to their shins. The whole village

built of pandanus and grass looked as if it were about founder in the sea of mud. The huts leaned drunkenly. There were piles of broken out ration boxes half submerged. The men were slimed from head to foot, for weeks unshaven, their skins bloodless under their filth. Lines of exhausted carriers were squatting on the fringes of this congregation eating muddy rice off muddy banana leaves. Their woolly hair was plastered with rain and muck. Their eyes were rolling and bloodshot with the strain of long carrying. Some of them were still panting.[11]

After having arrived at Eora Creek, Parer stayed to film while Chester and Osmar pushed forward to 21st Brigade HQ. Wilmot's account begins here.

'And Our Troops were Forced to Withdraw':

It usually took two hours to get to Brigade HQ, but we've been walking over three and we're still not there. We aren't making more than half a mile an hour along the single-file mud path beaten on the steep slippery mountainside by hundreds of Army boots. There are two streams of traffic where there's only room for one. Coming back is a line of troops who have just been relieved after a month's fighting near Kokoda. They are tired, muddy and unshaven. They're only kids of 19 and 20 but they've done a grand job and earned their rest.

Wilmot was describing the young soldiers of the 39th Militia Battalion. He had obviously done some homework concerning the 39th, as his comment 'they've done a grand job' would indicate. The dispatch continues:

There are wounded too. We've been passing them in ones and twos for several hours. They must be going through hell on this track, especially those with leg wounds. Some have been hit in the foot and they can't even get a boot on but they're walking back over root and rock and through mud in bare feet, protected only by their bandages. Here's a steep pinch and a wounded digger's trying to climb it. You need both hands and both feet, but he's been hit in the arm and thigh. Two of his cobbers are helping him along. One goes ahead, hauling himself up by root and branch. The wounded digger clings to the belt of the man in front with his sound hand, while his other cobber gets underneath and pushes him up. I say to this fellow, he ought to be a stretcher case, but he replies, 'I can get along. There's blokes here lots worse than me and if we don't walk they'll never get out.'

But they are being got out … now and then we pass a stretcher case. The stretchers are only two saplings with a blanket strung between them and sewn up with lawyer vine. But they do. It's hard enough to keep your feet with only a pack and rifle on your back. It's a miracle how they carry those stretchers. But they get through, even though it takes ten men all day to move one stretcher case back three or four miles. But the troops up forward are holding on, giving them time to get all the wounded out.

They put one stretcher down by the track for a moment to give the fellow a rest from the jolting. He's got a bedraggled half-damp fag in his mouth and he asks for a match. Mine are damp – they've been damp all week … but Ossie [Osmar White] has some waxies he's carefully preserved in an oil-silk tobacco pouch. We give him a light, roll another cigarette for him and he says, 'Thanks mate … a smoke helps a lot … I'll be OK now.' They lift him gently but he winces as the slow agonising jolting begins again.

Three striking issues emerge from the above passage. First, at that time, New Guinea Force HQ in Port Moresby – much less GHQ in Brisbane and less again the Australian public – had no concept whatever of the terrain, the track, and the challenge of evacuating the wounded. Thus, the Wilmot description of the wounded, although dramatic, is highlighting the key issue of logistics and planning. Second, although Damien Parer's film *Kokoda Front Line* would soon give the authorities and the Australian public a graphic visual account of the Kokoda Track fighting, Wilmot's dispatch is more detailed and reached a wider audience. To the uneducated, that is, everyone but the participants at this time, the notion that a conventional army stretcher would be useless in this environment would have been incomprehensible. Third, Wilmot is, probably unwittingly, helping to create the legend of the 'Fuzzy Wuzzy Angels', who worked in teams of 'ten' according to Wilmot, but in actuality mostly in 'eights' (one group of four for each stretcher handle, and another as the relief group of four for each stretcher).

Wilmot's dispatch:

Then a fellow I went to school with calls down the track. He used to be a good left-hand bowler, but he won't bowl for a while. 'How did you get that Bill?'

'Oh, we were out on patrol … trying to clear that ridge on the left … We got 'em off it … but three of the boys got knocked … We started to carry 'em in … but the Nips saw us and got behind us just at dark. First we knew was a shower of grenades. We blazed around and after a bit they pulled out, but it wasn't easy fighting and looking after the wounded too. They got 'Butch' and most of us got hit somewhere, but we carried 'em all back.' I watch him go off down the track … It'll be nearly a week before he reaches a hospital, and *he* has sound legs … for fellows with leg wounds and for stretcher cases it takes twice as long.

Wilmot's passage touches on one of the great tactical issues, and fights, of the Isurava battle: the canefield. Chester could not have known at the time that the brief encounter with his old school friend from the 2/14th was probably the first recounting of a critical fight at Isurava. Honner's 39th Battalion's B Company had originally occupied the canefield. When the 2/14th reinforced the 39th, Captain Nye's B Company later took over that position. Lieutenant Harold 'Butch' Bisset was one of Nye's platoon commanders. Peter Brune explains:

> When you fly by helicopter over this Isurava high ground [the canefield] you are struck by its isolation. It was part of an organised perimeter, but in this type of closed fighting the individual soldier, as the enemy gains ground under attack, fights an exceedingly personal war and is out of touch with the rest of his platoon, let alone the current standing of his company and much less his battalion. The high ground and its canefield had to be held. Lose it and lose Isurava.
>
> This isolation in terms of intelligence and communication and supply were the very three factors that cost Bisset (and many others) their lives. While distributing grenades and ammunition to his men he was mortally wounded by a burst of machine gun fire. As the enemy pressure mounted and their consequent gains in this vital area slowly increased, Bisset's men were forced to withdraw. This movement became a nightmare for the survivors of 10 Platoon as, burdened with their wounded, they struggled over uneven ground in the encroaching darkness, turning repeatedly to inflict delaying casualties on the enclosing enemy hotly pressing the pursuit. But amidst all this they carried the dying Bisset out with them.[12]

Wilmot's dispatch continues:

With wounded and troops coming back the track's crowded enough, but there are other troops going forward and parties carrying ammunition, food and most important of all mortars and their bombs. A wounded digger on his way back says to a mortar carrying crew, 'Get those up quick, sport … they were lobbin' four-inch mortars on us this morning from that ridge on the right … they couldn't shift us but we'd like to give 'em something back'.

From that same ridge now we can hear the methodical pop … pop … pop … pop … pop of a heavy machine gun. We meet an officer coming back from Brigade and he says, 'How the hell did they get that thing up there … they were shooting up Brigade with that this morning … they put some in the RAP and the doc got hit in both legs and a few of the wounded got hit again. Frank has a patrol out there now trying to clear 'em off the ridge.' But just before I leave Brigade, he says, 'We got a signal from him saying, "Japs all round us but can't see them … cannot repeat not clear ridge without another company" … And we didn't have another company to send.

'They're getting round on that side and shooting up this track from across the valley. When you get further along,' he says, 'you'll come to some open patches … they can see them and they're having a crack at 'em … Don't waste any time getting across and don't bunch when you get there … So long.'

But we don't get there … About five minutes later we run into Hugh, the brigade major, and Ben the 2 I/C of a Battalion. There's heavy machine-gun fire just over the ridge and every few seconds the valley rumbles with the crump of mortars. And the major says, 'It's no use your going forward, Chester, we're coming back … They broke through on the left of Crofty's crowd this morning and now they're swarming over the ridge above Brigade. They shot us up just before we left and we've sent the "old and bold" to clean 'em up. No doubt,' he says, 'they'll deal with this party but by tomorrow the Nips will be there in hundreds. Albert's bringing his Battalion back now and the others are going to make a clean break at dark and withdraw through 'em. I'm going back to reconnoitre the new positions. I think you'd better come back too.'

Wilmot is witnessing the hurried and pressured beginnings of a fighting withdrawal: 'Crofty' is Major Phil Rhoden, who assumed command of the 2/14th Battalion after Lieutenant-Colonel Key was lost. 'Ben' is Major Ben Hearman, 2/IC of the 2/16th Battalion. Wilmot's writing portrays the high drama of finding the next withdrawal position; of the Japanese mountain gun and their machine gun fire raking the Australians from the ridges around the valley; and the added trauma of 'Frank's'–Captain Frank Sublet, OC B Company 2/16th Battalion – uncertain position, out on the Isurava right flank trying to forestall a further Japanese advance through the 53rd Battalion, which has threatened to outflank and then cut off Isurava. 'Albert' is Lieutenant-Colonel Albert Caro, CO 2/16th Battalion. And the immediate and dramatic background to these events is the constant stream of stretchers moving back past them, and ammunition and supplies moving forward along that narrow, muddy 'funnel'. The wounded 'doc' was Captain Hogan of the 53rd Battalion – shot in both legs. Wilmot continues:

> So we turn back. The track's getting even more crowded now as the first of the withdrawing troops come back too. But there's no fuss … it's very quiet and orderly, just as it should be with good troops. But the evening mist is coming up so quickly that it'll be too late to reconnoitre positions if we don't hurry.

We climb a steep fold on the hillside and the Major says, 'This ought to do you, Ben ... put a company out there on the spur and another up on your left on the high ground ... and don't forget to send patrols out tonight to watch the top of the ridge, so they can't get round again. We've got to stop him here.'

'Do me best,' says Ben in his slow drawl. He's a great mountain of a man ... they call him the 'human tank' ... and the story is that when he was in Syria the Vichyites put so much lead into him that if he'd gone swimming he'd have sunk. He's quite unflappable but he says, 'I've only got two companies, you know ... Frank isn't back yet ... and you really need another Battalion to hold the ridge ... They won't get through us, but they might get round ...'

We go on ... looking for a place for Brigade HQ ... but there's nowhere where you can get off the track ... and it's raining now and getting even more slippery.

Then 25 yards ahead a shot cracks out and a khaki form slumps to the ground. It's an accident ... but a serious one ... An officer slipped ... the rifle he was carrying crashed down on a rock ... went off ... And we cover him with a blanket and send word back for the padre.

The officer was Captain 'Tubby' Jacob, OC C Company, 39th Battalion. He had relieved an exhausted young soldier of his rifle on the night of 30–31 August. Unbeknown to Jacob, the safety catch on the rifle was not 'on' and as Jacob slipped over a tree root the rifle discharged a bullet which hit him in the groin. Padre 'Nobby' Earl, 39th Battalion, a Catholic priest, read the Anglican Last Rites as Jacob's life passed. Originally a member of the 2/10th Battalion, Jacob had served during the Siege of Tobruk before fighting at Isurava with the 39th.

The dispatch continues:

It's almost too dark to see now and the six o'clock cricket which makes a noise like an air raid siren warns us how late it is. The track widens and we come to a small flat shelf at the side. The Brigade major says to me, 'This [is] about the best we'll get' … and then to his batman, 'Trapper … stand here, on the track and stop all Brigade personnel and anyone carrying rations' … and then to a signalman, 'Plug a phone in on the line there Mac, and let the Brigadier know where we are … he's still up forward.'

'I'll try sir,' says the sig., 'I've got a phone but I've gone and lost the earth-wire … Anyone got any wire?' … And a voice from the darkness says, 'I 'ave, but it's 'olden up me pants …'

'Well tie 'em up with a bit of creeper and gimme the wire; we gotta get the phone on.' The sig. twists the wire round a bayonet and jabs it in the earth. The other connection is a large safety-pin stuck through the covered signal wire.

But even with the phone on we can't find out much … the Japs have cut the line behind the forward companies. Last word was, 'All quiet … no contact … starting withdrawal 18.30.' Since then, silence. There's not even machine gun fire from there now, but we do know a Battalion HQ has been overrun, so maybe the troops will have to fight their way back in the darkness. It's pretty confused and no one really knows where the forward companies are. We do know that Don Company was swamped yesterday but they were still fighting late this afternoon in their old positions. There's less than half of B Company here, but odd parties are still fighting their way in, bringing their wounded with them when they can.

> Getting the wounded back is a serious problem now that we're withdrawing. An MO stumbles in to say that he still has 25 stretcher cases to get back. By the light of the flickering match with which he lights his cigarette I can see his face is tired and drawn … but he says, 'I'm going back to the creek to get some bearers.'
>
> But the Brigade major cuts him short, 'you can't go back tonight Rupe … you haven't been to sleep for three days … send someone else.' But the Doc won't have that … he says he has to see the hospital's cleared by dawn so as to make room for the new cases. He won't even stop to eat.

The medical officer mentioned above by Chester as 'Rupe' was Major Rupert Magarey. The incident Wilmot mentions above is but one of a number that Magarey was involved in at the time of the withdrawal from Isurava and then Eora Creek – hence Magarey's lack of food and sleep.

Wilmot's reference to a battalion HQ being overrun was not quite accurate. Lieutenant-Colonel Arthur Key's 2/14th Battalion HQ was pushed and dispersed off the track, not overrun. Wilmot continued:

> All through the night a stumbling procession moves back in dribs and drabs along the track … occasional stretcher cases … ammunition parties … troops withdrawing. The withdrawal's going very smoothly but there's still Frank's two companies across the creek on the ridge on the right. When the left flank was turned the Brigadier tried to warn Frank to withdraw, but before the message could be sent the Japs cut the phone line. Frank's force was out of touch and apparently the Japs were behind them, but we all knew he'd bring his men in somehow. The Brigadier had sent three runners over to tell them … but

could the runners get through? Would Frank know how to come back? These are questions that worry us as the hours drag by and no word comes in, except from the other companies who report they're back all right.

There were good reasons for the anxiety over Captain Frank Sublet's two-company force on the right flank at Abuari. First, the 2/14th had taken very heavy casualties at Isurava; second, the 2/16th would now be required to furnish much of the force for the ensuring fighting withdrawal; and last, significant numbers of troops would be needed for patrolling, ambush positions and the fighting. The loss of Sublet's two companies – half of the 2/16th's force – would have had catastrophic consequences for Maroubra Force. Chester continued:

> Dawn … and there's machine gun fire across the valley from where Frank was yesterday … enemy machine gun fire and still no word. Midmorning … and up the track comes a digger stripped of arms and webbing … he's been travelling all night with the news that the companies are safe … they'll be in this afternoon.

> Then another message: the Nips have hoisted their flag on the ridge where we were last night and a patrol reports they're swarming over it in hundreds. 'We'll turn the fighters onto them,' says the Brigade major as he goes to the phone and dictates a signal asking for air support. We wait and wait … straining our ears for the drumming of engines. There's not a cloud and the fighters'll have an open go if they come soon … At last … we search the skies … but there's only one plane … a recce to see if the weather's clear … and our hopes fall … By the time he can get back and the fighters can get here it'll be clouded over. Slowly we see our hopes fade as the clouds come down and

shield the enemy. Things are still going his way. He got in first
... he has the numbers ... and now he's getting little breaks like
this ... But he's still paying for every yard he advances ... he's
still being fought all the way by men who hate withdrawing and
refuse to admit defeat. Even though they've been forced back
they're determined, cheerful and unconcerned. You can drive
men like this back but you can't conquer them. Nothing tests
troops as much as a withdrawal ... and they're standing this test.
But neither they nor you want any more talk about 'glorious
withdrawals'. That's why I've tried to tell this story simply as
I saw it.[14]

Wilmot's 'And Our Troops Were Forced to Withdraw' was one of his finest dispatches. Written and probably recorded in Bill Mac-Farlane's jungle studio for broadcast on the ABC, it would have gone to air within days. Its impact would have been enormous. For the first time generalities and propaganda were replaced by a hard-nosed, dramatic account of war in a new and unforgiving environment, fashioned for a public craving for news of their sons, husbands, brothers and sweethearts.

However, Chester Wilmot's next piece of writing displayed a developed grasp of detail and analysis, which portrayed his professional growth that had begun in the Middle East and Greece, and had now matured in Papua. On 4 September 1942, at the urgent request of Generals Rowell and Allen, he wrote 'Observations on Operations of Maroubra Force.'

Wilmot began with an introduction which made five essential observations. The first concerned the two primary reasons why the Japanese had gained the initiative: the 'disorganisation of supply' caused by the destruction of the Dakota 'biscuit bombers' at Jackson's Drome outside Port Moresby on 17 August, which forced Brigadier Potts to delay his 21st Brigade's forward movement; and the ineffective patrolling by the 53rd Battalion on the right flank at Abuari, which in part caused the deterioration of the front at Isurava. Chester's first point was entirely accurate.

His second observation concerned the claim that Potts could not wrest the initiative from the enemy because he had to use his AIF battalions to extricate the 39th and 53rd Militia Battalions from Isurava. Nothing could have been further from the truth. The 39th Battalion had facilitated the arrival and occupation of the Isurava battlefield – it had not hampered it. And the 39th Battalion was not extricated – it stayed and fought and bolstered the 2/14th's defences. Further, it later withdrew in good order *with* the 2/14th from Isurava. One cannot help thinking that this information passed on to Chester by the staff of the 21st Brigade was a mixture of ignorance and a touch of militia bashing.

Wilmot's third observation was that the events described above caused Potts to commit his two AIF battalions piecemeal to the battle – company by company – and that he had been denied his third 21st Brigade battalion, the 2/27th, which was in reserve at Port Moresby. Fair points. However, Chester – and obviously his informants in the 21st Brigade – was quite wrong to assume that the addition of the 2/27th Battalion to Maroubra Force at this time could have forestalled a Japanese advance from Isurava. It might have delayed it, but it would not have stopped it. The Australians were outnumbered, outgunned and operating with a tenuous supply line.

Chester's fourth observation identified the Japanese superiority in camouflage and concealment and that they were prepared 'more scientifically' for jungle warfare. Again, constructive points. His fifth point identified the fact that the administrative or 'Q' work rather than the 'G' or tactical facet of the fighting was the key issue. Pithy and correct indeed. The Australians were unable to deploy the necessary numbers of troops at the right place at the right time, with sufficient food, water and ammunition – and with satisfactory means of speedy and efficient medical evacuation – to wrest the initiative from the enemy.

Chester then examined 'tactical considerations'. He noted the Japanese use of the high ground; he repeated the already mentioned point of Potts needing to extricate the militia battalions; but then, in a further error of fact, he criticised both the siting of and the nature of the 39th's trenches. As Chester was to point out in another dispatch, no battalion at Isurava had entrenching tools, and the fall of the vital canefield position occurred because of the overwhelming and repeated concentration of force that the Japanese were able to bring to bear. The canefield was always going to fall despite the bravery of both the 2/14th and 39th Battalions – ultimately it was simply a matter of persistence and time.

Wilmot's last tactical observation examined the role of the 53rd Battalion on the right flank: its inability to carry out its orders, and its lack of aggression. All too true. But neither Wilmot nor the 21st Brigade could have known of the circumstances of the raising of the 53rd, or its almost total neglect before the war came to Papua. One of its companies simply failed to turn up for the fight, while another failed to fight effectively because, quite simply, it hadn't been trained to. In fact, given Chester's highly developed sense of justice and forthright powers of both questioning and commentary, had he known of the disgraceful plight of the 53rd Battalion, he may well have written a dispatch that might have rocked both the authorities and the Australian public.

Wilmot then examined three further issues: camouflage, entrenching tools and the effects of exposure to the Kokoda Track environment. Camouflage and the need for entrenching tools have been identified, but Chester's comments on exposure were detailed. He talked of the constant wetness of the troops, the need for tents, waterproofing of gear and changes of clothing.

What is important – in the best traditions of sound journalism and history – is his use of highly informed sources. Discussing the issue of supply, Chester had interviewed Lieutenant Bert Kienzle, the ANGAU mastermind behind the 'Fuzzy Wuzzy' carrier line on the track, and the soldier who recognised the need for, and then found, the Myola dropping ground. For his exploration of the detail of the campaign, he interviewed Brigadier Arnold Potts. His extensive examination of the dropping of supplies at Myola and the whole logistical plan for the campaign was based on interviews with the 'Q' officers involved.

But to fully understand Wilmot's achievement one only has to compare the dates. 'And Our Troops Were Forced to Withdraw' was written on 9 September and his 'Observations on Operations of Maroubra Force' was written on 4 September 1942 – critically, *before* Brigadier Arnold Potts was ordered back to Port Moresby to report to Generals Rowell and Allen, *before* the 21st Brigade was relieved on the track, and *before* the 'Report into Operations – 21st Brigade Owen Stanley Campaign' was produced. While much of its content was therefore gleaned from the participants who would later write the 21st Brigade report, it was an original document – and a brilliant one. The 21st Brigade report explored many more issues than did Wilmot's – for example, intelligence assessments, and an examination of signals – but the point remains that Chester's 'observations' constituted a remarkable document. The fact that Wilmot wrote the 'Observations' before the dispatch is ample indication as to the pressing need he felt to get the report back to Rowell. In an interview with the author in 2003, Rowell's ADC, Gordon Darling, quoted Rowell as stating that if a member of his staff had produced a document as good as Wilmot's 'Observations', he would have promoted him to brigadier – fair praise. Rowell was so impressed with Wilmot's 'Observations on Operations of Maroubra Force' that he had the report circulated throughout the Australian Army, as well as to the Americans.

Within days of Chester's broadcast 'And Our Troops Were Forced to Withdraw' on the ABC, and his 'Observations' report for Rowell, two crucial battles occurred during the 21st Brigade's final fighting on the track. Those two conflicts unleashed a train of events at MacArthur's headquarters in Brisbane, and in Canberra, that caused an Australian command crisis the likes of which had not been seen before, and have not been seen since. And Chester Wilmot was to become a key protagonist.

14

THE FREEDOM OF THE PRESS

Wilmot was completing 'And Our Troops Were Forced to Withdraw' and the report for General Rowell when Damien Parer got back to Port Moresby. The last Wilmot and White had seen of the cameraman was when they had left him on the Kokoda Track at Templeton's Crossing, standing in the rain clutching his Newman camera in one hand, and his tins of exposed film in the other. Damien had just been told that George Fenton or Charley Maddern had arranged to have 1500 feet of film dropped to him so he decided to stay to cover the withdrawal. Somewhat apologetically, he had asked Wilmot and White if they could let him have a pair of socks, a spare shirt and some quinine.

Parer had been in a far worse state than he had revealed to his companions. He had come down with an attack of dysentery. Concerned that his condition would stop him filming, Parer had inserted a tube into his anus and ran it down his trouser leg into a bottle pushed into his sock.[1]

It was after he had parted from Wilmot and White that Damien had taken some of his most famous shots of the Papuan bearers carrying stretchers up the mud paths and across the streams. Throughout his filming, Parer's sequences reflected the concerns of his friends about the terrain, the foliage and the problems of supply. At Myola, even though he was short of film stock, Parer had photographed as many of the drops as possible as the planes came in at different heights. In addition, he shot close-ups of the packages after they'd landed. At that stage no one had any idea of the correct height for making those kinds of supply drops. When he had advanced with the 2/14th and 2/16th Battalions he had left the track and taken shots to show how the khaki uniforms stood out against the green of the jungle. Parer found a powerful climax for his film when he filmed the relief of the 39th Battalion by the newly arrived 2/27th at Menari. Included is a powerful shot of Lieutenant-Colonel Ralph Honner urging his men to forget they might have been let down by the 53rd Battalion on the right flank, and to 'remember we are all Australians'.[2] These 'ragged bloody heroes' seemed to Parer 'like a roll call on Anzac'.[3]

Almost as soon as he arrived at Moresby, the cameraman was hearing rumours that General Rowell was going to be relieved. Osmar White heard the story from Basil Morris and White told the author that he was certain Wilmot and Rowell were also aware of the speculation. Almost certainly this is why Parer decided to return to Australia with his film. He was so anxious to get away that he left some of the original dope sheets (shot lists) in Moresby. Rowell too may have had a hand in Parer's decision. The general was becoming increasingly concerned about wildly inaccurate reports about the campaign in the Australian newspapers and hoped Parer's newsreel would help correct these distortions – distortions that disturbingly seemed to be coming from MacArthur's headquarters.

When Parer returned to Sydney he was overwhelmed by the seeming indifference and complacency of the city – not an unusual experience for front-line troops returning on leave. As Parer poured all this out to Cinesound chief Ken G Hall, editor Terry Banks and contact man Stanley Murdoch in the screening room, either Banks or Hall – no one was sure afterwards – suggested that Damien introduce his own film on camera. At first he hesitated but

Hall insisted. 'It doesn't matter how badly you come out; you've got conviction in your voice and that's all that matters.'[4] As they crafted the narration Parer, who could be a shrewd political operator in a good cause, suggested a brief reference to the commanding general; so in went the line, 'When I got back to Moresby I was full of beans with the knowledge General Rowell was on the job and now we had a really fine command'.[5] Hall told the author later that at the time he had no idea what Parer was up to: 'If Damien wanted to praise the commanding general that was fine by me'.[6] Hall had his own motives. He wanted to use the newsreel to counter the way American successes – even fictional ones – had been boosted by MacArthur's communiqués. He was also annoyed by the way the Australian victory at Milne Bay, the first land defeat of the Japanese in the Pacific War, had been played down in the local media.

The success of *Kokoda Front Line* surprised everyone. On 17 September 1942 – the day it opened at the State Newsreel Theatre in Market Street, Sydney – the crowds extended around the corner into George Street. But it didn't stop there. The same footage, not quite as well edited, was used in the Movietone newsreel *Road to Kokoda*. Frame enlargements of Parer's shots were used to illustrate stories by Osmar White in the *Melbourne Sun* and *Daily Telegraph*. And of course Wilmot's powerful 'And Our Troops Were Forced to Withdraw' had been broadcast nationally on the ABC a few days earlier.

It seemed that the reporters had succeeded in informing the Australian public about the realities of war in New Guinea. And to cap it off the Japanese had been defeated at Milne Bay. However, anyone familiar with Australian military history of the 1940s would have been more than a little apprehensive. The victory at Milne Bay had been won by Major-General Clowes, who had been publicised as a rival to Blamey. Similarly, Rowell being praised on screens throughout Australia by a man fast becoming a national hero could be seen as threatening Blamey's position – getting too near the throne. Later when *Kokoda Front Line* was bought for the Australian Army as a training film, and troops were cheering the reference to Rowell, Blamey had all the prints withdrawn and the reference cut. (A 16 mm print with the cut is preserved in the Australian War Memorial.) Blamey had bitterly resented the 'Observations on Operations of Maroubra Force'. No sooner had Rowell circulated multiple copies than Blamey had them withdrawn and destroyed. The Americans, however, seem to have kept their copies.

Meanwhile, there had been a further crisis on the Kokoda Track during early September: an attack on the Australian positions at Mission Ridge-Brigade Hill near the village of Efogi, during which Brigadier Potts's Headquarters were nearly overrun.

The main feature of the Mission Ridge-Brigade Hill battle was the recurring effort by Potts to delay the enemy's passage to Port Moresby, while inflicting the greatest possible casualties, and thus taxing the Japanese lengthening line of communication and supply. In so doing, given that the enemy outnumbered Maroubra Force five to one, he could expect the usual Japanese response of heavy frontal attacks in unison with a determined and speedy outflanking movement. The tactical aim was therefore to hold until the position was untenable and then withdraw in good order. This had been done with great military finesse and determination from Isurava to Efogi. To withdraw too early meant a premature acquisition of ground for the Japanese; to withdraw too late was an invitation to the enemy to either surround and annihilate Maroubra Force, or cut them off from the Track – the one and only lifeline.

But by the time the Japanese had gathered outside Efogi, they too had refined their drill. Major-General Horii's assault near Efogi was this time characterised by a superbly synchronised frontal assault upon the fresh 2/27th at the forward Mission Ridge, and a strong attack upon Brigade Hill to the rear. The result was that the 2/27th held its embattled territory but was later cut off, while the 2/14th and 2/16th, after a desperate and bloodied attempt to clear the track between Potts and the bulk of his two battalions, were forced to regain the Kokoda Track by way of a circuitous route to the village of Nauro.

As a result of the failure to hold Mission Ridge-Brigade Hill, and the loss of the experienced AIF 21st Brigade's 2/27th Battalion, Generals Rowell and Allen ordered Brigadier Potts to report to them in Port Moresby. They replaced him temporarily with Brigadier Porter, who could look to the use of the fresh 3rd Militia Battalion, and the soon-to-arrive AIF 7th Division's 25th Brigade, which had arrived from Australia on 9 September. By the time Potts reached Moresby, Wilmot had reported to Rowell and Allen and the still very aggressive brigadier was able to fully brief his superiors and was promptly restored to command of the 21st Brigade.

When Brigadier Eather assumed command of Maroubra Force – his 25th Brigade, the 3rd Militia Battalion and the now composite 2/14th and 2/16th Battalion – he attacked near Ioribaiwa. Eather's offensive soon became a cause for concern. He requested permission from Allen to withdraw to Imita Ridge. This was granted.

However, the Japanese had reached the end of their tether. Confronted by a fresh force of four battalions; their defeat at Milne Bay; the resulting possibility of an Allied attack upon their rearward base at Buna; their tenuous line of communication; and the general debilitation of their troops, General Horii was ordered to withdraw over the Kokoda Track to the north-east coast's Gona-Sanananda-Buna beachhead.

Any fair and reasonable military assessment of Potts and Maroubra Force's fighting withdrawal on the Kokoda Track has to take into account that by the time the Japanese reached Imita Ridge, the average rice consumption was 2 *go* of rice per day (about 4 tablespoons in cooked form), which constituted around 550 calories. Further, within a month, they were engaging in cannibalism as a means of supplementing their diet. Potts had achieved his aim: deprive the enemy of ground and time and force a breakdown of his line of communication. He had succeeded. But Rowell and his brave subordinates had to deal with the perceptions of their allies and their military and political masters.

If the loss of Isurava and the later forced abandonment of the critical supply drop zone at Myola had shocked both New Guinea Force in Port Moresby, and General Headquarters in Brisbane, then the intense and bloody battle of Brigade Hill was profoundly disturbing. The notion that the three crack battalions of the 21st Brigade could be cut off from their line of communication, and, critically, that one of them – the freshly committed 2/27th – could have been lost from the campaign after only a few days of fighting seemed incredible. But when Brigadier Eather's first attempt at an advance came to grief at Ioribaiwa, and he sought and was granted permission to stabilise his front by a withdrawal to Imita Ridge, the panic at MacArthur's HQ in Brisbane reached considerable proportions.

What followed was arguably the most dramatic command crisis in Australian military history. The Mission Ridge–Brigade Hill battle was the first catalyst. Blamey had planned to visit Port Moresby before the politicians panicked. But as a consequence of a meeting of the Australian Advisory War Council on 9 September, he pushed his visit forward. Having already sent a reassuring letter to the Minister for the Army, Blamey arrived in Port Moresby on 12 September. At this time, Brigadier Eather was set to begin his operations at Ioribaiwa; Rowell had met with Potts and had been assured that with four fresh Australian battalions in the line and a long Japanese line of communication, the Japanese were now over-extended; and that critically, the fresh Australian force was now operating with a short line of communication. Tubby Allen recorded that 'all seemed pleased with the situation'.[7] In a letter to his old friend Cyril Clowes at Milne Bay, Rowell stated that he had 'had a pleasant day with the little man'.[8] At a press conference later in the day, Blamey told Chester and the other correspondents that Port Moresby was 'In no danger and I think we shall find that the Japs will be beaten by their own advance with its attendant problems of supply ... It will be a Japanese advance to disaster, an Australian retreat to victory.'[9] But in his usual incisive manner, and with tensions between he and Blamey never far from the surface, Wilmot asked Blamey if he thought the troops needed jungle uniforms. Blamey replied that they did not, that khaki had been designed in India, and that he had no evidence that the jungle in Papua was any different. Chester must surely have annoyed Blamey by replying that he could refer him to some hundreds who thought otherwise. Later Blamey was almost certainly even more annoyed when General Eichelberger, the new American field commander, took Damien Parer and Osmar White's advice to dye US uniforms mottled green instead of requesting a briefing from Blamey's own Land Forces Headquarters.

Having arrived back in Brisbane on 14 September, Blamey broadcast to the Australian nation the following day, praising Rowell and the troops. But his real problems began when he was required to report to the Advisory War Council on 17 September. Despite ill-informed questions Blamey backed his commanders and troops again.

This was Blamey at his best: he had gone to Port Moresby and satisfied himself as to the conduct of operations on the Kokoda Track; he had, most importantly, supported his commanders on the spot and he had further supported them politically and publicly in Australia. Both MacArthur's HQ in Brisbane, and the politicians in Canberra, should now have displayed the same commendable confidence and trust – but they did not.

On the very night that Blamey had supported those conducting the campaign, MacArthur contacted Prime Minister Curtin by 'secraphone' to inform him that despite the deployment of Eather's fresh troops, a further withdrawal had occurred at Imita Ridge. MacArthur told Curtin that Blamey should go back to New Guinea to 'energize the situation' and further, to 'meet his responsibility to the Australian nation.'[10] The Prime Minister had two choices: back Blamey or back MacArthur. He chose MacArthur. Curtin ordered Blamey to Port Moresby. Clearly, after the stormy Advisory War Council meeting, and his Prime Minister ordering him back to Port Moresby, Blamey knew his position was in real jeopardy. He therefore faced a further acid test – back Rowell or protect his own position. He chose the latter.

Blamey received Curtin's order to fly to Port Moresby on either the 17th or 18th of September 1942. Although he dutifully arrived in Brisbane on the following day, it would seem that he decided to buy time and hope that matters in the Owen Stanley Range might be resolved, that is, that Eather would begin to push the enemy back. It took Blamey a further four days to reach Port Moresby. On 20 September Blamey attempted to prepare Rowell for his visit by writing the following letter:

> The powers that be have determined that I shall myself go
> to New Guinea for a while and operate from there. I do not,
> however, propose to transfer many of the Advanced HQ Staff ...
> At present I propose to bring with me my P.A. [personal assistant]
> Major Carlyon, two extra cipher officers and Lieut. Lawson.
> I hope you will be able to house us in your camp and messes.
>
> I hope you will not be upset at this decision, and will not think
> it implies any lack of confidence in yourself. I think it arises out
> of the fact that we have very inexperienced politicians who are
> inclined to panic on every possible occasion, and I think the
> relationship between us personally is such that we can make the
> arrangement work without difficulty.[11]

Blamey's earlier visit to Port Moresby; his cordial relations with both Rowell and Allen there; his supportive national radio broadcast; his support of the command and troops in New Guinea at the Advisory War Council meeting and, finally, the above letter to Rowell would tend to portray a conciliatory Blamey – a commander who wanted to make the best of an awkward situation. But the fact remains that he should have stood up to Curtin and, having taken the above positive initiatives, followed his stance through to the end. Blamey was also to bring with him Colonel GH Rasmussen to replace Lieutenant-Colonel Fenton as censor, and had drafted new guidelines for correspondents. Clearly he intended to bring the annoying young Wilmot into line once and for all.

When Rowell received Blamey's letter in Port Moresby, the frustrating and humiliating events of Greece only about eighteen months before overwhelmed him. He sought the counsel of George Fenton. Rowell made it clear to Fenton that he would not tolerate Blamey's decision to take charge. The surviving fragments of Fenton's diary cast a new light on the command crisis. This is the entry for 25 September 1942:

> Saw General Rowell who said that he had a terrific argument with C-in-C who was determined to stay. Rowell said that he told C-in-C quite frankly what he thought of him, and was surprised that the C-in-C had put up with it. 'Any real man would have sacked me on the spot'. C-in-C had threatened him with retire [sic] list. 'I thought I might get out of it with a drop in rank.[12]

The following day, Fenton saw Rowell again, and wrote: 'Rowell seemed more depressed than previously ... I said it was essential that Wilmot should leave for the mainland that night. Wilmot was prepared to risk everything to help, and if he didn't go immediately the C-in-C could hold him up indefinitely.'[13]

Fenton then arranged for Chester's departure for Australia that night. He also gave Wilmot written instructions from Blamey concerning censorship of material for press and radio circulation. The material identified four scripts Chester had recently sent to Australia which had been banned. Blamey identified four areas where Chester had 'offended' his headquarters: giving information of value to the enemy; implying criticism of military direction and training methods; tending to lower morale of troops going to the area; and inaccuracy.

Chester would later write that these orders were designed to place Blamey beyond examination and criticism. Fenton's diary for 27 September reads: '0400 Chester left by bomber for south.'[14] The next day at 5 pm, Rowell rang Fenton. He said, 'The enemy has taken the initiative. There was a decisive action and a withdrawal was ordered. I leave by plane tomorrow at 8.'[15] Blamey had sacked Rowell.

Ostensibly, it would seem that Blamey had not decided to sack Rowell in the lead-up to their acrimonious meetings in Port Moresby. But there is evidence that rumours about Rowell's impending fate were circulating in Australia and Port Moresby, *before* MacArthur 'secraphoned' Curtin and *before* Curtin ordered Blamey to Port Moresby.

Rowell arrived in Sydney on 30 September 1942 and went straight to a meeting with Chester. He told the general that he had contacted CEW Bean, who was setting up a meeting with Prime Minister Curtin. At his meeting with the PM Wilmot made a strong case against Blamey. He described the widespread lack of confidence in the Commander-in-Chief throughout the Australian Army and urged him to reinstate Rowell. Curtin replied that the Australian Government knew everything he had told him about Blamey but the C-in-C had been so accurate in predicting the enemy's moves they could not afford to sack him. 'It is,' he added 'back him or sack him and we can't afford to sack him'.[16] In this Curtin was being somewhat disingenuous. Blamey's 'predictions' came from reliable intelligence estimates. Giving Blamey the credit for their work seems to have been Curtin's way of evading the issue of the C-in-C's unfitness for command.

During their interview, Wilmot mentioned he was preparing another version of his report on the New Guinea Campaign for the ABC. On 16 October, Curtin's private secretary contacted the ABC 'requesting a copy adding that as Curtin was Minister for Defence he was entitled to see it'.[17] Chester saw his opportunity to take on the C-in-C on the basis of his professional competence. Although never mentioned, the opening of these new observations was directed squarely at the failings of Sir Thomas Blamey. Repeatedly, Wilmot emphasised that the worst blunders occurred leading up to the campaign. In this context his opening to 'Observations on the New Guinea Campaign August–September 1942' was devastating:

> The situation, which resulted in the Japanese getting to within 35 miles of Port Moresby, appears to have been one which should never have arisen if enough troops, adequately trained and equipped, had been sent to New Guinea in time.
>
> After the Coral Sea Battle it was clear that we had a much better chance of holding New Guinea, and the Allied High Command took steps to strengthen our position there. To protect the right flank, airfields were built and a covering force (consisting of one AMF infantry brigade and some A/A gunners) was established at Milne Bay.
>
> Moresby was developed as a base for future offensive operations by increasing the number of aerodromes from two to seven.
>
> The Moresby garrison was increased from one Infantry Brigade Group to two and the A/A defences were considerably strengthened.
>
> As a first step towards driving the Japanese from their bases at Lae and Salamaua, it was decided in July to occupy Buna, and

a Militia battalion had already begun to march across the Owen Stanley Range to Buna when the Japanese landed there on July 22/23.

The importance of this landing was played down at GHQ and correspondents were told that the Japanese landing force did not exceed 2,500 and was probably smaller. (In fact, it is now estimated by New Guinea Force that the original landing force was more than 6,000). GHQ consistently belittled suggestions that this force could make any attack on Port Moresby and correspondents were encouraged to talk glibly about the 'impassable barrier of the Owen Stanley Range line'.

This seems to have led to some complacency in Moresby and at LHQ (Land Forces HQ) about the security of Moresby. The mountain barrier was relied on to protect it from landward attack, and the Milne Bay garrison with its aircraft was apparently considered an effective bar to any attempt by the Japanese to bring an invasion fleet round by sea. The result was that hardly enough was done to strengthen the Moresby garrison and defenses between the Battle of the Coral Sea early in May and the Japanese landing at Buna late in July.

During this period New Guinea was directly under LHQ and not under the command of any subsidiary formation. In May a move was made to put North Queensland and New Guinea under the command of First Army – on the ground that Moresby and Townsville are strategically linked. But the proposal came to nought.

One answer to the question why Moresby was not strengthened more is that it was regarded as being safe from landward attack and it was expected that putting troops and aircraft into Milne

Bay was a better means of stopping a seaborne invasion than strengthening Moresby. This proved to be right. In addition it was intended that Milne Bay should be the jumping off place for a seaborne force which could occupy Buna under air cover, provided by Milne Bay based aircraft.

This offensive plan went astray because:

The Japanese got into Buna first. (We certainly could not have saved Buna by putting a force in overland.)

The American attack on the Solomons took all available ships which might have been used for a combined counterattack against Buna and eventually from New Guinea.

Because this plan went astray and the Japanese pushed in in force from Buna, a threat developed to Port Moresby overland which otherwise would not have developed. Because it was presumed that Moresby was safe from overland attack:

No attempt was made to train any part of its garrison to fight in the mountains and jungle.

No tactical reconnaissance or survey of supply problems or tracks was made in the Owen Stanley Range.

This seems to have been an oversight for as there was an offensive intention we needed all the more to have troops trained for jungle fighting and it would at least have been as well to survey a landward route to Buna in case the garrison could not be maintained by sea, once established there.

From May to August there was an AIF division training in Queensland in country no way resembling the thick forest, jungle and mountain terrain of New Guinea. But the infantry reinforcements sent to Moresby were a not well trained and not very well disciplined Militia brigade. A warning as to their quality might have been obtained from the large number of troops (about 25%) who went AWL as soon as it was known that they were to go overseas.

The 7th Division was left in Queensland (with the exception of the brigade sent to Milne Bay *after* the Japanese landing at Buna). Not even advance parties, or staff officers were sent to the Moresby area to study local conditions, or make tactical reconnaissances.

The Militia brigade which went to Moresby did little more training than the brigade which had been there since the previous December. The training of both was seriously interfered with because anything from 800 to 1150 troops a day were engaged in unloading ships or working on the roads. By mid-July the two Moresby brigades had done little more than elementary infantry training and they had made comparatively little progress even in preparing defense works for the defense of Port Moresby from a seaborne invasion, which was their primary role.

However, they might be said to have been semi-trained for the task of fighting in the open light scrub country around Moresby. But they had had no training whatever in jungle warfare or in fighting in mountains, when the Japanese landed at Buna and pushed inland to Kokoda.[18]

Wilmot handsomely made amends to the 39th Battalion criticised in the first version of the report:

In these circumstances it is remarkable that the 39th Battalion, (AMF) the advanced elements of which met the Japanese near Kokoda about July 26th, should have done as well as it did. The troops were very young – the average age of at least one company was 21 and it included lads of 18 and 19. It is perhaps fortunate that during the next month the Japanese were not in a position to make a serious assault on the 39th Battalion's positions in the foothills of the Owen Stanley Range. This respite gave the Battalion a chance to learn something about jungle fighting. But they had to learn this *not* in training but in action. Moreover, they were handicapped by lack of supporting weapons. They had no mortars or Vickers guns, and *only one company* had steel helmets.[19]

The first sentence was probably based on a briefing from Rowell and emphasised the biggest mistake of the campaign: the failure to get a sufficient number of troops to New Guinea in time. The criticism was more devastating than Wilmot realised. MacArthur and Blamey had been in possession, two months earlier, of intelligence predicting a Japanese overland attack on Port Moresby. According to Peter Brune, even if the 21st Brigade could have been 'adequately trained and equipped' before leaving Australia, it was six solid weeks late. It should have been dispatched immediately after the Battle of Midway (6–8 June 1942). This would have seen it in Port Moresby by 1 July instead of mid-August. At the very least Brigadier Potts would have been able to reconnoitre the track and he would have had his complete brigade, as the 2/27th Battalion would have gone up with him. None of this is historians' hindsight. Rowell is on record as having said, in June 1942, that 'if we were where we should be, it would be in New Guinea with the 7th Division'.[20]

Therefore, Wilmot's criticisms of the failure to provide adequate jungle uniforms, proper rations and equipment, and training – as well as the the troops' belated arrival in New Guinea – was directed at Land Forces Headquarters: in other words, Sir Thomas Blamey.

Brune points out that Wilmot's comments reflected the 'Report into Operations – 21st Brigade, Owen Stanley Campaign'. When this report was first submitted, GHQ returned it and demanded it be rewritten. This rewritten version is to be found in the AWM. Brune, however, used the original for his groundbreaking *Those Ragged Bloody Heroes*.[21] Wilmot clearly won the argument but Curtin remained obdurate.

It was only a matter of time before Blamey moved against Wilmot. On 1 November, a week after he had returned to New Guinea, Wilmot was summoned into Blamey's tent. A transcript of the encounter survives.

> Blamey: I want to recall to you an incident which occurred in a Melbourne restaurant in May. It was reported to me then that you had alleged that there had been some improper dealings by me in the case of a motion picture contract in the Middle East and that I had benefited financially from these dealings. You also alleged that I had improperly interfered in stopping the court martial of an officer. Following this I asked our mutual friend, Mr Krcrouse, to see you and assure you that these allegations were unfounded and that you were behaving improperly in repeating them. Do you remember that conversation?
>
> Wilmot: I do but I do not recall the alleged restaurant incident and my recollection of the conversation is different.
>
> Blamey: We shall come back to that in a minute. During your conversation with Mr Krcrouse you said that you accepted my assurance and that you would not repeat these allegations. You also said that you appreciated the way I had handled the matter. Since then I have told no one of this conversation. Mr Krcrouse assures me that he told no one. Yet the fact that this conversation took place is known to at least three people. They can only

have got this information from you. During your recent visit to Melbourne my intelligence tells me that you discussed this matter with three people; you repeated the original allegations and revealed that this conversation with Mr Krcrouse took place. I have statements from three people and I understand from the same intelligence source that you have continued your interest in this matter with the object of having me removed from my position as C-in-C. Have you anything to say?

Wilmot: Yes, I have no recollection of the conversations you refer to.

Blamey: Will you say that you did not discuss this matter with anyone?

Wilmot: No I can't say that.

Blamey: Well that is all. You have endeavoured to undermine my authority as C-in-C. That is a serious matter. We should give thousands of pounds to have someone in your position in Japan trying to undermine the C-in-C there. Your accreditation to Allied Land Forces is forthwith cancelled. You will return to Australia at once. Fenton, will you please make the necessary arrangements. Good morning.[22]

Wilmot could recognise a trap when he saw it. Not only was Fenton there but also Herring, who had taken over from Rowell, and a stenographer. Fenton had survived Blamey's purge of Rowell men and was still an ally, but his work was being 'supervised' by Rasmussen. So Wilmot kept his mouth shut. It was believed in the Wilmot family that one of the very few people Chester discussed the picture contract with was fellow Melbourne Grammar 'old boy', Lieutenant-General Ned Herring.

One call Wilmot was able to make before leaving Port Moresby was on Colonel Charles Moses, the General Manager of the ABC, at the time serving in the AIF. Even though he didn't know Chester well, he immediately wrote him an enthusiastic letter of support for the commission. As Moses was under Blamey's command at the time, it says a great deal for his moral courage and his high regard for Wilmot. Chester broke the news to his father in a letter intended to allay the old man's fears but only succeeded in increasing his concern.

> I have a clear conscience – for I feel that when faced with a test in which I had to choose between doing what I thought was right and risking my job – and doing what I knew to be cowardly and keeping it – I have taken the risk. We have always said the only standard of a man in public life can accept is that he should do his duty fearlessly regardless of the consequences ... The point is that no one else could move in this matter. The soldiers are tied by the Army – the politicians didn't know – I was (as fate would have it) the only person with the knowledge and standing to act ... I have no self recriminations, except I might have been shrewder and more discreet but that is the fault of a young man in a hurry.[23]

At this stage Bung was not at all certain his son was right. He also sensed 'the boy' was alone and depressed. So he took *The Spirit of Progress* to Albury, changed trains, and met Chester at Central Station in Sydney. The two Wilmots then walked the streets from coffee shop to coffee shop as Chester poured out the story to his father. Once convinced, Bung became a superb devil's advocate as they explored every possible argument. When Bung left for Melbourne he was convinced his son had a very good case. 'The case' was, however, too much for the 'girls' in the ABC offices who had to type it. 'We can't have them reading that', exclaimed Bearup.[24] So he approached the formidable Betty Cook and asked her to do the typing. She was the first woman graduate in economics from the University of Sydney and was at the time Moses's special assistant. For this stage of his fight for vindication Wilmot was to have nothing but the best.

The memo entitled 'Withdrawal of My Accreditation' is a remarkable document. It answers Blamey's charges; chronicles the trail of events between Blamey and Wilmot from the Middle East to Papua; examines Blamey's alleged corruption; and, critically, deals with the confrontations between Blamey and a number of his senior commanders during this period. As background to the memo, Wilmot stated that: 'Although the alleged statements regarding the motion picture contract were cited as the reason for the action taken by the C-in-C, it is well known among the AIF that the conflict out of which this has arisen began in the Middle East. The matter can only be seen in perspective if the background is known.'[25]

Chester then proceeded to cite the confrontations between himself and Blamey. The first was Mr Spender's visit to Palestine at New Year 1941. Blamey, through the censor Fenton, ordered Wilmot to go to Palestine to film speeches by him and Spender. 'I protested that my duty was to go back to Bardia. Captain [Fenton] referred the matter to Gaza and I was told that it was General Blamey's orders and that I had no right to query them.'[26]

Wilmot's next point concerned a broadcast by a Mr McGibbon:

In May 1941, Mr. SJ McGibbon came to Cairo on behalf of the Government. He was disturbed by what he saw and in a broadcast script which he dictated to me and which I submitted to censorship he roundly denounced the 'old men' of Cairo, who with their 'ladies' were leading a peacetime life and taking afternoon siestas form 1.30 till 5.30. The script was referred by the censor to General Blamey who took it as a personal attack on himself and I am told he regarded me as one of the inspirer's [sic] of the script.[27]

This incident would have been a very sensitive one for Blamey. It was known all over the Middle East that Blamey was indulging in a 'vigorous' social life; seen in civilian attire enjoying sleazy bars; and engaging in frequent 'womanising'.

The next Wilmot transgression involved his script on Crete. Blamey resented the fact that Chester had met with Wavell for 'one and a half hours' and had agreed to 'take up certain matters in it' with Blamey. Further, 'officers on General Blamey's Headquarters warned me that he strongly disapproved in principle of submitting any criticism at all'.[28]

Wilmot's fourth point was that he had written two broadcasts about the AIF Reinforcement Depot. In them he 'criticized the standard of reinforcements arriving from Australia'.[29] He also praised the work of General Robertson. Blamey resented any criticism: 'he said that it was not a correspondent's job to be critical at all.' Blamey 'killed the script', and there was 'no mention of General Robertson'. Wilmot then pointed out that 'the same material appeared in Australian papers ... with credit given to the General himself.'[30] Blamey had seen Robertson as a future rival for his position. After an impressive performance in North Africa, Robertson was hospitalised with a varicose vein condition. He did not gain an active command for the rest of the war.

Chester Wilmot's next point was that due to the incidents above, he was not popular with Blamey when he returned to Australia: 'In April 1942, speaking of Middle East War Correspondents to Mr. Errol Knox, General Blamey said – 'We had a good lot of correspondents in the Middle East, except for young Wilmot. He gave us a lot of trouble – too mischievous. I gave him two chances there; he won't get a third here.'[31]

Chester then turned to the Kokoda Campaign. His comments brought into sharp focus the difference in attitude between Rowell and Allen on the one hand, and Blamey on the other:

> On my return from the Kokoda Front, General Rowell ... and General Allen ... asked me to make a report on what I had seen and on certain deficiencies in training and equipment which had become evident.
>
> I attempted to cover these in a report which was sent by General Rowell to General Blamey's Headquarters with a recommendation that it be widely circulated.[32]

Wilmot then pointed out that as Blamey was not present at his HQ upon receipt of the report, it was duly reproduced and circulated. Upon his return, Blamey 'ordered every copy recalled'.[33] The fact that Rowell and Allen digested it, and the Americans, and that II Australian Corps HQ distributed it also, would seem to indicate that it contained useful information – except in Blamey's eyes. Wilmot then described the fate of his first four broadcasts on the campaign. They were submitted to MacArthur's HQ and the 'State Publicity Censorship in Brisbane ... The scripts were passed by GHQ substantially unaltered'.[34] But when the scripts were presented to Blamey's HQ they were 'killed'. Wilmot then received a guideline for future scripts which we have previously identified.

Chester then went on to discuss the issue of his 'friendship' with General Rowell, arguing that it went beyond the personal and served the national interest:

> My friendship with General Rowell from whom all correspondents had received much help here and in the Middle East, apparently made me suspect also. When I left Port Moresby the day before he [Rowell] did this suspicion was no doubt increased. Evidently General Blamey ordered his Intelligence Officers in Melbourne to furnish him with a report on my activities during [Wilmot's] absence. At any rate General Blamey told me he had received such a report.

My interest in General Rowell's cause was not based merely on personal grounds, though I did feel that he was being unjustifiably victimized. It was based on much broader considerations of general national interest. These led me to take action in a matter which may be considered a mere army affair, but which I regarded as of national interest far transcending the immediate personal issues involved.[35]

Wilmot then pointed out that Rowell's staff officers asked him to act in not only Rowell's interests but in the interests of the army, arriving at what he considered the heart of the matter:

Quite apart from the loss of General Rowell, the national issue, I believe, is this. In two years with the AIF I have come to realize that the Australian Forces are seriously handicapped by the widespread lack of faith in General Blamey. In two years I have heard him denounced in the strongest possible terms in messes and private conversations by senior officers, who had no interest in supplanting him, by junior officers and by ordinary diggers. I have never once heard him defended by any but his own close friends.

By the end of last year in Palestine he had lost the confidence of even ordinary troops. Officers and other ranks had seen him at cabarets in Tel Aviv and Cairo in civilian clothes. There was free talk of scandals about the picture contract, the laundry contract and the canteens – especially the beer and liquor shipments. There were whisperings about what was alleged to have happened in Greece when allegedly the General left early and precipitously [sic] against the advice and in spite of the pleading of his senior officers.

I do not know the full truth of these matters, but they were being discussed and the very fact these rumours were current seriously undermined the confidence of officers and troops in their Commander. It is not of great importance whether or not the Army's lack of confidence is justified. The important thing, I believe, is that they have no confidence in General Blamey either personally or as a soldier.

Another reason for lack of confidence is that there is a widespread feeling among senior officers that those Generals who show signs of rising to heights from which they might threaten the throne of the C-in-C have been kept down or pushed aside into some unimportant job. This is evident in the cases of Generals Lavarack, Rowell and Robertson. It is freely and widely stated among senior officers that we have suffered militarily because of the antagonism between General Blamey and many of his senior commanders. It is alleged within the army – rightly or wrongly – that General Morris – a junior and admittedly a second rate commander – was left in command in New Guinea until the situation got really bad, because General Blamey was reluctant to appoint a strong man for the job. These dissentions and rivalries have seriously divided the Australian Army for some time and have caused increasingly grave concern among responsible officers.[36]

Wilmot then pointed out that he had sought the counsel of Dr CEW Bean, the Official Australian Historian for World War I, and Dr Evatt, concerning the issue of correspondents having the right of criticism. According to Chester, both thought Blamey's 'instructions regarding criticism too severe'.[37] Both men also questioned Wilmot about the Blamey–Rowell clash.

After commenting on another clash with Blamey over a dispatch, Wilmot then addressed the issue of Blamey's reasons for his disaccreditation:

General Blamey chose to act against me on grounds which superficially at least did not involve the freedom of the press. His charge is that I have tried to undermine his authority as Commander-in-Chief by repeating allegations about the motion picture contract.

But even this issue is not purely personal. This involves a correspondent's freedom of enquiry into matters of public interest. Correspondents recognize the Army's right to restrict by censorship what is published or broadcast. But to my knowledge this is the first time that the Army has tried to restrict enquiry by taking disciplinary action. Throughout the Middle East campaigns it was generally recognized that there was nothing to stop a correspondent gathering material and submitting it for censorship. The restrictions were only imposed on a publication.[38]

Chester then pointed out that when he had returned to New Guinea a further restriction had been placed on correspondents that had not existed in the Middle East: they were not permitted to enter the office of any staff officer at New Guinea Force HQ. He pointed out that in all other campaigns, correspondents were permitted to do so; that they were usually allowed to see operational and intelligence reports 'and as a rule nothing was withheld from them'. 'Such freedom of movement and contact', thought Wilmot, 'are essential if correspondents are to remain well enough informed to report objectively.'[39]

Wilmot then summarised his arguments:

1   That I was rightly concerned in enquiring into the matter of the motion picture contract.
2   That even if it were not proper for me to continue my interest in this matter, this was not sufficient grounds for my disaccreditation.

3   That the picture contract, though cited as the reason, was not the main reason for the action taken against me.
4   That the real reason was my insistence on the right of a correspondent to criticize and to enquire freely and the fact that I had been critical of the military conduct of the war in New Guinea and when I could not get my criticism published, I had gone to the Government.
5   That this is not just an individual case affecting me alone. The basic freedom of correspondents in General Blamey's command is at stake. If this is unchallenged he has succeeded in placing himself above criticism.[40]

The memo was submitted to the Commission. This time Wilmot won the argument.

No one quite knew what to do about Blamey but they affirmed the commission's confidence in their reporter. Years later the author asked Sir Charles Moses why he supported Wilmot against the Commander-in-Chief in wartime. Moses replied, 'Chester was so level-headed that if he said Blamey was corrupt, he was!'[41]

15

A DANGEROUS SUBVERSIVE AND A COMMUNIST

The ABC Board may have believed Wilmot was right in his dispute with Sir Thomas Blamey but they were not prepared to take a public stand against the Commander-in-Chief. In a tortured paragraph to his father, he described the board's convoluted reasoning:

> I think they started from the premise that they couldn't win anyway. They argue – even if you are right – the government would have to make any final decision and that would mean choosing between B [Blamey] and you: unless they were prepared to sack him they would have to side with him and Ford has indicated they 'are not going to sack General B because C W [Chester Wilmot] wants that done.' Cleary [the chairman] also feared that the newspapers wanted to use an ABC case 'so they can drop it without losing face if the fight goes against them.' They may want to take a crack at Blamey but they also see a chance for doing some harm to the Commission.[1]

Chester didn't accept this. If the ABC wanted to stand up to Blamey and the Australian Government, it could. 'But they have never fought anything in recent years and they are now so weak with the Government and the Press that they can't do anything strong ever again.'[2] However the board did say that, 'the best answer we can give to B [Blamey] is for us to employ you in the most responsible capacity possible – to keep you on air; that clears you personally and it more than clears you … if we send you as a correspondent to another theatre'.[3]

And there were other overtures. Chester was tentatively offered a position with the *Sydney Morning Herald* through Gavin Long. However, when he had lunch with the editor, although Wilmot was told they would like to take up his case, there was no straightout offer. A definite offer did come from Brian Penton, the editor of the *Daily Telegraph*, but Chester knew that editors and newspaper proprietors had their own scores to settle with the government. They bitterly resented the often petty and ludicrous censorship administered by the Department of Information (DOI). Wilmot shared their irritation with the department. His letters are full of complaints about the often absurd cuts demanded in his scripts. In addition, the DOI had frustrated his attempts to interview Damien Parer when the cameraman had returned from covering the guerrillas on Timor. But Chester didn't want his own case to be used in the newspapers' feud with the department and the government. This conflict was to explode in April 1944 over a political dispute with Arthur Calwell, the Minister of Information, when Commonwealth and State censors suppressed all the daily newspapers in Sydney, all the afternoon papers in Melbourne plus Adelaide's only evening paper. The newspapers won that battle when the High Court issued an injunction preventing the censorship of editorial opinion.

Chester did not at first realise that the most powerful weapon in his dispute with Blamey was his observations on the New Guinea campaign. In what seems to have been a meeting at a Melbourne club, Brigadier Charles 'Gaffer' Lloyd told Bung that the disaccreditation had nothing to do with the picture contract, 'it was the

Report'.⁴ 'But,' the elder Wilmot responded deftly, as he skillfully tried to draw out his old acquaintance, 'the report was completely objective.'⁵ Lloyd replied that Blamey was afraid the politicians would get hold of it and use it against him. And indeed major Labor figures Eddie Ward and Jack 'Stabber' Beasley, both on the Advisory War Council, loathed Blamey. From the outset, however, Chester had decided this second report should remain confidential. It was a principled decision by an honourable man.

Despite the support of friends like Tubby Allen and Gavin Long, Chester was lonely and depressed. He missed the AIF and the war: 'I've grown up with this show, my best friends are there.'⁶ Edith was not with him in Sydney as she had gone back to Adelaide to be with her parents for the birth of their first child. In one letter to her, Chester mentioned [sic] that Allen and his wife, 'a delightful littley woman'⁷, had offered to put Edith up. If this was a hint that she should join him in Sydney, it was ignored.

At this time Chester was doing regular broadcasts for the ABC. The head of talks, BH Molesworth, would ring in the morning and ask him to do the commentary that night. Chester explained to his family that 'Moley doesn't give any orders in the ordinary sense … [He] says … it looks like North Africa is in the news … I'd like you to talk about Rommel's retreat – it's all worked out on the basis of discussion.'⁸

From time to time in Molesworth's absence, Chester acted as temporary head of Talks. Later he was to develop the prestigious 'Guest of Honour' broadcasts. However, despite all the outward signs of the commission's confidence in 'their Mr. Wilmot', it was still not enough.

His frustration at this time can be gauged from a revealing anecdote by journalist and broadcaster Frank Legg. Prior to his own posting to New Guinea, Legg had come to ask Chester about the role of a radio correspondent. As Legg recalled:

A dangerous subversive and a communist

When his secretary, an amiable girl, brought in our afternoon tea, she asked lightly. 'And how's the war going to-day, Mr. Wilmot?' Chester, ignoring his tea, strode to the wall, pulled down a map of Italy and plunged straight in. 'There's a very interesting report from Italy this morning,' he began. About an hour later he snapped up the Italian map, and before his secretary could escape, had pulled down a map of Russia. 'On the Eastern Front …' he boomed.

After another two hours fascinated and exhausted I broke in. 'Sorry to interrupt, Chester,' I said, 'But perhaps your secretary might have an appointment or something.'

'Good heavens, is it as late as that?' Wilmot asked, and immediately apologized to the girl. 'It's all right Mr. Wilmot,' she said faintly. 'It's been most interesting.' Then she fled.[9]

To make matters worse, early in 1943 the ABC closed down the Broadcast Unit in New Guinea, as the reporting restrictions instigated by Blamey had stifled the unit's ability to get enough stories. Wilmot's commentaries were little more than intelligent speculations based on written communiqués or dispatches from other reporters such as Legg.

* * * *

It was inevitable that Wilmot would have considered writing a book of his wartime experiences sometime during his career. Fellow correspondents Alan Moorehead, Quentin Reynolds, Alexander Clifford and Richard Dimbleby were already publishing their own accounts. Chester had already read a draft of a manuscript by Gavin Long and thought he might be 'able to do better'. However, a glance at his notebooks indicates that from the outset he had in mind something more ambitious than a description of his adventures.

Wilmot first thought he might need more on Crete and Syria, but decided to concentrate on Tobruk. He was later to remark that Tobruk was the crucible that eventually produced *The Struggle for Europe*. In the closed world of the desert fortress, he had been able to research earlier events in the siege, not just as a broadcaster but also as a historian. Molesworth provided him with an office and a secretary while Chester assembled his notebooks and the scripts of his broadcasts. He now shaped this material into a series of continuous narratives that would be discussed in the evenings with Mervyn Scales, a new friend, who like Chester was staying at the University Club. A quiet, unassuming man with an incisive, critical mind, Scales was a documentary film producer, whose meticulousness and insistence on accuracy were similar to Chester's. He proved to be an invaluable sounding board. Damien Parer also 'read bits of it and was most helpful'.[10]

The writing came easily. Over about four days, 12 000 words on the Battle of the Salient were completed; 'what a sweat – the first continuous account', Chester wrote proudly to the family.[11] Unlike most of the other correspondents whose books tended to be reminiscences of their experiences covering the campaigns, Wilmot was mainly writing straight history. Colonel John Treloar, Head of Military History and Records, agreed to give him access to the relevant files in Melbourne and Chester planned to research these records on his way to see Edith in Adelaide when it was time for her to have the baby. He was also getting material from participants. His recent visitor, Frank Legg, had been a sergeant in Tobruk. He described for Chester how tired the troops were when they first reached the desert fortress. Major-General JH Lavarack, commander of all the forces in Cyrenaica after the capture of Generals Neame and O'Connor, provided Wilmot with a report on the decision to hold Tobruk. In addition, the general gave Wilmot copies of his correspondence with Wavell along with other confidential papers.

A dangerous subversive and a communist

Almost certainly Lavarack was his main informant for this passage:

> In a battered house in Tobruk on the 8th, Wavell and Lavarack met Morshead and Lloyd and the senior surviving officer of 'Cyrcom' (Brigadier G Harding). Harding outlined the position and asked whether they were to hold Tobruk. Wavell did not reply at once. He took out his eyeglass, polished it, and asked for a map. He studied this for a few minutes and then announced Lavarack was to take command in Cyrenaica and a stand was to be made at Tobruk. 'There is nothing,' he said to Lavarack, 'between you and Cairo.'
>
> Then he took three sheets of note paper and pencilled for Lavarack [six] brief, broad and not too optimistic instructions.[12]

Lavarack gave Chester permission to use a photostatic copy of these orders as an illustration for the book. To counter the threat from Rommel, Wavell had held back Lavarack's 7th Division from Greece. Blamey 'blew up' when he got the news. He was in part mollified by a conciliatory dispatch from Wavell and a personal visit from the C-in-C. As we have seen Blamey was able to persuade Wavell not to appoint Lavarack to the command of Western Desert Force. Sir Thomas tried to cover his tracks by suggesting to his disappointed subordinate that Lavarack had missed out on the appointment because he had recommended that a two-division reserve be retained in Tobruk. This was denied by Wavell when Lavarack wrote asking him to clarify the situation. Without revealing anything about Blamey's mean-spirited intervention, Wavell praised Lavarack's conduct of operations. This too was shown to Chester, who quoted Wavell at the conclusion of the passage describing how Lavarack's early decisions contributed to the successful defence of Tobruk. This was in Chester's words:

a ticklish part of the book ... In the first five days Lavarack was there and made a number of important decisions which time has proved correct. On some of these LJM [Morshead] opposed him, but will not now admit it ... and most of those in the know are taking Morshead's side because he is up and JDL [Lavarack] is down. I sent my manuscript to JDL, who is a most difficult man to please – and he sent it back with a very nice letter with only the most minor suggestions for changes. What I wonder now, if he is pleased LJM will not be, but he can't deny the truth of the facts I have stated for I have quoted written documents. I am pleased to be able to do this for *Salt* [the army paper distributed to the troops] had an article recently written by Gaffer Lloyd and in it L [Lloyd] gives all the credit for the early days to Morshead and none to Lavarack and makes statements that are directly opposed to the documents e.g. Wavell wrote out the instructions for Lavarack and gave the orders to him. Lloyd says W [Wavell] gave the orders to M [Morshead]. Wheels within wheels.[13]

Chester may even have known that Lavarack had written to Morshead about this same article complaining it had 'slurred over his connection' with the siege. In 1944 Morshead wrote a bitter letter of complaint to the director of Army Public Relations, JH Rasmussen – the same man Blamey had taken to New Guinea to 'supervise' George Fenton – over a supposedly 'self aggrandizing' letter Lavarack wrote to Kenneth Slessor.

In spite of this rivalry Morshead seems to have made no attempt to influence Chester's treatment of the early days. The book was judiciously even handed about both men. Lavarack was described as 'one the finest military brains Australia has produced'.[14] Morshead was 'something of a martinet' but was 'just as critical of himself as of his men'.[15] Wilmot included a few pointed reminiscences about the general's pedantic corrections of his scripts. 'He disliked slang and at one time suggested a Digger in a broadcast should talk about "men" not "chaps" and about "devitalizing minefields" not "delousing" them'.[16] However, Morshead could hardly have complained about Wilmot's summing up: 'In Morshead Australia has found another fine citizen soldier – a man with a profound sincerity, honesty, and strength of purpose, and with more experience now as a fighting commander in this war and the last than any other Australian.'[17]

Wilmot still defended the Greek venture. He insisted that after reaching Benghazi

> it would have been a grave mistake to have attempted a further push westwards to Tripoli when it was known Hitler was going to attack in the Balkans ... It is widely believed ... that if there had been no expedition to Greece, Wavell could have held Cyrenaica, and could also have gone onto Tripoli and could have swept the Axis from North Africa two years before the Allies eventually did. This view springs from either wishful thinking or ignorance. I believe that even if Wavell had had available all the troops and equipment that went to Greece, the Axis could still have retaken most of Cyrenaica before the middle of 1941.[18]

When he wrote this Wilmot did not know that General O'Connor was to blame himself for the rest of his life for not ignoring Wavell's orders and taking Tripoli. Indeed this 'Forgotten Victor' of the desert war was to say as much on Thames' 'The World at War' shortly before he died. Rommel agreed with him. As he wrote in his account of the war in Africa,

> When a commander has won a decisive victory – and Wavell's victory over the Italians was devastating – it is generally wrong to be satisfied with too narrow a strategic aim ... Troops who on one day are flying in wild panic to the rear, may, unless they

are continually harried by the pursuer, very soon stand in battle again, freshly organized as fully effective fighting men.[19]

Wilmot would not have known about the German general's views until the 1950s when his friend Basil Liddell Hart edited *The Rommel Papers* (1953). By then Chester must have realised that he had overestimated the strength of the Afrika Korps. Also he would have learned that the Germans had not received any special training in desert warfare as stated in *Tobruk*.

Nevertheless, *Tobruk* remains a classic of Australian military history. Wilmot incorporated the social history and observation from his scripts to portray the diggers of the garrison. In fact, his censored 'In a Dugout in Tobruk' finally made it into print. This was interwoven with an exciting narrative of the battles that he had pieced together from participants and the war diaries together with a vivid account of his own experiences during the siege. Moreover, the last thirty pages include one of the best brief accounts of the Crusader Offensive and the break-out from Tobruk ever written. Chester confided to Edith that this was very difficult to get right. (Hardly surprising; at different times both sides were confused about the state of the battle.) The notes on the dust jacket of the original edition put it best: '*Tobruk* is neither a personal story nor a full military history, but an attempt to record what took place in and around Tobruk in 1941.'[20] Chester could not resist mildly rebuking his colleagues' accounts of many of the same events by getting whoever compiled the blurb to include this sentence: 'Those interested in the campaign itself and the men who fought it will find it refreshing to read a book by a war correspondent who writes about the war and not the correspondent.'[21]

Early in 1943 Chester took some long-overdue leave. As he wrote to his sister Jean:

The child was due to arrive on or about February 1st and reckoned I should get over here about a week beforehand. My leave began on January 16th and I bowled over to Melbourne to spend a week or so there collecting material for my book. I got to Melbourne on the 17th Sunday and rang Edith that night. She didn't breathe a word about the possibility of the snippet appearing ahead of schedule though at that time they thought it might. However an hour or so after I spoke to her on the phone they whisked her off to the hospital and the child 'bounced out' – to use Edith's lurid language – at 4pm on the 18th ... From my point of view the whole arrangement was magnificent – painless paternity if you like. No pacing the floor for hours and all that.[22]

It was a baby girl. The Wilmots christened her Jane Morris Wilmot. It was both an easy and fitting naming: Edith liked both names, Chester's mother would be suitably impressed, and Edith's mother was to be no less proud with her maiden name being adopted as the child's middle name. For all his flippancy Chester was overwhelmed at becoming a father. He wrote to Edith: 'To be away from you today of all days is just too terrible and agonizing – my heart has been thumping against my ribs all day when it wasn't in my mouth – I could hardly speak when your littley [sic] mother rang me this morning – she too was almost incoherent with excitement.'[23] Almost certainly he was also profoundly relieved. Earlier Edith had had misgivings:

> Life is rather lousy at present because I don't know whether I am pregnant or not and the suspense is what I imagine Hell is like – an ever lasting dreary fear haunting your day and night ... If by any chance I am pregnant or when this doctor tells me I am – I shall [sic 'go'] me straight off to another kind of doctor and have a small but expensive operation – Don't worry I'll be alright and you did promise (on the Sunday under the pine trees) that I

could finish my course this year and that I needn't have a child until that was done – so I know you won't go back on your word now.[24]

Chester's reply has not survived. Almost certainly he would have been appalled. Of course Edith did have the child and proved to be a devoted mother. So Chester probably convinced her that she could have the baby and complete her course. But in 1942 for a woman of Edith's class and background, and the daughter of a clergyman, to even contemplate an abortion was extraordinary. Clearly for all the warmth of her letters, Edith was reluctant to begin the marriage. She may have been passionately in love with Chester, but even after they were formally engaged Edith still felt she really didn't know him. This had been brought home to her when before the wedding night he asked if she minded if he wore a red nightshirt.[25]

In some ways they were quite a modern couple. There was never any question of Edith giving up her career as a social worker for marriage. After falling pregnant Edith not only completed her course but continued to work. More conventionally, she returned to her family in Adelaide for the birth. The arrival of the baby seems to have resolved any lingering doubts Edith had about the marriage, at least for the moment. Later in the year they had found a small house in Lane Cove, a northern Sydney suburb. Soon Chester was sending his family the usual maps, floor plans and descriptions of their new dwelling.

* * * *

Late in 1942, Bob McCall, Deputy General Manager of the ABC, wrote a private letter to Brigadier Errol Knox, the newly appointed Director-General of Army Public Relations. Errol Knox was anything but a Blamey stooge. Before the war he had been Managing Editor of the *Argus* and was a friend of Wilmot senior. It was to him Osmar White had written early in 1942 describing the foul-ups in censorship in New Guinea. In his letter, McCall sought Knox's views concerning a solution to the Blamey–Wilmot conflict.

Knox's reply was promising. He welcomed McCall's initiative and stated that he held Wilmot in high regard, and had been greatly upset by what had happened. Although he regarded Wilmot's behaviour towards Blamey as 'foolish and rash and indiscreet ... the door was not necessarily closed'.[26]

On hearing this, Bung decided to take a hand and saw Knox, who repeated what he'd said to McCall. Then there was a mysterious intervention by a senior officer in 'another service', identified in Chester's letters only as 'another bloke', who seems to have been close to Blamey.[27] This 'bloke' told Chester that the Commander-in-Chief bore him no lasting ill will and had acted in self-defence and more in sorrow than in anger. Knox and the 'other bloke' indicated that if Wilmot wrote an apology to Blamey he would be reaccredited. Much as he wanted to return to the AIF, Chester remained wary; there were important principles at stake.

Chester was not prepared to back down on this just to get his accreditation again. However, he knew that even though Blamey's behaviour about the picture contract was suspicious, he had gone beyond his evidence. So he decided to make what amendments were necessary about the films, but to stand firm about everything else. He tactfully dissuaded Bung from writing to Blamey, promising his son would not offend again and rejected some his father's suggestions for his letter.

Chester also rejected Knox's suggestion that he should say a correspondent should be completely loyal to the C-in-C and should never criticise without the C-in-C's consent. Wilmot was determined not to sacrifice the independence that Bean as Official Correspondent had fought for in the Great War. And 'Charlie' Bean, now located in a house at Mowbray Road, Chatswood on Sydney's North Shore, had become one of Chester's close advisers.

As these negotiations developed Charles Moses also played an active role. He had returned as General Manager with the rank of Colonel after Curtin wrote to him personally urging him to come back to the ABC. Anxious to get his best broadcaster into the field he employed his formidable charm to persuade Chester to include some more conciliatory passages in the final version. No copy of the actual letter has survived but it must have been dispatched late in January 1943. Knox suggested that after suitable intervals, Wilmot apply for reaccreditation and in April, Moses made the application on Chester's behalf. Nothing was heard from Melbourne for some weeks, so Moses decided to see Blamey himself. His ostensible reason for undertaking the trip to Victoria Barracks, Melbourne was to discuss the ABC's Army broadcasts.

After their business was completed Moses said: 'About young Wilmot, a rather impetuous young man, but about his reaccredidation.'

'I wouldn't think of it,' Blamey replied.[28]

'It was a double cross,' Moses said when the author interviewed him in 1983, still visibly angry after forty years.[29]

He returned to Sydney to find a scrawled letter from Blamey formally refusing to restore Wilmot's accreditation. 'I've got his apology which isn't good enough. He can't have his accreditation. Wilmot is a dangerous subversive and a communist.'[33]

Moses didn't leave it at this. He and Syd Deamer, Head of ABC Public Relations, took up the matter with Prime Minister Curtin. By now Blamey had told the PM that Knox didn't have any right to make the promises he did. 'These vendettas have got to cease,' Curtin told Moses and Deamer. 'Wilmot and Blamey will have to sit down and have a cup of tea'.[31] 'I wonder if there will be a shorthand writer behind the door,' Chester remarked when told about this, recalling the way Blamey had ambushed him in New Guinea.[32]

Nothing came of Curtin's intervention. The Commander-in-Chief remained obdurate and Curtin let him get away with it. This sort of behavior was typical of Blamey. It was never enough to defeat

A dangerous subversive and a communist

someone; he had to destroy them. As Curtin said later, 'He is a good hater.'[33] But Chester was quick to discern there was another motive behind this coerced apology. It was the film.

The film in question was the AWM's *Sons of the Anzacs*. It was to be a follow-up to the outstanding success of *We of the AIF*, produced in 1939 from official films taken during the World War I. Urged by their new Acting Managing Director, Arthur Bazley, the AWM Board decided to produce a sequel covering the activities of Australia's forces in the present war. There had been a whole range of films taken by cameramen in the Historical Records section of the Australian Army headed by the managing director of the AWM, Lieutenant-Colonel John Treloar, who was filling a similar role to Bean in the previous conflict. As well there were the films shot by the DOI Unit first set up by Damien Parer and then headed by Frank Hurley. Much of this had been used in the newsreels as short news items but not as a continuous narrative. Cinesound and Movietone, who produced the newsreels, had been unwilling to pay to send their own cameramen to the Middle East or New Guinea. So with a few exceptions the bulk of the war footage belonged to the Australian Government and was destined for the AWM. It was this material Bazley intended to use for *Sons of the Anzacs*.

The AWM wanted Chester Wilmot to write and speak the commentary. 'Having been with the AIF as the Commission's representative from the beginning he seemed best fitted to the task,' Bazley was to write later. Chester of course accepted and easily obtained the month's leave from the ABC that everyone expected would be all that was needed. Within weeks of his appointment Lieutenant-Colonel Treloar had been dispatched by Blamey from Melbourne with a copy of Chester's apology to show to the Minister for the Interior and chairman of the AWM Board, Senator JE hawes. As Wilmot had been disaccredited Blamey insisted he ought not to be allowed to write the commentary for the film. As a result Bazley was ordered to suspend all work on *Sons of the Anzacs*. Treloar even urged Bazley not to tell Wilmot what had happened. Clearly annoyed at Blamey's intervention, Bazley decided to consult Dr Bean, still very influential in the affairs of the War Memorial. On his advice a guarded message was conveyed to Chester about the problem with his accreditation. At this stage nobody seems to have told either Bean or Wilmot about Blamey and Treloar's intervention. So Moses on Chester's behalf informed Bazley that the problem with his accreditation would soon be resolved. The board then decided to continue assembling the footage and wait until Wilmot was available to write the commentary. Indeed Collings advised him in May to apply for reaccreditation.

But when Bazley discovered Blamey had rejected Wilmot's application he decided to take the matter to the Prime Minister. (How much the acting director knew about the double cross is not clear, but a furious Moses was keeping no secrets.) First Bazley consulted the Crown Solicitor, who informed him that Wilmot had a prima facie case against the AWM for breach of contract. This was all the leverage Bazley needed. He briefed the PM's private secretary and prepared a memorandum. At the last minute the possibility of Wilmot taking legal action was dropped from the memo but was included in a covering letter by Collings. Curtin was left in no doubt that the matter could end up in court. The PM consulted Collings, Minister for the Army Frank Ford and Deputy Prime Minister Ben Chifley – a staunch supporter of Chester's – before telling the AWM that he could see no reason why Wilmot should not work on the project.

Ironically it seems never to have occurred to Chester that he had a case against the AWM and almost certainly neither he, nor anyone at the ABC knew about Bazley's actions until later. Blamey on the other hand must have been frustrated and furious. The last person he wanted relating the story of Australia at war was Wilmot. In fact, Chester's role in the production of the film was to become much greater than anyone had imagined.

16

SUCH A COMPLETE VICTORY

Chester started work on *Sons of the Anzacs* for the second time on 20 September 1943. His first task was to screen the footage taken by the official photographers that Neville Bletcher and Arthur Higgins had edited. Chester was appalled. After going through some 200 000 feet Higgins and Bletcher had compiled a work print of 12 000 feet. It contained so many inaccuracies that Chester was compelled to take the print apart and re-examine it shot by shot. As Wilmot explained to Arthur Bazley:

> This has been inevitable, for we found in the case of the attack on Bardia ... that nearly 50% of the shots in the working print were clearly identifiable as having been filmed elsewhere, mostly at El Alamein, a number of American tanks which were not in the Middle East until a year later were shown operating in the Battle of Bardia; some men were shown – rightly – wearing battledress and greatcoats, others in different shots were in shirts and shorts.[1]

Chester, who vividly remembered the bitter cold of the first desert battle, clearly found this ridiculous. Even worse were 'a number of false impressions'. The edit suggested that at Bardia 'the Australians were supported by masses of tanks of many different kinds',[2] when they had at most twenty. A Kittyhawk bomber was being made ready for action in one shot but the plane into which the pilot climbed was a Tomahawk and turned into a Kittyhawk again when it took off. 'Inaccuracies such as these would have made the film a laughing stock not only of airmen but of every small boy,' Chester observed trenchantly.[3] In his letter outlining these problems Wilmot pointed out that the DOI had only supplied 'dope sheets' (shot lists) for about 20 per cent of the film it had sent them. Chester, who had been present when much of the material had been shot, did his best to identify sequences using internal evidence. Fortunately, Damien Parer was in Sydney staying down the road at the Wynyard Hotel, a few hundred yards from where Wilmot was working in a 5-foot by 15-foot room in the Commonwealth Bank building. He was able to check through his own films with Chester, Higgins and Bletcher.

Arthur Higgins was an old friend and mentor of Damien's. They had worked together on Charles Chauvel's *Heritage* when Higgins had been director of photography and Parer his assistant. Almost certainly Damien would have told Chester about Higgins's importance in the Australian film industry. The veteran cinematographer had been Raymond Longford's cameraman in the silent era and had photographed *The Sentimental Bloke* (1919), which by 1943 was regarded as a classic. This was probably why in his letters to Bazley, Wilmot praised the way Higgins and Bletcher made the necessary changes, and emphasised they could not have done any better without proper documentation. Nevertheless, Chester seems to have been more than a little high handed and tactless in his efforts to make the film as accurate as possible. At the second screening of the original assembly he stood up and gave a long speech outlining what needed to be done. From a rather plaintive letter Higgins wrote to Bazley later, this did not go down well. This was not the only example of Wilmot's tactlessness. Stephen Stack, the AWM's Film Officer – a warm supporter of Chester's – was mildly reproachful when the broadcaster went straight to Bazley to arrange for Mervyn Scales's secondment to the project.

Wilmot did go through channels, however, when he tried to borrow Parer's friend Ron Maslyn Williams from the DOI for a few days. Williams had been a producer with the Film Unit in the Middle East and had written extensive dope sheets for Parer and Hurley's films. The official explanation from the head of the Department, RE Hawes, was that Williams was too busy. But there is reason to believe the DOI was hostile to the project. In a letter written to Parer in late 1944, Williams apologised to his friend for blocking a later attempt by the War Memorial to make a film with Parer about Australians serving in Europe, because they did not want government films to be made by anyone other than the Department of Information. Moreover, in mid-1943 the DOI was making *Jungle Patrol* from a concept first suggested by Parer. Although a very different sort of film, *Sons of the Anzacs* might have been seen as competition. In any case the department would undoubtedly have been hostile to the cameraman's involvement as there was a very public dispute at the time between Parer and Hawes. Ever since his return from the Middle East in early 1942, Damien had been fighting for improved pay and reasonable expenses not just for himself, but for all the other cameramen and still photographers. It had reached a climax in mid-1943 when the DOI had victimised two of Parer's friends. Damien had responded by resigning, hoping by doing so, that pressure might be placed on the Department. Chester had supported him as best he could by broadcasting an interview with the famous cameraman. It had to be scripted but by adroitly varying the pace of his questions Chester made most of it seem spontaneous. In a deft sideswipe at the DOI, they pointed out that *Kokoda Front Line*, which had just won an Academy Award, had nearly not been made when the department ordered Parer south just as he was about to climb the Kokoda Track.

During the preparation for the program Damien must have

told Chester that the action in the newsreel *Men of Timor* had been staged. Certainly it was mentioned by Parer during the interview. This was an important issue for *Sons of the Anzacs*. Bazley and especially Bean – still a major influence in the institution he had founded – were far ahead of most filmmakers of the 1940s in insisting on absolute accuracy in documentary film. For Bean, manipulating the photographic image was the same as distorting a historical source. Chester and Damien agreed with him.

Of course, Wilmot had been worried about re-enactments in documentary film since he had investigated the making of Robert Flaherty's *Man of Aran*. Consequently he and Scales decided to remove all the staged scenes from *Sons of the Anzacs*, including the Timor footage. Discarding this material created some gaps. These were replaced by maps. Scales also suggested they use a sand map to explain tactics in the desert. This proved very successful with an anonymous 'officer', back to camera, tracing the movements of the Australian, German and Italian forces in the sand with a pointer. They also found some German newsreel showing the build-up before the first attack on Tobruk, including some striking shots of Rommel. This enabled Chester to tell at least part of the story from the enemy's perspective.

One of the reasons Wilmot had been so difficult as they assembled this 'first edition' of *Sons of the Anzacs* – 'a holy terror' Scales described him later – was that the War Memorial had committed to a 19 November 1943 screening at the Sydney Town Hall, which gave them very little time to recut the film. This premiere, or preview as it turned out, proved to be a disaster. While the film was being screened individual reels were still being processed and sent from the laboratory by motorcycle messenger. The sound was distorted and some of the maps were out of focus. Edith was sitting next to the Lord Mayor of Sydney feeling, as she said later, so terribly sorry for Chester, who had been working from 9 am to 11 pm for weeks to get the film ready.

Such a complete victory

In fact, the situation was not nearly as bad as it seemed. The distorted sound was caused by the Town Hall's notorious acoustics – there has always been an echo that muffles any form of amplification – while the maps could be easily photographed again. Indeed when Bazley saw the film he was delighted. But Wilmot and Scales believed there was considerable room for improvement. Even though the young actor Peter Finch's delivery of Wilmot's narrative, especially in the lighter passages, provided an agreeable contrast to Chester's authoritative style, they both believed there needed to be greater variety. Fortunately, when the revised version of the film was being made in early 1944, Damien Parer was back in Sydney. He was now working for Paramount News so there was no danger of the DOI sabotaging anything he might do for the AWM.

Parer had been a great success when he had introduced *Kokoda Front Line* on camera; and equally effective when he had done the same for Cinesound's *Assault on Salamaua*. Damien was still very attached to the story of men of the 2/3rd Independent Company who had featured in the newsreel. The cameraman had decided to become part of the units he was photographing. It had grown out of an earlier idea to make an infantry film. 'Just one section. Show that extraordinary comradeship there [that] is not grown in any other unit … Use three or four characters … show them on patrol, wary, experienced,' he had scrawled in one of his notebooks.[4] For this last assignment for the DOI he had gone over the Bulldog Track – in some places a worse track than Kokoda – and filmed the 58/59th Battalion and the 2/3rd Independent Company in the so-called 'Battle of the Ridges' outside Salamaua in New Guinea. He had covered an attack on Bobdubi Ridge – from a distance; Damien didn't trust the troops. But he had gone in with the experienced 2/3rd when they assaulted the Timbered Knoll, and had captured some of his most powerful action footage. Wilmot and Scales decided to get Damien not just to supervise the editing, 'so there will be no plurry muck ups boys'[5], but to narrate the segment as well. The sequence closely followed an outline the cameraman had prepared when he was making up the dope sheet which had made it clear that there were two engagements depicted in the film. Even though when they were cut together in the newsreels it had much greater impact, for Parer and Wilmot this was still a distortion, and was corrected in their version of the material.

For the final attack they even employed accurate recreations of the sounds of the weapons used by the Japanese and Australians. Chester prepared a commentary giving the general strategic background, but Damien stalled on the pronunciation of several phrases, and with his difficulties increasing, Scales suggested they run the rough cut again so he could describe the action in his own way. Damien settled into his seat and soon lost all sense of his immediate surroundings. Scales remembered him saying, 'There's poor bloody old Jock on his stretcher, machine gun got him'. ('Jock' was Jock Erskine, who had probably been killed by inexperienced militia troops as he was returning from a scouting expedition.) 'There was a woodpecker over that ridge – got Robbie – there he is being bandaged – some other blokes copped it too', Parer exclaimed.[6] He even recalled exactly what was said when one attack was blocked: 'That way is suicide we have got to go round'.[7] All this was taken down in shorthand so Chester could weave this more personal response into his broader treatment.

What the filmmakers hadn't counted on was that Damien was about to get married to Marie Cotter. According to Chester she was 'a very sensible lass' and very much in love with his friend, so it was not that much of a surprise when the following day Parer burst into the cutting room, tossed his bag in one corner, cap into another and announced, 'Well, chaps, getting hitched on Thursday, wacko, the diddle oh.'[8] That finished any work for the day as they all went out to celebrate.

Parer tried to record the new narration on the Wednesday afternoon but his mind was on other things. 'Tell you what, mate,' Parer exclaimed after a particularly disastrous rehearsal, 'Nuptial Mass is about 9.30 tomorrow morning, takes an hour, that's 10.30. Be here by half past 12 with nothing on me mind but this and we'll do her then!'[9] Parer was as good as his word. 'I've a vivid recollection of Damien as we recorded him intent and confident giving everything he had, and it was much, to the job in hand … on his wedding day a gift to the Diggers he loved,' Mervyn Scales recalled.[10] As he spoke the commentary Damien wondered if this more personal style was going to work. It was after all quite unusual for 1944. As it turned out, his honest response to the images helped make the sequence the highlight of the film. As soon as the recording was completed Wilmot and Scales rushed Damien off to a cocktail party at the Cotters' tiny Wollstonecraft flat. It was turning into quite a wild party with nearly 200 of the couple's friends and family crammed into the small space when the married couple slipped away to catch the train to Orange for a brief honeymoon.

* * * *

Late in 1943 Moses heard that Blamey was planning to use the Manpower Act to draft Wilmot into the army. 'A latrine unit was waiting.'[11] Without telling Chester he cabled the BBC: 'Wilmot available'. The BBC had been interested in Wilmot almost since Richard Dimbleby had tried to recruit him in the Middle East. Recently it had been particularly impressed with the reports on New Guinea he had been doing for it on the short wave. With the Burma front becoming more important, Wilmot's experience of jungle fighting seemed ideal to the British. Soon a cable arrived asking the ABC if Wilmot could be released to cover Burma for the BBC. However, they needed the PM's permission. Curtin sat on the request for a month, then refused. 'I have considerable doubt as to the propriety of Mr Wilmot's selection for this appointment … I feel it would be better not to proceed with this appointment,' he wrote.[12]

Clearly the PM felt he could not allow Wilmot to leave the country without Blamey's approval.

Chester decided to have another try at persuading Curtin. In January 1944 he and Edith attended the Annual Political Summer School for the ABC in Canberra. Wilmot used the opportunity to arrange an appointment with the PM. Curtin listened courteously to Wilmot's argument, thought it over, then sent a message via his secretary stating the answer was no. This was confirmed in writing in a letter to the ABC. Edith was with Chester when Curtin's refusal was phoned through to their hotel. She recalled him slamming his fist into the palm of his hand exclaiming, 'I'm going to get through this somehow!' Wilmot did not tell Edith about his next moves. First he went to see Kenneth Slessor and told him that he now had the full story about the picture fraud and would give it to him if Blamey continued to prevent him from taking up the British offer. Would Slessor write the story?

After his return from the Middle East Slessor had been targeted by Army Public Relations and forced to resign. What is more he had despised Blamey ever since he had seen him 'jazzing' in a Cairo nightclub. Slessor had given vent to his feelings in one of the two poems to come from his experiences in the war, 'An Inscription for Dog River' (the other was 'Beach Burial'). A footnote to the title placed the poem in context:

> At this point the hills approach the sea and rise high above the river; together they form a very serious obstacle which had to be negotiated by every army marching along the shore. Here the Egyptian Pharaohs therefore commemorated their successes, and their example was followed by all subsequent conquerors, Assyrian, Babylonian, Roman (and French) down to 1920 ...
> In 1942 General Sir Thomas Blamey had an inscription cut to celebrate the capture of Damour by Australian troops under his command.[13]

The conclusion had been devastating. The men had given everything to their general except their respect. He was more than willing to make Wilmot's exposé a companion piece.

Chester's next contact was Robert Menzies. This would seem to be a strange choice. Menzies had been instrumental in getting Blamey appointed in the first place. But he had written to congratulate Chester on his broadcasts from the Middle East. They also knew each other socially. When Menzies had been Attorney-General of Victoria, Janie Wilmot had hosted a formal luncheon in his honour. Although they were political opponents Menzies was on good terms with John Curtin. Wilmot never divulged what he said to Menzies. In the best traditions of the Melbourne establishment he probably asked for his fellow Victorian's assistance and indicated there was now conclusive proof of Blamey's corruption. Menzies saw Curtin almost immediately. A few days later the PM wrote to the ABC withdrawing all the government's objections to the BBC appointment.

What had Chester found? Probably he discovered that Australian distributors had made mint prints of all the new releases available to the AIF free of charge and that instead of screening them for the troops Blamey had given them to Albert Shafto to run the films in his chain of theatres in the Middle East. In the 1940s this would not have been all that difficult to track down. Almost certainly this was why Blamey warned off Chester in the first place. It was Ken Hall who first told the author about the prints and he worked closely with Damien Parer, who was of course a mate of Wilmot's. Even if Chester had not found out through Damien, the fact that distributors had donated films to the AIF would hardly have been a secret. And once he had that piece of the puzzle a reporter of Wilmot's experience would have had little difficulty in finding proof of Blamey's corruption. What is certain is that he told Slessor he had conclusive evidence and that within a week Wilmot had permission to take up the BBC appointment.

In the midst of these negotiations a cable from the BBC came cancelling the Burma assignment and offering Wilmot a position with 'War Report', the team of broadcasters being assembled to cover the invasion of Europe. Wilmot decided to travel to Britain through America. They closed the Lane Cove flat and Edith and Jane went back to Adelaide to stay with Edith's parents. There were two triumphant farewells at the Sydney ABC offices. Bill MacFarlane, who had become a firm friend since their days in the Middle East, told a series of funny stories about working with Wilmot. This was probably the source of the famous anecdote in which Bill complained about being tired and Chester thundered accusingly, 'What is it I saw you doing between two and four o'clock this morning.'[14]

Almost immediately after Wilmot left for Britain Charles Moses got a phone call from Sir Thomas Blamey. 'I hear Wilmot is going to the BBC,' he barked. 'That's true.' Blamey was clearly furious. 'I don't approve, I don't approve!' Moses was beginning to enjoy himself. 'The ABC is modelled on the BBC, Sir Thomas, and we always like to help them whenever we can.'[15] This only served to make Blamey even angrier. Moses was a far more skilful in-fighter than the Commander-in-Chief had ever encountered in the Australian Army, as anyone who crossed the General Manager soon discovered. He realised that Blamey's next move would be to write to the BBC and the British Army. So Bob McCall was enlisted to write to the BBC explaining there was a personal dispute between Chester Wilmot and Sir Thomas Blamey and any queries about Wilmot were to be referred to General Rowell at the War Office. Like Chester, Rowell had been vindictively pursued by Blamey, who had tried to get him reduced from lieutenant-general to his substantive rank of colonel. In spite of this, he had been seconded to the British Army and made Director of Tactical Investigation, which was to play a key role in the planning for D-Day. Blamey did indeed write to both the BBC and the British Army trying once again to remove Wilmot's accreditation. His letters were referred to Rowell. With great relish Rowell gave Chester a glowing endorsement.

Blamey's pursuit of Wilmot now went back to where it started with *Sons of the Anzacs*. The second version of the film had been in general release for some weeks when it was screened for the Commander-in-Chief in Melbourne on 8 August 1944 at the Ministry of Munitions Theatrette. By then Chester was broadcasting regularly on the Pacific Service of the BBC. At first Blamey only suggested alterations and improvements. Scenes of troops playing two-up should be deleted; there should be more animated maps; it was unfortunate that the trumpeters in the opening should have been so unsoldierly in their deportment. All this was faithfully relayed by Treloar to Bazley. Then Bazley heard that Blamey had told journalists in Melbourne that he (Blamey) had banned *Sons of the Anzacs*. The Commander-in-Chief then wrote directly to Senator Collings. The letter was vintage Blamey.

> The film appears to me to contain so many factual inaccuracies and to fall so far below the standards one must set for historical records of this type, that I appointed a committee of officers to examine the film from every angle ... The report indicates that quite a large proportion of the errors are errors in commentary and I suggest that the best method of approaching the problem is for you to forward to me the typed script of the commentary for investigation and checking by my committee, with a view to correcting misstatements and generally presenting a more correct and more balanced story of Australia's War Effort. The corrected script could then be returned to you for your further consideration, after which you may think it desirable that the whole film should be rebuilt.[16]

In fact the committee did not find any inaccuracies. It only made some comments about the length and 'the failure to present to the public the strategical or tactical or practical programme planned by the command'.[17] Then followed a list of positive material for the new commentary that included: 'With the assumption of command by the Commander in Chief on 23 September 42, plans were made for deliberate offensive action aimed not merely at defeating the enemy in the ridges but eliminating him from the whole of Papua.'[18] This was nothing more than another weak attempt by Blamey to claim to have 're-energised the situation' after sacking Rowell.

If Blamey thought he could undercut Bazley by writing to his minister, he was mistaken. Collings referred the letter to Bazley. Exasperated by the Commander-in-Chief's interference with Wilmot's appointment, he took nearly three months to reply. His letter dismissed all the objections in the report and implicitly refused to let Blamey's committee anywhere near the film. Even now *Sons of the Anzacs* remains an impressive achievement. Wilmot did far more than write the commentary. It is the most accurate treatment of actuality footage to be found in any wartime film of the period. Fifty per cent of the film was shot by Damien Parer. Unlike most newsreel cameramen he shot in sequences, and whenever possible, Chester exploited this to create a strong narrative. Wilmot's commentary has great authority but is never intrusive. He was content to amplify the images and place them in context. Chester never quite realised how good *Sons of the Anzacs* really was, but Damien Parer did, and wrote to Bazley praising the way the sand map and the graphics had been woven into the narrative.

When he was walking the streets of Sydney, explaining to Bung why he had supported Rowell, Chester could never have believed he would win such a complete victory over such a powerful enemy. And the irony is, but for Sir Thomas Blamey, Wilmot would never have gone to the BBC's 'War Report', or have written *The Struggle for Europe*.

17

BROADCASTING AS AN ARM OF WARFARE

When Chester walked into the BBC headquarters at Portland Place in London in May 1944, much had changed since he had last worked there. In 1937–38 Broadcasting House had been a gleaming white ocean liner of a building with a foyer that was virtually an art deco temple to broadcasting. The corporation founder, Sir John Reith, a 6-foot-6-inch Scot nicknamed by Churchill 'Old Wuthering Heights', occupied a third-floor office where staff approached his desk over a carpet that seemed as large as Mussolini's in the Palazzo Venezia. Reith ruled the corporation with an iron hand and with, perhaps, a touch of fascism. He did, after all, keep Churchill and other opponents of appeasement off the air for nearly eight years. Reith's policies on programming were resolutely high minded and dictatorial, given the BBC's virtual monopoly of broadcasting. He didn't believe in catering to popular taste. Reith's dictum was 'He who prides himself on giving the public what he thinks it wants is often creating a fictitious demand for lower standards which he will then satisfy'.[1] The Director-General had no doubt what the public ought to hear and, predictably, was uncomfortable with listener surveys. Certainly there was some high-class programming during the Reith era, particularly in music, although the corporation didn't go as far as Moses and Cleary, and set up orchestras all over the country.

But Reith's BBC never seemed to belong to the people. For many it was too 'toffee nosed'. Anonymous announcers spoke in clipped upper-class 'Received English', and the programs mainly talked down to their audiences. 'Never forget,' Reith told one young recruit, 'the BBC is not an organ of mere entertainment.'[2] By 1944 Reith was long gone. He had left in 1938 to take up a well-paid position in industry, although the former Director-General still cast a long shadow.

* * * *

When Chester joined 'War Report' the walls of Broadcasting House were pitted with small craters and the white surface had been darkened with camouflage paint. There were armed guards on the main doorway and in the foyer sandbags partly covered the murals. He was also probably required to show a pass of some sort – all signs that by 1944 the corporation was regarded as vital to the war effort.

In many ways World War II was a radio war. It has been estimated that during the war around 75 per cent of houses in the United Kingdom owned radio sets or, as they were known then, 'wirelesses'. In Germany nearly every house had a radio thanks to the government subsidies – although tuning in to the BBC was a capital offence! Listening to the radio was a far more focused and communal experience than it is now. There were no programs for the very few who had television sets. After the outbreak of war transmission to the 25 000 TV sets in Britain was turned off. Radio was therefore the British people's principal source of entertainment and information. The BBC was also part of the propaganda war. When William Joyce, soon to be known as Lord Haw-Haw, began broadcasting from Radio Hamburg, he was countered by postscripts following the nine o'clock news that asserted British values. They were delivered by public figures such as the actor-director Leslie Howard,

Robert Donat, the star of *Goodbye, Mr Chips*, and, most famously, the novelist and playwright JB Priestley. However, when his vision for a New Britain took on a slightly socialist tinge and Conservative MPs complained, Priestley was taken off the air by order of the Ministry of Information.

The BBC also broadcast extensively to Europe from studios in Bush House in Maida Vale. When Chester joined the corporation it was transmitting programs in thirty-nine languages. The cool objectivity and honesty of BBC News meant it was trusted throughout Europe. When 'War Report' went to air the program was talking to a family by a London fireside, to a little group in a Midlands pub, to a party of soldiers gathered round a radio truck, to seamen, to French, Belgians and Dutch listening under the shadow of informers and the Gestapo, reaching even clandestine sets known to be in prison camps throughout Germany. Eventually the audience in Britain alone was estimated at ten to fifteen million.

The skills and experience that went into the creation of 'War Report' did not come easily. Chester's friend from the attack on Tobruk, Edward Ward, and Bernard Stubbes along with the usual cumbersome radio equipment had been with the British Expeditionary Force when the Germans attacked in France, but only managed a fragmentary coverage. Their reports had been included in the news broadcasts. Sometimes they were attributed and read in the studio; often the voices of the correspondents were used. The problem for the corporation was that because of the prewar agreement with the newspapers it was only slowly developing a news service of its own. War Correspondent and broadcaster Frank Gillard estimated the staff for News at that time was only seven. This caused many of the problems Richard Dimbleby was grappling with when he first encountered Chester in the Middle East.

However, it turned out the corporation learnt a great deal from Dimbleby's unfortunate experience. He had been among the first to record a commentary against the authentic sounds of a real battle.

Chester was a close second with his description of an air-raid on Tobruk harbour punctuated by the sounds of bombs exploding in the water. This use of authentic battle noise was to become a trademark of all the 'War Report' broadcasters, especially when the BBC monitors discovered the German correspondents were recreating their battle effects in the studio. It was also clear that if they were going to get anything like adequate coverage they needed to employ teams of reporters. This had been advocated by Richard Dimbleby since the late 1930s but back then no one had wanted to listen. The highly successful coverage of El Alamein and the subsequent battles by skilfully placed men like Howard Marshall and Godfrey Talbot demonstrated that relying on a single 'BBC Observer' as they had with Dimbleby was absurd.

Other important contributions to the development of 'War Report' came from Frank Gillard and General Sir Bernard Montgomery. Gillard was a former schoolteacher who had joined the BBC in the late 1930s. By 1943 he had built up a considerable reputation as a war reporter. In an interview with the author, Gillard related the challenge facing the BBC both in terms of its procedures and its equipment:

> We were, in a way, in revolt against the rather conventional ideas of the news management people in London, the news editors, who thought that the way in which you report a war by radio was in the same way that you report a war by newspapers, by print. In other words, you observe what's happening, you go back to some place and write up an account of it, you then get that censored, and by some means or other you get that back to London in your own voice if you can, but if that's not possible it doesn't matter, an announcer can read it for you. And I in particular, I don't want to take personal praise for this in any way, but I was the one of the three who was left high and dry on these matters, and I insisted that radio was a medium with a potential far

beyond that of the press. And they're different, they're different, a different potential. Whereas the press and printed word could convey somebody else's impression, the reporter's impression of what happened, radio had the ability to take the listener right into the thick of the action and all the noise, and the hub bub, and the pandemonium and the chaos and the shouting and the explosions and the yells of the commanders ... You could convey, you could send over the air to the listeners at home by their firesides and you could really take them for a few minutes into the heart of the battle. And I thought that that's what radio ought to be doing.[3]

If the 'heart of the battle' was to be reached and recorded, then the use of recording trucks in the immediate battle zone was a handicap. Consequently, Gillard regularly bombarded the BBC with memos urging the corporation to develop some kind of portable recorder. Not only would that enable the reporter to capture the immediacy of the battle, he would be able to dispatch the recording either directly to the BBC, or to a station to be transmitted to London. Moreover, Gillard advocated a team approach. When the new Director-General of the BBC, William Haley, visited Italy and discussed with Gillard and General Montgomery arrangements for correspondents on 'War Report', the two BBC men told Montgomery that they needed a team to cover every aspect of the invasion. Moreover, the BBC could not be treated as just another newspaper with one reporter for one paper. It was the national broadcaster. There was a nod. Then they said they were developing a mobile recorder – another nod. Finally, somewhat apprehensively, they put the argument for a mobile transmitter. Again Montgomery nodded. Gillard had never believed Army Signals would countenance another independent transmitter in their area. But Montgomery had agreed to exactly that. Later the Field Marshal, as he had become, told Gillard why:

I went through the last war and finished as a Lieutenant-Colonel and never saw my Commander in Chief. I was determined that was not going to be the case with me. Now I can rally my men and I do that through you. Broadcasting is an arm of warfare. It is vital that the men are properly informed so that they have confidence and their morale is high.[4]

At the time each detail of the agreement reached by Montgomery and the BBC men was the subject of long and hard negotiations in London. But once Haley and Gillard had Montgomery on side many of the difficulties disappeared. Not long after the technical department produced its first mobile recorder, known as the 'midget'. It was an 18-inch by 2-foot box, rather like the portable record player people took on picnics. There was a wind-up motor and a needle that cut the acetate disc when one was placed on the turntable as the reporter spoke into the microphone. According to Gillard the machine was far from ideal: 'Individual discs only recorded for two minutes and you could bet one in three of the discs would fail to record and since there was no replay facility you never knew which one it was.'[5]

The midget was first used in action at the Anzio beachhead by Wynford Vaughan-Thomas in late January 1944.

Therefore, when Chester arrived in London four months later on 2 May 1944, he was about to become part of an organisation that through its wide and varied programming, had won the affection of its home front listeners and was trusted throughout Europe. If he was about to work for an establishment that had significantly refined its technical knowledge, then a number of its correspondents – and certainly Wilmot himself – had also refined their craft. 'War Report' and its reporters were about to attempt to cover the largest and most ambitious amphibious landing in history.

* * * *

Planning for a cross-Channel invasion of France had begun in March 1943 under the command of Lieutenant-General FE Morgan. At the Casablanca Conference in January of that year, Morgan was appointed Chief of Staff to the Supreme Allied Commander (Designate), which became known as COSSAC. His orders were to form an Anglo-American HQ for the Supreme Commander (still to be chosen), and to prepare a plan for a crossing of the English Channel. The codename for the invasion of France was Operation Overlord, whilst the landing on the beaches was christened Neptune.

Morgan and his COSSAC staff were confronted with numerous problems for Neptune: the size of the invasion force needed to form and hold a bridgehead; where to land such a force; and, after the landing, the need to provide a speedy build-up of men and material to initially hold the bridgehead and then facilitate a break-out. COSSAC's original force estimate was limited by the then available resources – particularly in terms of landing craft – to a movement of two airborne brigades and three seaborne divisions across a 25-mile front. While the Germans anticipated an Allied landing at the Pas de Calais, between the mouth of the Somme and Dunkirk – the shortest route across the Channel – COSSAC chose Western Normandy, between Caen and the Cotentin Peninsula.

General Dwight D Eisenhower's appointment as Supreme Commander of the Allied Expeditionary Force (SHAEF) was made public on Christmas Eve 1943. His senior commanders would be General Bernard Montgomery, commander of ground forces for Neptune; General Omar Bradley, commander of the American Army Group; Air Chief Marshal Leigh-Mallory as Air Forces Commander; and Admiral Sir Bertram Ramsay as the Naval Commander. Air Chief Marshal Tedder was appointed as Eisenhower's Deputy, and Lieutenant-General Bedell Smith became Eisenhower's Chief of Staff.

Eisenhower and Montgomery almost immediately demanded and won an increase in the size of both the landing force and the

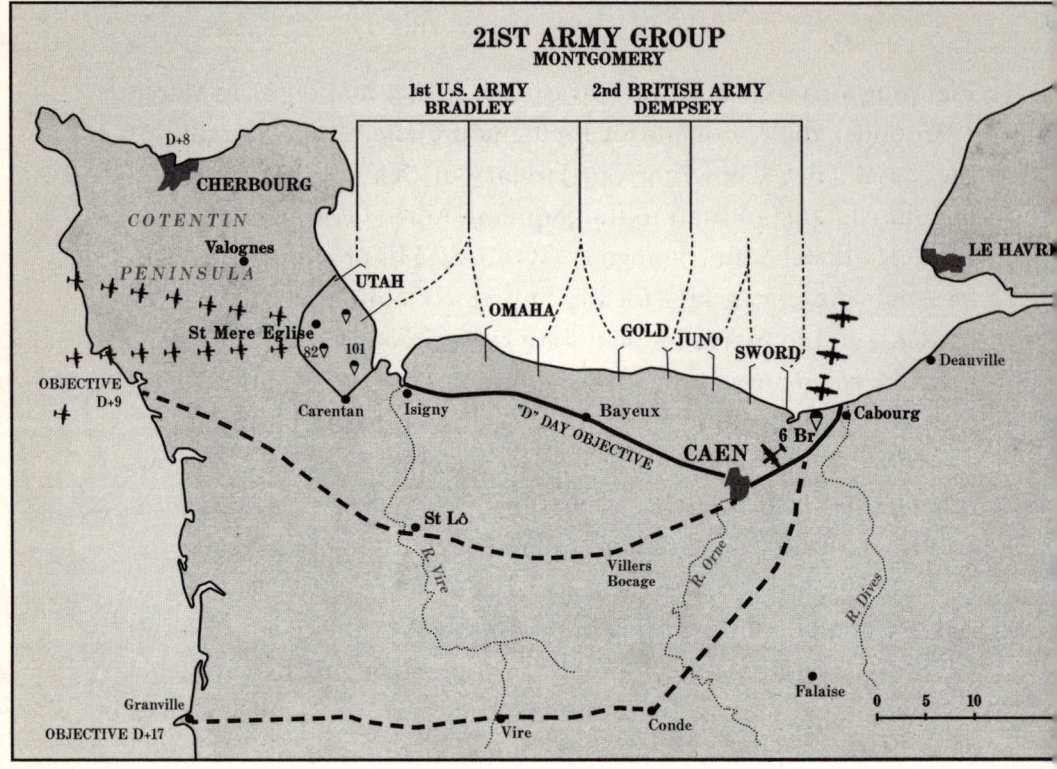

Operation Neptune: D-Day

front for Neptune. The original two airborne brigades and three seaborne divisions across a 25-mile front became three airborne divisions and five seaborne divisions across a 50-mile front. The Normandy coast was divided into five beach landing sectors, codenamed Utah and Omaha for the American landings, two British beaches codenamed Sword and Gold, and one Canadian beach named Juno. The landings were to be undertaken in two parts: the airborne assault was to consist of the British 6th Airborne Division, which was to capture – intact – the bridges at the Benouville-Ranville crossing on the Orne River, to then defend its gains from an anticipated German armoured counterattack and, finally, to cripple the German artillery at the Merville battery, which had the potential to fire upon Sword beach. The American 82nd and 101st Airborne

Divisions were tasked with objectives west of Utah beach. In all, the British, American and Canadian airborne troops numbered around 24 000, and were to be landed just after midnight on D-Day.

Montgomery planned that by the end of D-Day two bridgeheads would be formed: the first between the Vire and Orne rivers, extending from Caen to Bayeux and to Isigny; and the second stretching from the coast of the Cotentin, north of the Vire River, and forming a line from the Carentan Canal to beyond the River Merderet. He anticipated that by D + 8 that beachhead should be extended northwest, west and south. Wilmot would later record that:

> On the left flank the role of the I British Corps was to hold Caen and the open ground immediately south of the city as a pivot and as a bastion, which must at all costs withstand the counterattack of the enemy's main panzer reserves stationed in the area Chartres-Paris-Amiens-Rouen.[6]

From the centre of the bridgehead the US V Corps and British XXX Corps was to secure the high ground running from St Lô to Caumont and thence to Villers-Bocage, to prevent German shelling of the Allied harbours and thus facilitate a rapid build-up of supplies. On the right flank the US VII Corps was to attack west and close off the base of the Contentin and drive north to sieze Cherbourg. With that centre captured, General Bradley's 'full strength would be concentrated for a southward drive to expand the bridgehead into a substantial lodgement area.'[7]

If this increase of the initial lodgement area succeeded, Montgomery planned that by D + 50 with the arrival of Patton's US Third Army and the Canadian First Army, the Allies might hold an area 'including the Brittany Ports and extending south to the Loire and east to the line Deauville-Tours'.[8] Finally, by D + 90 the Allies were to be established 'along the Seine, across the Paris-Orleans gap and down the valley of the Loire to the sea'[9].

In order to gather and deploy the extra landing craft and divisions needed for the expanded plan, Overlord was delayed from May 1944 to the June moon period. Elaborate deception plans were put in place to convince the Germans that the Normandy landings were a ruse, and Allied air and naval superiority were brought to bear for the interdiction of the Channel and the German line of communication in France. In all 160 000 Allied soldiers were to land on D-Day: around 73 000 Americans; over 61 000 British; and around 21 400 Canadians. The risks involved were enormous and the potential for disaster great – the recent pages of history bore ample testimony to the crippling casualties involved in both airborne operations and amphibious landings. Winston Churchill has best described the British apprehension prior to, and during the COSSAC and SHAEF planning for D-Day:

> Thought arising from factual experience may be a bridle or a spur ... while I was always willing to join with the United States in a direct assault across the Channel on the German sea-front in France, I was not convinced that this was the only way of winning the war, and I knew that it would be a very heavy and hazardous adventure. The fearful price we had had to pay in human life and blood for the great offensives of the First World War was graven in my mind. Memories of the Somme and Passchendaele and many lesser frontal attacks upon the Germans were not to be blotted out by time or reflection.[10]

Clearly, the sheer magnitude of the Overlord and Neptune Operations dictated that if the BBC was to adequately cover them, then its number of correspondents in the field would have to increase markedly. In an interview with the author, Frank Gillard identified the coverage required:

Instead of having one BBC reporter with each army, we had twenty-seven altogether that day. We had a reporter on each of the five beaches; we had reporters with the gliders – Chester Wilmot; we had Guy Byam with the paratroops, he went in with them; we had reporters in all the bombing flights; we had reporters out at sea with the attacking naval craft; we had reporters out with the merchant fleet bringing in the supplies; we had reporters at Monty's Headquarters, that was where I was; at Ike's Headquarters, at everybody's Headquarters! So that we really had the place saturated with BBC people and we really had the equipment we needed (A) to record whatever was going on, whatever we could do to produce in the way of pictorial illustration of what we were talking about, and (B), the transmission facility to get it back to London. At last! Perfection![11]

Therefore, while much of the credit for this massive undertaking was due to the BBC technicians and their development of the midget recorder, General Montgomery's full cooperation and permission for the BBC to employ its own transmitter – and his employment of it as a medium to communicate with his army – constituted what Gillard described to the author as 'broadcasting as an arm of warfare'. But it was one thing to have the right number of correspondents spread across critical parts of the Neptune Operation, but quite another to guarantee the quality of their work. Frank Gillard recalled:

The BBC ... had to recruit a very large number, twenty or more fresh people, fresh journalists coming in to the BBC, to become BBC war correspondents for the last phase of the war. Well, they came in very raw, they came in off Fleet Street mostly. They knew nothing about war reporting ... they had to be taught it, and they had to be taught it in a hurry, and they had to be taught to look after themselves, because if you're a really active war correspondent and you're in a forward area, you'll jolly soon be booted out and sent back somewhere or other unless the commander on the spot knows that if there is a problem, you can look after yourself – you're not going to be a passenger, that's the point ... So the newcomers had to be taught all those things ... they had to be taught how to become a member of the army family, if I could put it that way.[12]

* * * *

Wilmot was given an even more enthusiastic welcome from the BBC than he had received in Australia when he had returned from the Middle East in 1942. He was met by the Director of the Pacific Service, George Ivan Smith, and taken straight to Broadcasting House to meet the Administrative Head of 'War Report', Malcolm Frost, and the new body's Director, Howard Marshall. Wilmot had previously encountered Marshall during his last visit to London when he had joined the BBC's commentary team for the cricket. Almost immediately Frost asked Chester what he would like to cover: 'Land Forces, not Navy or Air.' 'What about Airborne?'[13] Frost added that while the details were still secret it was a very important assignment for which they needed an experienced reporter. Chester tentatively agreed. He was, as he confided to Edith, very frightened and wondered, now he was a father, if he was entitled to go on such a hazardous assignment.[14] Wilmot was also worried about Blamey, who was visiting Britain with Prime Minister John Curtin. Unaware of how effectively the C-in-C's attempted intervention with the British Army and the BBC had been quashed by Moses, Chester feared that even at the last minute 'the little man' might step in. He soon realised that such fears were groundless.

Wilmot had presented the PM with a copy of *Tobruk*, and when he next saw Curtin, the PM told him that he had not had time to read the book yet but had asked a 'mutual friend' to give him an opinion. Chester also raised some of the allegations made against him by Blamey.

During these official visits to Britain and the USA Curtin – a recovered alcoholic – was becoming increasingly concerned about Blamey's heavy drinking. There was one last encounter. Chester was walking down a corridor in the Savoy when he saw Blamey coming out of a room. Determined not to give way Chester continued walking. Blamey turned around and went back into the room.

After further consideration, Wilmot was even more worried about going with the airborne forces after he went to the War Office to get Rowell's advice. His old friend seemed to think the idea could indeed be crazy. Rowell must have known that the recent airborne assault on Sicily had incurred appalling losses with nearly half the gliders being dropped in the sea. Close as they were, Rowell could never have divulged that sort of information to Wilmot. But soon after, he arranged for Chester to meet the commander of the British Airborne, Lieutenant-General 'Boy' Browning. In 1944 Boy, as he had been nicknamed from his earliest days in the army, was regarded as the father of the airborne forces. In fact the idea had originally been Winston Churchill's, but the force would never have existed but for Browning's relentless advocacy and the wide range of contacts that he seemed able to deploy at will. He was an imposing man, very handsome, with a strong face and a clipped moustache. Married to novelist Daphne Du Maurier, the general had been one of the real-life models for the brooding Max de Winter in his wife's bestseller *Rebecca*.

Browning was always immaculately turned out and when he met Chester would probably have been wearing the distinctive maroon beret and shoulder patches he had devised for the airborne forces. A stickler for spit and polish – his military career began in the Grenadier Guards – Browning with his challenging manner and affected voice seemed to be a stereotypical upper-class British officer. This was, however, not how he appeared to Wilmot. In the brief description of their meeting that he wrote to Edith, all Chester mentions is the enthusiasm with which the 'Big Chief' outlined the importance of the airborne's mission on D-Day and how he went out of his way to allay the reporter's concerns. Browning then arranged for Chester to observe the 6th Airborne's last exercise before the invasion. It is likely Browning also told Rowell in confidence that at least some of the disasters in Sicily had occurred because his advice had been ignored.

Although *The Struggle for Europe* includes a marvellously evocative description of what it was like to go into action in a glider, Chester left no description of the gliders themselves, when he first saw them. This may have been not to alarm Edith any further. He had already apologised enough for going with the airborne forces in the first place. Sergeant Jim Wallwork of the 6th Airborne gave this description to the American historian Stephen Ambrose of a Horsa glider: 'It was like a big black crow. When we first got in, before we ever flew and felt the controls, saw the size of the flaps, we were very impressed particularly as we were going to have to fly it.'[15] The seats in the cockpit were side by side and 'very big'. Visibility through the front and side was excellent. Each pilot had proper dual controls. It was, according to Wallwork, like flying an aircraft except the engine was ahead in another aeroplane. The glider was tugged on a rope that had a 'Y' arrangement. The films of take-offs show a line on each wing that came together in front of the nose then became a single line to the aeroplane doing the tugging. There was a telephone line along the rope making voice communication possible between the glider and the tug. The only problem for Chester was that the glider had nothing like the stability in flight of an aircraft. As he'd made his usual good impression on the 6th Airborne officers and men Chester seems to have had no trouble in persuading them to let him go up on numerous flights while he put discs on the midget and tried to get the machine to record – all without much success. He described the experience to Edith:

> Before D-Day I carried out several tests in the air with Bill Griffith – the English County cricketer who came to Australia with the English Cricket team about 1936 and whom I met then. He was marvellous and did all sorts of things to test recordings. Actually the glider flies higher than the tug to avoid the slipstream and the pilot uses elevating flaps all the time to keep him above it. The really thrilling time is when the glider lets go the tug and flies alone. When, as the tug goes on, the glider loses speed rapidly. For a few seconds you feel as though you are being dragged backwards but then you get a most wonderful sensation of being buoyant and free – and the air is yours – you are riding on your own power and the power of gravity. If the glider begins to lose speed you just put the nose down and dive a few hundred feet to enough speed to pull out level again.[16]

He found that while it was impossible to record when the glider was diving, there seemed to be no problem when they were flying level. But the midget continued to malfunction.

Convinced the machine was faulty, Chester took it back to the BBC and called in the engineers, who made some further adjustments. Finally, it seemed to work and he quickly returned to the exercise. The 6th Airborne knew all about getting unfamiliar equipment to work and Chester's determination to make certain this new portable recorder operated properly seems to have impressed everyone. They also liked the way he did his best to familiarise himself with every aspect of the operation. On the last day of the exercise, General Browning came down for a final inspection, and formally presented Wilmot with the maroon beret of the airborne forces. This meant a great deal to Chester. When he was fighting to get his accreditation back he longed for the time he would be able put on his war correspondent's uniform again. Now not only was Chester back in uniform, but was entitled to wear the headgear of an elite formation, without of course the cap badge. Later in the war it came to signify that he had been among the first correspondents to land on D-Day.

★ ★ ★ ★

When Chester was assigned to the Airborne Division he had only a vague idea when and how his recordings would be broadcast. In fact the BBC had decided 'War Report' would go to air at 9.15 pm following the by now famous 'Nine O'Clock News'. It was to be presented by the BBC's principal announcer, John Snagge, one of the most famous broadcasters on the BBC. He was chosen at the corporation's insistence to make the historic D-Day announcement on the morning of 6 June at 9.32 am British Double Summer Time. According to his own account, Snagge was only handed the official wording written on a pink card at 9.15 am in the cubicle beneath the press room at Supreme Headquarters in Bloomsbury, where the broadcast originated. He scribbled the opening himself and was on the air seventeen minutes later as the planes of the invasion force droned overhead.

'War Report' anchored by Snagge was broadcast for the first time that evening. It had its own studio, LG1, and down the corridor LG14, where the programs were prepared. Laurence Gilliam, the Head of Features, and Don Boyd of Talks were to take it in turns to edit the program. Each had a distinctive style, and Snagge has described how, as the program developed, insiders were able to pick whether it was a Boyd or Gilliam night. Both were equally as good. According to the official history of 'War Report', the news bulletin was intended to give an objective statement of the major facts:

> The roving man with the microphone gave the authentic
> context, the setting the mood, the significant small incident,
> the very stuff of reality, as it was experienced by the men who

fought across a particular meadow under enemy fire, and were sometimes scared and sometimes brave and often hungry and often tired.[17]

The whole program was designed to run for fifteen minutes so individual items were supposed to be approximately three minutes long. Inevitably the big stories were longer and on those nights 'War Report' would run over. Stories were shared with 'Radio Newsreel', which was broadcast to the Armed Services and, if it was important enough, a report would go straight into the news.

Although Chester had been accustomed to writing quite substantial dispatches in the Western Desert, dispatches he had been easily able to transpose into *Tobruk*, or use as articles, this briefer format was not difficult for him. Wilmot was already practised at describing action, and his debating training enabled him to ad lib brief commentaries and summaries with ease. Another advantage was that his copy was difficult to cut: the paragraphs deftly interlocked and as his prose was always concise he was able to exercise some control over how his material would be used. According to John Snagge, during the great days of 'War Report' staff would always be relieved when they heard Wilmot was coming on line at 5 pm with three minutes, as it would give them a good start for a strong program.

* * * *

Frank Gillard and Chester Wilmot were assigned two of the key reporting roles for the BBC coverage of Operation Neptune. Gillard's role further demonstrates the razor-edged anticipation of just how precarious the operation was perceived to be at the time:

> I was with Monty. The BBC, when we were planning the last stages of our coverage of D-Day, the BBC said, 'Well, we do

have to face the possibility that it will be a failure.' The landings in Normandy. You'll remember that Eisenhower also took that precaution. 'If it is a failure, the man who will have to decide on how to handle it on the ground is Montgomery. And therefore, it is very important for us to have somebody at Montgomery's side who Monty knows, and Monty will be candid with, and who can really give us a first-hand and authentic account of what's happening and the precautions that are being taken and so on. So Frank, as much as you may like to be on the beaches on D-Day, you'll in fact will be with Monty …'

That night, that is on the eve of June 6–7, without telling anybody at all, he [Montgomery] stole away taking only Johnny Henderson, his ADC. They boarded a destroyer … and he therefore, by the next morning, the next day, was in Normandy. And when I discovered that I was pretty cross![18]

Chester Wilmot was destined to have no such ill luck. Gillard vividly remembered Chester just prior to D-Day:

I must have first met him [Wilmot] at [the] final training exercise just before D-Day. I knew his reputation very well, I think he probably knew mine. We met on terms of equality. Not in any sense at any time of competition – never … I found him very congenial, cordial, talkative, but I liked that … but he was always worth listening to, that's the point. He knew what he was saying, he was a very, very experienced war reporter …
I thought without any question at all, he intellectually, in terms also of courage and bravery and determination, he was head and shoulders above most of us, he really was.[19]

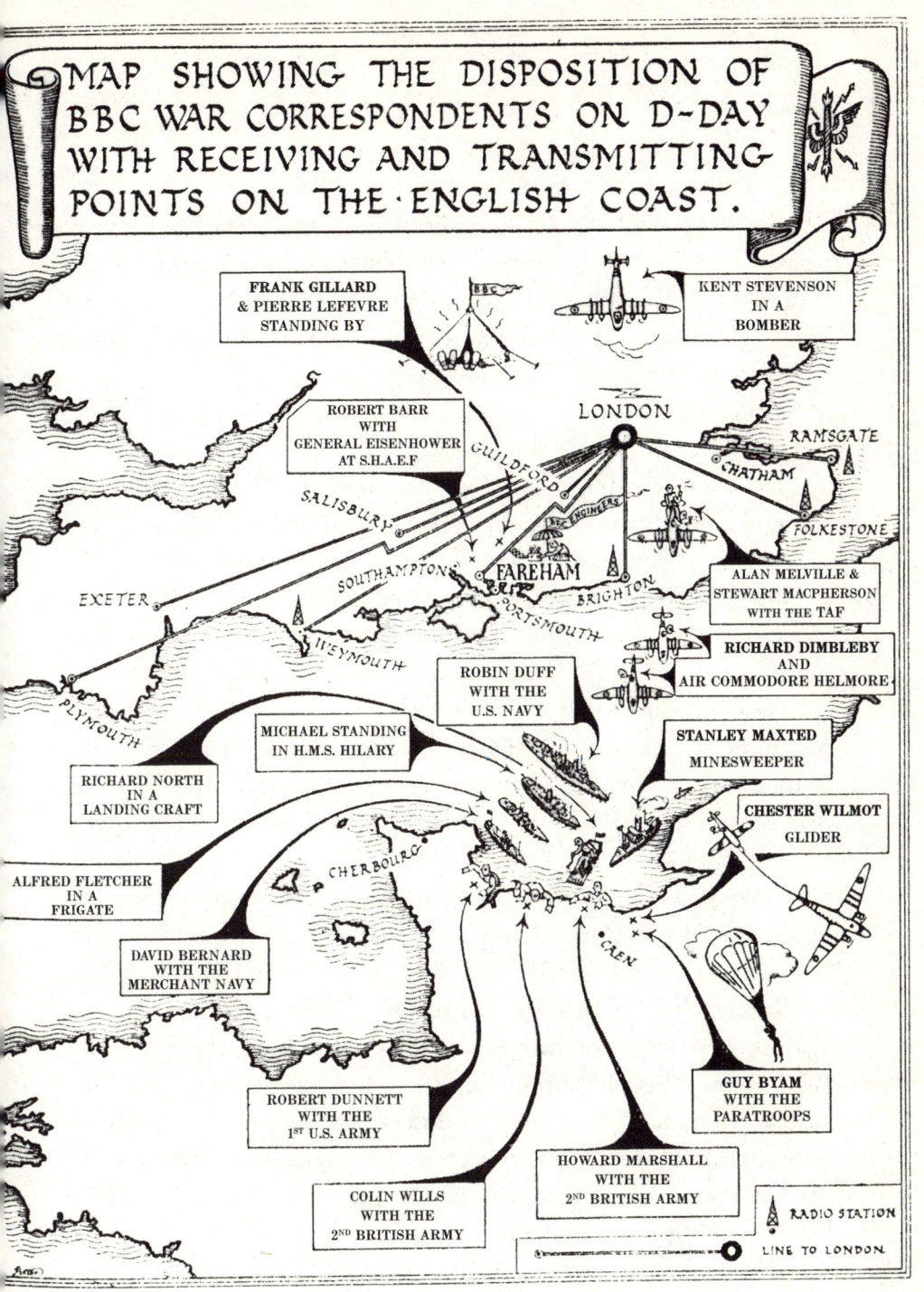

D-Day: The BBC Coverage

★ ★ ★ ★

Wilmot was not told about the Airborne's objectives for D-Day until he was invited with the other correspondents into the tent of the commander of the 6th Airborne, Major-General Richard Gale, and briefed on the whole divisional plan. Chester liked Gale. He later described him in *The Struggle for Europe* as

> tall spare and ramrod straight, with ruddy face bristling moustache and bushy eyebrows, Gale looked a 'Poona colonel' every inch, but this first impression was misleading. When he spoke, the power of his blunt but lucid words revealed a man who could both devise a plan of daring originality and imbue his men with the confidence and courage to carry it out.[20]

As Gale explained it, the 6th Airborne's tasks were, between midnight and dawn of D-Day, to capture, intact if possible, the bridges on the only through-road over the Orne River and the canal between Caen and the sea. As well, Gale's force was to destroy a coastal battery capable of firing on Sword Beach, where the British forces were to land at dawn on 6 June 1944. The objectives were to be secured by two brigades of parachutists and a small glider-borne force. By the middle of D-Day they were to be reinforced by the 1st Special Service Brigade. Six of the gliders were to crash land against the defences of the bridges and seize them by a *coup de main*. By dropping this division behind the coastal defences north of the British, Canadian and American forces landing on the Normandy beaches, Montgomery hoped to forestall any counterattack on the flank of the invading force. Effectively the 6th Airborne was to hold the open flank of the bridgehead.

Chester was to accompany the divisional headquarters, which were to leave Harnley airfield two hours after the pathfinders, who were to guide the division to its landfall. He carefully placed a disc on the midget and recorded his first broadcast of the campaign. It was from 'somewhere in Britain on the eve of Invasion. This is from one of the many airfields from which the first wave of the invasion is being launched to-night.'[21] Wilmot then went on to describe Gale's last speech to his men in which he outlined the broad plan:

> I don't think the Hun'll expect us to land where we are going to land. He's obstructed the whole area so thoroughly that no doubt he thinks no one but a bloody fool would try to go there; but I'm going. The general stepped down from his rostrum: a thousand soldiers whipped off their berets and cheered.[22]

After describing how the troops made up their battle kits, Wilmot briefly sketched in the effect on the men of the postponement of the invasion because of the weather:

> The last few days of waiting have been long drawn out. As the sky clouded over and a gusty wind whipped across the airfield during the weekend, the troops' faces lengthened. The day they thought was the day came and went, and this morning dawned blustery as before. But about noon the word came, and long faces broke into broad smiles.[23]

This description of troops eager for battle was almost certainly exaggerated. Chester himself was more than a little apprehensive. His throat was sore so after breakfast, he had gone to the RAF mess and 'steamed and gargled'. Most probably this was due to nerves. In his notes Chester described the 6th Division only as 'relieved' with 'the long strained faces' he observed earlier in the day now gone. 'Everyone is putting on a forced air of breezy casualness but we are all keyed up,' he wrote in his notes on the airborne invasion.[24]

Even more frightened was David Woodward of the *Manchester Guardian*, an old friend and colleague from the Western Desert. He had heard about the disaster in Sicily and faced with the prospect of battle he lost his nerve. Woodward was about to pull out when Chester took him aside and took him around the hangars telling him what an important story this was and that it was a great opportunity for both of them. It was just what was needed. Woodward made the jump successfully and filed his story. Wilmot seems never to have mentioned his intervention to anyone – it is not even in his notebook. The story only surfaced when it was related by Woodward himself in the BBC memorial program after Wilmot's death.

Late that evening, Chester made a final test on the recorder, noting 'it works or seems to' and then drove over to the glider. He roped the midget into seat four over the landing gear ('more wheel danger,' he thought) and stacked the gear under the seat. 'The discs are doped, numbered and ready – test cuts OK,' he wrote, noticing that the seats opposite were taken up by motorcycles and two folding bicycles. Chester quietly hoped that the securing chains would hold.

Chester watched as Gale farewelled the Pathfinders. Last cups of coffee were drained, cigarettes extinguished and the men clambered into the aeroplanes. Engines roared into life, a signal flashed from the control tower and the six Albemarles thundered down the runway. The drone of their engines had no sooner faded than the throb of aircraft engines filled the night as 1100 transports from airfields all over England, carrying British and American paratroopers, took to the air. The planes climbed and circled over the darkened countryside, their red and green navigation lights 'twinkling like fireflies'.[25] Then just after 11.30 pm the lights moved into formation and faded into the south. Ninety minutes later it was the turn of the Divisional Headquarters.

Gale's departure exuded optimism. Air Commodore Dennis Wheatley, the best-selling novelist whose Gregory Sallust spy series anticipated James Bond by over ten years, came to see the general off. He brought a bottle of 'delicious hock' that was sampled on the spot, and movingly presented Gale with a Crusader sword. At the

Broadcasting as an arm of warfare

door of the glider the station commander gave the general a jar of treacle, to which he was known to be very partial. Chester was to go in the next lift with twenty-six troops and a new friend he had met during the exercise, Brigadier Hugh Kindersley. An imposing figure with his guardsman's moustache and medal ribbons from the Great War, he was going in ahead of his brigade to meet the men when they landed in Normandy. Chester was the last to climb into the glider and joined British Public Relations Officer Peter Cattle forward on the port side near the pilots – a prime position to describe the action. The troops were singing 'Annie Laurie', 'Mountains of Mourne' and 'Land of Hope and Glory', as Chester eased himself into what remained of seat four.

At 1.25 am on 6 June 1944, the tow car began to drag them in the wake of the gliders ahead, each attached to its transport aircraft, the British-built twin-engined Whitworth AW 41 Albemarle. Every twenty seconds Albemarles roared down the strip with the Horsas in tow. Wilmot's glider swung onto the tarmac. While one of the pilots tested the intercom, the glider was attached to the tug for launching. The plane's engine roared, the rope tightened and they were moving; sliding down the runway past the line of guiding lights. The Albemarle was still on the ground but the glider lifted, bucketing as they rose above the slipstream and then the plane was also airborne. Chester could see the lights of the other planes and gliders ahead. He took a last look at the aerodrome and they were on their way.

Chester Wilmot was about to cover the biggest story of his life.

18

HELLO BBC! HELLO BBC!

Twenty-seven of the airborne infantry together with their Div HQ staff officers sat quietly alongside in the glider, their backs to the fuselage. Soft rain bounced on the perspex of the cockpit. All they could see was the guiding light of the plane that was towing them, flying just below. The big questions in everyone's minds, Chester scrawled in his notebook, were:

> Do the Bosche know they're coming? What will the flack be like? Will the parachutists have cleared the poles [that Rommel was known to have erected]? Will their arrival have warned the Germans? Will the Germans have moved their troops to attack the drop zones before [they] got there? Will the drop zones be obstructed by mines, booby traps and wires?[1]

A break in the clouds provided a last brief glimpse of the south coast of England, from which the invasion fleet had sailed. Chester heaved himself to his feet and, as Peter Cattle shone a carefully covered torch on the machine, he placed a disc on the midget to record a half-minute item. Another break in the clouds and the men saw the dark water of the English Channel flecked with the creamy wakes of countless ships. As the glider passed over the massive invasion convoy below, Chester cut a second disc. Around 3 am, just as the disc on the midget's turntable finished, the darkness was stabbed with streaks of light: red and yellow tracers from the guns on the coast at Le Havre.

A sudden explosion seemed to come from inside the glider. In the excitement Chester nearly missed seeing the coast of France. He placed a fresh disc on the turntable, stood up and flicked the switch on the microphone:

> This is Chester Wilmot broadcasting from a glider bound for France and invasion. We've just passed over the coast of France and all around us along the coast ack-ack fire is going up – away to the right of us and off to the left but in front of us there is nothing coming up at all. I can see way off to the right the river that is our main guide for coming into the landing zone. And there now I can see the light that is to guide us in.[2]

Peter tapped Chester's leg to warn him to switch off. There was a harsh crack and a vivid flash as an ack-ack shell hit the glider. The glider bucketed around as Chester placed a new disc on the machine. He was just getting it going when the pilot turned around and called: 'I'm letting go now, hold tight!'

As the midget was beside him, Chester couldn't strap himself in so he stopped recording and wedged his feet against the three motorcycles lashed against the opposite fuselage. There was a sudden backward surge as the glider lost speed and 'hovered like a hawk prepared to strike'.[3] They went into a slow gliding descent. The roar of the wind dropped to a murmur as they glided smoothly towards the drop zone. Then there was a sharp banking turn. With sinking stomachs and bursting ears they pulled out of the dive. Chester's glider was skimming the ground about to land when out of the night another glider came straight at them. The pilot lifted sharply and let it sweep under their nose before they touched down with a jolt after a 'violent lurch to starboard' on a ploughed field. Chester glanced at his watch; it was 3.21 am – they were only two minutes late. Shouts and cheers came from the troops in the glider. 'This is it, chum, I told you we wouldn't have to swim,' came a voice from the darkness. Cattle and Chester untied the midget recorder and scrambled into the cornfield.

They were surrounded by the wreckage of the gliders that had landed earlier, all in far worse condition than theirs. It seemed that the daring plan Gale had outlined so enthusiastically had failed. But when Chester looked more closely things looked better. As they moved towards their rendezvous at Ranville Church, he could see that forty-nine of the seventy-two gliders that according to the plan were to touch down in this field had landed accurately.

Men were climbing out of the splintered wrecks, slashing at the wooden fuselages to free jeeps and guns. Chester found out later that ten of the fifteen anti-tank guns survived – not a bad ratio for an airborne landing. The German flak guns were still firing into an empty sky but there was little sign of any other fighting. All he could hear was the rustle of the troops moving through the cornfield, a muttered curse from a soldier stumbling, the sound of jeep motors bursting into life.

Wilmot did not record his famous broadcast at the doorway of the glider as portrayed in the spectacular and very moving display at the D-Day Museum at Portsmouth. But he certainly spoke soon after landing when some quick repairs to the midget had been completed.

> With grinding brakes and creaking timbers we jolted, lurched, and crashed our way to a landing in northern France early this morning. The glider in which I travelled came off better than most. The bottom of the nose was battered in … the wings and tail assembly, but she came to rest on her three wheels even though she had mowed down five stout posts that came in her

path, and virtually crash landed in a ploughed field. No one was even scratched. We shouted with joy and relief and bundled out into the field. All around us we could see silhouettes of other gliders twisted and wrecked – making grotesque patterns against the sky. Some had buried their noses in the soil; others had lost a wheel or a wing; one had crashed into a house; two had crashed into each other. Yet as we marched off past those twisted wrecks – thanking heaven for our good fortune – troops were clambering out as casually as they might leave a bus …

But as we moved off the landing zone we were promptly reminded we were still in the middle of enemy territory. We could hear Germans shouting excitedly at a church nearby, starting a car driving furiously off. A quarter of a mile from us a German battery was firing out to sea … from positions all around us German ack-ack batteries sent up streams of tracer. The airborne forces had gained their first foothold in France by a daring night landing … but all of us knew it would be harder to hold the ground than to take it.[4]

They were ordered to lie in a ditch and watched as several men with sten guns pushed their way through one of the hedges and moved towards the church. There was a burst of machine gun fire as they reached a crossroads. They took cover in a hedgerow and waited as it gradually grew lighter. More gunfire: bullets zipped over their heads. From further up the road came the sound of a familiar voice: 'Don't you dare argue with me – Richard Gale – get on I say get on!' the general bellowed.[5]

Chester found out later that a runner had come with news that the village of Ranville was free of the enemy and Gale was urging on a column of jeeps and guns. Using his toggle as a halter, he was leading a splendid chestnut horse that he'd found grazing on the landing zone. 'Take care of this animal', he said to his ADC. 'It's

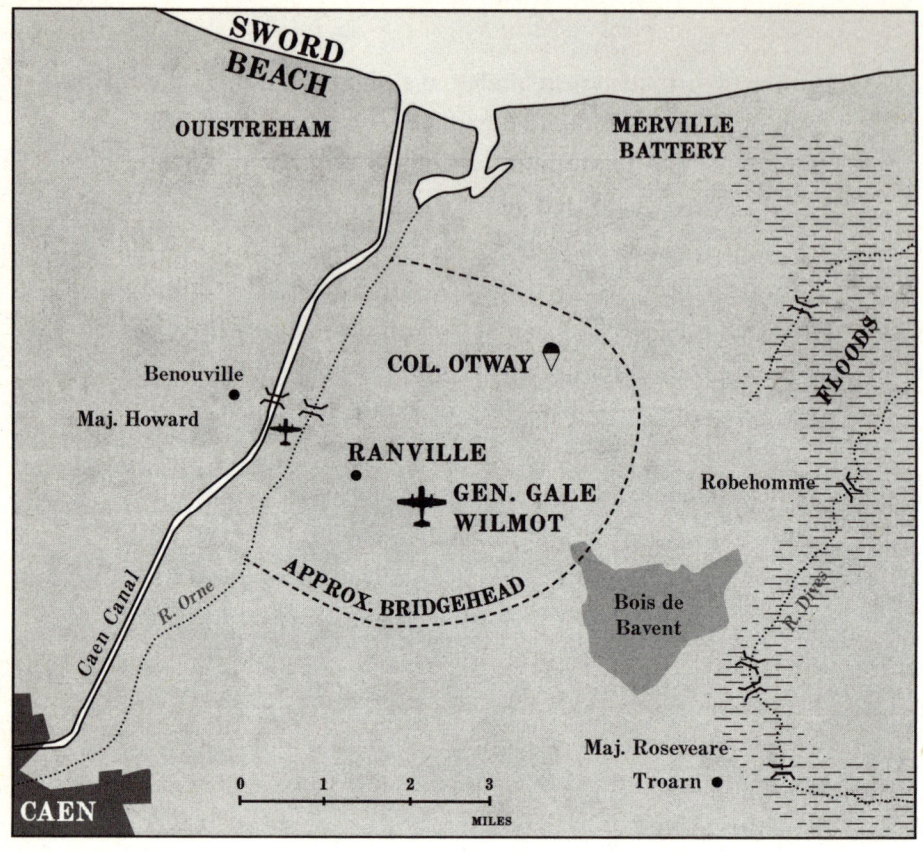

Chester Wilmot: Dawn on D-Day

a fine morning for a ride.'[6] There was a burst of laughter from the troops – a much-needed release of tension. Gale was always good at the theatre of command. Then from overhead there came the thunderous roar of the Lancasters bombing Ouistreham and the beaches. As Wilmot's party moved up the hedged lane the ground seemed to shudder beneath their feet.

Flying in the first of the gliders in his 'lift', Gale had experienced a less hazardous flight than Chester. It was dawn when Gale and his party reached the chateau at Ranville and knocked on the door. The householders were very frightened and 'had not the remotest idea what it was all about'.⁷ Soon the 6th Airborne's Divisional Headquarters was being established.

When Chester arrived the offices had already been set up. Jeeps were streaming into the chateau's grounds. The signallers were working under the trees. At 7 am Gale held a brief press conference with Chester, Leonard Mosley of the *Daily Sketch*, and the young, dashing Guy Byam of the BBC. Byam had cracked his coccyx in the jump and was suffering a delayed reaction from the injury. However, this didn't stop him from recording a riveting description of his experience. Gale told them that two of the important bridges over the River Orne and the canal had been captured and the small bridgehead on the east bank was being held. He was going over to see for himself.

At the bridges Gale and one of his brigade commanders, Brigadier Nigel Poett, swagger sticks beneath their arms, nonchalantly walked around talking to the men in their trenches. Even though there were still snipers in the area they then crossed one of the bridges just before a fire fight broke out with a German barge sailing up the River Orne. To the immense relief of the horrified battalion commander he was able to get the senior officers into cover. Chester described the scene at the Divisional Headquarters in *The Struggle for Europe*:

> Into this bedlam rode General Gale fresh from a visit to the captured bridges. At the top of the front steps he paused and looked around his newly won domain, across the field strewn with parachutes of many colours, across the glider landing zone to the wooded ridge where already he hoped a parachute brigade was established. As he turned in through the door he muttered half to himself:
>
> 'And gentlemen in England now abed ... shall think themselves accursed they were not here.'⁸

David Woodward of the *Manchester Guardian*, the reporter Chester had steadied on the airfield at Harwell, must have felt that at least some of his fears had been justified. When his glider crash landed the man next to him was killed and Woodward's right wrist was fractured. Then, as he made his way to Ranville, Woodward was hit by sniper fire. It was only a minor head wound that he was able to get dressed at a first aid post. But Woodward felt battered and weary as he made his way up the driveway of the chateau. The first thing Woodward saw was a park bench with a press flag tied to it. Beneath it was a trench that had been dug by Chester and Leonard Mosley. It was too small for all three of them – both Wilmot and Woodward were rather burly – so together with Guy Byam they took refuge in the chateau where a press room had been set up.

The Germans were counterattacking. Woodward recalled Chester coming into the correspondents' room and announcing calmly, 'The German tanks are just down the road. They will probably be here in half an hour. I think we've had it.'⁹ The sounds of gunfire increased and the correspondents headed to the cellar to write their dispatches. Later they were followed by a steady stream of wounded. Outside there was heavy mortaring mixed with high-velocity shells.

As he watched the situation develop Gale believed the artillery fire was coming from the west of the canal from the high ground north of Caen. The main attack, as he'd anticipated, was from the south. They discovered later the attacking troops were from the formidable 125th Panzer Grenadier Regiment. Although the assault was skilfully delivered and well supported, the Germans failed to break through the line which was being held by the 12th Battalion. The tank that had alarmed Chester did get to the outskirts of Ranville, but was forced to withdraw and by 1.00 pm the area was clear. There were no further attacks that afternoon but the situation was still precarious. Then they heard the dull roar of approaching aircraft. Chester set up the midget on the top step at the entrance to the chateau, placed a disc on the turntable, flicked the switch on the microphone, and began to describe the scene.

> It's just about nine o'clock in the evening and a whole mass of gliders has just come in having been towed across the channel from Britain. They've received a particularly severe welcome from the German ack-ack defences and the flak has been going up from all around us because we are jammed on two or three sides by the Germans. The gliders are sweeping around us overhead and coming into land. There is no prepared airstrip and the gliders just have to take their chance in amongst the poles and the wrecked gliders that came down last night. And above are the Spitfires providing them with fighter cover. But not much is needed because there has been no sign of the Luftwaffe today. Here come more gliders sweeping low as the ack-ack rises to a new and greater fury.[10]

As Chester recorded his description mortar shells crashed around the British Headquarters. The Germans also targeted Ranville village and the landing zone. Jack Norris, the artillery commander, received a 'terrible throat wound. None of us thought he could possibly survive,' Gale was to write later, '[but] he did.'[11] Jerry Lacoste, the intelligence officer, was also hit and one of the provost men standing just behind the general was killed. That evening there was an attack on the bridges with fighter bombers. A 1000-pound bomb scored a hit but bounced off without exploding. Throughout the evening and into the night the Airborne's bridgehead was bombed and mortared continually. Nevertheless, the arrival of the reinforcements had considerably strengthened the British position.

The next day Woodward decided to return to England. The reporter was unable to write and was in far worse shape than it seemed when he had joined Wilmot and Mosley outside the chateau. Somehow he was able to transmit the story of the capture of the bridges. It appeared on the front page of the 7 June 1944 edition of the *Manchester Guardian*. Woodward also took Chester's discs back with him. They were first broadcast in 'War Report' on 8 June. Edith heard them on the Pacific Service of the BBC shortly after. From Chester's point of view his most important listeners were the airborne troops themselves. Hearing an account of their exploits on the BBC only a few hours later not only boosted morale, it made it much easier for Chester to get further stories.

The next major story Wilmot recorded was of the capture of the Merville battery early on the morning of 6 June.

> On rising ground near the coast east of the River Orne there was a strong German battery position. Its guns were sited to fire along the beaches on which the Third British Division was to land. It was a prime task of the Sixth Airborne Division to capture that battery before dawn … Parachutists were to do the job, but in the darkness and bad weather the paratroops were widely scattered and only 150 reached the rendezvous for the attack in time. The colonel couldn't afford to wait for others, so went in with what he had. The battery position was strongly wired and mined, but they blew the wire with Bangalore torpedos and the first assault dashed in over the mines regardless of those that burst … and regardless too of the machine gun posts, they raced for the guns in their concrete emplacements. They got there … blew up the guns while the second assault wave fanned out inside to silence the machine guns. This took all the colonel's men and just as he went in he was warned that two German platoons were advancing up the road behind him.
>
> At that critical moment help came in from the skies. The original plan had provided that as the enemy went in, three gliders should swoop down out of the night and land right inside the battery position and take the defenders in the rear.

> But the night was so dirty that the gliders couldn't find their targets ... one pilot took a chance and crashed his glider into an orchard right on the edge of the enemy position. As it landed the Germans turned their machine guns onto it ... some men were wounded, the glider caught on fire ... but the rest rallied by a warrant officer, went straight into action to deal with the German reinforcements. For over an hour they held them off, while the main party mopped up the Germans in the battery itself. At 4.45 am, with only a quarter of an hour to spare the position was ours ... 150 men had done the job of a battalion. The colonel fired a success signal and dispatched a carrier pigeon off to England with the news.
>
> The courage that took the battery was the courage that's held this flank.[12]

This was the first account of the desperate fighting at Merville anyone heard, and it was a brilliant broadcast; but Chester couldn't tell the whole story. Of the 150 men who 'had done the job of a battalion', half were killed or wounded. Almost certainly, when Chester encountered the men of the 9th Battalion and their commander, Lieutenant-Colonel Nigel Otway, they would have been bitterly angry with the air force because of the chaotic drop. As Wilmot was to write in *The Struggle for Europe*:

> The Lancasters' bombs fell more than half a mile from the target, narrowly missing the reconnaissance party which was then en route to the battery position. Five gliders carrying the battalion's anti tank guns jeeps and explosives broke their towropes in a squall and plunged into the Channel. The drop was little short of disastrous. Nearly half the battalion landed in or beyond the flooded swamps of the Dives. One 'stick' was dropped thirty miles away and Otway's own party came down

beside the HQ of a German battalion and he was lucky to reach the rendezvous at all.[13]

The RAF's blunders were even worse than Chester realised. It would later transpire that of Lieutenant-Colonel Otway's 750-strong 12th Battalion, at least 192 were never seen again – alive or dead. In his *Dawn of D-Day*, published in 1959, David Howarth revealed that navigators had mistaken the River Dives for the River Orne, and that men were either dropped in the sea or 'more likely the ghastly quagmires of the Dives closed over their heads'.[14] Moreover, not only was Otway dropped near the German HQ, but because of the evasive actions the pilot insisted on taking to avoid the flak, the colonel was the only one to parachute out of the aircraft. The pilot had to go back four times over the zone to drop the rest of Otway's stick. In 1944 Chester was probably aware of at least some of this darker story, but including such details in a BBC broadcast would have been unthinkable. Still, Wilmot was right when he described the 9th Battalion's seizure of the Merville battery as a great feat of British arms.

In spite of the danger Chester enjoyed his time with the 6th Airborne. 'I never had such good facilities … they gave us a jeep. We were told everything,' he wrote to Edith,[15] the memory of being banned from interviewing senior officers in New Guinea still rankling. He was even more flattered when Gale told the colonel of his reconnaissance regiment: 'Tell him what you told me – he's almost one of my staff now.'[16] It must have seemed like old times with Rowell and Allen.

On Monday, 12 June 1944, Chester and Leonard Mosley decided it was time to return to London. Wilmot's midget had broken down and Mosley needed to file his stories. They were farewelled by a crowd of senior officers at the headquarters. Among the men he visited before his departure was Hugh Kindersley, who had flown with him in the same glider. Chester promised to phone his wife as soon as he got back to the BBC. By a tragic irony, half an hour after she received the call, Brigadier Kindersley was seriously wounded. As Wilmot drove back to the coast,

> the roads were packed with traffic – guns tanks, mobile workshops … coming forward; empty vehicles going back; and along the side of the narrow, muddy roads, lines of infantry … the green fields [were] studded with dark shapes, camouflaged shapes, dumps of ammunition and guns, vehicles and tanks.[17]

Chester believed that since he had been able to visit the beaches two days before the expansion had been 'tremendous'. He was certainly right about the logistical build-up. About the same time Richard Dimbleby had broadcast a similar report describing the supply ships from the air. But as Chester was to discover when he researched *The Struggle for Europe*, much of the optimistic tone of the reporting of these early days, including his own, was unwarranted. The landings on the American and British beaches were a near-run thing. Had the Allied deception plan that persuaded the Germans the real invasion was to be across the Pas de Calais and that the Normandy landings were a feint failed, or if Rommel had been at his HQ in France and had been able to get the panzers to the beaches, it could have been a very different story. But as it was, by 12 June 1944, Ground Forces Commander General Montgomery had established his beachhead. Wilmot and Dimbleby's impression of vast amounts of supplies heading for France was accurate: 326 000 men, 54 000 vehicles and 104 000 tons of stores had been landed successfully.

Wilmot was back in London that night. He found the BBC's coverage had 'wiped the floor' with that of the newspapers. Major print correspondents and rivals from the Western Desert, such as Ronald Monson and Alexander Clifford, had not been to France at all. Chester was also something of a hero at the BBC. He was the only correspondent who had been able to get his midget to work.

With Wilmot's return to London there were some large gaps in the ranks of correspondents with 'War Report'. Guy Byam was still 'bomb happy'. Howard Marshall had gone in with the British troops on D-Day and had been dumped into the sea twice! He did manage to get to a microphone, his clothes sodden and notes ruined, to ad lib one of the highlights of the 'War Report' D-Day coverage; but after Marshall went back to France again and returned he was exhausted and had been in England since the 8th. Frank Gillard had followed Montgomery to France and was at the general's Tactical Headquarters at Creully, setting up the BBC's transmitter in the tower of a nearby chateau, and was yet to begin transmitting stories. Consequently the corporation was anxious to get Wilmot back to Normandy. Unfortunately, once they managed to get him on a transport along with the much-needed new transmitter, the ship was delayed. Wilmot, still very much ahead of the game, relaxed, caught up with his sleep, and wrote to Edith:

> My darling one – at long last I've managed to get back to a typewriter for you … I'm feeling really magnificently well though I haven't had much rest … the sense of achievement is so great that tiredness doesn't seem to matter. Oh Darling, I hate being away from you and Jane, but this is really worth it. It must put me right back on top in Aust and must give our friend [Blamey] a g[rea]t deal of concern and annoyance. (I get rare pleasure out of thinking that every time he listens to the radio news of the second front, he has to listen to the hated name.)[18]

* * * *

Throughout June 1944 there were four attempts by the British Forces to seize the town of Caen, including the Villers-Bocage envelopment of 13 June. Although the Allies inflicted heavy casualties on the Germans, none of the operations was successful. Soon after returning to France, Chester was covering these operations. From his base at Bayeux, one of the few towns that had been captured undamaged, he described for Edith a typical day as a war correspondent, broadcasting for both 'War Report' and the Pacific Service of the BBC:

> Up 7.30, breakfast at the pub – off by jeep to a press conference that gives us the latest information. Back to the transmitter. Write 150–250 words on the situation, add this to a piece say, 350–450 words written the night before (usually a colour piece) – get the whole thing censored and go on the air to Australia at 0946 local time. That is quite a rush but it's been working. Then off by jeep ... to do the rounds of the four headquarters, Divisional and Brigade as necessary.[19]

Wilmot found his stories in two ways. The first was to 'go out ... in search of the highlights of the previous day and night's fighting'.[20] He'd pick up leads from the early morning press conference and track down the participating units. Chester would use the rapport and trust he'd built up with officers and their soldiers to piece together his story. Later he tended to avoid the press briefings 'because any question I ask gives the other reporters leads to my stories'. But it was his second method that was the ultimate challenge. When it came off it provided the most graphic, dramatic and immediate stories. Chester described it as going 'up to where things are expected to happen that day'.[21] In fact, it meant taking calculated risks to get close enough to the action to get the story he wanted. He then reported about what he saw succinctly in three or four minutes. This is what made Wilmot a bastion of 'War Report'. Chester described one such example to Edith:

> One day last week I arrived near the front and found that at 6.30 am some anti-tank gunners had knocked out four German

tanks. I took the midget up to the gun positions, set it up in an old German trench where the German tanks were lying and interviewed a sergeant who KO'd the first three shots he had ever fired. That disc was relayed over the channel to London later in the day and was on the BBC that night. We were really rather lucky finding the sergeant still in the same place – also lucky that three Germans in a trench 50 yards away were not bloody minded. We were just finishing recording when two officers came snooping around looking in the abandoned German trenches and they found these Huns lying low ... they were then captured.[22]

★ ★ ★ ★

While the British and Canadians were engaged in their slow, costly and seemingly fruitless advance upon Caen during June 1944, progress in the American sector had also been slow. Late that month Montgomery had ordered General Dempsey and his British Second Army to continue to advance in, but primarily hold, the Caen sector. Meanwhile General Bradley's American First Army was to turn on the left in the Caumont area and to the south and east to gain a general line Caumont–Vire–Mortain–Fougères. After gaining that line, Bradley was to deploy one of his corps to turn onto the Brittany Peninsula and the remainder of his Americans to stage a strong thrust south of the Bocage country to successively capture Laval–Mayenne and Le Mans–Alencon. Montgomery ordered these operations to commence on 3 July.

Although General Bradley had a significant superiority in men (around fourteen divisions to six), and greater firepower across a roughly 50-mile front, the terrain favoured the defenders, who, Hitler had ordered, were to yield not an inch of ground. After a week of desperate fighting Bradley's First Army had made only modest advances. Chester Wilmot covered a number of their engagements during the attempted break-out. His dispatches vividly described the difficulties Bradley experienced. His dispatch of 6 July 1944 explained:

> The country through which the Americans are fighting their way south is much more difficult than it looks on a map. The base of the Cherbourg Peninsular is 37 miles wide from coast to coast, but this 37 miles is so broken up by swamps and flooded river valleys that in the narrowest part there's less than 10 miles of dry land ... and the worst part of the front is the section south of Carentan, where the road to Periers runs between two broad swamps along a strip of firm ground which is only a mile and a half wide.[23]

Chester identified the resulting bottleneck; the fact that only one decent road ran through that bottleneck; that the Germans had felled trees and laid them across the side tracks; and, finally, that their anti-tank and machine gun emplacements made progress very slow.

During a dispatch the next day, Wilmot observed the Americans' crossing of the River Vire and their subsequent attacks upon the German high ground to eliminate their shelling of those crossings. He succinctly noted the longer term consequences:

> Although the American thrust southward hasn't been rapid the German reserves have been fully taxed. They've been switching reserves from sector to sector as first one thrust developed and then another. They've been robbing Peter to pay Paul and tonight both Peter and Paul must be calling out for more reinforcements as the American pressure southward continues.[24]

Chester's dispatch the following day, 8 July 1944, not only gave further evidence of the pressure on German reinforcements, but also showed that he must have been well briefed by the Americans. He identified the SS 2nd Panzer Division as being the German reserve against the advancing Americans, and said that 'this division has not been sent as a whole in one area' but that 'various elements have been pushed up to plug widely separated gaps in the line, which must now be strained almost to breaking point.'[25]

* * * *

By mid-July everything was coming together for Wilmot. Gillard had arranged for him to do regular commentaries on the news for 'War Report', and his reputation had been further enhanced by the broadcast on the Nebelwerfer (a German rocket mortar launcher with a distinctive moaning sound that Wilmot had been able to record for the first time) and, judging by the BBC's internal memos, the success of the D-Day dispatch. Finally, on 16 July 1944, Chester met General Bernard Montgomery. It was a particularly auspicious occasion; the presentation of medals to the 6th Airborne Division and Lord Lovat's commandos. Wearing his maroon beret, Chester was introduced to Monty by General Gale, who emphasised that the correspondent had landed with the Airborne on D-Day.

Montgomery was in good form. After congratulating the troops, he told a gruesome story about a fanatical SS officer who said he would rather die than accept a transfusion of British blood. 'So he died!' said Monty to loud cheers.[26] Needless to say, Chester wanted the speech for the BBC. Montgomery agreed to let him record the occasion but placed the discs under a temporary embargo. Chester packaged up the discs and enclosed a letter informing Marshall, now directing the unit in France, about the embargo: 'These cannot be broadcast – at least not yet – they can be broadcast subsequently if we get a script transcribed to Monty of the parts he wants used.'[27]

Despite Wilmot's clear letter, two nights later extracts from his recording of the ceremony went to air on 'War Report'. Montgomery was furious. He had been listening to the broadcast at his tactical HQ and immediately contacted Brigadier Neville, the head of the Publicity and Psychological Warfare Department. It was decided that Wilmot was to be sent back under escort to Britain until the matter could be investigated. Meanwhile, Chester was on a hilltop preparing to describe the opening moves of what was to be known as Operation Goodwood. The recording van had been parked in a nearby sunken road and Wilmot planned to spend the night in a slit trench so he and his engineers could set up the recording gear before dawn. Chester had also borrowed two signal sets along with the operators from 6th Airborne. He had managed to get the frequencies of the main units taking part and he wanted the engineers to record the inter-tank talk on the radio sets. At midnight Chester went back to 6th Airborne's HQ. A message was waiting for him stating that a public relations officer was coming to take him to Second Army HQ. When he found out about the 'War Report' broadcast, Chester rang the Chief Public Relations Officer and read out a copy of the letter that had accompanied the recordings. The PR Chief agreed to allow the correspondent to stay on the hill until morning.

Chester was still on the hill with General Gale when the mass air attack prior to the launching of Operation Goodwood came over:

> Hello BBC! This is Chester Wilmot broadcasting ... on the eastern bank of the Orne overlooking Caen and the country east of Caen. The R.A.F. has just begun a tremendous bombing raid on this area between Caen and Troarn. It's just about a quarter to six now in the morning, and the sky is thick with ... flares ... have been dropped by the Pathfinders and Caen itself is now completely blotted out by the smoke and each of the explosions.[28]

The sound of the recording still survives and it is very impressive. He was, of course, describing the controversial virtual obliteration of Caen that was to be discussed at length in *The Struggle for Europe*.

Chester returned with his escort to BBC HQ to wait for Howard Marshall, who had taken up the matter with Montgomery. The news was devastating. Marshall informed Wilmot that he was to return to England immediately. In a letter to the BBC's controller of news the next day, Marshall made it clear that Chester's fate hung in the balance:

> The C-in-C has decided, and will not be persuaded otherwise, that Wilmot must return to England immediately, whether he is guilty or innocent, and that Neville must enquire thoroughly into the facts. If Wilmot is innocent, he can return immediately; if he is 'guilty', he must never return to this theatre of war.[29]

The flight to England was a nightmare – 'one of the worst journeys of my life', Chester told Edith. Memories of New Guinea and Blamey flooded back. He had been disaccredited once and he knew a second disaccreditation would certainly finish him. Although he had covered himself with a copy of his letter written to Marshall about Monty's embargo of his broadcast, his mind raced with horrendous – if unlikely – scenarios. What if his plane was shot down and he should fail to have the chance to vindicate himself? In the end, would Blamey be proved right after all?

Four memos written by Marshall to the controller of news, at the BBC, portray the former's professional incompetence and his initial failure to grasp the consequences of his actions for both Wilmot and 'War Report'. On 18 July in a letter given to Chester to take back to London with him, Marshall described the episode as 'a storm in a tea-cup', and said that it could be resolved by 'tactful handling'. In the following sentence, he stated that 'if things look like hanging fire, it is absolutely vital that we have a substitute for Chester out immediately'.[30] The point is that the potential for 'hanging fire'

– and, by extension, Chester Wilmot's career – was completely of Marshall's making. Two things saved Wilmot: his copy of his original letter, and Marshall's soon-to-be given admission of responsibility for failing to enclose Chester's letter. This evidence was more than enough to clear Wilmot with Neville. But there was a far wider issue at stake.

During a meeting with Mongomery on 19 July 1944, Marshall was told that he, (Monty) was 'greatly concerned about the danger of giving news about so important an operation to the enemy, a danger much increased by the speed of up-to-date radio communications'.[31] Monty was in fact informing Marshall that he was not prepared for 'War Report' to be giving the enemy an up-to-date situation report every night at 9 pm! Given the fact that the German communications had been hard hit, and that 'the news of the battle was not getting back from the front to their army commanders nearly as fast as it was to ours', he could not afford to take 'the slightest risk of telling the Germans anything they did not know'.[32] Monty's angst was entirely understandable. At that very time, Monty said, the British were engaged in an operation south-west of Caen; that the BBC had been briefed that the operation was not a major attack but a deception attack; and, as the BBC had 'virtually said so', it had therefore compromised his plan. Marshall was told that Monty was 'not blaming the BBC for making the statement, but pointing out how the most innocent remark, duly passed by censors, might … do irreparable damage'. And Monty was not prepared to take chances: he banned BBC broadcasts and print news for 24 hours, 'except colour stories'.[33] Montgomery was coming to terms with the new speed of communications that on the one hand could be used to both inform and rally his army, but on the other could cause serious breaches of security.

It was the beginning of the end for Marshall. For the moment his lapses had been overlooked. His famous voice, especially when describing the cricket, had become a BBC institution. Nevertheless as far as the military was concerned, one more indiscretion and he was finished. Only weeks later, desperate to be first with the story of the capture of Paris, Marshall went to air live without a censor. As a result he was suspended from working in Europe for six weeks. Still supportive, the BBC argued that if broadcasters could get to Paris so should the censors. But as Chester pointed out in a letter to Edith, the censors had literally been in the next street. Although he was still referred to as the director of 'War Report', Marshall was effectively finished with the organisation he had helped to set up. After the war the golden-voiced broadcaster continued to excel as a cricket commentator.

* * * *

When Brigadier Neville rang Richard Dimbleby (who was filling in as Traffic manager at the BBC) with the message exonerating Wilmot he had some additional information for the broadcaster:

'If Chester Wilmot likes, he may see the Commander-in-Chief when he returns to France.'

'You mean surely,' replied Dimbleby, 'if the Commander-in-Chief likes, Wilmot may see him.'

'No,' said Neville, 'I mean what I said, if Wilmot wants to see General Montgomery, the General would be glad to see him.'[34]

Chester was of course delighted. The meeting took place at Montgomery's Tactical HQ, where the general and his team of young liaison officers monitored every phase of the current fighting. Overlooking Monty's caravan was the tower of the chateau where Frank Gillard had set up one of the BBC's transmitters. Chester realised all was well when Monty offered him tea and then went on to explain that he could not allow a speech to be broadcast that he had embargoed, so, as Chester had seemed responsible, he was sent back to England until it could be investigated. 'I know it is not a good thing for a correspondent to be sent back from a theatre of operations, but at the time there was no alternative,' said Montgomery.[35]

Then followed any war reporter's dream: a discussion of the campaign by the Commander-in-Chief. Monty explained why the Germans would not mount a counter-attack, and discussed how the Caen battle would affect the campaign as a whole. He then asked Wilmot why he thought the London papers had made such a fuss about the failure to capture Caen. 'They speak as if we were going well and then failed.' Feeling he had to be absolutely honest, Chester told Montgomery that it was the use of the word 'breakthrough' in the original communiqué which had resulted in headlines such as 'Monty Does It Again', and 'Monty Breaks Through'.

'Well, that is largely my fault', replied the general. 'I drafted the original communiqué and when I said "breakthrough", I didn't realise the press and public would jump to such conclusions.'[36]

Some days later Chester received a letter from Montgomery stating how glad he was to have been able to apologise personally for the inconvenience he had caused the reporter. As a peace offering Monty enclosed a signed photograph of himself. Chester then took a hand in the dispute over the 'breakthrough' in his dispatch of 24 July 1944:

> I'm afraid that there has been a certain amount of public confusion because the term 'breakthrough' was used in the first official announcement ... after that hopes ran higher than was justified. From the start the offensive had limited objectives. We had aimed to do three things – the first to extend our bridgehead on the east back of the Orne beyond Caen ... second to destroy the German forces in this area ... to bring to battle the armour,

which is the core of Rommel's reserve. There was no intention of sending British armour thrusting on and roaming beyond the Orne and Caen.[37]

Almost certainly this was based on the briefing from Montgomery himself and reflects the scaled-down objectives the general had introduced just before launching the attack. Montgomery's briefing and Chester's subsequent dispatch are interesting. There is more than a hint of the general manipulating the correspondent, but from Wilmot's perspective, there came two positive outcomes: after a career-threatening dispute with the general he had had the opportunity to develop a positive relationship with him and as a direct result he simply got a great story.

But an intriguing train of events occurred at the time of the embargo on Wilmot's dispatch, his subsequent briefing by Montgomery upon his (Wilmot's) return from England, and Chester's despatch concerning the 'breakthrough' at Caen.

The supposed 'breakthrough' by the British at Caen – codenamed Operation Goodwood – was to have been synchronised with General Bradley's planned break-out from the American sector (Operation Cobra). Goodwood had originally been planned for 18 July 1944 and Cobra for the 20th. Some measure of Montgomery's success in drawing the majority of German manpower and resources onto the Caen sector may be gauged by the fact that as both operations commenced, General Dempsey's British Second Army comprised fourteen divisions facing an equal number of enemy divisions – and 600 tanks – while General Bradley's First Army, numbering fifteen divisions (with a further four divisions under General Patton in reserve), was to confront nine German divisions.

Although General Bradley had intended to launch Cobra on 20 July, poor weather had delayed the operation until the 25th, the day after Chester's meeting with Montgomery. Cobra was a resounding success. In *The Struggle for Europe*, Chester would record that the

Hello BBC! Hello BBC!

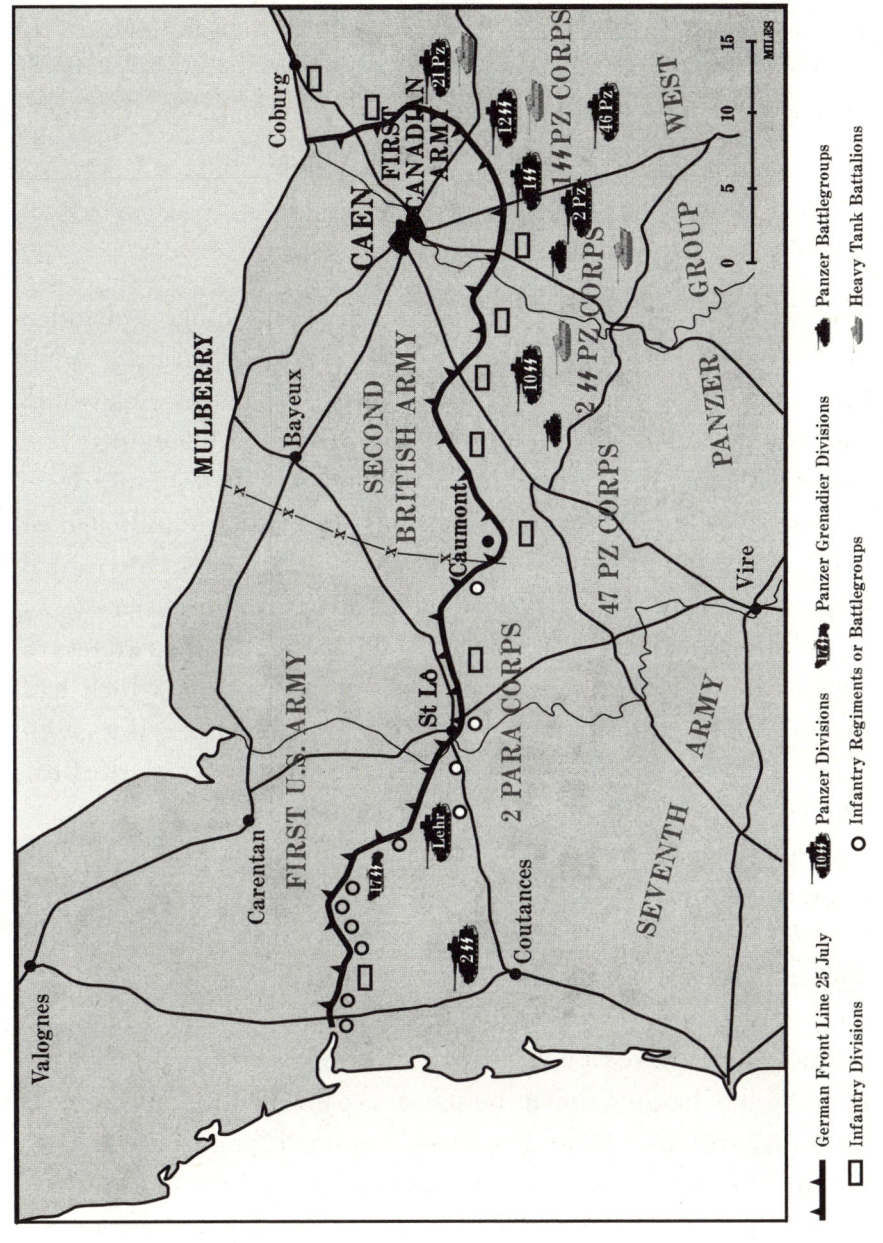

Goodwood & Cobra: 25 July 1944

critical day was 27 July, when 'the two armoured divisions of the VIII US Corps broke through from Periers and Lessay and swept down upon Coutances, which was captured during the afernoon. The remnants of a half a dozen infantry divisions were cut to pieces.'[38]

★ ★ ★ ★

The Battle of Normandy, almost seven weeks long, concluded on 19 August 1944. In the end, it was a crushing defeat for Adolf Hitler's 'Fortress Europa': estimates of the German losses would vary between 300 000 and 400 000; approximately 3000 guns were either destroyed or captured; over 1000 of their prized tanks were destroyed; around 40 of their divisions were either eliminated or badly mauled; and twenty of their senior commanders (divisional commanders and above) were either killed or taken prisoner.

During that campaign Chester Wilmot had, despite two return trips to London, completed well over 100 dispatches, which had begun with his action-packed landing behind the enemy lines with the 6th Airborne, through operations in the Caen area with the British 21st Army Group, and also on occasions with the Americans.

Just before he had returned to France, there had been a terrible engagement outside Villers-Bocage. On 13 June 1944, SS Captian Michael Whitman was leading a group of five from the 501st Heavy Tank Battalion when he saw a halted British column of tanks from the 7th Armoured Division just beyond Villers-Bocage. 'They are acting as if they have won the war already,' muttered his gunner, Corporal Woll. Charging down the stationary line, Whitman slammed shell after shell into armour and trucks at nearly point-blank range, finally ramming a last Cromwell tank aside that was blocking his path. In the High Street of Villers-Bocage Whitman destroyed three tanks of the County of London Yeomanry Headquarters Group.[39]

The attack by a single German Tiger Tank effectively destroyed the spearhead of the British offensive. It demonstrated the disparity between the German and British equipment. As Max Hastings observed in his groundbreaking *Overlord*: 'The British authorities were at pains to stifle any public debate about the shortcomings of their tanks, although these were well-known throughout the British army.'[40]

In fact both Prime Minister Churchill and Secretary of State for War, PJ Grigg, were at worst lying, or at best being evasive. Churchill claimed that British armour was at least equal to the forces of any other country in the world while Grigg regularly insisted that the public discussion of this issue was not in the public interest.

It is against this background that Wilmot's contemporary reporting of tank engagements for the BBC has to be understood. 'The Strength and Weakness of Our Tanks':

> We've now reached a stage in the Normandy campaign, when we can use our tanks to better advantage than we've been able to do before. The area we're fighting in now – the Bocage country – is not ideal for tanks, but it is the most suitable country we've struck so far for our tanks. In the open cornfields, east of Caen, our armour was brought to a standstill by the German anti-tank screen. The anti-tank gun is still the master of the tank and in open country it's impossible for tanks alone to deal with dug-in anti-tank guns, or tanks used in an anti-tank role. That was the prime reason why our tanks couldn't break right through in the Caen sector …
>
> But in the centre of the Allied line, in the area south and southeast of Caumont, the country is open enough to allow tanks to manoeuvre across country … but not so open that the German anti-tank guns and tanks can get long fields of fire. The Germans haven't enough anti-tank guns and tanks to hold every road and lane. Because their tanks are slow and not very manoeuvrable, they tend to stick to the roads and they can't move quickly to counter our outflanking. Consequently our tanks are able in this terrain to

manoeuvre into position to attack the vulnerable flanks of the Panthers and Tigers, without exposing themselves to the superior German fire-power.

> Since 'D' Day I've talked to many of our tank crews and senior commanders about the relative merits of different types of tanks fighting in Normandy. Their views amount to this … you can't have heavy protective armour, as well as speed and manoeuvrability. You can't have a high rate of fire with a gun of long range and great hitting power. There is no ideal, all-purpose tank, but our tank crews consistently say on that the nearest approach to one is the German Mark V – the Panther.[41]

In great detail, Chester then assessed the relative merits of the German and Allied tanks using four criteria: the quality of their guns, their armour, their mechanical reliability, and their speed and manoeuvrability:

> To sum up – I think we may say this. Where you need fire-power and defensive armour, the Germans still have the advantage, but in conditions, which allow the use of numbers, speed and manoeuvrability, our tanks can be used more effectively …
> We must remember that as the front lengthens and the battle becomes more and more one of movement and manoeuvre, the particular qualities of our tanks will become more important. We'll be able to counter the German advantages to some extent by bold and skilful use of our superior numbers.[42]

Did Wilmot get this dispatch to air? The surviving copy in the Liddell Hart Archive is longer than a 'War Report' dispatch, but it was marked for both the BBC and the ABC. This meant that it was intended to be broadcast on the Pacific Service as well as in some other BBC slot such as 'Radio Newsreel', free of the time constraints of 'War Report'. However, there is no censor's name on the copy, but nor does any kind of stop appear. So on balance it seems as though Chester may have got it to air.

While Chester Wilmot was gathering his information, journeying to numerous battlegrounds, and filing or recording his stories for the BBC, issues of tremendous importance were happening around him.

During his time covering the Normandy campaign two matters of critical importance occurred: the first was Wilmot's continued development as a war correspondent and historian, and the second was the beginning of a number of contentious Allied differences of opinion and personal rivalries which would continue to be debated not only until the end of the war and for some time after it, but to this very day. Chester Wilmot's *The Struggle for Europe* would provide the initial basis for the debate. In fact, the debate itself would, for many years, be identified as the 'Wilmot Thesis'.

The Normandy Campaign gave rise to a series of controversies that linger today. The first was the conduct of the campaign itself: the performance of the British and Canadians at Caen, and of their commander, Montgomery; the decision at the end of September 1944 to replace Monty as Land Forces Commander with General Eisenhower; the consequent command decisions by Eisenhower on the future conduct of operations; and the implications of those decisions upon the destiny of postwar Europe. Whilst these questions will be examined in detail in our account of Wilmot's writing of *The Struggle for Europe*, their genesis in Normandy deserves some comment.

Chester Wilmot's coverage of operations in the Caen sector of the Normandy Campaign were many and varied. However, it is difficult to ascertain how much he knew at that time of the controversy of Caen: the notion that Montgomery had stated that Caen was to be captured around D-Day + 1. It was not. Montgomery drew harsh criticism from the Americans and a number of English senior officers for claiming after the war that 'everything had gone to plan'. As the campaign unfolded, Montgomery changed his plan. Not unlike in his 'crumbling' operation at Alamein, he drew the vast majority of the German armour and infantry strength onto his Caen sector, wore the Germans down during limited operations such as Epsom and Goodwood, and thus facilitated the American break-out. To the 'uneducated', these operations were seen as a failure to capture Caen. To Montgomery they were a part of a necessary war of attrition that finally allowed for the resounding success of General Bradley's Cobra operation – the break-out at Normandy.

When the possibility of a complete German disaster was narrowly missed by the Allies' inability to completely close the 'bag' at the Falaise Gap, the Americans blamed the English and the Canadians' perceived slow pace and their commander's caution. The final American Caen criticism consisted of postwar claims that there had been both an unequal contribution to the eventual victory in Normandy and an unequal sacrifice. This caused British resentment. The Battle for Normandy unleashed a whole chain of events that were to heighten the bitterness and controversy which began in Normandy, debates and resentment that would continue to the fall of Berlin, and postwar. And out of these contentious issues Chester Wilmot would be among the first to record not only the history of the Allies' return to Europe, but the postwar consequences of their military and political decisions.

★ ★ ★ ★

Chester Wilmot often began his broadcasts for 'War Report' with 'Hello BBC! Hello BBC!' On the one hand, such a 'call sign' was as much an enquiry or plea asking, 'Are you there?' But, by the early weeks of the campaign in Normandy during June–July 1944, this 'call sign' had become a familiar signal that the BBC was about to play a broadcast not just of mere facts or generalisations, but of incisive journalism delivered from the battlefront.

19

VIVA BBC!

For all Chester Wilmot's appearance of robustness – the square jaw, the authoritative manner, the good-humoured shouts to friends and colleagues as he departed the correspondents' billet – his health was always uncertain. Some close to him noticed hints of strain: the slight wheeze as he puffed on the ever-present pipe or the dark smudges under his eyes. Chester did his best to make light of his frequent breakdowns. There were optimistic letters to Edith and the family about how he was recovering in some military hospital or nursing home or friend's house together with mouth-watering descriptions of how well he was being fed. There was little or nothing about how dangerous some of these attacks undoubtedly were.

In mid-August the pressures of reporting the Normandy fighting finally caught up with him. First, there was a highly undignified boil on his nose. Chester was inclined to make light of it, but the medical officer insisted he go to hospital. There followed the usual sanitised descriptions in letters to Edith. No sooner was Wilmot out of hospital than he came down with dysentery. This was much more serious. Chester did not write about it at the time, only making a few allusions later; clearly he did not want to worry anyone. He was cured by a dose of the drug sulphanilamide, which was quite effective, but the side effects caused irritating stomach upsets for the next two months.

Uncertain stomach notwithstanding, Wilmot was able to accompany the Second Army in its drive to the Belgium border. By 1 September 1944 Chester was reporting:

> The British Second Army is going hell for leather for the buzz-bomb bases. The troops know that their task is to get the flying bomb sites and there's no holding them. Already British columns have over run five sites the Germans had prepared for the launching of flying bombs and one that was to be used for V-2. And this afternoon I was with one of our armoured columns which had crossed the southern border of the Pas de Calais. And as they advance FFI [Free French] come in every few hours with the location of another launching site and dumps of flying bombs themselves.
>
> The Germans have had no chance to prepare defences for their precious victory weapons. We are in the Pas de Calais already … and their army in north-western France is disorganised and demoralised.[1]

The day of the broadcast Chester had driven in a column that was racing through the French countryside. He was told that at 7 am the British armour had advanced from the Amiens bridgehead in three columns. As the troops overran one village the Germans fled to the next:

> In the middle of the morning they had reached the line of the main road from Doullens to Arras just in time to intercept the garrison of Doullens as it tried to race across their bows. The tanks had some good shooting. Those vehicles which weren't shot up crashed into the ditches beside the road … and the tank

crews raced in to grab their prisoners. Almost every village and wood yielded up a small bag of prisoners, and as the tanks raced on the Maquis were beating the wood flushing the Germans. Three times I saw them coming in with groups of more than a hundred. Very few of the Germans attempted to fight and the columns just kept racing on … By the time I had to turn back to make this broadcast the tanks were north of Arras.[2]

Getting back to make his broadcasts was a major problem. The second BBC transmitter mounted on a heavy lorry could be as much as 100 miles behind the advancing troops. The new Corps commander, Lieutenant-General Brian Horrocks, helped by providing Wilmot with a light plane that would fly low over the countryside until the pilot spotted a field close to where the transmitter had been set up. Still, if the weather was poor, instead of the 35-minute flight there was a hazardous three-hour drive by jeep to Brussels.

Chester told his listeners that the swift advance was largely due to Horrocks:

> In Horrocks the new Commander of XXX Corps, Montgomery had a man with the drive and enthusiasm the hour demanded. Horrocks had commanded a brigade in Montgomery's division, before Dunkirk and, when Montgomery went to the Middle East he had brought out Horrocks to command XIII Corps at Alamein … He had been seriously wounded during an air raid on Bizerte and for a year had been in hospital … When Montgomery needed a new commander for XXX Corps, Horrocks came at once. Within a few days his fresh and fiery spirit had transformed the Corps. A tall, lithe figure, with white hair angular features, penetrating eyes and eloquent hands, he moved among his troops more like a prophet than a general.[3]

As Chester shuttled between the forward troops and the transmitter the general had ordered the 11th Armoured Division to drive on in the late evening and through the night of 29 August 'to bounce the Germans out of Amiens before they can blow the bridges'. Long columns of tanks, guns, trucks and carriers wound through the narrow village streets. Two German tanks vainly tried to block the advance but were blasted aside. By morning the British armour was rumbling over the cobblestones of Amiens and the bridges had been captured intact. With the fall of Amiens and the capture of the German commander as his headquarters were overrun, the Allies reached the Belgium frontier, one day's march from Brussels.

In an interview with the author, Frank Gillard pointed out that the BBC had three teams covering the Allied advance. One, under Howard Marshall, accompanied the American Third Army's assault upon Paris. The second, under Wilmot and Stewart MacPherson, was responsible for coverage of the crossing of the Seine, and the advance through Belgium to Brussels. According to Gillard, his third team had the 'easiest job': the coastal thrust where the flying bomb sites were located. Eventually they all met up in Brussels.

By then Gillard was effectively director of 'War Report' after Howard Marshall's gaffe in Paris, even though Marshall was to retain the title until the end of the war. Wilmot was greatly relieved. He didn't trust Marshall after the Montgomery affair. Chester found Gillard 'a pleasant chap – quiet efficient never rushed (Oh, how I envy him), most hard working'.[4] He believed that Gillard thoroughly deserved to have charge of the unit in the field and that the correspondents were much happier because Gillard 'thinks of the unit as a unit' and, in an obvious reference to Marshall, that some of them were no longer engaged in 'great personal broadcasts on great occasions'.[5]

Chester arrived in Brussels with the tanks of a reconnaissance regiment. Before they had even reached the centre of the city his jeep was swamped with flowers and presents as the crowds shouted

'Viva BBC!' One elderly lady wearing the medals of 'another war' pressed a package of two cigarettes into his hand – the only present she had. The police had to form a cordon while Chester found the midget's microphone, placed a disc on the turntable and shouted a brief description. The sound survives but he had to record a fuller account later.

> Their [the troops'] main trouble was not dealing with the scattered German resistance but getting through the crowds who thronged the roadsides every mile from the frontier to Brussels … cheering laughing shouting people with wild delight in their voices and tears of joy in their eyes. As the news of our coming spread like wildfire from village to village along the main roads from Tournai to Brussels, Belgian men grabbed their hidden arms and went hunting for the Germans …
>
> And so it went on until we came to Brussels itself and here our welcome was wildest of all. There had been Germans in the street only an hour before and not a flag had been in sight, but by the time we arrived every building was plastered with flags and streamers.[6]

Arguably the most satisfying moments of the whole advance were experienced by General Horrocks. For his formal entry into Brussells Horrocks arranged something special. A Belgian brigade was attached to his corps and when he entered the city the general was escorted by Belgian troops. To the cheers of the crowd Horrocks pointed to his escort and repeatedly shouted '*Belge!*'

Chester found the Belgian welcome far more moving and unreserved than their reception in France. With their martial traditions the French had felt it should have been their own soldiers who liberated them, not the British. To say this on air, however, was hardly appropriate when the BBC had just covered General de Gaulle's entry into Paris and the moment when he had been nearly killed by snipers in Notre Dame. Wilmot did, however, include the observation in *The Struggle for Europe*.

Swamped by the crowds Chester finally took refuge in the police station. He had arranged for some tanks to go to the Brussels radio station. The BBC transmitter was now 200 miles away in France and this was their best chance to get their stories back. Then Wilmot was told that before they withdrew the Germans had blown up the station. However, there were other transmitters in Belgium. They had been dropped by the RAF to the White Army – the Belgium resistance – now very visible in the streets rounding up alleged collaborators.

Throughout his career Wilmot seems to have possessed extensive intelligence contacts. It probably began with his reports to the Department of Foreign Affairs on conditions in Europe and Asia during the debating tour. At the BBC he was surrounded by intelligence operatives as the corporation broadcast coded messages to resistance groups throughout Europe. In addition, by now Chester had the confidence of Field Marshal Montgomery and was close to his Chief of Intelligence, Edgar 'Bill' Williams. So it is not surprising that almost as soon as he arrived at the BBC's temporary headquarters at the Hotel Metropole, a 'lawyer' arrived to take him to a cache of White Army transmitters. The 'lawyer' led Chester to a back street of the fashionable Avenue Louise, then through an old garage and into a garden behind. This garden was built into the side of a hill with stone steps leading to the terrace of another garden next door. Halfway up the steps a rusted iron door was set into the face of the wall. Chester's guide pushed on the door and it creaked open and they stepped into a dark chamber.

As he looked around and adjusted his eyes to the darkness Chester could smell the damp. The only light seeped out from a small hole on the far side, where some bricks had been removed to provide a crawl space for one man. The hole led into a room of 8 square feet hollowed out of the hillside that was packed with radio equipment. Some of the parts, Chester was told, had been smuggled out of factories; others had been dropped by the RAF. The transmitter had been assembled so it could be used to coordinate a rising by the White Army. It was of no use at present to either the resistance fighters or Chester as it required further testing. However, when Chester was taken to the attic to meet a young Belgian known only as Polka, there seemed to be some hope. On the table in front of him was a transmitter built into a suitcase. He and his radio had been parachuted into Belgium in May. Polka had been more or less on the run ever since, setting up his transmitter in one place for ten minutes to get off or receive messages, then swiftly moving to another location lest he be located by the German direction finders. Now with the Germans out of Brussels he was at the disposal of the BBC. So the first message from Brussels was in morse; and for three days Chester was transmitting in cablese. Chester's first roughly typed message for transmission concisely summed up the situation.

URGENT DESPATCH FOR BBC RPT BBC FROM CHESTER WILMOT

Brussels September 6 censored by Adams one

British armoured columns ... have fanned out from Brussels and Antwerp STOP Germans are still bewildered and disorganised but east of Louvain they have had time to blow some bridges and around some towns suicide garrisons have formed islands of resistance [sic] which have not been easily overcome but between these islands there is little or nothing and they can be safely bypassed by armoured columns and dealt with by motorised infantry who come up later STOP There is still no sign the Germans trying to organise defenseline this side of Rhine ...

Yesterday our troops occupied Lille and today armoured columns met little opposition STOP Swift thrust carried them forward fifty rpt five zero miles STOP They've now reached outskirts famous mediaeval city of Gent rpt Ghent 35 miles northeast of Brussels this advance has so widened and strengthened original narrow salient now no chance Germans escaping from pocket formed when British Second Army cut through to Antwerp STOP Message ends. Chester Wilmot.[7]

The broadcasters were more fortunate than the print journalists. After being taken to the Hotel Metropole by tram – the owner of the company offered them the use of the equipment and drove the tram himself – they typed up their stories and were then flown some 200 miles to the transmitter.

But Gillard, Wilmot and the rest of the BBC team desperately needed to get on the air. Finally, Belgian National Radio came to the rescue. The Germans had not blown up the studios as first reported. Instead they had tried to flood them. But Belgian Radio's chief engineer had intervened. He'd been in hiding for four years and had long expected the Huns to try something like this. The veteran engineer smuggled himself in and foiled the German attempt. Although the Germans had taken the transmitter, the Belgians had been secretly building their own. Within 48 hours of the liberation their equipment was operational and for three weeks Belgian National Radio kept the BBC reporters in contact with Broadcasting House.

Chester soon came to understand how much the BBC had come to mean to the Belgians. He had just finished using the suitcase transmitter behind Avenue Louise when he was confronted by a very small, very polite boy. The conversation went something like this. Boy: 'Good morning. Are you the BBC?' Chester: 'Yes I am.' Boy: 'My mother would like to meet you. Will you please come with me to my home?' 'Thank you very much,' replied Chester with grave politeness and followed the lad to a pleasant house where he was introduced to a charming family who soon adopted him as 'their Tommy'. Apart from a description of how the mother took him out to buy a dress for Jane, Chester included few details about his benefactors in his letters to Edith. Almost certainly this was because there was a brief romance with someone either within or close to the family. Frank Gillard told the author that Chester had a girl in Brussels, 'but I didn't enquire into his affairs anymore than he did into mine'.[8]

It was through this family and their friends that Chester came to hear stories such as these. Describing how her husband had come home from a liberation party one lady told him that her husband was 'rather gay' and

> as he came into the house he heard the BBC midnight news full on. He rushed to the set and switched it off. Then he realised he no longer had to fear. It is the most popular pastime in Brussels to listen to the BBC with the windows wide open. It reminds us that we are free.[9]

Chester used such stories in his broadcasts.

* * * *

According to General Horrocks, it was at this stage that 'those responsible for the higher direction of war in the west faltered'. As he was to describe the situation in *Corps Commander*:

> First of all we were ordered to halt, since we were outstripping our administrative resources, which we were still receiving from the beachhead some 300 miles away. We were told that supplies, particularly of petrol were running short. This was a tragedy because as we now know, the only troops available to prevent us reaching the Rhine were one German Division, the 719th

composed of elderly gentlemen with stomach ailments, and who had hitherto been guarding the coast of the Netherlands and had not seen a shot fired in anger, plus one Battalion of Dutch SS and a few Luftwaffe detachments …

Although the order came to us from my immediate boss General Dempsey, Commander of the Second Army … I think it was the direct result of the broad front strategy insisted on by Eisenhower for political reasons.[10]

The broad front strategy versus the narrow thrust approach advocated by Montgomery was to be examined in detail by Chester when he came to write *The Struggle for Europe*. Chester was to vehemently support Montgomery. But as early as 1944 reporters like Wilmot and Gillard, who were close to the field marshal, were well aware of this dispute as well as the American dissatisfaction with the supposedly slow British attacks on Caen.

Even in 1944 Gillard and Wilmot believed Montgomery was right and had little regard for Eisenhower. Gillard: 'He didn't look like a fighting soldier. We saw very little of him and he had no time really to talk to people like me. There was always something sleazy about Eisenhower. We knew about the affair with his chauffer and it didn't go down well.'[11]

Chester did come to modify his views about the American general later in the war, but the British reporters couldn't help comparing Monty's studied informality and frequent appearances in the front line with Eisenhower's near invisibility. As one British soldier put it, 'When things were at their worst you'd look up and there would be Monty'.[12] Horrocks, too, in the words of his biographer, 'led from the front'. Earlier in the campaign when RAF bombloads mistakenly fell on his troops, Horrocks piloted a light plane into the RAF formation that was following behind and let off flares to direct the planes to the right targets. The British reporters' high opinion of both men was to influence their coverage of the invasion of Holland soon to be known by its codename Market Garden.

* * * *

At 1.30 pm on Sunday, 17 September 1944, Chester found General Horrocks standing on a slag heap beside the Meuse-Escaut Canal. The general told Wilmot he had just received word that everything was going to plan. Consequently he had decided to begin the ground attack at 2.35 pm. His powerful field glasses trained on the white road ahead, Horrocks outlined Montgomery's plan to Chester. At that moment over 1000 troop carriers and nearly 500 gliders were heading for Holland. This aerial armada carried almost three divisions which were being dropped along the line of Eindhoven–Nijmegen–Arnhem with the task of capturing the road bridges over the Maas, the Waal, the Nederrijn and five other waterways. The armoured and motorised columns commanded by Horrocks were to drive north from the Meuse-Escaut Canal to the Zuiderzee. As Wilmot summed it up later in *The Struggle for Europe*: 'With this one sabre stroke Montgomery intended to cut Holland in two, outflank the Siegfried Line and establish Second Army beyond the Rhine on the northern threshold of the Ruhr.'[13]

To cover the air drop Gillard had assigned Guy Byam, now fully recovered from his D-Day injury, and Stanley Maxted. Maxted was a craggy Canadian with a long career in radio as a singer, actor and programmer. He had served in the Great War, and at nearly fifty claimed to be the oldest of the war reporters. When he first arrived at Arnhem Maxted was seen walking down a line of Canadian paratroopers peering intently into their faces. Then he stopped abruptly and stuck out his hand to one of the paras. 'Hello, son,' he said.

'War Report' also covered the flight of the Airborne Army from the air. Stewart MacPherson took off from Belgium in a scout plane to meet the air armada. At first all he could see were fighters; then

MacPherson's pilot shouted, 'Look straight ahead!'

> The sky was black with transport aircraft flying in perfect formation. They were completely surrounded by Typhoons, Spitfires, Mustangs, Thunderbolts and Lightning fighters. The transport planes were in the middle with their fighter cover flying at three different heights ... The armada flew on and everywhere you looked were aircraft – Allied aircraft. As my pilot shouted at me, 'No room up here for Jerry!'[14]

Accompanied by one of the BBC's engineers Chester took his midget up into an observation post in the most northerly village the British held and recorded a commentary on the barrage that opened the attack:

> Hello BBC. This is Chester Wilmot broadcasting from an observation post on the border of Holland, in the bridgehead which British Second Army troops gained at Escaut-Meuse Canal [*sic*] only a few days ago. Troops of the British Second Army are now fighting forward from this bridgehead and into Holland ...
>
> As the tanks move down the road, they have been shooting out yellow identification smoke to warn any Allied aircraft around that these are British tanks which are moving up the road ... Those hard cracks are the four point two mortars going off from the wood just in front of me; and with my glasses I can see the gunners pressing their fingers in their ears as the mortars go off.[15]

He stayed the night at one of the Corps Headquarters and the next day, Monday, 18 September, pushed on to the village of Valkenswaard, the first sizeable place in Holland the Allies had liberated. There was a murmur in the crowd of villagers when they recognised

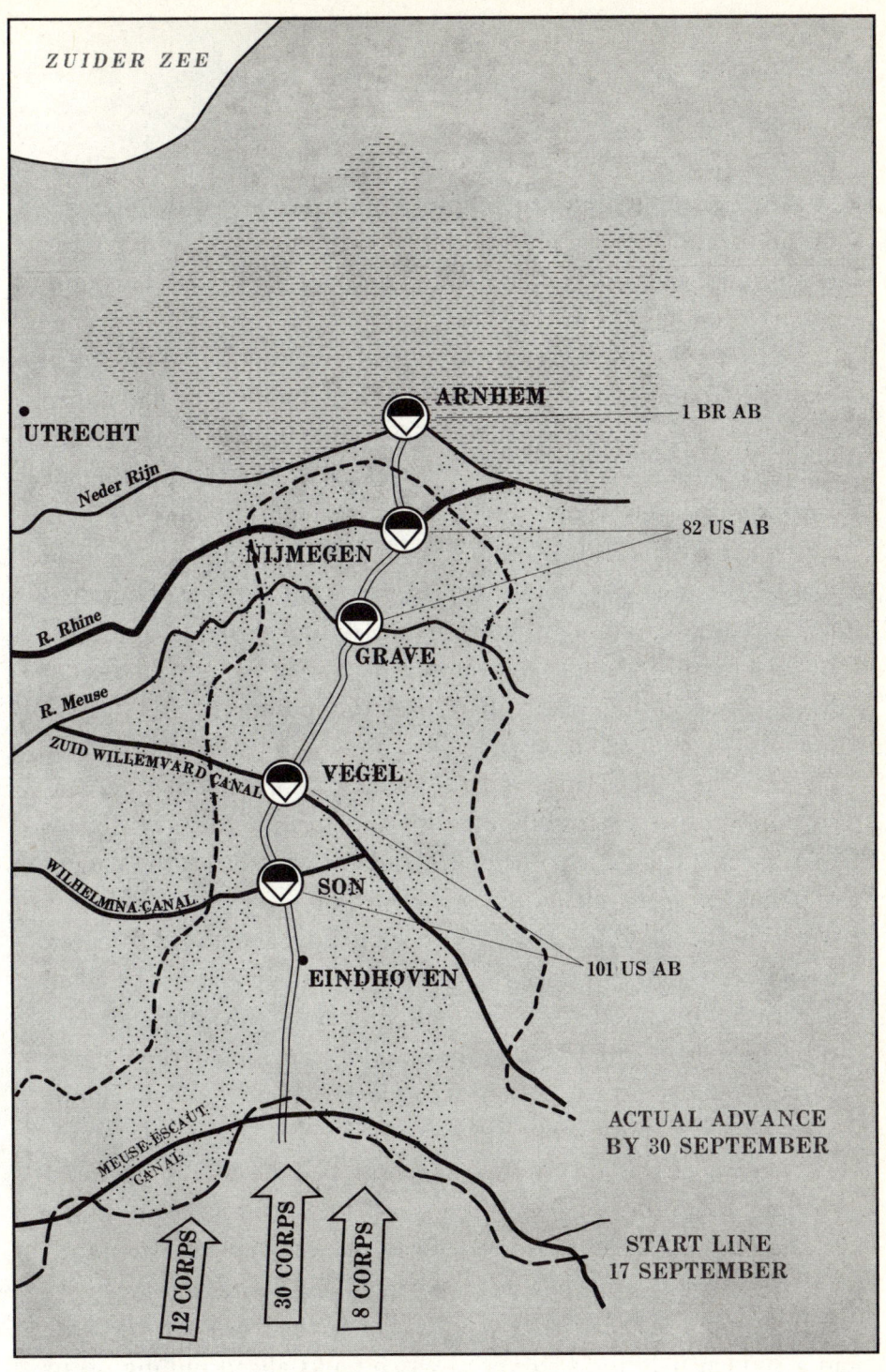

Operation Market Garden

the BBC jeep. Within a mere 30 minutes of his arrival in Valkenswaard, 'a couple of dozen people' who had followed the progress of the invasion by listening to the BBC greeted him, and Wilmot felt 'humble to think people risked their lives day in and day out to listen to you.'[16]

Chester recorded a very emotional Dutchman who described how the 'Tommies' had come to the village. By noon he had nailed down the story of Valkenswaard and headed back to Corps Headquarters to pick up the plane Horrocks had laid on for him; he landed in Brussels 35 minutes later. He assured Edith that 'it's quite a simple business really, you just fly straight up and down the road that is the main axis. Usually we cruise along at a couple of hundred feet and as Belgium is absolutely flat … it is lovely flying country.'[17] By then the arrangement was that the plane that brought Chester to Brussels would then take Gillard back to the front. At this stage of the campaign it was impossible to record anything but pure colour pieces in the field because of the censorship. It was not that the censorship was bad. Chester thought it was better and more intelligent than he had experienced before. But there was always the danger of giving away the tactics if a reporter did a story blind. This was why Wilmot and Gillard had to go back to broadcast to 'War Report' from Brussels. At this stage the BBC transmitter could not be taken any further forward because it would drown out the army signals.

The following day Chester recorded the opening of the Belgian Parliament. On the way back he was asked by Army Public Relations to escort a WAAF officer to Eindhoven. The WAAF, Joy Nicholson, was later to tell the story of their adventures on the BBC's memorial program to Wilmot in 1954. Wilmot and Nicholson had come down to the front in separate Austers (light planes) then transferred to Chester's BBC jeep. They were moving along beside a vast convoy of three-ton trucks carrying supplies. Then the truck convoy came to a sudden halt and Chester saw two tanks ahead pulling off to the side of the road. Then a fleet of military police on motor bikes poured down the road shouting, 'Jerry's coming … Jerry tanks'. Deciding this was no time to have a WAAF officer on his hands Chester swung the jeep around in a driveway only to find after he had made his turn that the whole convoy of 3-ton trucks had followed suit and were speeding south in the opposite direction.

The scare was soon over, the convoy turned back and the rest of the drive to Eindhoven was peaceful. But as they were reaching the outskirts of the town in the late evening an aircraft flew low over them. 'German,' shouted Chester. 'They couldn't have been such bloody fools not to have taken the airfield.'[18] A parachute flare dropped, lighting up the old town, and they heard the crump of the bombs. Chester pulled into the side of a block of flats and they piled out of the jeep and took refuge in the hallway. Finding themselves too vulnerable, they went down into the cellar where some of the families from the apartments had taken refuge. Chester, who knew a little Dutch, began questioning their companions. They told him that earlier in the day the people of Eindhoven had been celebrating their liberation, dancing on the pavements, singing, blowing whistles and banging toy drums. Joy and Chester could see they still had marigolds and grated carrot in their buttonholes and hair – anything that was the national colour of orange. In the late afternoon had come the flares followed by the bombs. Chester cleared a space on the cellar floor and plotted out the action based on their information. Eindhoven was represented by his beret and Nijmegen by Joy's hat; fruit jars (the cellar served as a storage area) stood in for the Allies and Germans, with some tulip bulbs in the corner representing the airfields and dropping zones.

Then they heard a series of bomb blasts. One hit the block of flats; another fell on the trucks packed in the square outside. After an hour Chester and the others realised the bursting ammunition in the trucks had set fire to the top of the building. Cries were heard from a flat above. Chester at once took charge. He organised relays of rescue squads; his official driver and a corporal climbed up the drain pipe and through a window into the burning flat where they found two dead and five wounded. They managed to lower them in blankets to those waiting below. The whole building was about to blow up but there appeared to be no way to move the injured. The corporal found a Dutch ambulance in a nearby street and they carried the wounded to safety minutes before the building collapsed. Later Chester insisted to a horrified Edith that he had really only been helping carry the wounded out five minutes before the building came down and so there was no real danger. She seems to have remained unconvinced.

As Gillard and Wilmot reported on its progress Horrocks's corps pressed on to Nijmegen. Until then they had been advancing more or less according to plan. Then they found themselves in the middle of a battle. But there had been a fatal delay in moving against Nijmegen and that had given the Germans time to concentrate their forces. Now they were going to stand and fight. The tank column halted and Chester watched the spectacle with Captain Lord Carrington. Between them they drank Carrington's last bottle of liberated champagne. As with almost everything about Market Garden, it was a matter of bridges, and here there were two bridges across the Waal, an imposing road bridge and a rail bridge. Both had to be captured before the Allied forces could relieve the Airborne troops at Arnhem who were fighting desperately on yet another bridge.

During the night of 19–20 September 1944, Horrocks and Browning planned a simultaneous attack from the north and south upon the Nijmegen Road Bridge, while the American 504th Parachute Regiment was to cross the Waal a mile downstream and capture the northern end. At the same time, British Grenadier Guards and a battalion of paratroopers were to assault the southern defences.

The crossing of the Waal by the 504th is one of the most celebrated feats of the Arnhem battles. Since it was an American operation, Chester did not use it for his broadcast but passed on the information to CBS correspondent Bill Downs. Downs's description of these events became a classic of American war reporting. Understandably Chester wanted to cover the exploits of the Grenadiers who were about to take the road bridge. This dispatch was to become one of Chester's most famous broadcasts.

> The American paratroops cleared the southern part of the park and the British went for the block-houses and the fortified knoll right near the bridge itself. The tanks smashed a way through the block-houses. They put armour-piercing shells through the concrete and the sandbags and then fired with high explosive inside. They carved large gaps in the walls so infantry could move from house to house under cover. In some houses the Germans held out until the Tommies were near enough to blind them with smoke grenades and blast the pill boxes with piat bombs. Then at last they were through to the edge of the park and only the fortified knoll lay between them and the end of the bridge.
>
> In small groups of half a dozen or so they formed up in the wrecked houses; fixed bayonets, drew safety-pins from grenades, and then burst out into the open, with Vickers guns mounted on the roofs firing over their heads. The Germans below ground had every protection. But they couldn't stand this sudden onslaught. The leading British company commander was killed by a German only twenty yards away. But his men raced past him and into the German trenches. Then the hunt began. As one of the platoon commanders said to me later, 'It was like flushing bolting foxes …'
>
> Once the block houses and the knoll were captured and as soon as the Americans had silenced the last anti-tank gun down the park, the way was clear for the tanks to rush the bridge. At seven o'clock just as it was getting dark, five British

tanks made their run. As they got near the bridge they were fired on from the other side of the river, but they were ordered to keep going regardless of the fire, to push on across the bridge. As the two leading tanks roared down the long straight 600-yard stretch of bridge, guns on the far right kept firing. Germans in the girders let loose with machine guns and bazookas. But the tanks went on. They shot straight through a gap in the concrete road block at the northern end of the bridge and went on up the road. They got through. But beyond the bridge the next two tanks were shot up; and when the fifth one reached the northern end its commander realised there was no one else there. And so he stayed there. And for half an hour his tank held the bridge alone until the American paratroopers got through to support him.[19]

The commander of the lead tank was Captain Carrington, with whom a few hours before Chester had been sharing that last bottle of champagne, and undoubtedly he was the source of many of the details in the story. Chester now had a great story of British prowess to match Bill Downs's description of the American boat crossing, but how was he to get it to a transmitter?

By now it was late on Sunday, 24 September 1944. Downs's account had reached the BBC already but they were still waiting for Wilmot's report in London. The Germans had cut the road behind the Nijmegen party but Chester was still able to get to his plane, and then drove at high speed into Brussels. But he still had to get his copy censored. That proved relatively easy, but by the time the censor had finished the only transmitter available was MCN – the transmitter was nicknamed 'Mike, Charlie, Nan' – located 10 miles outside Brussels. MCN had just completed its test transmissions, which meant by then no one in London would be listening. Peter Herrin, the engineer in charge of MCN, was driving back to Brussels when an oncoming car pulled in front of him.

'Hey, are you BBC?'

'Yes.'

'We've got to go back, this dispatch is urgent'.

Herrin realised it was Chester Wilmot. Since MCN was assumed to be silent, Chester broadcast on a medium wavelength audible to ordinary listeners in Britain, asking them to let the BBC know that Chester Wilmot was desperately trying to get through. Within five minutes the BBC's switchboard at Broadcasting House was jammed. But by the time the BBC was receiving Wilmot direct 'War Report' had finished. In any case, to the group listening in the control room, the quality was dreadful. Then one of the senior engineers used a morse key to instruct Herrin to adjust the frequency. The transmission cleared and they were able to record the dispatch for broadcast the following night.

As Market Garden began to unravel Chester did all he could to ensure that the courage of the British troops was recorded accurately. When CBS correspondent Bill Downs in a 'War Report' broadcast confused the attack by British tanks and American paratroops on the railway bridge at Nijmegen with the later British assault by British tanks and infantry on the road bridge, Chester protested to the BBC Traffic Manager. It was a grave injustice to the British forces who had in fact stormed the southern end of the bridge. Wilmot sorted it out with Downs and presumably it was put right in a subsequent 'War Report'. All that survives now are both men's splendid accounts of American and British courage that appear in the 'War Report' anthology of correspondents' dispatches.

By 25–26 September the Airborne Division that had been dropped at Arnhem was slowly being wiped out. It was then that, as Frank Gillard told the author:

> BBC in London sent me a signal ... 'retrieve Maxted and Byam.' What did they think I was going to do for God's sake? No movement could take place in daylight ... and night after

night I was there up and down, on foot and in my jeep, hoping I would find Stan Maxted, hoping I would find Guy Byam ... On the very last night in the darkness I found Stan Maxted. And Maxted's first words to me were, 'You'll never see Guy Byam again.' And I said, 'Why not?' And he said, 'Guy got impatient, he wouldn't wait and he dived in the river and he swam ... he'll never make it.[20]

Gillard drove Maxted to Eindhoven, where the BBC transmitter was, and Maxted did a 'brilliant broadcast'. Then Gillard announced he was going to drive back to Brussels. When they got back to the Metropole there was Guy Byam sitting in the main entrance hall looking, it seemed to Gillard, 'as if he had just stepped out of an army outfitter's department in the most expensive part of London'.[21] Almost immediately they were flown back to London. That evening, 27 September, twirling his beret in his hand Maxted was in Studio LG1 broadcasting live on 'War Report'.

> About five kilometres to the west of Arnhem, in a space 1500 yards by 900, on that last day, I saw the dead and the living ... those who fought a good fight and kept the faith with you at home, and those who fought magnificently on. They were the last of the few. I last saw them yesterday morning as they dribbled into Nijmegen ... If they hadn't held that horde of enemy force at Arnhem, that force would have been down at Nijmegen upsetting the whole apple cart.[22]

Maxted was followed by the young and passionate Guy Byam:

> They came out because they had nothing left to fight with except their bare hands ... The men had been fighting without food and practically no water, fighting an enemy whose growing strength was always in our midst, fighting with small arms

against armour ... Then the division heard they were to be evacuated. They hated to go because they were not beaten, but they got ready, smashed their equipment, the meagre equipment they had left. They put sacking over their shoes and prepared for their last ordeal.[23]

Then 'War Report' played the recordings they had made on the spot including the despairing moment when Stanley Maxted saw desperately needed supplies land in the wrong place and out of reach. While it was brilliant documentary radio, it was much more than that. Maxted, Byam and later Wilmot, when soon after he pieced together a dispatch on the last days at Arnhem, were creating a legend of an heroic British defeat. Later, when Chester came to describe 'Market Garden' in *The Struggle for Europe* he was to be more critical.

20

UNHAPPY PHRASES

Chester arrived back at Croydon with Alan Moorehead and Alexander Clifford at about 6 pm on 28 September 1944. There had been a lull in the fighting and he was still feeling the after effects of the sulphanilamide drugs that had been used to clear up the dysentery. Like everyone else who had taken part in Operation Market Garden, Chester was very tired. But within hours he was caught up in the usual war correspondent on leave rush: dinner at the Ritz, drinks later with the producer Sydney Bernstein, who was soon to work on a film exposing the atrocities at Belsen for which Alfred Hitchcock was a consultant. The following day Chester was at the BBC. He gave a half-hour review of the battle at Arnhem to the editors that complemented Stanley Maxted and Guy Byam's dramatic appearance in the studio a few days earlier. Chester also went out of his way to brief the Controller of News, AP Ryan, about the BBC's responsibility for news on the continent. He described some of the problems in his first letter to Edith after coming back from Europe.

> I'm afraid the BBC's reputation [is] so high … [that] even if it says something is 'unconfirmed from official sources' Belgians and Dutch take it as gospel just because the BBC gives it its cache[t] … After we got into Antwerp long before we went into

Unhappy phrases

Holland BBC put out a story that we'd crossed the border and were in Breda – as a result Dutch partisans in nearby towns rose up and people put out their flags. Actually the report had not come from any correspondent or SHAEF but from the Dutch Government in London, which had been misled by a signal from an agent in Holland – we now believe the agent was a phoney and that the story was a German inspired ruse for the very purpose of bringing about the premature rising. [Chester's sources were correct. The entire Dutch network had been blown.] This is on the RECORD Prince Bernhard – [Princess] Juliana's husband – who commands the Dutch Forces of the Interior, sent for me and asked me to correct the story.[1]

AP Ryan was a powerful figure in the wartime BBC and had a high opinion of Wilmot. The briefing, which coming from anyone else (Dimbleby, for example) might have been resented was, it seems, a great success.

By the following week Chester was typing a long series of airmail letters to Edith from 'a lovely old pub in Bray' near Oxford (though in reality he was sleeping in a nearby home that supplied special accommodation when the inn was overcrowded). Free from the tensions of war reporting, and with the defeat of Germany inevitable – the setback at Arnhem notwithstanding – Chester was pondering his future.

After posing all sorts of alternatives – Burma, the Pacific – in one rather disorganised letter, he told Edith that he wanted to stay working in London as a freelancer for the BBC while supplementing his income with assignments from the newspapers. Chester had already politely declined a lucrative offer from *News of the World* – at twice his present salary – as he 'didn't want to work for a paper like that'.[2] Chester's commitment to quality journalism and public broadcasting remained firm throughout his life.

Above all he wanted Edith and Jane to join him in London and for months afterwards his letters were filled with lists of people she needed to contact so as to arrange passage. Chester was, of course, missing his family but Edith's veiled descriptions of Jane's aggressive behaviour worried him. The child was obviously very intelligent but wasn't talking and was nearly impossible for Edith or her mother to control. No one had yet realised the girl was profoundly deaf. There was a rumour in the Wilmot family that Edith had contracted German measles from one of the children she had been visiting for her social work diploma in the early months of her pregnancy. If true, it explains some of the later problems in the marriage, as Chester had been against Edith doing field work while pregnant.

Some months later, after recovering from another asthma attack, Chester sent Edith an account of his adventures covering an attack on a canal crossing in Belgium. Driving his jeep to the front with his engineer Syd Gore, who was following in his BBC truck, Chester came across an old colleague and friend. George Silk was a New Zealand photographer and friend of Damien Parer who had joined the Australian Department of Information and covered the war in the Middle East and Greece and later New Guinea. After a dispute with the DOI, Silk was now working for *Life* magazine. Wilmot naturally invited Silk to tag along to capture the action in photographs. Chester's detailed account of the canal crossing is easily the best description of how he reported action. The troops were attacking from the Wert region towards Venlo.

> It was really a terrific party – there were more than four hundred guns supporting the attack and in addition several squadrons of tanks were lined up on our side of the canal to fire in the barrage and then move up to support the infantry, who were also to be aided by crocodiles – flame throwing Churchill tanks. In addition Bofors, ack-ack guns and Vickers magazines were to fire over the infantry's heads – making quite a party. From the Brigade we moved on along an even worse track to the Battalion

HQ about 500 yards from the canal bank and asked where we could safely take the truck and what OP [observation post] I could use. They pointed to a farm house a couple of hundred yards down the road and said I could get up on the roof with an arty OP officer.[3]

When Wilmot had covered a canal crossing before he had moved the sound truck up on dead ground. The canal was in raised banks and 'so one was protected from view and fire'.[4] This time to his horror he was to discover there was no raised bank and they had left the great lumbering truck in full view of the enemy.

Thinking the approach was covered we drove up; I found a place on the roof of a farm with an arty [artillery] OP officer. [The attack] went with a swing and we had a wonderful view until the smoke screen blew back in our faces ... I saw the tanks and infantry assemble behind the farmhouse, described the infantry marching by and the tanks going with them – the assault boats going off on the backs of the bren gun carriers – the flame throwers going into action.[5]

Chester felt the 'only snag' was that the sound background seemed so poor and he wondered why his engineer had not employed two microphones: one for the commentary and the other for the noise of the battle.

In an interview with the author in 1996, George Silk described these events and emphasised that neither he nor Wilmot had questioned the other's decision to remain at the start line or Silk's decision to go forward. However, when he saw Silk's splendid sequence of stills showing the last assault boats going into the water with the flames from the flame throwers in the background and the Germans coming out of their foxholes, Chester rather wished he had gone forward with Silk. But for all this boyish excitement, Chester never saw the war as anything other than a tragedy, and his broadcasts were always sober and objective. The description itself is an invaluable record of how an experienced and very professional broadcaster brought a sound portrait of battle into living rooms throughout the world and managed to stay alive.

Wilmot then received letters from his father and Edith telling him that Damien Parer had been killed in the Pacific while filming US Marines on Peleliu. After the death of his sister, it was the second great bereavement of Chester Wilmot's life. At first he couldn't find the words, but soon cabled Marie Parer – 'the sensible lass' he'd liked so much when Damien had first introduced her as the girl he was going to marry. Edith, always at her best in these situations, had already sent a letter of condolence. A few days later Chester wrote this tribute to his parents and more or less repeated it in his reply to Edith:

> I am most distressed about Damien and haven't been able to get him out of my mind ever since I received your letter. I knew nothing about it at all, for there has been nothing in the papers here. What a terrible tragedy for he was such a fine man as well as a brilliant photographer. He made the camera speak as no other man I have ever known and his films gave an immortal portrait of the Australian soldier of this war – he was a great artist as well as a most sympathetic human being and it was because he felt so deeply that he was able to get so close to the men and catch their spirit in his lens … You know I tried to persuade him to be more careful now that he wasn't working with the AIF, but he didn't know what fear was, and he was never content with anything but the best. Of course, a good photographer like Damien had to run more risks than the ordinary correspondent and he would never have been happy if he hadn't been right in the thick of things, but at this stage of the war things can get too thick.[6]

By late October Chester seems to have overcome the worst of his asthma and was on his way back to Europe. Before leaving he had begun to set up a new life in Britain. Nothing was final but AD Peters, his literary agent, had signed a contract on his behalf for a book on the Western Front. The publishers were WH Collins, one of the best in Britain. Chester was to get '300 pounds advance, more if I want it – 15% on the first ten thousand 20% on the rest'.[7] Many of the well-known correspondents had already written books. These were, on the whole, autobiographical accounts of events as experienced by the reporters. Impressed by Chester's *Tobruk*, Collins wanted him to go further and write his book from the documents – 'how the invasion was planned, how carried out'.[8] Wilmot had always been instinctively a historian who needed to understand and explain the events he was reporting. *Crusade in Europe*, the provisional title of the proposed book, would provide the ideal opportunity.

November 1944 saw the beginning of the bitterest winter Europe had experienced since the beginning of the war. Wilmot was covering Montgomery's 21st Army Group's operations to clear the Germans from south-west Holland. They were fighting over waterlogged ground crossed by canals, many of which had been deliberately flooded. It was disturbingly like the Western Front in the Great War. The infantry's only protection was in ditches half filled with water. Chester watched the men slithering into these ditches, often sinking deep in slush. 'The days are long, the news is flat and it is difficult to get anything into "War Report". I feel mentally stale and unable to rouse any enthusiasm',[9] he wrote to Edith.

Frank Gillard, who was attached to the newly promoted Field Marshal Montgomery's Tactical Headquarters, was having a better time – at least he was aware of some of the behind-the-scenes tensions and intrigue. Monty was quite open about his contempt for Eisenhower's broad front strategy. As he saw it Generals Omar Bradley and George Patton were essentially fighting separate battles; there was no plan, no strategy and definitely 'no grip!' Gillard and the other correspondents didn't write about any of this at the time. 'It would never have passed the censor,' the veteran correspondent told the author.[10]

Montgomery made a final effort to change Eisenhower's broad front strategy. On 29 November he suggested that a conference be held between Eisenhower, Tedder, Bradley and himself, for the purpose of discussing the current situation, which would then enable Eisenhower to issue his plan for the final assault upon Germany and the end of the war. The conference was held at Maastricht on 7 December 1944. During the discussion, Montgomery advocated the Allies' strategic thrust should be aimed at the Ruhr and that the passage to that prize should be operations conducted to the north of it – where the ground would facilitate mobile operations and thus a speedy end to the war. To achieve this objective, Montgomery argued that Bradley's US 12th Army Group and the British 21st Army Group should be deployed for this northern thrust. He further stated that these operations should be conducted under the command of either Bradley or himself.

Eisenhower refused. The broad front strategy was to stand. Thus, on 7 December 1944, at the conclusion of the Maastricht conference, the situation was that General Bradley's 12th Army Group was split into two main formations, and both poised to resume the offensive. But between them, occupying a gap of some 100 miles in the Ardennes, were deployed a mere five divisions of General Middleton's US VIII Corps. Coupled with the vulnerability of this broad front strategy was the Allied belief that the Germans would await an Allied crossing of the Roer River before unleashing any reserves that they might have built up – a German offensive was not contemplated.

On 16 December 1944, the Germans, their movements masked by the snow, attacked through the Ardennes at the gap held by the US VIII Corps. Hitler had amassed seventeen divisions and mounted a major offensive that plunged deep into Allied-held territory creating the bulge in the American lines that was to give the battle its name. Later when Chester was able to examine the US intelligence assessments he discovered they had been concentrating on the very real problems facing the Germans, but had failed to consider what the enemy might do.

* * * *

Hitler had two motives for an Ardennes offensive – one military and the other political.

The German plan adopted the age-old principles of war, concentration of force and surprise. Three armies were deployed across a 75-mile front from Monschau in the north to Echternach in the south: the principal or northern thrust was to be undertaken by

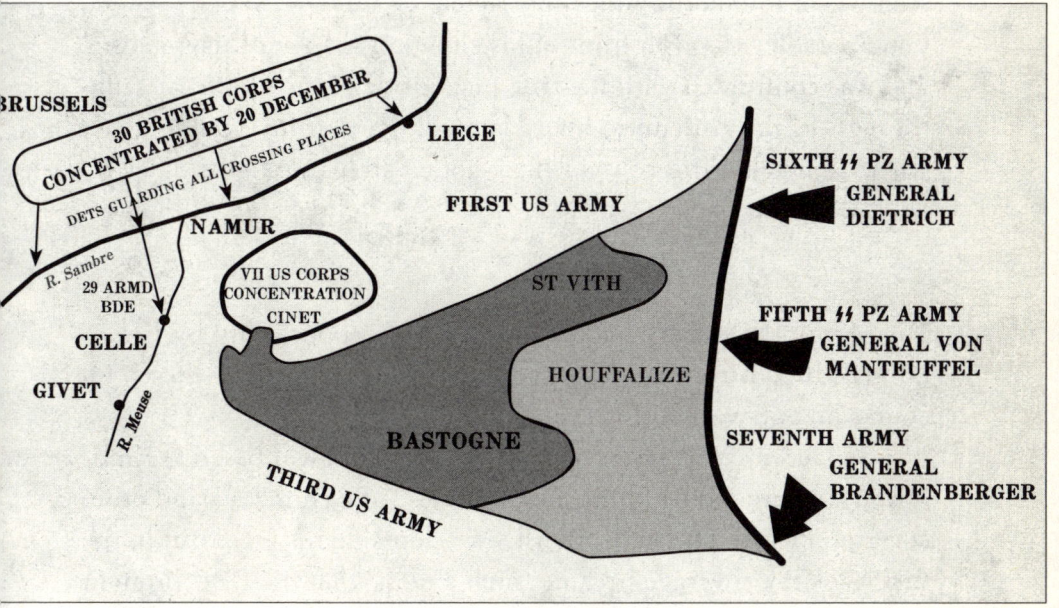

The Ardennes – the site of the German's last offensive of the Second World War

the SS Sixth Panzer Army, commanded by General Sepp Dietrich, across the Meuse and then north-west to Antwerp; the southern offensive was undertaken by General Erich Brandenberger, whose Seventh Army was to cover the flank from Luxembourg to Givet; and the central thrust was allotted to General von Manteuffel's Fifth Panzer Army, which was to strike through Namur and Dinant and on to Brussels.

Hitler's generals thought the operation far too ambitious and unlikely to succeed in reaching their distant objectives, but Hitler hoped for a political outcome of equal importance to his military plan: the fragmentation of the Western Allied armies and their political will. The German build-up of men and material was brilliantly hidden from Allied intelligence, and the first days of the offensive were screened from air reconnaissance by the poor weather.

The German concentration of force and the sudden and unforeseen use of it took the Allies completely by surprise. When General Omar Bradley stood in front of his situation maps in Luxembourg, and was confronted with the true magnitude of the German breakthrough in the Ardennes, he exclaimed, 'Pardon my French – but where in hell has this son of a bitch gotten all his strength?'[11]

* * * *

For Monty the enemy had been given this opportunity by Eisenhower's broad front strategy: 'you can't be strong everywhere'. Of course no one was writing that either.

By December Chester had left Brussels and was based at Eindhoven surrounded by 'quite an entourage' of technicians and other correspondents. The new offensive was outside his area. But in the first week the coverage became 'such a mess' that the BBC brought him down to coordinate the correspondents and engineers. Chester was encouraged to reserve for himself the military commentaries on the battle as a whole. Effectively the Australian was running the show. Driving his new Humber over icy roads from one sector to the next Chester was able to assemble a richly varied coverage.

American forces north of the German thrust were fortunate they were commanded by Montgomery. Eisenhower had made the decision to place the Field Marshal in command of the northern sector with great reluctance and it was never forgiven by General Omar Bradley most of whose forces, with the exception of Patton's Third Army, had come under Monty's command. But Bradley's Headquarters were too far from the battle and Eisenhower himself was at the Trianon Palace Hotel near Versailles, and neither had anything like adequate communications. In addition, the one piece of intelligence SHAEF had received was that English-speaking German commandos in American uniforms were trying to assassinate the Allied leaders. Consequently both generals were confined to their headquarters under heavy guard.

Montgomery was having none of this. He ordered one of his staff to get the largest Union Jack that would fit on the bonnet of his heated Rolls-Royce, and also called for eight motorcycle outriders. His entourage then roared into General Courtney Hodges's 9th Army Headquarters, and it seemed to one observer 'like Christ come to cleanse the temple'.[12] But however much his actions may have been resented later, Montgomery's authoritative intervention was accepted at the time with gratitude and relief. As the Field Marshal saw it, there were plenty of American troops available to counter the German attacks: they only needed organisation – 'tidying up the line', he called it.[13] To do this Montgomery was quite prepared to yield ground if it meant saving lives and putting troops in better defensive positions.

Absolutely crucial in countering the German attacks was the break in the weather that came on Christmas Day 1944, which gave the Allied air forces the opportunity to strike at the enemy's main strengths. In a broadcast that went to air on 29 December, Chester summed up the situation.

We can see now the effect of these air attacks in what has happened and is happening beyond Rochefort. The [German] reinforcements haven't arrived, and those reconnaissance tendrils which were pushed out towards the Meuse have withered for lack of nourishment and are now being lopped off and destroyed. Here, our people are on the offensive and the enemy is being driven back from the Meuse towards Rochefort. And so we have this position along the front. At the western end of the salient the Germans are being forced back. On the southern flank we have a solid wedge driven in as far as Bastogne, so at its waist their salient is now only eighteen miles wide. On the northern flank where they've put in the main weight of their best panzer divisions, one strong attack north-west of Lierneux in the middle of the line was repulsed on Tuesday. North-west of Grandmenil, where they've been trying their way up the road to Liege, their attacks have been held, and here the enemy now shows signs of weakening under our counterattack. The relief of Bastogne combined with the holding of our positions near Grandmenil has so pinched in the German salient that von Rundstedt's troops west of this narrow waist must be feeling very uncomfortable; and this is specially so because of our air attacks on their supply lines.[14]

Now the British were fighting alongside the Americans. Until then Montgomery had held the British forces in reserve and allowed the Americans to fight their own battle. As a precaution the British Second Army had moved to cover the Meuse in case German forces reached the river. Montgomery, however, had no intention of letting the German thrust penetrate further. When Brian Horrocks romantically suggested they let the Germans through and defeat them on the field of Waterloo, Monty at once sent him on leave. But now the British Second Army came into play. Chester's broadcast on 5 January 1945 described how the battle unfolded:

Unhappy phrases

British troops are fighting alongside the American First Army in our offensive against the western end the northern flank of the German salient in the Ardennes. It was British armour and infantry which captured the two villages south of Rochefort on Wednesday, and yesterday another British force joined in the attack on the Americans' right. East of Marche they pushed the Germans back nearly a mile, with a series of thrusts into the hills along a five- to six-mile front ...

When the Germans broke through in the first week-end of their offensive, Field Marshal Montgomery at once brought the British Divisions south in case the Americans needed them and, as the German threat developed, the roads leading back into Belgium were packed with British convoys day and night. It is remarkable how quickly and efficiently we moved thousands of troops with all their guns, tanks, ammunition, and engineering supplies. The Belgians lined the roads and cheered the Tommies, as the convoys moved towards the new front.

The troops forgot about their Christmas plans, and in the rain and sleet they dug defensive positions in the valley of the Meuse. The men who had helped liberate Belgium were determined that they would not let the Germans come back. But, as it turned out, the main German assault towards Liege was held by American troops alone, and until Christmas Day the British forces had only the role of a long stop. By then the Germans had captured Rochefort, and had sent a series of armoured columns probing towards the Dinant sector of the Meuse. British tanks, self propelled guns, and motorized infantry were sent to support an American division in dealing with these. The combined allied attack brought disaster to the Germans ... The Germans were stopped, and most of them were surrounded. We're counting the wreckage in this area west of Rochefort now, and we've already counted lying there, derelict and abandoned, 81 German tanks, 7 assault guns, 74 other guns, and 405 vehicles. In this action the Germans lost the bulk of one Panzer division and the westward thrust towards the Meuse was finally stopped.[15]

The day after this broadcast on 7 January 1945, Field Marshal Montgomery gave a press conference about the battle. His notes are published in his memoirs and there is a transcript of the broadcast Chester recorded for the BBC. Reading these now, it is difficult to see why reporters sympathetic to Montgomery such as Frank Gillard, Alan Moorehead and Chester himself, were so horrified. On the face of it, Montgomery gave a perfectly straightforward account of the battle, deplored press criticism of Eisenhower, and concluded with a tribute to the Supreme Commander as the leader of the team. But the correspondents knew how deeply the pride of the American High Command had been affronted by the need to call in Montgomery. No one outside the inner circle of British Government and High Command knew that Montgomery had actually secured Eisenhower and Bradley's grudging agreement to a narrow front strategy, agreements they reneged on almost as soon as they reached the comfort of their respective headquarters. But everyone realised how irritating some of Monty's statements were to the wounded sensibilities of the American generals and their staffs. In *The Struggle for Europe* Chester singled out some of the Field Marshal's more 'unhappy phrases'. He said, 'When the crisis came national considerations were thrown overboard', a statement which the Americans regarded as a suggestion that Eisenhower had called in the best man. Montgomery also declared that his first task had been to 'tidy up the battlefield' and he spoke of the operation as 'one of the most interesting and tricky I have ever handled'.[16] The situation was made worse by Nazi black propaganda. As Chester explained,

Unhappy phrases

My dispatch to the BBC was picked up in Germany, rewritten to give it an anti-American bias and then rebroadcast by Arnhem Radio, which was then in Goebbels's hands. Monitored at Bradley's HQ, this broadcast was mistaken for a BBC transmission and it was this twisted text that started the whole uproar.[17]

The 'whole uproar' was to involve much more than American hostility towards Montgomery over a press conference. The Battle of the Bulge cost the Americans around 80 000 casualties in killed, missing, wounded and captured – the highest number of casualties suffered by them during the war; it cost them approximately 800 tanks; and, of critical importance, it cost the Allies six weeks of bitter fighting before they regained their pre-Ardennes line. What might have occurred in the political landscape of postwar Europe; the relative performances of the key Allied commanders from Normandy to Berlin; and a number of Allied political decisions would become the subject of bitter claims and counter claims by the participants and historians for years to come, and would influence the so-called 'Wilmot Thesis'.

* * * *

Much as he had come to like Montgomery, Chester in 1944 was still an impartial observer. His conclusions about the Anglo-American alliance and the strategy adopted in Europe and the Battle of the Bulge itself were to come later, after he had undertaken a close examination of the documents and interviews with participants for *The Struggle for Europe*.

A side effect of the press conference was that Bradley demanded his HQ should be covered by a BBC representative. So Frank Gillard was transferred to the Americans. As a result Chester would now come to report on Montgomery and the British Second Army at even closer quarters.

21

SO BIG WAS WILMOT'S STORY ...

Seven days after Montgomery's press conference Chester recorded a twelve-minute dispatch on the so-called von Rundstedt Ardennes offensive. Almost certainly it was based on briefings from a highly placed source at the Field Marshal's Tactical Headquarters, probably Monty's Chief of Intelligence, Edgar Williams. The dispatch was a remarkably acute analysis, and it is easy to see why it was allowed to take up more than half of the program's fifteen minutes. Chester began by outlining the enemy's objectives as he saw them. The Germans, Wilmot argued, were attempting to anticipate the Russian winter offensive and avoid having to fight on two fronts. They therefore needed to put the Allies on the defensive by concentrating their forces and thrusting deep into the American lines. Politically this would drive a wedge between the Allies so the Germans could secure a separate peace with the USA and Britain that would exclude Russia.

By 15 January 1945, the date of the broadcast, Wilmot was able to make a good case for the failure of the German offensive. They had not reached Aachen or the Meuse; all they had succeeded in doing was creating a bulge in the American line. Chester admitted the Germans had overrun several American divisions but then argued that the enemy's strategy had taught the Allies a decisive lesson. Von Rundstedt had concentrated his strength on a narrow front. Therefore to defeat him, the Allies had to switch tactics and move away from advancing from a broad front to fighting the enemy on the same narrow front. Naturally, there was no mention of the earlier dispute between Eisenhower and Montgomery over the issue, but Chester was clearly arguing the British case. He had subtly moved from being an impartial observer and reporter to an advocate. However, the broad front continued to dominate Allied strategy. When he came to describe the campaign in the Rhineland for *The Struggle for Europe* Chester was less critical of Eisenhower's planning for the invasion of Germany, which was essentially a compromise. In *The Struggle for Europe* he outlined Eisenhower's plan to develop operations in three phases:

> Phase 1: Montgomery was to seize the west bank of the Rhine from Nijmegen to Düsseldorf, after clearing the Lower Rhineland with converging attacks – from the Reichswald by First Canadian Army and from the Roer River by Ninth U.S. Army, which was to remain under his command for the Rhine crossing. During these operations, apart from capturing the Roer dams and covering Ninth Army's southern flank, Bradley's forces on the Ardennes front were to maintain an aggressive defence.
>
> Phase 2: While Montgomery was preparing for a set-piece assault across the Lower Rhine, Bradley was to secure the west bank from Düsseldorf to Coblenz. For this purpose First Army was to drive its left wing through to Cologne and then strike south-east into the flank and rear of the Germans in the Eifel. Thereupon, Third Army was to take up the offensive, attacking eastwards from Prüm to Coblenz.
>
> Phase 3: While Montgomery was assaulting the Lower Rhine, the Third and Seventh American Armies were to clean out the

Moselle-Saar-Rhine triangle, and secure crossing places on the Mainz-Karlsruhe sector for the forces which were to carry out the southern envelopment of the Ruhr.[1]

Much to the reporters' dismay, after the Ardennes offensive, the BBC temporarily suspended 'War Report' for six weeks (from 4 February to 23 March). Just why is not clear, but the program had its share of enemies among the bureaucrats. However, Wilmot continued to send back dispatches of approximately the same length, confident they would get into other programs such as 'Radio Newsreel', 'Radio Weekly', the 'Pacific Service' or 'Unit Spotlight'. He recorded profiles of individual units and a series of dispatches on the Battle of the Cologne Plain as Montgomery's forces fought their way to the Rhine. In early March 1945, Chester also wrote his first piece of outright propaganda since he had worked for the Department of Information in Australia. There had been a campaign in the British press to have Montgomery made Ground Forces Commander. If Monty was good enough to take over during the crisis then, the press insisted, he should be retained once the situation had been restored. When this did not happen there were inevitably lingering doubts about the competence of the American commanders. It was these doubts the dispatch was endeavouring to counter.

> Hello BBC! This is Chester Wilmot speaking from Field Marshal Montgomery's Headquarters on the Western front, where Allied troops now command most of the west bank of the Rhine from Cologne to Arnhem ... Of course we mustn't forget that this last barrier [the Rhine] is the greatest obstacle our troops have faced since we attacked the Atlantic Wall on D-Day. But even from this side of the Rhine our guns can shell the industrial heart of Germany, the Ruhr; the very streets of the Ruhr will be under rocket and machine-gun fire from

Thunderbolts, Typhoons and Spitfires, operating from airfields only a few minutes flight away.

Chester then 'explained' the delays and disappointments of late 1944 and early 1945.

All this means that in the past three weeks we've witnessed in the Cologne Plain one of the decisive battles of the war, and a striking victory for Montgomery and his American, British and Canadian troops. This victory is the reward of a lot of things but basically it's the reward of waiting, not being idle while you have to wait. Last September we had high hopes that the war could be finished in a couple of months. The Germans in the west were on the run, and if the Arnhem operation had been a complete success, we might have kept them running.

But when that didn't come off, I found the people in England were rather critical, rather impatient, because the Army hadn't finished the war. But we know now that we couldn't have finished Germany last year … By waiting through the winter in the West, we've been able to gain a much cheaper victory and a much more timely victory then we could have gained if we'd tried to deliver the so-called 'final blow' last year. We've been impatient here, and you at home have been impatient, because there's been so little progress these last few months in terms of miles. But even though we haven't been advancing very much in the West; we've been doing something equally important; we've been destroying Germans and turning the balance of striking power in our favour. That's the achievement of the winter – the turning of the balance of striking power.

The dispatch went on to make the most of the German failure in the Ardennes.

Last November the Americans launched an offensive with five armies attacking. In France they reached the Rhine; in Germany they reached the River Roer. Small gains on the map, perhaps, but in defending this ground we know now that the Germans lost about a quarter of a million men – two hundred and fifty thousand – enough troops to make up twenty-five German divisions at present day strength.

In spite of these losses the Germans were still able to launch their Ardennes offensive; but here again they lost far more than they gained. In that attack they must have lost the equivalent of ten divisions. Into that abortive venture, von Rundstedt sent almost the whole of his armoured reserves in the west, including the Sixth Panzer Army that he'd so carefully built up as his strategic reserve. That came out of the Battle of the Ardennes with its manpower well down, with most of its armour destroyed, and with its morale seriously weakened.

And I believe that this attack was a blessing in disguise. Montgomery had planned to launch the Canadian Army and the 9th Army in an attack towards the Rhine at the start of January. These armies were to carry out just the plan that they're now completing. But if there'd been no Ardennes battle, and we *had* attacked in January, the German opposition would have been extremely tough. The whole of the 6th Panzer Army would have been waiting for us in the Cologne plain. As we attacked through the Reichswald and across the Roer River, we'd have been met by counter-attacks from von Rundstedt's tactical reserves; reserves which hadn't been mauled in the Ardennes fighting. We'd have been fighting in bad weather and with little air support. And if we had got to the Rhine, it would have been only after a long, costly battle.

That enforced wait has saved us many lives.²

Chester did not mention the massive casualties sustained by the Americans; nor did he even suggest that the German offensive became possible when the Americans 'thinned out' the Ardennes sector as part their broad front strategy. Rather it is implied that a German attack was only to be expected and that it had all worked out for the best. Nothing was said about the American blunder prolonging the war.

Two months earlier Chester was advocating Montgomery's narrow front strategy. Having lost that argument Wilmot had of necessity become a propagandist for Allied unity. The dispatch was calculated to allay doubts about the US leadership, deftly implying that all was well because Montgomery was playing a major role. The broadcast then went on to emphasise the German weakness and the impact of pressure from the Russians. Chester was always uncomfortable writing propaganda, even when it was combined with valid analysis, as was the case here; but given the tensions between the Allies since the Ardennes, Wilmot clearly saw it as his patriotic duty. A real discussion about the issues could wait.

As the British 2nd Army Group and the American Ninth Army together fought their way to the Rhine, Charles Moses arrived in Brussels. The ABC General Manager had been attending a Commonwealth Broadcasting Conference in London. Once the conference was over Moses persuaded the BBC to temporarily attach him to the 'War Report' Unit as one of the reporters covering the Rhine crossing. Chester enjoyed showing his old boss over the front, but some of the other reporters were less welcoming. When Moses asked why, Chester explained that due to the intense competition to get stories into 'War Report', if the BBC broadcast one of Moses's stories, it meant one of the others would miss out. On the other hand Moses – Lieutenant-Colonel Moses as he had become after commanding a battalion on the Sanananda Track in Papua New Guinea – was an excellent broadcaster with a firm grasp of military tactics. He was to make an impressive contribution to the 'War Report' coverage of the Rhine crossing even though he was more than a little apprehensive. As Moses confided to the author, 'After all the hazards of organising the Gordon Bennett escape from Singapore I'd have felt very silly if anything had happened to me when I was decked out as a war correspondent'. Much as he enjoyed Moses's company, Chester had to tactfully dissuade him from taking charge of the BBC's coverage of the battle.

Montgomery's plan was for the British Second Army to cross the Rhine to the north of Wesel from positions near the towns of Rees and Xanten on the west bank. The plan was so precise that Chester was able to organise a full coverage of nearly every aspect of it. Stewart MacPherson was on a hill near Calcar that looked down the Rhine Valley and also onto Rees. He later moved to another vantage point at the Commando HQ. Chester decided to record his broadcast from a tower 300 yards from the river bank. The 15th Scottish Division was to cross in Buffaloes after an eight-hour barrage. Wynford Vaughan-Thomas went in one of the Buffaloes accompanied by his brother, who was the brigadier commanding the division. (This was not revealed in the broadcast. Vaughan-Thomas mentions it in his memoirs.) The air drop supporting the ground attack a day later – Operation Varsity – was to be covered by Richard Dimbleby in a Dakota and Stanley Maxted in a glider. Chester himself was to go up in a spotter plane with a wire recorder.

Field Marshal Montgomery had always been determined to bring as many of his men back with him to Britain as he could, and in this, the last set-piece battle he would ever fight, Monty was taking as few chances as possible with the lives of his soldiers. As night came on 23 March 1945 the whole 22-mile front on the west bank of the Rhine erupted. 3500 field guns opened fire simultaneously together with 2000 anti-tank guns, mortars and rocket projectors. Did the spectacle remind some of the veterans of the all-night bombardment the night before El Alamein and the sound of the pipes in the clear desert air? As before, British troops were to jump off first and Chester was to begin his coverage with the pipes of the Scottish regiments playing the men into their assembly areas. At precisely 9 pm Chester looked down from the tower, flicked the switch on the microphone of the midget his engineer Harvey Sarney had set up, and began recording his description of the assault. Despite having been in hospital with asthma a few days earlier, Chester's voice was strong and clear:

> Hello BBC, this is Chester Wilmot taking up the story of the Rhine crossing from the observation post in the tower of a building looking down on the Rhine itself. The tower I'm speaking from is 300 yards from the river's edge and that river at the moment is a sheet of burning water, because above it are streams of tracer shells and Bofors guns and machine guns. We're putting down a pepper pot, a shower of shells and bullets on the enemy's forward defences from machine guns and Bofors guns while the 25-pounders and the heavier weapons pound away at the enemy gun positions and mortar positions further back. Although the moon is pretty well blanketed by the fog and the smoke that is lying in the river valley as a result of the 45 hours' bombardment that's gone on already, the river is brilliantly illuminated by the streams of tracer shells and bullets …
>
> Now all around this tower and in this town and in the fields beyond, are the waiting troops who are about to cross; men sitting waiting patiently in their Buffaloes, their amphibious vehicles packed and armoured. Already those Buffaloes are moving down towards the water's edge …
>
> A few minutes later, after I saw those Buffaloes disappear over the edge of the bank on this side and go down into the water,

I didn't catch sight of them again, because apparently they came up behind a clump of trees and went straight across to the other side and they were shrouded from my view by this small clump, and the river is no longer illuminated by the streams of Bofors shells which were marking the crossing places, and so it just appears as a thin grey line between two darker banks. I can still see the Buffaloes moving along between the trees on the bank on this side, but they disappear around behind and after that I don't see them as they go across the river, they get lost in the darkness and the smoke or else they are hidden by the trees.

Chester moved to a field where the Buffaloes were being reloaded after returning from crossing the river and described a team loading a 6-pounder gun up a narrow ramp into the rear of one of the carriers. An hour and a half later he saw the Buffaloes and their loads making their second crossing of the Rhine: 'The officers in charge of the bank control are waving them forward with lights; they follow a trail of green lights that wind away across the fields, and there they go off again for their second trip across the Rhine for tonight.'[3]

At a position near Wilmot's Charles Moses found the German return fire coming straight at him. He kept his voice even but when Moses and the author played a recording of the broadcast in the 1980s he pointed out there were tiny halts in his delivery as bullets came in his direction.

Montgomery planned to support the Rhine crossing with an air drop a day later by the US 17th Division and the British 6th Airborne (with whom Chester had landed on D-Day). In overall command was Major-General Ridgway but his deputy was another acquaintance of Wilmot's, Major-General Richard Gale. Gale had studied Operation Market Garden and was grimly determined not to make the same mistakes. The airborne forces were due mid-morning. Flying just below them was Chester in a light spotter airplane clutching a wire recorder:

So big was Wilmot's story ...

And now here come the gliders ... coming in as thick as flies; an absolute swarm of them flying right above my head now; I can't even see where the swarm finishes, because they're swallowed up in the smoke over to the west. And the head of the column is swallowed up in the smoke on the far side of the Rhine. And as the gliders come in, a few hundred feet below them are the parachute Dakotas coming back.

This Armada of gliders and transport aircraft absolutely fills the sky; and now here's another aircraft from which the crew has baled out; it's a Dakota which has been hit; there go the five members of the crew, and they're coming down safely, while the Dakota slips towards the ground on this side of the Rhine. Another crew has been saved, but another plane has been lost.

We're straggling again and we're heading back towards the Rhine, looking into the areas in which the parachutes are being dropped.

As the transport aircraft swing north, over the dropping area, we see a trail of white blobs, as the parachutes open and the men drop, and then we see them just as they fall a couple of hundred feet, and then the parachutists are swallowed up in the clouds. There doesn't appear to be very much flak coming up at the aircraft, but – because I can't see any tracer coming through the smoke or going out into the clear sky above it. But evidently there is plenty of flak hidden there in the smoke, because I see another aircraft coming out smoking; it's apparently all right, but it must have been hit.

Here's another wave now, coming in lower than the others coming in actually underneath us. The waves which have come in so far have been above the level at which we're flying; now this wave is coming round, swinging very low, over the Rhine, and being swallowed up in the smoke cloud on the far side. Meantime, flying, skimming along only a few hundred feet above the ground, are other aircraft that are coming back after completing their mission.[4]

The recordings were directly transmitted through the BBC's powerful mobile transmitter Mike Charlie Nan (MCN) or packaged up with as much explanatory material as possible and flown back to London. Applying techniques developed for the BBC's coverage of the D-Day landings to a single battlefield enabled the combination of multiple perspectives, the authentic experiences of a number of the reporters and the sense of immediacy to take listeners into the event itself. This 'actuality coverage' was recognised at the time as groundbreaking radio, with some editions of 'War Report' running for thirty minutes (at least twice the normal length of the program) as the BBC cut from each report, creating a montage of sound that is as riveting now as it was for listeners in March 1945.

Operation Plunder was both a set-piece battle and a public relations exercise for Montgomery's forces at a time when the British part in the campaign was being downgraded. Chester did have some criticisms of the operation but these were confined to *The Struggle for Europe*. There he was to point out the Americans also had forces over the Rhine, and that the disintegrating German forces were particularly vulnerable to the improvised American tactics, implying that Monty's set-piece battle may not have been entirely necessary. Nevertheless as Wilmot recorded:

> At the end of that day [24 March 1945] Montgomery's forces were six miles east of the Rhine. During the next forty eight hours, while Montgomery's engineers were constructing bridges … the British and American bridgeheads were linked and expanded and the German armour which attempted a counterattack was thrown back.[5]

Moreover, casualties were low and a lot of British and American soldiers owed their lives to Montgomery's meticulous planning and professionalism. Operation Varsity may have been costly, particularly in the lives of the glider pilots – the fragments of film captured by the very brave official cameramen show some horrendous crashes – but this time the planning was faultless and all the objectives seized. Was it some kind of compensation for the blunders of Operation Market Garden? While no one said anything at the time, judging from his memoirs, the thought was definitely in the mind of General Gale.

* * * *

As the British forces fought their way deeper into German territory towards Berlin, Wilmot covered their progress in a series of dispatches transmitted directly to the BBC via MCN. MCN was mounted on two 7-ton trailers hauled by 3-ton trucks. It had replaced the more mobile but less powerful MCO in late September 1944. At first MCN was expected to take three days to move from one location to another but eventually the task was reduced to ten hours. This enabled Chester and his team to maintain a continuing coverage of the Second Army's drive through northern Germany towards Berlin. As well as the usual descriptions of battles the war reporters were discovering the cesspit that lay beneath Nazi Germany. Chester's dispatch describing the liberation of Stalag XIB and Stalag XXX seethes with suppressed anger.

> Only this morning, when tanks of the 8th Hussars reached these two camps near Fallanbostal, 35 miles south-east of Bremen, they found that our troops (the prisoners) had already taken charge of the camp and interned their German guards. An Airborne Sergeant-Major, an ex-Guardsman, was in command, and the British guards were as spick and span as any parade-

ground troops. Their boots were polished, their trousers pressed, and their belts and gaiters blancoed. The British troops had taken over the German offices, and their liberators found clerks busy typing out nominal rolls on German typewriters.

The prisoners had been running the camp since last Friday, when three-quarters of the German guards departed, leaving a skeleton force of 60 to carry on. For the past four days, German and British troops have been on guard together, but this morning the Germans were disarmed.

This afternoon, at Stalag XIB, I saw some of the 20,000, and learned from padres, doctors, and NCOs how they'd been treated. They told me that in this camp there were 4556 British troops, and 2428 Americans. Of these 6700 [sic] more than 1000 are in hospital suffering from wounds, injuries or starvation … Here in this camp I saw clear evidence of the German neglect and wanton disregard for the lives and health of their prisoners. Of the 4250 British prisoners, some 2500 have come into the camp in the last three weeks. The Germans have marched them from Poland, lest they should be set free by the Russian advance. Ten days ago in this camp, there were 3000 other British and American prisoners who had made this terrible trek from Poland; but when Second Army crossed the Weser, the Germans put these 3000 on the road again, and set them marching back towards the Russians. They were determined to stop the 3000 being liberated because they were airmen and paratroops. How far they'll be able to march I don't know, for I saw today the pitiable condition of those who have already made the nightmare journey. I saw them in hospital – drawn, haggard, starved, starved beyond description – limbs like matchsticks, bodies shrunken till their bones stood out like knuckles. The doctor in charge of them said to me, 'Nothing has kept these men alive except Red Cross parcels and their own spirit …'

> I wish those people who think the Germans should be treated lightly, had seen what I saw today. But I saw also the something that was inspiring and encouraging. All this German oppression and brutality and starvation hadn't been able to kill the spirit and self respect of these men of Arnhem, men of Crete, of Dunkirk and Calais, men of Bomber Command and the 8th Airforce [sic]. They'd managed to rise above their sordid environment and today, those of them who were on guard or on duty, were as smart and soldierly in their bearing as they were the day they were captured. They were proud that they had their own camp running when our tanks got there. They felt they had almost liberated themselves. And this afternoon they had the supreme pleasure of watching their German guards being marched away to our prison cage, and as they watched, they cheered.[6]

On 15 April 1945 Chester, Richard Dimbleby and Wynford Vaughan-Thomas were at the Press Centre when a report came that there was a camp down the road. Dimbleby joined a platoon of soldiers and a military doctor to inspect the camp. He thus became the first reporter into Belsen. This is some of what he sent back to London.

> I picked my way over corpse after corpse in the gloom, until I heard one voice rose above the gentle undulating moaning. I found a girl, she was a living skeleton, impossible to gauge her age for she had practically no hair left, and her face was only a yellow parchment sheet with two holes in it for eyes. She was stretching out her stick of an arm and gasping something, it was 'English, English, medicine, medicine,' and she was trying to cry but she hadn't enough strength. And beyond her down the passage and in the hut there were the convulsive movements of dying people too weak to raise themselves from the floor.

In the shade of some trees lay a great collection of bodies. I walked about them trying to count, they were perhaps 150 of them flung down on each other, all naked, all so thin that their yellow skin glistened like stretched rubber on their bones. Some of the poor starved creatures whose bodies were there looked so utterly unreal and unhuman that I could have imagined that they had never lived at all. They were like polished skeletons, the skeletons that medical students like to plan practical jokes with.

At one end of the pile a cluster of men and women were gathered round a fire; they were using rags and old shoes taken from the bodies to keep it alight, and they were heating soup over it. And close by was the enclosure where 500 children between the ages of five and twelve had been kept. They were not so hungry as the rest, for the women had sacrificed themselves to keep them alive. Babies were born at Belsen, some of them shrunken, wizened little things that could not live, because their mothers could not feed them.

One woman, distraught to the point of madness, flung herself at a British soldier who was on guard at the camp on the night that it was reached by the 11th Armoured Division; she begged him to give her some milk for the tiny baby she held in her arms. She laid the mite on the ground and threw herself at the sentry's feet and kissed his boots. And when, in his distress, he asked her to get up, she put the baby in his arms and ran off crying that she would find milk for it because there was no milk in her breast. And when the soldier opened the bundle of rags to look at the child, he found that it had been dead for days.[7]

When the recording reached the BBC they refused to broadcast it until the story was confirmed by the newspapers. An outraged Dimbleby rang Broadcasting House and told the newsroom if the story did not go to air he would never make another broadcast in his life. Finally a truncated version was included at the end of 'War Report'. Then Chester took a hand. An extremely rude memo was dispatched in which Wilmot denounced the program as the worst he had ever heard, said that Dimbleby's report was the only redeeming feature and demanded to know why they were trying to bury one of the finest stories of the war. Almost immediately a placatory letter came back explaining that a senior producer had come into the studio just before 'War Report' went to air and bumped Dimbleby's piece to the bottom of the program and would he (Chester) 'please explain' to Dimbleby. Soon after the full report went to air.

Wilmot never wrote anything about Belsen although he and Montgomery also visited the camp. Colleagues who saw Wilmot on his return described him as pacing around whistling, unable to type. In his papers there is a copy of a detailed official report on the camp. Belsen seems to have been the great unwritten story of Chester's life; an unacknowledged influence on everything he was later to write about Nazi Germany.

The BBC decided they needed Richard Dimbleby to cover Berlin. It could have been an apology of sorts for the way he was treated over the Belsen story but his combination of sincerity and passion was exactly what was needed. By then it was clear neither the Second Army nor the Americans were going to take Berlin. Eisenhower had signalled Montgomery that Berlin was no longer a military objective. Worse still, in an appalling political blunder, Eisenhower had telegraphed his intentions to Stalin. Instead of supporting a balance of power, the traditional British policy for centuries, the United States was collaborating in Russia's creation of satellite states throughout central Europe. Displaying a political acumen with which he is not often credited, Montgomery sent the British 11th Armoured Division racing to Lübeck to block any Russian move into Denmark. Effectively the Field Marshal sealed the Soviet Union into the Baltic. Not surprisingly Monty was to receive a hero's welcome when he entered Copenhagen. The implications of the chess game now being played between the Allies could not be explored in 'War Report' but were to be examined in detail in the book that became *The Struggle for Europe*.

On 1 May Chester and some of the other correspondents were in a 'little German village,' listening to the German stations that called themselves Bremen and Hamburg when the program was interrupted. Wilmot described what followed in a brief dispatch.

> That was at 9.40 pm British time. We were listening to a war commentary in English – the commentary usually given by Lord Haw-Haw, but after last night, when Haw-Haw was drunk at the microphone, the Germans put on another spokesman … another traitor … He was in the middle of a sentence when there was a disturbance in the studio – it sounded at first as though shells were bursting just outside it … The speaker paused … went on again … there were more muffled explosions … and his voice faded out … And then the announcement from the main German station … 'Our Fuhrer Adolf Hitler this afternoon has fallen defending to the last [the German] … Chancellery against the Bolsheviks.'
>
> Then Grand Admiral Doenitz announced that the Fuhrer's mantle had fallen upon him … and the struggle against Bolshevism, in which the Fuhrer had died a hero's death, must be continued. After Doenitz own broadcast there came an order of the day from Doenitz to the German people, ending with the plea that only by unquestioning obedience to his orders could Germany be saved from chaos and destruction.[8]

Dönitz, as he stated in his memoirs, published in 1958, was desperately trying to make a separate surrender to the Allies while continuing to fight the Russians. In Wilmot's papers there is a transcript of a short dispatch describing some of these attempts which seems not to have been filed.

> The official British attitude is that as these two Armies are still engaged in fighting the Russians, we can't accept their surrender, and in any case their commanders are in no position to hand over the armies to us. And so tonight in the woods and villages between the Baltic and the Elbe there are tens of thousands of Germans from Army Group Vistula vainly trying to find someone who will accept them as prisoners. Their Commanders have surrendered; their staffs have disintegrated; only those units still in direct contact with the Russians continue fighting, – fighting rather than yield to the Red Army.[9]

On the same day Wilmot heard the German broadcast, Montgomery's Tactical Headquarters was moved to Lüneburg Heath. Two days later Chester was the only 'War Report' correspondent in camp when the first German peace emissaries came. They were all big men facing the much shorter Field Marshal who was at his most casual wearing corduroy trousers, a grey turtle-neck and of course the black beret. 'Who are you? ... I've never heard of you', Monty barked. They replied they wanted to surrender all the German armies in the north. He replied with a diatribe about Belsen and the destruction of Coventry, adding that if unconditional surrender was not forthcoming in 24 hours he would unleash on them 1000 bombers day and night. Accompanied by two of the liaison officers the Germans went back to their headquarters to get Admiral Dönitz and Field Marshal Keitel's authority for the surrender terms. Chester was able to talk himself into accompanying them. It was supposed to be officers only but the red beret he had worn since landing on D-Day and a greatcoat borrowed from an officer made him appear to be a captain. They found Keitel in an office at the end of a long corridor, his Field Marshal's baton on the desk in front of him. 'The terms will be honoured in the letter and the spirit,' he replied when told of Montgomery's demands. When they returned to the Tactical Headquarters, Chester went to Montgomery's caravan and asked the Field Marshal if he could record the surrender for broadcast on the BBC. 'We'd better rehearse,' Monty replied. So they went over to the tent, army blankets were put on the table, and they went through the exchanges while Harvey Sarney set up the microphones. The recordings made the following day went live into 'War Report' that evening. This is a transcript of what went to air.

> Hello BBC, Hello BBC, this is Chester Wilmot speaking from the 2nd Army front in Germany. This is not so much a description of what happened this afternoon, but the actual thing – recorded at Field Marshal Montgomery's headquarters this afternoon. The full ceremony which took place when the German plenipotentiaries came to sign the instrument of surrender. I've just got to the transmitter and so I haven't had time to edit these recordings and will play them to you as we recorded them on the hill of the Luneburg Heath this afternoon at Field Marshal Montgomery's headquarters. There is an opening description of the arrival of the plenipotentiaries and then you hear Field Marshal Montgomery himself reading the terms of surrender. These are the recordings we made:
>
> Hello BBC this is Chester Wilmot speaking from Field Marshal Montgomery's Tactical Headquarters on a high wind-swept hill on the wild Luneburger Heath near the River Elbe.
>
> It's ten minutes past six on Friday May 4th; the hour and the day for which British service men and women and British people throughout the world have been fighting and working and waiting for five years and eight months.

So big was Wilmot's story ...

The Commanders of the German forces opposing Field Marshal Montgomery's 21st Army Group have come to this headquarters today to surrender. The plenipotentiaries are: General Admiral von Friedeburg, Commander in Chief of the German navy, who succeeded Admiral Doenitz in that post then Doenitz became the new Fuhrer. With him are General Kinsel Chief of Staff to Field to Von Friedeburg, and another staff officer.

They came here yesterday hoping to parley – to talk terms. But they were told to go back and return today with power to make unconditional surrender. They have come back – through the lines again today to make that surrender. And now we're waiting for them to come through the trees that surround Field Marshal Montgomery's headquarters in the field.

And now von Friedeburg is entering General Bergonzoli's caravan, the caravan that was General Bergonzoli's before it was captured by the British in 1940–41. He has gone inside. He stood for a moment at the door, saluted, and walked in.

The four other Germans also saluted and they're now standing at the bottom step. They're standing underneath the camouflage netting screen, and ten yards away to their right is a Union Jack flying in the breeze and they're just saluting Field Marshal Montgomery under the shadow of that flag which is honoured by the troops to whom they're surrendering today.

The caravan in which this final conference is being held is the caravan which the British troops captured from General Bergonzoli when they first destroyed an enemy army in this war, the army of Graziani Cyrensiona in February 1941. In that caravan, a souvenir of the first victory in this war, the discussions leading to our final victory are now taking place, and in a few moments Field Marshal Montgomery and the German plenipotentiaries will move to a tent where the final ceremony of signing will take place. It's now twenty minutes past six, the discussions have been short and to the point. Admiral von Friedeburg has stepped down from Field Marshal Montgomery's caravan and he is now walking over to the tent where the signing ceremony will take place with the other plenipotentiaries and Field Marshal Montgomery is following behind carrying the instrument of surrender which they have agreed to sign. Now inside the tent which is an ordinary camouflaged army tent, the five plenipotentiaries are standing round the table, an ordinary army table covered with rough army blankets. Field Marshal Montgomery enters, they salute and he sits down.

Field Marshal Montgomery: Now we've assembled here to-day to accept the surrender terms which have been made with the delegation from the German Army.[10]

At that moment the line went dead. There was, according to John Snagge, panic in LG1, the main studio for 'War Report'. Instead of saying, 'I'm sorry, we seem to have lost the line we will try to get it back,' the announcer then terminated the program: 'That is the end of tonight's "War Report". Somebody said, 'That has torn it.' Then followed 'a babel of blaming'. The BBC switch was jammed with phone calls demanding to know what had happened. Meanwhile Mike Charlie Nan came back on line and the whole act of surrender was recorded. So big was Wilmot's story that the 'War Report' producer demanded a break into regular programs. The request went all the way to the Director-General. An hour later 'War Report' was back on air. Montgomery was heard continuing:

So big was Wilmot's story ...

I will now read out the terms of that instrument of surrender of all German armed forces in Holland, in north-west Germany, including the Friesian Islands and Heligoland and all other islands, in Schleswig-Holstein, and in Denmark to the Commander-in-Chief 21st Army Group. This to include all naval ships in these areas. These forces to lay down their arms and to surrender unconditionally. All hostilities on land, on seas, or in the air by German forces in the above areas to cease at 0800 hours British Double Summer Time on Saturday the 5th of May 1945. The German Command to carry out at once and without argument or comment all further orders that will be issued by the Allied powers on any subject. Disobedience of orders or failure to comply with them will be regarded as a breach of these surrender terms, and will be dealt with by the Allied Powers in accordance with the accepted laws and usages of War. This instrument of surrender is independent of, without prejudice to, and will be superseded by, any general instrument of surrender imposed by or on behalf of the Allied Powers and applicable to Germany and the German Armed Forces as a whole.

The instrument of surrender is written in English and in German. The English version is the authentic text. The decision of the Allied Powers will be final, if any doubt or dispute arises as to the meaning or interpretation of the surrender terms.

That is the text of the instrument of surrender and the German delegation will now sign this paper, and they will sign in order of seniority and General Admiral von Friedeburg will sign first.

After each of the German delegates wrote their signatures listeners heard again Field Marshal Montgomery's hard, clear voice: 'That concludes the surrender.'

22

A RATHER DIFFERENT SPECTACLE

On 25 May 1945 Chester Wilmot made the last broadcast from the mobile transmitter MCN: 'Mike Charlie Nan'. By then it was located near Montgomery's headquarters at Lüneburg. 'The war is over the job is done,' he told listeners in the UK, Europe, the Pacific and the United States. Chester went on to describe how at first 'War Report' had used MCO, a small, highly mobile transmitter, to carry the dispatches from the beaches. But as the 'triumphant march' of the Second Army had taken the BBC correspondents further away from London, a more powerful transmitter was needed: MCN. It was, he explained, late September before the station was on air at a location near Brussels. Soon after came Wilmot's famous appeal for 'any British listener' to phone the BBC and tell them MCN was trying to get through with one of the great stories of Arnhem.

The day before this last broadcast Chester had achieved a world scoop: the suicide of Reichsführer of the SS, Heinrich Himmler. The Allies had been very anxious to capture the mass murderer they believed was directly responsible for the millions of dead in the concentration camps they were discovering as their armies advanced into Germany and the occupied countries. Himmler, they knew, had held a wide range of appointments in the last days of the German Reich. He had even been given a military posting as commander of Army Group Vistula, the forces tasked with countering the Russian advance on Berlin. After proving totally inadequate as a general Himmler tried without success to negotiate with the Allies. Since the surrender Chester had been reporting on various attempts by the Second Army to capture him. They discovered later that British military police had just missed the Reichsführer when he had gone to Flensburg to offer his services to Admiral Dönitz. When the Admiral heard Himmler wanted to see him, he placed a loaded pistol beneath the papers on his desk, and told him bluntly there was no place for him in the government. Ironically, while the British were scouring Flensburg for Himmler, he was virtually in custody unrecognised. As Wilmot reported,

> The beginning of the end came on Monday evening – May 21st, when Himmler and two of his SS staff in civilian clothes were stopped by British troops making a routine check of all civilians crossing the bridge at Bremervörde, the bridge over the canal that links the Elbe and the Weser west of Hamburg. Himmler was wearing a civilian suit and was disguised with a black patch over his right eye and had shaved off his moustache. When asked who he was, Himmler said his name was Hizinger and he produced papers showing that he'd been discharged from the army. This at once roused the suspicion of the guards on the bridge. For the German Army has been ordered not to issue any more discharge papers. Himmler had been too clever.
>
> The guards called in the Field Security Police. They didn't recognise Himmler as the man for whom all the Allies were hunting, but his answers to their questions made them suspicious and they sent him back for special interrogation. He spent Tuesday and Wednesday being moved from one prisoner of war cage to the next until he reached the 2nd Army cage yesterday evening.

At 2nd Army last night he again escaped recognition but when he realised he was being put aside for special interrogation, he sent his adjutant to seek an interview with the camp commandant. To him Himmler announced his identity. He took off his eye shield and it was immediately apparent to the British Intelligence Officers there that he was telling the truth. This was confirmed when he gave his Party number, SS [number], date and place of birth and most important of all, his signature. All squared [with] our records.

He then requested to be taken to a senior British Officer. This was agreed but just as he was searched again for weapons and poison in his kit a small phial of poison [was found] hidden in a small brass case.

He was then made to dress in a British army issue cloths – except that he was given no trousers or coat. Then wrapped in a blanket he was driven to 2nd Army HQ. There he was again searched for poison ... searched by a doctor ... thoroughly. After searching his body, the doctor told Himmler to open his mouth. He did. The doctor saw nothing but told Himmler to move near the light. He moved and the doctor put his index fingers inside Himmler's mouth. As he did so Himmler jerked his head back ... bit down on the doctor's fingers ... and the doctor saw a small black object flash across Himmler's mouth ... the black object was the head of a phial of cyanide.[1]

Wilmot had been allowed to check the body for himself:

He was lying on the floor where he fell last night covered with a blanket and clad otherwise only in a British army shirt and a pair of grey army socks.

A rather different spectacle

There is no doubt that that was Himmler ... there was the crooked nose, the receding chin, the flabby jowls, the high sloping forehead and the thinning hair. He'd shaved off his moustache, but that was never a distinctive feature. His notoriously shifting eyes were closed behind his transparent horn-rimmed glasses; his hands were folded across his chest.[2]

That story was on air at 8 pm, the very minute it was released to the world media. The BBC had beaten all the other news services. MCN also transmitted Chester's recording of Sergeant Major Edwin Austen's eye-witness description of Himmler's death, cutting only Austen's last words: 'and I spat in his eye'.[3]

Before the war the corporation had virtually no independent news service and had been forced to rely on the newspapers and the wire services for their news bulletins. Now the BBC was breaking its own stories. However, for all its achievements during the war, the BBC was still stubbornly class conscious. But Chester remained the egalitarian Australian. His final broadcast from MCN concluded with a tribute to the technicians.

> And now with perhaps the last great war story broadcast from Germany, MCN is packing up and going back to England. But we Correspondents and those of you who've listened to us and the men we've brought to the microphone should be grateful to the engineers who've operated MCN ...
>
> And now MCN is closing down, but it's only right that the engineer in charge of it, Geoffrey Herrin, should call our London Station, and have the last word.
>
> Herrin: Hello Mike Charlie Mike 4 – this is Mike Charlie Nan 4 – This station is now closing down – thanks very much for

all the help from your end. Mike Charlie Mike – this is Mike Charlie Nan 4 closing down. Over and out.[4]

The sound of this last broadcast from MCN survives. It was one of Chester Wilmot's finest dispatches with Geoffrey Herrin's last words underscoring, as nothing else could, the magnitude of the BBC's technical achievement.

* * * *

Chester's regular employment with the BBC ended with the war. But there were still stories the corporation wanted him to cover and Wilmot had a lucrative book contract. In addition he could make more money working for the BBC as a freelance than if he was on staff. So he resisted indirect pressure from well-meaning family friends who urged him to return to Australia and go back to the law. He did contemplate a brief journey back to report the end of the war in the Pacific. But as a journalist and historian his subject matter was in England and Europe. This was why Chester wanted Edith to join him as soon as possible. Travel in wartime was severely restricted and for nearly six months Chester had sent lists of contacts for Edith to try, all to no avail. Finally, Edith secured passage for Jane and herself on the cargo vessel *Rangatiki*. By 1945 the voyage was reasonably safe. They were to travel across the Pacific through the Panama Canal into the Atlantic and then on to Britain. But it was still a difficult passage for Edith and Jane. Two-year-olds are difficult enough, but Jane's as yet undiagnosed deafness made her very hard to manage in the confined spaces of a long sea voyage. When the ship finally reached Britain, Chester found Edith in a line at the purser's office while his daughter was beating up the other children on the boat. He could see the voyage had exhausted Edith and quickly took Jane in hand. Before long the delighted little girl was climbing all over her father and to Edith's horror even somersaulting off his shoulders.

A rather different spectacle

When Chester first planned to bring his family to Britain he had asked his wife whether she wanted to live in London or the country. Edith barely hesitated before deciding on the country. Chester had always wanted to live in an English village and work in the city so he quickly started house hunting in towns and villages near London. He could afford a car and was an expert driver easily able to undertake long drives. About this time Chester joined the Savile Club. To attract interesting members, traditionally the club kept fees and subscriptions low, both of which made stays in the city when researching the book or working at the BBC relatively easy. Edith quickly mastered British rail timetables and was visiting London herself even before they had moved into the new house. It was a world portrayed in countless British novels and films of middle- and upper-class life and soon Edith came to feel at home. Moreover, Chester's position had its privileges. A few days after arriving in London he had taken her to see John Gielgud in *Hamlet*. Gielgud was one of the great Hamlets of the twentieth century and it was the last time the great actor was to play the part on stage. They saw it from the fourth row courtesy of the BBC. A few months later Chester managed to get them seats for two other famous productions, *Henry IV* parts one and two at the Old Vic with Laurence Olivier as Hotspur and Shallow and Ralph Richardson as Falstaff. Even at the time they both knew they had witnessed theatre history. Before long Edith was writing to her family about how 'we in Britain' saw things, describing visits to art galleries and long drives with Chester in the countryside where they hurried through 'dreary mining towns'.[5] Not that either of them ignored the darker side of postwar Britain. Edith always remembered the flat desolation of the blitzed suburbs she saw with Chester from the top deck of a bus on their first day in London.

For Edith the Labour victory in late 1945 was a shock. They were staying with some of Wilmot's cousins in the South Riding village of Scorby. It had been a Tory stronghold for years and everyone was devastated. Putting aside his own left-wing sympathies, Chester assured the family that with the support of the British middle class, the country was ready for socialism. Undoubtedly his own feelings were mixed. He admired Churchill as a war leader but supported the ideals of the welfare state. The unexpected victory of the socialists must have seemed to him the beginning of the more equal and just world he had hoped would come at the end of the war – views that infuriated Edith, who never took his idealism seriously. But could the British Labour Party handle the complicated European and transatlantic postwar diplomacy? Chester was not sure.

When he returned to Europe to collect material for the book in early August 1945, Wilmot retained his BBC accreditation as a correspondent, but with the obligation to send them an occasional story – at freelance rates. The corporation files indicate Chester was a hard bargainer. He usually got what he asked for because, in the words of one memo, 'he is the best'.[6] Chester still had the German Volkswagen that the BBC had 'liberated' from the Germans garaged in Brussels, so his journey began there. He was in Holland when news of the dropping of the atomic bombs and the Japanese surrender came. Almost immediately he was inundated with requests for stories about the victory celebrations. Not only did he make a 'killing' on them financially but collected some useful information for the book. In Germany he found the boundaries between the Russians in the east, the Americans to the south and the British in the west were being firmly established. The divisions that had fought in this last battle for Germany were still there but many of the Americans were due to return to the United States. So after writing to the commanding officers, Chester embarked on a three-week tour of the American zone, allowing two days for each division. As he explained to Edith: 'First I get the story from eye witness accounts and documents. I then tackle the divisional general and shoot various questions at him, find out what he considers were the problems and critical points and the reasons for success or failure … this gives

A rather different spectacle

me the inside story of what went on in the commander's mind.'[7] Throughout this dredging through documents Chester could not help remembering his training with Ernest Scott. 'We hated those essays that had to be based on original sources but thank God for Scotty now.'[8]

By September he was back in England. Before leaving Germany he had contacted General Eisenhower, who had suggested he send a questionnaire. Later that month he was back to get his answers.

> Ike was wonderfully frank. He told me why he had to postpone D-Day from May to June, what happened on the nights of 3 June and 4 June when it was postponed again and then put on. We discussed our strategy and tactics and that of the Germans in Normandy and afterwards, and talked at great length about the Ardennes. All this time he was pacing up and down the room talking in his vivid direct way and this went on for two and a half hours.[9]

In *The Struggle for Europe* Chester was to be very critical of some of Eisenhower's decisions but he seems never to have lost his respect for the man. The day he saw the American commander, Ike had relieved General George S Patton of command of the Third Army and as Governor of Bavaria, essentially for failing to implement the de-Nazification program in his area. Patton had been guilty of yet another indiscretion but the general's sympathy for former Nazis was the real reason Eisenhower had acted. Chester approved and said so in a broadcast for the BBC that evening.

When Wilmot returned to England, he had to confront a major problem with Jane. In spite of her obvious intelligence she was still not talking. The problem was solved when Richard Dimbleby dropped by to meet the family and suggested Jane might be deaf. They immediately followed up on Richard's lead. There was a quiet talk with a Mrs Hartley, a teacher of the deaf in the village where they were staying. After spending some time with the girl her opinion was that Dimbleby might be right. A visit to a specialist followed. He discovered that Jane could hear only certain frequencies. This partial hearing may have been why the condition had not been diagnosed earlier. Edith was shattered. How had she missed discovering this herself? Chester ignored Edith's self-reproach and just said, 'Let's make her the best little deaf girl we possibly can.'[10] Reading between the lines of his letters home it is clear he believed his wife was on the verge of a nervous breakdown. Chester insisted Edith pick somewhere she would like to go for a holiday before they tackled Jane's problems. During Chester's time in the Middle East they had made a pact to share every detail of their respective experiences in war and on the home front, but during the last months of the war Chester had not been able to write as fully and frequently as he would have liked, and Edith wanted to share these experiences too. So she asked to be taken to some of the places from which he had been reporting only a few months before. The Ector family, who had befriended Wilmot in Brussels, were delighted to put them up, friends agreed to look after Jane and within days Chester had bustled Edith onto the boat train for Paris.

Judging from Edith and Chester's letters home this was one of their happiest times together. The Ectors were delighted to see Chester again. Whenever there had been a free moment from reporting the war he had come over to spend time with the children. Chester had been missing his family but the youngsters were delightful personalities, as Jane was to find when she stayed with them later, and the children treated him like a long lost hero. 'My father always kept his friendships in good repair,'[11] she told the author. Edith found her schoolgirl French of little use, but Chester soon recovered his fluency. Even when uncertain he would speak as quickly as possible because 'they like it that way'. Edith delighted in hearing from Wilmot's friends in Brussels some of the stories he had not been able to tell her. One she particularly liked was about the time the BBC truck had been parked outside the hotel where the correspondents were staying when the Allied Forces entered Brussels and the crowds kept calling for their favourite broadcasters: Frank Gillard and Chester Wilmot. As there was no one else from the corporation there Chester had to go out and acknowledge the cheers alone.

The liberated Volkswagen was garaged in the city so Chester was able to take Edith on long drives over the battlefields of France, Belgium and Holland with the BBC plates on the car virtually guaranteeing them a warm welcome wherever they went. There were still many signs of the warfare that had raged across the Belgian and German landscape. Many of the battles had taken place in some of the most beautiful countryside in Europe. Almost certainly never far from the couple's minds were the images of the flattened, blitzed areas Chester had shown Edith on their first day in London. The tragedy of war seemed to be all encompassing.

On their return to England they placed Jane at a local school. She was making a great effort to lip-read and trying to speak. But even though Jane was doing well, Chester and Edith were advised she would make greater progress at a specialist institution. After some investigations they enrolled her in the Royal School for the Deaf in Manchester. It was rather forbidding in appearance and she would have to become a boarder, but the school had a good reputation and the children were treated with great sensitivity and understanding. They were also very generous with each other. Soon Jane felt at home there and began to speak more fluently. Ultimately, she became 'the best little deaf girl' her father had hoped for. At the time of writing, Jane Wilmot Crane, OBE is a lawyer and a vigorous activist for the deaf community.

During his journeys in Germany researching the book Wilmot began to feel a certain compassion for the defeated people. He remembered the glittering Berlin of 1938 and was repelled by the appalling devastation wrought by the strategic bomber offensive. One incident stayed in his memory. It was the sight of starving men and women bidding on a street corner with their jewellery and ornaments for a piece of fish that had been produced from a bag by a Russian serviceman. Chester was disgusted by the lavish party he had been compelled to attend the same evening. He told Edith that consuming that much food in such circumstances was indecent. Chester saw the bunker where Hitler had committed suicide and toured the devastated suburbs. Although it was the capital of the Third Reich, Berlin was a tragedy. Berliners had never supported the Nazis and as far as they dared had treated Hitler, Göring, Goebbels and the rest with civilised contempt. Nuremberg, where Chester went to cover the war crimes trials, was different. The city had been ardently Nazi since the mid-1920s. It was there the party rallies had been staged. The last time Wilmot had been in Nuremberg was for the 1938 rally when he had been 'ashamed to be an Englishman', because of Britain's betrayal of Czechoslovakia.

He was not ashamed now. In a thirteen-minute broadcast for the BBC Wilmot told the story of that last rally and then he concluded by describing a recent visit to the Zeppelin field and compared it with what he had seen at the 1938 rally:

> One day I went out to the Zeppelin Field to watch Hitler inspect 50 000 workers of the Labour Corps. The Zeppelin Field was a huge arena built by the Nazis and holding about a quarter of a million spectators. It was packed three hours before Hitler arrived, but thousands stood patiently in the cold and rain, sang militant songs, chanted Nazi war cries and periodically shouted the German equivalent of 'We want our Fuehrer.' An hour before he was due to arrive the various Nazi delegations to the rally began to arrive ... then came the Fuehrer and the Nazi big shots with a screen of armoured cars and outriders and a fleet of great sleek Mercedes Benzes; as the Fuehrer appeared the air was split with the mass roar of 'Sieg Heil – Sieg Heil!' And then the cheer leader led the crowd in the parrot slogans of the year 'Ein Reich

A rather different spectacle

Ein Fuehrer' and so on. Then the workers marched in, stripped to the waist, carrying shovels at the slope and moving with military precision. Hitler addressed them, the crowd listened in devoted silence and then broke into another frenzy of cheering and incantation until the great black cars slipped the new Messiah and his apostles away.

To-day I went back to the Zeppelin Field which [is] now renamed Soldiers Field, and it's the sporting headquarters of the Third American Army, in place of the swastikas is the Third Army sign, a big white A in a red circle standing for Army of Occupation. In one corner of the field is a baseball diamond and the great signboard where the Nazi cheer-leader would burst the next slogan for the crowd to chant, that is now a baseball scoreboard: right next to the Zeppelin Field is the stadium where the Nazis held some of their rally festivities. In this stadium I watched a rather different spectacle than the one I saw in 1938. It was an American football game between the 1st Division and the 42nd. And true to American custom, each side had its band, its flags, its cheerleaders. But the flags were those of the regiments and the 48 states of America ... Outside the stadium a line of German prisoners of war who keep this ground tidy, stood back while American generals and colonels rode off in a fleet of great Mercedes Benzes that had once been black. We drove from the Zeppelin Field up into the ruins of Nuremberg, and the beautiful old city I'm afraid has been almost completely destroyed by fire bombs.

Nuremberg is more badly damaged than any big city I've seen except Berlin and Cologne ... People are still trying to live among the ruins, but the glory that was Nuremberg is gone for ever, and the Tower of Torture is one of the few old structures still more or less intact. It stands as a reminder [that] the crimes for which the Nazis are to be tried in Nuremberg, have their roots deep in the past, in that strange contradiction in German character between the cultured and the brutal. Because of that I feel that here we're not only putting on trial the twenty-five Nazi war criminals who've been indicted, but we're also passing judgement upon that element of aggressive brutal militarism which has been Germany's evil genius for so long. The Nuremberg trial is an attempt to establish a precedent for the punishment under international law of those who wage aggressive war. This I think makes the Nuremberg trial something far more than the last rally of the Nazi party. Here we may be able to lay the first foundations of a new system of an international justice.[12]

The trial took place in the Palace of Justice in courtroom 600. Five Sherman tanks guarded the court house and the whole area was protected by US troops. Among the twenty-five accused were some familiar faces from the surrender: Grand Admiral Karl Dönitz, Hitler's designated successor; the Minister for War in the Third Reich's last government and the Head of Oberkommando der Wehrmacht (German Supreme Command of the Armed Forces, or OKW), Wilhelm Keitel; Alfred Jodl, former Chief of the Operations Division of OKW; Albert Speer, the Minister of Munitions, who had obligingly handed Chester the production figures for the last year of the war; and a direct adversary of the BBC, Hans Fritzsche, Head of the News Division at the Ministry of Propaganda. As well there were the prominent Nazis, Hermann Göring, Commander of the Luftwaffe and the Führer's designated successor until April 1945 when he fell out with Hitler; Rudolf Hess, Deputy Führer until he flew to Scotland in 1941 on a peace mission; Ernst Kaltenbrunner, the highest ranking SS leader to be tried; and Joachim von Rippentrop, Minister of Foreign Affairs 1938–45. In addition, there were some ambiguous figures such as Baron Konstantin von Neurath, Minister of Foreign Affairs 1932–38; Erich Raeder, C-in-C of the German

Navy 1928–43; Franz von Papen, briefly Chancellor of Germany in 1932, the Ambassador to Austria 1934–38, and the ambassador to Turkey 1938–44; the banker Hjalmar Schacht; and the nauseating anti-Semitic propagandist Julius Streicher.

The trial began on 20 November 1945 with a day-long reading of the indictment. The charges were participation in a common plan or conspiracy for a crime against peace, planning and initiating aggressive war, war crimes and crimes against humanity. The next day the prosecutor, Supreme Court Justice Robert H Jackson, opened the case for the prosecution. Delivered in measured tones it was one of the great speeches of the proceedings. He made it clear that there was no intention of incriminating the whole German people. 'If the German populace had willingly accepted the Nazi program, no storm troopers would have been needed in the early days of the Party and there would have been no need for concentration camps or the Gestapo.'[13] Jackson mentioned 'incredible events' that he had at first not believed himself; then he read from reports of the paramilitary SS groups following the military into the Soviet Union with the mission of rounding up and killing Jews, Gypsies and other groups thought hostile to the German people. Later Jackson quoted from SS General Jürgen Stroop's report on the destruction of the Warsaw Ghetto. Chester managed to get a copy. It is a horrifyingly repulsive narrative. There is overwhelming evidence of the courage of the Jewish resistance but Stroop could not admit this even to himself because they were 'Jews and cowards'. The Chief Prosecutor then quoted from the military records to illustrate the charge of waging aggressive war. There followed a chilling account of medical experiments in Dachau. Jackson's peroration was particularly moving. He told the Tribunal that 'the real complaining party at your bar is Civilisation', finally concluding:

> Civilisation asks whether law is so laggard as to be utterly helpless to deal with crimes of this magnitude by criminals of

this order of importance. It does not expect that you can make war impossible. It does expect that your juridical action will put the forms of international law, its precepts, its prohibitions and, most of all, its sanctions, on the side of peace.[14]

Chester could only have heard part of the speech but was very impressed. He had been called in at 24 hours' notice when the assigned BBC man fell ill. Wilmot landed in a snowstorm without a pass, managed to get a temporary pass then got the BBC engineers to vouch for him and took over the coverage watching from a glassed-in booth over the courtroom. The following day the notorious concentration camp film was screened. Many of the defendants turned away from the horrifying images and refused to watch. Then the prosecution began to read one document after another into the record. At the first opportunity Wilmot sought an interview with Jackson. The Chief Prosecutor explained that by making the case with documents, they wanted to put on the record full evidence of the Nazi crimes against their own people, as well as against humanity.

> We must have this proof on the record in our own country – the USA – proof from the Nazi documents here in Europe there was a great evil power at work that we were morally obliged to fight. And when ten or twenty years on, when the apologists for Hitler in Germany or the isolationists in America tell people there was nothing bad in the Nazi system and America was dragged in by Britain into the European War unjustifiably, the proof will be there to refute the myths.[15]

Wilmot thoroughly approved and made arrangements to get his own copies. He was in charge of the coverage of the verdicts and sentencing. So important was it considered that he was able to persuade the BBC Foreign News to charter a plane to fly discs of the recordings of his reports to Paris, where they were played over a BBC transmitter to London. Wilmot then decided to try to get the corporation to broadcast the sentencing itself. He persuaded one of the judges – probably the alternate justice, Sir Norman Birkett – to write an outline of the final proceedings and send it to Broadcasting House. Chester had a lot of influence with the BBC and his proposal was accepted. However, the climax of the broadcast – the actual sentencing – nearly didn't get to air. Wilmot was in the middle of his preliminary commentary when an American military policeman pushed past him and looked through the open observation window above the dock. He then tried to get Chester to shut the window even though he had permission in writing to have it open. He pointed to the notice but the MP would not move. 'Finally, still carrying on the commentary and holding the mike in one hand I led the dumb bugger by the arm to the notice on the wall, jammed his nose into it then led him out the door and went on with my broadcast.'[16] Chester took careful note of the reactions of each of the defendants as they heard their sentences: 'Herman Goering death by hanging, Wilhelm Keitel death by hanging.' In spite of their crimes, the broadcast recorded that the twelve sentenced to death accepted their fate with great dignity.

* * * *

Early in 1946 the Wilmots moved into the former servants' wing of a large country house in Buckinghamshire. A storeroom was converted into a study for Chester and he commenced writing the book then titled *The Great Crusade*. An exasperated Edith brought him regular cups of tea as he struggled to find his first sentence. Finally, at the end of the day, it came. 'In the summer of 1942 four hundred million people lay under the yoke of German rule.' His wife's memoir reveals little understanding of what it took to write a book like *The Struggle for Europe*. But had Edith read closely what followed that initial sentence she might have learned.

In the summer of 1942 four hundred million people in Europe lay under the yoke of German rule. The empire of Adolf Hitler, then at its greatest extent, stretched from the Mediterranean to the Arctic, from the English Channel to the Black Sea and almost to the Caspian. Between the Pyrenees and the Ukrainian steppes there was no other sovereign state but Switzerland. Even Hitler's partner, Mussolini, had been reduced to the role of a puppet. In the ancient capitals of Europe – in Athens, Rome and Vienna, in Paris and Prague, Oslo and Warsaw – all other voices were drowned by the voice of Nazi Germany. The spearheads of Hitler's panzer armies had reached the Volga and were within striking distance of the Nile. Far to the west his U-boats had carried the German offensive to the Atlantic coast of North America and into the Caribbean. In the east his new ally, Japan, had engulfed the colonies of older empires, gained command of Asiatic waters and borne the Rising Sun into the Indian Ocean. The possibility that Germany and Japan might join forces east of Suez could no longer be disregarded. In three years of war Hitler had been denied victory only in the sky above London and in the snow outside Moscow.[17]

Chester Wilmot was about to write a major military and political history of the Western Allies' final triumph in Europe. And a month earlier, a letter had come from a man who knew a great deal about writing military history. His name was Basil Liddell Hart.

23

PASSING TO THE OTHER SIDE

Captain Basil Liddell Hart had been one of the most celebrated military writers of the 1920s and 1930s. Military Correspondent for *The Daily Telegraph* (1925–35), and for *The Times* (1935–39), the author of a series of books on military history and theory, he had been the ultimate insider. Liddell Hart advised senior army officers and politicians such as David Lloyd George, and, during the Munich crisis, Winston Churchill. He also influenced the development of the tank. One of his disciples was Sir Percy Hobart, the inventor of the famous 'Funnies' used to great effect on the beaches on D-Day. In 1946 his reputation was in decline. Curiously, this advocate of tank thrusts deep into enemy-held territory had failed to predict the war of movement when Germany invaded France in 1940. Liddell Hart had also been an opponent of total war, believing that Britain's only choice was to secure a negotiated settlement. Later when America came into the war he was a critic of the strategic bomber offensive and of the demand for unconditional surrender. When Hart contacted Wilmot he was in the process of restoring his reputation through a series of interviews with the captured German generals. A broadcast by Wilmot concerning the 20 July 1944 bomb plot to kill Hitler had interested him, and he wrote asking for a copy.

There was an exchange of letters followed by a meeting and

soon they were sharing information. Liddell Hart wanted some of the material Chester had collected in Europe, while Chester needed to see the transcripts of the interviews with the generals, so he could tell the German side of the story. Wilmot was engaged in an extended retrospective on the war, which was to become a major work of military history and grand strategy. Liddell Hart, author of many surveys of military history from Alexander the Great to Napoleon and the American Civil War, was concerned with a close historical analysis of decisions seen through the eyes of the German commanders. The two men possessed very different personalities: Wilmot was intense, argumentative, usually brandishing a pipe for emphasis, but always deferential to older men; Liddell Hart was immensely tall, and talked in half-sentences through an unlit pipe clenched between his teeth. They soon became close friends and colleagues. Fortunately for the historian, they lived in different parts of the English countryside, and one can trace something of their relationship through their correspondence. There were, of course, drives for lunch at each other's houses and meetings in London at their clubs, and their wives became friends. But their intellectual engagement was embodied in their letters and comments on each other's work.

Like so many of his generation Liddell Hart was shaped by his experiences in the Great War. As a young officer he endured a series of concussive injuries that took him out of the line. Then after returning to duty he was gassed on the first day of the Somme. This saved his life as his battalion was almost entirely wiped out. When Liddell Hart came to study the strategy of the war, first as a staff officer, and then as a military writer after his enforced retirement, he became a trenchant critic of frontal assaults and, inevitably, the British Commander-in-Chief, Field Marshal Haig. From a survey of decisive battles in history that were viewed in the light of his experience of the Western Front, Liddell Hart evolved his concept of the indirect approach: 'In strategy the longest way round is often the shortest way there; a direct approach to the object exhausts the attacker and hardens the resistance by compression, while an indirect approach loosens the defender's hold by upsetting his balance.'[1]

Direct attacks against an enemy, he argued, almost never work and should never be attempted. To defeat an enemy one must upset his equilibrium. This is not accomplished by the main attack but before; so the main attack can succeed. Chester, who very early in their relationship had asked Liddell Hart to send him a copy of *The Strategy of Indirect Approach*, was to follow closely these ideas for his analysis of American and British strategy.

For Liddell Hart, battles were mind games: 'the issue of battle is usually in the minds of the opposing commanders not in the bodies of their men'.[2] This was not as cold blooded as it might seem. Strategy and manoeuvre were for him ways to limit casualties. In his wartime edition of *The Strategy of Indirect Approach*, Liddell Hart even praised Hitler's use of indirect methods in politics and military strategy to achieve his objectives without bloodshed. He was of course not endorsing Hitler's aims – Hart was anything but a fascist. However, his portrayal of the minds of Hitler and the General Staff seems to have influenced Wilmot's treatment of how the Führer's stop order to the German Army allowed the British Expeditionary Force to escape at Dunkirk and saved Britain.

Liddell Hart had closely questioned the German generals as to Hitler's motives. First, he established that it was indeed the Führer who had given the order, and not Field Marshal von Rundstedt, Commander of Army Group A. (Winston Churchill was to state in Volume Two of his *History of World War II* that the halt order was on the Field Marshal's initiative not Hitler's.) Liddell Hart's interviews with the generals, including von Rundstedt himself, established that it was indeed Hitler who gave the order. In his book *The Other Side of the Hill*, which Chester proofread, Liddell Hart carefully weighed the evidence from his interviews, and concluded Hitler may have wanted to conciliate Britain, something Churchill was reluctant to acknowledge. Chester based his narrative of the same events in *The Struggle for Europe* on Liddell Hart's transcripts combined with his own research into the OKW archives. This gave him the key for the theme of the first half of the book, summed up in the sentence 'Germany's defeat and Europe's liberation began at Dunkirk'. Throughout his later research for his book, Wilmot used Liddell Hart's contacts with the German senior officers. Von Rundstedt's Chief of Staff, General Westphal, told them both about the Field Marshal shouting 'Make peace you fools' into a phone line to Hitler's headquarters at a bad moment in the Normandy Campaign. Wilmot used it to great effect in the book while Liddell Hart passed it on to the screenwriters for *The Desert Fox*, a semi-fictional film about Rommel. Chester avoided anything like Liddell Hart's personal involvement. Hart sent food parcels to the general's families in Germany and even secured a decent bed for von Rundstedt in his captivity. Wilmot was suspicious of the Field Marshal, believing he could have taken a stronger stand against Hitler's excesses. He did, however, correspond with Manfred Rommel, who extracted the German tank figures from his father's papers for him.

When Chester came to the Battle of Britain his narrative was based on the research for a program of the same name that he had written for Laurence Gilliam in 1947. It used the real words of the participants, only they were spoken by actors. This dialogue was linked by an authoritative narration delivered by Chester himself. The format had been pioneered in America by *The March of Time*, which dramatised the news of the day with semi-fictional exchanges. Gilliam, when he first devised the BBC version early in the war, made his programs more authentic. Subsequently, Chester's scripts often 'published' original documents for the first time. Fortunately the sounds of these broadcasts survive. Carefully rehearsed and superbly timed, they work equally well as documentary and radio drama.

On 22 January 1948 Wilmot took his research further and interviewed the head of the Fighter Command in the Battle of Britain,

Air Chief Marshal Lord Dowding. They met at the Army and Navy Club. Chester's notes state:

> Dowding is a quiet rather diffident Scot. He looks more like a professor than an airman and is certainly the student rather than the man of action. However he does unbend as he warms to his subject, but the ordinary person meeting him for the first time would find it difficult to get through his reserve. A casual acquaintance would certainly feel the nickname Stuffy was well applied.[3]

Chester then recorded a concise briefing by Dowding on his difficulties when he assumed command. '[He] said that his chief worry throughout the years of preparation and even after Dunkirk was that he could never get from the Air Staff an assurance guaranteeing a certain number of squadrons for Home Defence.'[4] Dowding related the now famous story about Churchill being

> insistent that more fighters should be sent to France and the cabinet supported it. [Dowding] had drawn up a graph showing that if the casualties continued at this scale [they were losing thirty planes a day], the complete force of Hurricanes would be destroyed in six weeks. At the crisis of the meeting, when Churchill seemed sure to prevail, Dowding got up walked round to Churchill's chair lent across and put on the table in front of him this graph. That decided the issue. The cabinet gave the order that no more squadrons would leave for France beyond the eight half squadrons which it had promised to send in reply to Reynaud's plea the previous day.[5]

The incident appears in nearly all the later accounts of the Battle of Britain but Chester must have been one of the first outsiders to hear about it. He was also aware of the controversy over the employment of big wings. Air Vice Marshal Trafford Leigh-Mallory believed the best strategy was to assemble wings of Hurricanes and Spitfires so they could intercept the enemy planes on their way back from their targets. Dowding and Air Vice Marshal Keith Park insisted the enemy should be engaged piecemeal as soon as the planes were identified on the radar. Indeed Wilmot's script dramatised this piecemeal interception with both Park and Dowding portrayed in the program. The intrigues around this dispute had led to Dowding's premature retirement after winning the Battle of Britain. Chester did not discuss the controversy in *The Struggle for Europe*. He concentrated on the scientific background and the tactics of the air battle itself, emphasising the decisive part played by Dowding. In doing so, Wilmot beat Churchill to his own story. Churchill had been unhappy with the way Dowding had been treated by the Air Ministry and originally intended to make amends in *Their Finest Hour*, the second volume of his history of the war. At the last minute he was persuaded to follow the ministry line. There was a brief tribute to Dowding's strategic insight and that was all. It was a decision Churchill came to bitterly regret. The first major writer to do justice to Dowding's role in the battle was Chester Wilmot.

From the first Chester wanted to interview Field Marshal Montgomery. When he had been in Europe Monty had politely declined but had allowed his staff to open his files to the reporter. His excuse was that he was writing his own book, *Normandy to the Baltic*. In fact it was compiled from the Field Marshal's files by his Chief of Operations, Major-General David Belchem, a mate of Chester's. A few months later a signed copy of the book had arrived, and not only did Chester send a thankyou note; he raised the question of an interview. Edith related what followed in a letter to her mother.

> It's Saturday, and Jane and I have had a quiet day and Chester a most interesting one. His day began with a telephone call …

When he answered the phone a voice barked, 'Is that Chester Wilmot?' Chester replied that it was and the voice barked again, 'This is Field Marshal Montgomery speaking …' and Chester rapidly thought now which of my friends is pulling this 'swifty' … but to his amazement it was the man himself inviting Chester to Hindhead, Surrey, on Saturday …

So Chester set off by car at 9 am sharp and when I remarked that it was an early start for an 11 o'clock appointment Chester said he was taking no chances – when one is late for Monty, Monty is very charming but one is not given another chance to be late or anything else! …

Montgomery lives with some friends who run a very good 'prep' school of 73 boys, large, pleasant old house, chapel (with Montgomery's swords), very good playing fields, garden and so on. Montgomery has a wing of the house and his famous caravan is in the garden. He spends all or most of his leave at Hindhead for he has made his home with these friends, the Reynolds. Major Reynolds, the headmaster was with Montgomery in the Great War. Chester said Monty was at his best, completely charming and unaffected, and he is more than ever convinced that Montgomery's apparent love of fame and limelight is only because he feels it helps in the job of a commander. For himself, he wants nothing but an utterly simple life.

Chester was very pleased for at long last he was able to get his hands on 'the directives', and now he hopes to be able to squash (in his book) the American claim (put forward by Ralph Ingersoll and others) that Montgomery failed at Caen and that the American Armies won the battle of Normandy and most of the others as well by quoting directly from these directives that Montgomery sent to his generals before the battles in question.

So we will see. For a long time Chester has been after these directives but permission had always been refused – I'm sure they'll add a lot of value to the book.[6]

Ralph Ingersoll was a journalist who had been attached to Omar Bradley's headquarters and had just published *Top Secret*, a virulently anti-British personal account of the war in Europe. As well there had been *My Three Years with Eisenhower* by Harry Butcher, Eisenhower's aide, equally anti-British: all part of the war of the books over Anglo-American strategy that was beginning far earlier than anyone had expected. At the time Montgomery could not go public. But he could put his case through a Chester Wilmot.

Chester began by asking about the general strategy. Speaking of Normandy Montgomery said, 'Ike and the Americans generally never understood the Normandy strategy. In his dispatches to the War Department Ike says quite definitely that the original plan was to break out at Caen, and drive for the Seine ports and Paris; this is nonsense.'[7] Later he admitted that

> of course we would have liked to get Caen on the first day and I was never happy about the left flank until I got Caen. But the important thing on this flank was to maintain our strength so that we could not only avoid any set back, but keep the initiative by attacking whenever we liked. On this flank ground was of no importance at all. I had learnt in the last war the senseless sacrifice that can be made by sentimental attachment to a piece of ground.[8]

This last sentence is underlined in Wilmot's transcript. Doubtless it reminded him of Monty's insistence during the Battle of the Bulge that American troops were not to be sacrificed simply to hold territory.

When Chester had examined all the documents concerning

Monty's Normandy strategy he found they put the Field Marshal's comments about Caen in a new light. By then he was aware of Montgomery's statement that he wanted to draw the German armour onto his front and destroy them while the Americans under Bradley broke out on the right. As Chester wrote to Liddell Hart,

> There is no doubt that the intention to hold on the left and break out on the right was the basis of his conception and appears in the very first documents in February. For instance the 2nd Army outline plan dated February 21st defines the Army's objective in these words 'The ultimate object of 2nd Army is to protect the flank of the United States Armies while the latter capture Cherbourg, Angers, Nantes and the Brittany ports. There is no intention of carrying out a major offensive until the Brittany ports have been captured.'
>
> And yet the Chief Historian of the RAF said to me yesterday – 'Of course Monty's original intention had been to break out to the East and capture Le Havre', and went on to say that this policy was only changed after D-Day.
>
> However I can find nothing in the early documents about any deliberate plan to compel the enemy to commit all his armour against the British. In his two main speeches to his Commanders he speaks in rather negative terms of the 2nd Army's task, declaring in one case – 'The army will pivot on its left and offer a strong front against any movement toward the lodgement area in the east.' At this stage he seems to have thought of Dempsey's role as that of blocking rather than attracting and destroying the enemy's armour.[9]

There had of course been a change of plan and Montgomery always insisted all his battles went according to plan. Wilmot's account of these 'modifications' in *The Struggle for Europe* is a model of tact.

> He did modify the means he sought to achieve [his main strategic purpose]. After the war was over, anxious to defend himself against American criticism he asserted 'the operation went exactly as planned.' In making this claim, Montgomery does himself less than justice, for his real genius as a commander was shown in the way he varied his day to day policy to meet the unpredictable situations caused by bad weather, by Hitler's suicidal policy of fighting for every yard, and by tactical failure and slowness on the part of British and American troops.[10]

Shortly after the interview Chester persuaded Monty to take part in a dramatisation of the Battle of El Alamein. They naturally wanted him to deliver the speech he had made to the Eighth Army officers when he took over command. Montgomery gave Chester his notes which with some emendations were included in the script. Underscored in Wilmot's copy were these lines: 'Here we will stand and fight; there will be no further withdrawal; I have ordered that all plans and instructions dealing with further withdrawals are to be burnt, and at once. We will stand and fight here. If we can't stay here alive, then let us stay here dead.'[11]

When Chester showed these notes to Liddell Hart he replied that he thought Monty's allusions to his predecessors 'caddish'. He was a friend of the former C-in-C, Sir Claude Auchinleck, and his Chief of Staff at the first Battle of El Alamein, Eric Dorman-Smith. Chester responded that he thought the remarks were justified by the circumstances that existed when Montgomery took over. However, he removed from the script the following paragraph in the original speech.

> I do not like the general atmosphere I find here. It is an atmosphere of doubt, of looking back to select the next place to

which to withdraw, of loss of confidence in our ability to defeat Rommel, of desperate defence measures by reserves in preparing positions in Cairo and the Delta. All that must cease let us have a new atmosphere.[12]

Montgomery went in to the BBC studio to record the speech. The first take was flat and no one quite knew how to tell the great man. Chester took over. He went up to Monty and said, 'Field Marshal when you gave that speech it changed everything in the Middle East. Now we want to hear that in your voice.'[13] Montgomery said 'Right' and proceeded to electrify the control room with his delivery. Wilmot had evoked what method actors call 'emotional recall'. For a few moments the Field Marshal was back at his headquarters instilling new life into the Eighth Army. The sound has been preserved and even today hearing Montgomery's voice combined with so many fine radio actors of the period can be very moving. There was a repeat performance of sorts when Monty delivered an abbreviated version of his briefing before D-Day. Again, under Wilmot's tactful guidance he was very good.

By now Chester and the Field Marshal were friends. In a characteristically brief letter before he left as Chief of the General Staff to visit Australia, he informed Wilmot that he was going to visit his father. Before long a letter from Bung was on its way to England describing the meeting. It was arranged by Rowell, who was now Chief of the Australian General Staff. (The British had wanted to keep him but Prime Minister Ben Chifley was having none of it.) Montgomery apologised for bringing Bung into Government House then went out of his way to stress how important Wilmot's services had been during the war. 'I saw him as part of my staff.'[14] Monty had sensed how shaken a very conservative man like Chester's father had been by the disaccreditation and was doing his best to heal the old wound.

The meeting came at a fortunate time. Bung, afflicted by a lethal combination of heart trouble and bronchitis, was failing. The family always received regular family letters from Chester, but Jean, who was staying with the family, sensed their father would like to receive a personal letter and contacted her brother. He wrote immediately, evoking all their old comradeship saying how much he was looking forward to yet another frank talk when he returned to Australia. When the letter arrived Bung was in hospital and had lapsed into a coma. Jean took the letter in anyway and found her father was not only awake but had rallied. 'Of course I have been unconscious I'm in different clothes.'[15] With great pleasure he settled down to read his son's letter. Bung died that night.

With books being published criticising British strategy, Wilmot had to come to terms with the rival American and British plans. From the outset he had been given access to confidential communications in Montgomery's files, but he still needed to put some direct questions to Monty. They met at Dover House on 23 March 1949. In the course of the interview the Field Marshal made these pointed observations:

> I advocated the appointment of a Land Forces Commander in Chief because I considered the whole command set up was fundamentally wrong. There was no one who could give complete and undivided attention to the day to day direction of the land battle as a whole. Eisenhower could not do this. He had not the experience, the knowledge; the organisation or the time. He should have been devoting himself to questions of overall strategy, to political problems, to problems of inter-Allied relations and military government, and to the general direction and coordination of the effort of all three services. Instead he kept trying to run the land battle himself. Here he was out of his depth, and in trying to do this he neglected his real job on the highest level. In trying to direct the strategic and even the tactical development of operations, he lost sight of overall strategy, and of political objectives.

> I believe he knew in his heart that the right strategy was to concentrate everything behind a thrust for the Ruhr, but because he did not feel able to stop Patton, he persuaded himself both thrusts could succeed and his chief administrative officer, Humphrey Gale, must bear a great responsibility for advising him wrongly. In the last week of August and in the first week of September [1944] he was quite confident he could close up to the Rhine throughout its length on a broad front. His [Eisenhower's] basic conception of war was all wrong. He did not really understand the principle of concentration and he was very unhappy if he did not have any troops who were not actively engaging the enemy.[16]

Chester was convinced, and he began to shape an eloquent vindication of the narrow thrust strategy. The Americans, he argued, were anxious to use their power and numbers to finish the war and bring the troops home even if fewer returned because of their generals' willingness to incur heavy casualties. The British preferred the indirect approach, a war of manoeuvre, guile and balance. Even as Chester was developing this theme, influenced by the book Liddell Hart had sent him, the ground was shifting under him. More documents were becoming available and more participants were publishing their recollections. Omar Bradley's *A Soldier's Story* with its attack on Montgomery appeared in 1949. Robert E Sherwood's *Roosevelt and Hopkins* came out the same year and threw new light on the Allies' relationship with Stalin by including details of the Yalta Conference. Chester, who had thought to finish his book with the Nuremberg trials, now realised he needed to incorporate at least some of the grand strategy.

His publisher WH 'Billy' Collins always believed *The Struggle for Europe* was going to be a bestseller and he could see Chester was swamped by his sources. There was a spacious attic office at Collins available and his struggling author needed an assistant. Chester was quickly moved into the attic and Therese Denny, a young Australian who was freelancing celebrity interviews to the BBC and the ABC, was hired. Professionally she was exactly what Chester needed. As he was later to tell her sister, Therese could see the pattern in a mass of diverse sources and suggest to him the structure of the chapter. She could also laugh him out of his psychological asthma. 'That's enough wheezes for this chapter'. At some stage during their collaboration they fell deeply in love. From the beginning Chester made it clear he could never leave Edith but there is no doubt about the sincerity of his feelings. For Therese it was her first love. Years later she obliquely revealed to a family member something of the intense physical pleasure she experienced during their affair. Therese could understand Chester's asthma – an affliction which irritated Edith. Like Chester, she had been very sick as a child. There had been a nearly lethal bout of scarlet fever and she had survived a polio attack. Therese was not crippled by the virus, but her legs were differently shaped. She was usually photographed in the long, well-cut straight dresses fashionable in the 1940s and early 1950s.

Among clouds of tobacco smoke from Chester's pipe, and Therese's ever-present cigarettes, they crafted the further dimensions of the Wilmot Thesis. Eisenhower's contacts with Stalin over Berlin were still secret but the book contains trenchant criticisms of the Supreme Commander's failure to realise the city was a vital political objective. Wilmot was not suggesting the Allies should have reneged on their agreements and held on to the city. But as the Russians were breaking the agreements they had made at Yalta the possession of Berlin, he argued, could have induced them to keep their word. And there was always the matter of prestige. Once the Russians captured Berlin there was no doubt who was the dominant power in Europe. We know now that is the way Stalin saw it. He did not believe Eisenhower's assurance that the Americans thought the city was of no strategic value and ordered his commanders to speed up the advance.

Chester's portrait of a naive Roosevelt trying to come to a sensible agreement with Stalin and a realistic Churchill already aware of the Russian danger may be a little overdrawn, but the sources he was using were still incomplete and the evidence of the President's hostility to Britain and, at times, Churchill came from a highly indiscreet memoir by his son.

The most criticised passages in *The Struggle for Europe* are where Wilmot applies the indirect approach to the Balkans. It is very clever debating. Chester's main support is the American Commander Mark Clark and the idea that there should have been diversionary attacks in the Balkans to draw off German resources does seem plausible. The main counter argument is that the terrain in the Balkans is fiendishly difficult. Chester was on stronger ground when he argued against the resources poured into 'Anvil', a landing in the south of France after D-Day. The British had resisted the operation from the beginning, and believed its resources would have been better employed in strengthening the thrust into Germany from Italy.

In late 1950 Edith went with the children to Australia. Chester's mother had been demanding to see her grandchildren and was putting the pressure on as only she knew how to do. Edith had become increasingly exasperated by the way she and the family were shut out by her husband's work on the book. Almost certainly she did not suspect there was an affair with Therese. But Chester's young assistant was helping him in his work in ways his wife never could. For Edith the only way to resolve the situation was by making a dutiful visit to Australia. There was no breach. It was arranged that Chester would join her when he finished the book. She was not to see him for a year.

Chester and Therese conducted their affair with great discretion. There were no public outings. When he had to take Therese to an interview with Sir Brian Horrocks at the House of Lords she brought a celebrity friend as cover, the film actress Valerie Hobson.

Horrocks sensed there was something between Chester and Therese but rather enjoyed meeting the glamorous Miss Hobson. As Chester battled to finish the book, Edith's regular letters were insisting he join his family in Australia for her brother's wedding in Adelaide. Much as he cared for Therese he did not want to break up his marriage and he still had to complete the manuscript. Finally, Billy Collins agreed to allow him to do the last work on the book by mail. By then Chester had recruited Edith's younger brother Graham Irwin, who was studying history at Clare College, as a researcher. Liddell Hart agreed to check the proofs and in July 1951 the author departed on a four-day flight to Melbourne. Edith was 'shattered' when she realised how much Chester still had to do. 'I could never forgive myself for the pressure I had exerted on Chester to come to Australia in time for the family wedding.'[17] He was working to a tight schedule because Collins's promotional campaign depended on a January publication. Galley proofs went back and forth from Melbourne and London. Liddell Hart sent over his corrections saving Chester from many a blunder. Chester was tired and depressed and battling hay fever. Edith guessed he was missing Therese but feared to question him too closely. Therese Denny's family believe they had ended the affair before he left for Australia. When he fell behind Therese went to Collins herself and got Chester a week's extension. As the pressure mounted, Edith finally got to work on the book, correcting even more galley proofs and plying her husband with tea, black coffee and whisky as he worked through the night. Finally, *The Struggle for Europe* was completed and Chester and the family returned to London on the *Stratheden*. Therese's youngest sister, Marie Kennehan, was also travelling to London. Chester had been told she was aboard and sought her out to tell her how much he owed Therese for her help with the book. Marie knew about the affair and felt awkward – especially when Edith appeared with the children – but she appreciated the gesture.

The launch at the Dorchester Hotel, where Wilmot gave a

speech outlining the themes of the book, was a great success. He had, of course, arranged for a copy to be sent to Field Marshal Montgomery, who wrote back on 20 January 1952.

Dear Chester,

I must thank you for the book and sometime I will get you to inscribe it for me. I have read it and consider it to be excellent in every way. It is very well presented and is the best critical analysis of the war in Europe, political and military that I have seen. Indeed I think it is a classic, and will be considered as such for many years.

The general theme seems to me to be twofold.

1   The political contest between Stalin and Roosevelt-Churchill.
2   The military contest between myself and the American generals.

Stalin won his contest.

I am not certain who won the military contest but you make it very clear who was right!

I, of course can make no comment for publication as I am serving under Eisenhower in what is in effect an American HQ. But when I am free to speak I shall give my own views on your book in no uncertain voice![18]

Montgomery's memoirs, published five years later, did indeed make his case 'in no uncertain voice', but perhaps his finest compliment to Wilmot was that in the Arnhem chapter he quotes and endorses the book's criticisms of the mistakes in the planning, many of which were his own.

The Struggle for Europe was indeed everything Montgomery said it was. What is more, it was an enormous success on both sides of the Atlantic. For most British critics, Chester was seen as a powerful ally of Winston Churchill, whose multi-volume *History of World War II* was appearing regularly in the late 1940s and 1950s. Written in collaboration with a syndicate of writers Churchill's history was a justification of Britain's and his own role in defeating Hitler. We know now that it was a semi-official narrative based on the memos Churchill wrote while in office. These had to be cleared by the Cabinet Office, which would often persuade him to modify both the documents and his narrative so as not to embarrass the government or Britain's allies. Wilmot was held in such high regard that he was shown top secret documents that he was unable to quote. But he was under no obligation to avoid offending the Americans – or anyone else for that matter. But the curious relationship between *The Struggle for Europe* and Churchill's histories is illuminated by Chester's account of his only meeting with the great man.

> The invitation to lunch came through Randolph Churchill whom I knew in the Middle East and he came with me to Chartwell – Winston's lovely old house in Kent. There we lunched in state – including one bottle of hock, two bottles of champagne, and for Winston cointreau followed by whisky and soda. Winston was most complimentary about the book, although disagreeing with my interpretation of what he wanted to do in the Balkans – and asked me to autograph his copy. He admitted that he hadn't yet finished reading it but said, 'When I start on a chapter I never put it down till I've finished. You've told me a great many things I didn't know and you have done splendid service to the cause of History.' He drew on his cigar. 'After my custom I first studied the

index to see how copious were the references to myself, and looked to see whether they were friendly or inimical. I found the result of the perusal highly gratifying. But in your generous appreciation of myself I fear you have been unfair to my friend Roosevelt.[19]

Churchill's warmth was genuine and there is good reason to believe he was grateful to Wilmot for many passages in *The Struggle for Europe*. Clearly it was a book of its time. It spoke for a Britain in decline that needed affirmation of its leaders' courage and wisdom during a war in which they had effectively saved Western civilisation. We know now that the coming of the Cold War was a more complex process than Wilmot described. But he and his friend Basil Liddell Hart were undoubtedly right in criticising the Allies' insistence on unconditional surrender and the failure, largely by the Americans, to think beyond victory over Nazi Germany. Wilmot rightly saw Stalin's Russia as a tyranny and deplored the USSR's dominance of so much of Europe.

The Struggle for Europe was, and remains, a classic: it is narrative history at its best; the campaigns are brilliantly described; and Wilmot subtly employs Liddell Hart's theory of indirect approach to illuminate British and US strategy, and never forgets the economic and logistic issues. One of Chester's great strengths as a historian and a man was that he was never afraid to draw conclusions from the evidence. He was also unafraid to modify his views in the light of new evidence. A revised edition of the book was being planned almost as soon as the first edition was published.

Chester was always a formidable debater but it was invariably civilised debate. He might have disagreed with Eisenhower but immediately accepted Therese Denny's suggestion to invite him to review the book. He liked Monty but was not blind to his faults and the great soldier, untypically one has to say, did not resent Wilmot's criticisms.

The Struggle for Europe had the kind of reception writers dream about. Good reviews flowed, especially in England, and the book achieved instant bestseller status. There was an 80 000 presale alone, and this did not take into account the US market. Chester was able to buy a country house with room for Geoffrey born in May 1952 in Cuddingham, yet another romantic village. There were numerous lucrative assignments from the BBC and Chester became the Military Correspondent of *The Observer*. He was never quite sure it was going to last, so installed a piggery in the grounds of his new house – just in case.

Chester had been a pioneer of television documentary. Unfortunately none of his work survives. The practice then was to film on location and to broadcast the footage with a live studio narration. Reportedly Chester was brilliant at matching words with images. In the autumn of 1953 Wilmot was commissioned to make a series of documentaries on the Far East and South-East Asia. For ten weeks he and the BBC's television cameraman Arthur Englander toured the capitals filming and collecting material. Chester parted with Englander in Bangkok and flew to Sydney to anchor the Queen's Christmas message. It was a prestigious assignment. Queen Elizabeth and Prince Philip were on their first Royal Tour and she was to broadcast from New Zealand while Chester was to narrate from the ABC studios in Sydney. Typically he was still working on the narration two minutes before the program went to air. It was, of course, a great success.

Chester was to return to Britain on Flight 781, a British Airways Comet flying from Singapore to Rome, and from there to Heathrow Airport in London. On 10 January 1954, at 0950 GMT wreckage from the airliner was seen crashing into the sea off the island of Elba. At 1.30 pm a horrified Edith, who was to meet the plane with Jane and Caroline, saw the flight taken off the arrivals board at Heathrow. It was later determined that the cause of the crash was in-flight metal fatigue, resulting in explosive decompression. In other words the Comet blew up – Chester would have been killed instantly.

On 27 January 1954, a memorial service was held for the life of Chester Wilmot at All Souls, Langham Place, London. During the service this line adapted from John Bunyan's *Pilgrim's Progress* was read out: 'So he passed over, and all the trumpets sounded for Mr Valiant for Truth on the other side.'

NOTES

Full details of the sources cited in these notes can be found in the Bibliography. The bulk of the quotations of Wilmot's dispatches are from the revised texts in Neil McDonald (ed.), *Chester Wilmot Reports*. They are filed in the Chester Wilmot Series in the National Archives of Australia in Sydney. The author's photocopies of the dispatches will be lodged with the Papers of Chester Wilmot at the National Library of Australia.

1 First things
1. Chester Wilmot, *The Struggle for Europe*, p. 237.

2 The shop
1. RWE Wilmot to Chester Wilmot, Papers of Chester Wilmot, National Library of Australia (hereafter cited as Wilmot Papers), series 1, folder 3.
2. RWE Wilmot to Chester Wilmot, Wilmot Papers, series 1, folder 3.
3. Chester Wilmot to Jean Bemis, Wilmot Papers, series 1, folder 3.
4. This and other Santamaria quotations throughout the chapter are from Bob A Santamaria, interview with the author, 1996.
5. Bob A Santamaria, interview with the author, 1996.
6. Edith Wilmot, memoir.
7. WM Maidment (associate professor of English, University of Sydney, 1970s and 1980s), conversation with the author.
8. Fay Woodhouse, 'A Place Apart'.
9. Sue Ebury, *Weary*, p. 73.
10. Bob A Santamaria, interview with the author, 1996.
11. Edith Wilmot, memoir.
12. RWE Wilmot to Chester Wilmot, Wilmot Papers, series 1, folder 3.
13. George Johnston, interview for 'Portrait of Chester Wilmot', BBC Home Service Basic, 1954.
14–16. Bob A Santamaria, interview with the author, 1996.
17. Arthur D Innes, *A History of England and the British Empire*, p. 5.
18. Stuart Macintyre, *A History for a Nation*, p. 103.
19. Stuart Macintyre, *A History for a Nation*, p. 106.
20. Bob A Santamaria, interview with the author, 1996.

Notes

3 Half-cocked college guys
1 Raymond Edward Priestley Papers, University of Melbourne Archives.
2–7 Fay Woodhouse, 'A Place Apart'.
8 Chester Wilmot to Jean Bemis, Wilmot Papers, series 1, folder 15.
9 Wilmot Papers, series 1, folder 15a.
10 Raymond Priestly Papers, Melbourne University Archives, diary.
11 Wilmot Papers, series 1, folder 15.
12–17 Wilmot Papers, series 1, folder 7.
18–23 Wilmot Papers, Series 1, folder 8.
24 Wilmot Papers, Series 1, folder 11.
25 Ibid.
26 Wilmot Papers, Series 1, folder 17.
27 Wilmot Papers, Series 1, folder 12.
28 Ibid.
29 Chester Wilmot to Raymond Priestly, Wilmot Papers, Series 1, folder 20.
30–32 Wilmot Papers, Series 1, folder 7.

4 Ashamed to be an Englishman
1–9 Wilmot Papers, Series 1, folder 8.
10 G Ward Price, *Year of Reckoning*, p. 165.
11 G Ward Price, *Year of Reckoning*, pp. 166–167.
12–14 Wilmot Papers, Series 1, folder 8.
15 GER Gedye, *Fallen Bastions*, p. 18.
16 Gitta Sereny, *The German Trauma*, p. 6.
17–19 Wilmot Papers, Series 1, folder 8.
20 Hugh Stewart (BBC producer, 1930s), personal communication to the author, 1975.
21–23 Wilmot Papers, Series 1, folder 8.
24–28 Wilmot Papers, Series 1, folder 9.
29 Basil Wright, conversation with the author, 1981.
30–46 Wilmot Papers, Series 1, folder 9.
47 John Wheeler-Bennett, *Munich*, pp. 90–91.
48–65 Wilmot Papers, Series 1, folder 9.
66 John Wheeler-Bennett, *Munich*, p. 170.
67–71 Wilmot Papers, Series 1, folder 9.
72 Thomas Blamey, Australian War Memorial.
73 Winston S Churchill, *The Second World War*, vol. I, pp. 293–294.

5 Two captains and a mister
1 Wilmot Papers, NLA MS8436/1.
2 Edith Wilmot's recollections in this chapter are from Edith Wilmot, memoir.
3 Ibid.
4 Ibid.
5–7 Wilmot Papers, Series 1, folder 24.
8 Wilmot Papers, Series 1, folder 24.
9 See Peter Rees, *Bearing Witness*, pp. 357–380; Ross Coulthart, *Charles Bean*, pp. 312–318.
10–20 Wilmot Papers, Series 1, folder 24.

6 A lot of little cuts first
1 Neil McDonald (ed.), *Chester Wilmot Reports* (hereafter cited as *CWR*), pp. 16–17.
2 *CWR*, pp. 16–17.
3–5 Wilmot Papers, series 1, folder 24.
6 *CWR*, pp. 16–17.
7 Ivan Chapman, interview with the author, 1986.
8 Stuart Braga, *Kokoda Commander*, p. 80.
9 Gavin Long, *To Benghazi*, p. 79.
10 Ibid.
11 Sydney F Rowell, *Full Circle*, p. 50.
12 Chester Wilmot, *Tobruk*, p. ix.
13 Wilmot Papers, series 1, folder 24.
14 Ibid.
14 Alan Moorehead, *A Year of Battle*, p. 23.

7 I could 'ave been a blinkin' General
1 Alan Moorehead, *Mediterranean Front*, p. 109.
2 Alan Moorehead, *Mediterranean Front*, p. 110.
3 Ibid.
4 Wilmot Papers, series 1, folder 24.
5 Ibid.
6 CWR p. 26.
7 CWR p. 28.
8 CWR p. 29.
9 CWR p. 30.
10 Ibid.
11 CWR p. 28.
12 CWR p. 29.
13 CWR pp. 30–31.
14 Ibid.
15 CWR p. 31.
16 Brian Bond, *Liddell Hart*, p. 55.
17 Basil H Liddell Hart, *Strategy*, p. 376.
18 Ibid.

8 Caught in the open
1 Correlli Barnett, *The Desert Generals*, p. 40.
2 Correlli Barnett, *The Desert Generals*, p. 28.
3 Wilmot Papers, series 1, folder 24.
4 Ibid.
5 *CWR*, pp. 32–33.
6 Wilmot Papers, series 1, folders 30–43.
7 Wilmot Papers, series 1, folder 26.
8 Chester Wilmot, *Tobruk*, p. 36.
9–12 Chester Wilmot, dispatch, 'The Capture of Bardia', 10 January 1941, Australian Archives, SP300/4.

Notes

13	Wilmot Papers, series 1, folder 26.
14	Ibid.
15	*CWR*, pp. 65–71.
16	Ivan Chapman, conversation with the author, 1985.
17	HB Gullett, *Not as a Duty Only*, pp. 14–15.
18	Wilmot Papers, series 1, folder 26.
19	Chester Wilmot, *Tobruk*, p. 3.
20	Chester Wilmot, *Tobruk*, p. 5.
21	*CWR*, pp. 65–71; 'What I Saw at Tobruk', 24 January, 1941; Australian Archives, SP300/4.
22	Chester Wilmot, *Tobruk*, p. 27; 'What I Saw at Tobruk', 24 January, 1941, Australian Archives, SP300/4.
23	Ibid; *CWR*, p. 64.
24	Ibid; *CWR*, pp. 68–69.
25	Edward Ward, *Number One Boy*, p. 151.
26	Chester Wilmot, *Tobruk*, pp. 55–56.
27	Wilmot Papers, series 1, folder 25.
28–31	Chester Wilmot, dispatch, 'After the Fall of Derna', Australian Archives, SP300/4
32	Chester Wilmot, dispatch, 'Last Roundup in Cyrenaica', 7 February 1941, Australian Archives, SP300/4.
33	Kenneth Macksey, *Beda Fomm, the Classic Victory*, p. 135.
34	Ibid.
35	Kenneth Macksey, *Beda Fomm, the Classic Victory*, p. 139.
36–41	Wilmot Papers, series 1, folder 26.
42	Correlli Barnett, *The Desert Generals*, p. 58.

9 A desire to seek the underlying causes

1	Clement Semmler (ed.), *The War Diaries of Kenneth Slessor*, p. 267.
2	Wilmot Papers, series 1, folder 26.
3	*CWR*, pp. 112–113.
4	Chester Wilmot to Edith Irwin, Wilmot Papers, series 1, folder 26.
5	Chester Wilmot, dispatch, 'A Letter from the Front', Australian Archives, SP300/4.
6–13	Family letter April 1941, Wilmot Papers, series 1, folder 26.
14	Lawrence H Cecil, Report to the ABC, Australian Archives, SP300/4.
15	Dispatch 'A Letter From the Front', Australian Archives, SP300/4; *CWR*, p. 120.
16	Dispatch 'Monastir Gap', 17 April, 1941, Australian Archives, SP300/4; *CWR*, pp. 122–123.
17	Ibid.; *CWR*, p. 124.
18	Ibid.; *CWR*, p. 127.
19	Ibid.; *CWR*, p. 128.
20	Ibid.
21	Family letter April 1941, Wilmot Papers, series 1, folder 26.
22	Lawrence H Cecil, Report to the ABC, Australian Archives, SP300/423.
23	Family letter April 1941, Wilmot Papers, series 1, folder 26.
24	Ron Maslyn Williams, interview with Tony Morphett, c. 1980.
25	Ibid.

26–30	Rowell to Gavin Long, 20 January 1947, Records of Gavin Long, Australian War Memorial.
31	Stuart Braga, *Kokoda Commander*, p. 126.
32	Wilmot Papers, series 1, folder 44.
33–35	Records of Gavin Long, Australian War Memorial.
36	Sydney Rowell, interview with Ivan Chapman.
37	David Horner, *Blamey*, p. 198.
38	Peter Charlton (historian) related the story to Peter Brune, Ian Bowring (of Allen & Unwin) and the author.
39	Edith Wilmot supplied a copy of this letter to the author in 1989.

10   Sand in their shoes

1	Clement Semmler (ed.), *The War Diaries of Kenneth Slessor*, p. 271.
2–4	Clement Semmler (ed.), *The War Diaries of Kenneth Slessor*, p. 270.
5	Ivor Hele, interview with the author and Gavin Fry, 1992.
6	Ivan Chapman, conversation with the author, 1991.
7	Wilmot Dispatch, 'Air Power and the Greek Campaign', 5 May 1941. *CWR*, pp. 153, 154, 156, 157. The censor cuts are marked on the original.
8	Ibid. p. 154.
9	*CWR*, p. 156.
10	Ibid.
11–14	*CWR*, p. 157.
15	Wilmot Papers, series 7, folder 8; *CWR* p. 159.
16	Dispatch 'Air Power and the Greek Campaign', Australian Archives, SP300/4.
17	Ibid.
18	Family letter April 1941, Wilmot Papers, series 1, folder 26.
19	Ibid.
20	Chester to his father, Wilmot Papers, series 1, folder 25.
21	David Horner, *Crisis of Command*, p. 120.
22–25	David Horner, *Blamey*, pp. 211–212, 213.

11   We are slow to learn

1	*CWR*, pp. 187, 189.
2	Chester Wilmot, *Tobruk*, pp. 251, 254–256.
3	Chester Wilmot, *Tobruk*, pp. 110, 111.
4	*CWR*, pp. 212–217.
5	Chester Wilmot, 'In a Dugout at Tobruk', dispatch, National Library of Australia, Papers of John Latham 1009. The dispatch was enclosed with a letter to George Fenton. Chester Wilmot series 1.
6	Wilmot Papers, series 1, folder 27.
7	*CWR*, p. 221.
8	Chester Wilmot, *Tobruk*, p. 99. The 'fucking bunnies' was revealed by Chester in a telephone conversation with Ivan Chapman.
9	*CWR*, pp. 243–245.
10	Chester Wilmot, *Tobruk*, pp. 294, 301, 302.
11	Chester Wilmot, *Tobruk*, p. 302.

12 CWR, pp. 257–261.
13 Wilmot Papers, series 2, folder 79.

12 Syd is coming
1 Wilmot Papers, series 1, folder 48. Similar observations were made by Alan Moorehead in *A Year of Battle*, 1943.
2 Peter Brune, *A Bastard of a Place*, p. 54.
3 Peter Brune, *A Bastard of a Place*, p. 55.
4 Peter Brune, *Those Ragged Bloody Heroes*, p. 15.
5 Peter Brune, *A Bastard of a Place*, p. 55.
6 Ibid.
7 Edith Wilmot, memoir.
8 Ibid.
9 Wilmot Papers, series 2, folder 1.
10 Wilmot to Molesworth, Australian Archives, SP300/9.
11 Edith Wilmot, memoir.
12 Ibid.
13 Peter Brune, *Those Ragged Bloody Heroes*, p. 43.
14 Peter Brune, *A Bastard of a Place*, p. 98.
15 Wilmot Papers, series 2, folder 1.
16 Ibid.

13 Unnecessary Australian graves
1 Gordon Darling, interview with the author, 2003.
2 Osmar White, *Green Armour*, p. 152.
3 CWR, pp. 285–288.
4 Osmar White, *Green Armour*, pp. 156–157.
5 Gordon Darling, interview with the author, 2003.
6 Ibid.
7 Osmar White, interview with the author, 1983.
8 Osmar White, *Green Armour*, p. 160.
9 Peter Brune, *Those Ragged Bloody Heroes*, p. 90.
10 Peter Brune, *Those Ragged Bloody Heroes*, p. 81.
11 Osmar White, *Green Armour*, p. 159.
12 CWR, pp. 297–309.
13 Peter Brune, *A Bastard of a Place*, p. 148.
14 CWR, pp. 305–316.

14 The freedom of the press
1 Father Ferdinand Parer (Damien's brother), interview with the author, 1983.
2 Jack Sim, interview with Chris Masters.
3 Dope sheet, *Kokoda Front Line*, Australian War Memorial.
4 Ken Hall, interview with the author, 1982.
5 Damien Parer, *Kokoda Front Line!*, transcription.
6 Ken Hall, interview with the author, 1982.
7–9 Peter Brune, *A Bastard of a Place*, p. 243.

10	Peter Brune, *A Bastard of a Place*, p. 245.
11	Peter Brune, *A Bastard of a Place*, p. 246.
12–15	George Fenton, diary.
16	JDB Miller, interview with the author, 2007. Miller, an ABC reporter, encountered Wilmot in the foyer of Parliament House, Canberra, immediately after Chester's interview with Curtin.
17	Australian Archives, SP 300/9.
18	*CWR*, pp. 360–363.
19	*CWR*, p. 364.
20	Sydney F Rowell, *Full Circle*, p. 110.
21	Brune was given a copy of the original by Captain Ken Murdoch, staff captain, 21st Brigade, in October 1987.
22	Wilmot Papers, series 2, folder 9. A copy of the transcript is in Edmund Francis Herring, State Library of Victoria, and is reproduced in John Hetherington, *Blamey*, pp. 401–403.
23	Wilmot Papers, series 2, folder 2.
24	Betty Cook, conversation with the author, 1983.
25–40	Chester Wilmot, 'Withdrawal of My Accreditation', Australian Archives, SP300/4.
41	Charles Moses, interview with the author, 1983.

15 A dangerous subversive and a Communist

1–3	Chester to his father, January 1943, Wilmot Papers, series 2, folder 11.
4	Wilmot Papers, series 2, folder 8. See also series 2, folder 7a.
5	Ibid.
6	Letter to family, Wilmot Papers, series 2, folder 3.
7	Letter to Edith, Letter to family, Wilmot Papers, series 2, folder 3.
8	Wilmot Papers, series 2, folder 3.
9	Frank Legg, *War Correspondent*, p. 21.
10	Wilmot Papers, series 2, folder 3.
11	Ibid.
12	Chester Wilmot, *Tobruk*, p. 81
13	Wilmot Papers, series 2, folder 3.
14	Chester Wilmot, *Tobruk*, p. 114.
15	Chester Wilmot, *Tobruk*, p. 110.
16	Chester Wilmot, *Tobruk*, pp. 110–111.
17	Chester Wilmot, *Tobruk*, p. 114.
18	Chester Wilmot, *Tobruk*, p. 63.
19	Basil H Liddell Hart (ed.), *The Rommel Papers*, p. 96.
20	Chester Wilmot, *Tobruk*, dust jacket.
21	Ibid.
22	Wilmot Papers, series 2, folder 3.
23	Ibid.
24	Edith Wilmot, letter to Chester Wilmot, copy kindly supplied to the author by Jane Wilmot-Crane.
25	Edith Wilmot, memoir.
26	Chester to his father, April 1943, Wilmot Papers, series 2, folder 3.

27	Ibid.
28	Charles Moses, interview with the author, 1983.
29	Ibid.
30	Blamey letter, Australian Archives, SP300/9.
31	Wilmot Papers, series 2, folder 11.
32	Ibid.
33	Family letter May 1944, Wilmot Papers, series 3, folder 1.

16 Such a complete victory

1–3	Memos concerning 'Sons of the Anzacs' are filed in the AWM, 50/5/51/10 and 1006918.
4	Damien Parer Papers, State Library of New South Wales.
5–10	Mervyn Scales to AW Bazley, 6 June 1949, AWM PR84/389.
11	Charles Moses, interview with the author, 1983.
12	Wilmot Papers, series 2, folder 7.
13	Kenneth Slessor, *Selected Poems*, p. 126.
14	John Hetherington, *Australians: Nine Profiles*, p. 108.
15	Charles Moses, interview with the author, 1983.
16–18	Film – 'Sons of the Anzacs', Australian War Memorial.

17 Broadcasting as an arm of warfare

1	Asa Briggs, *The History of Broadcasting in the United Kingdom*, vol. 2, p. 258.
2	Wynford Vaughan-Thomas, *Trust to Talk*, p. 125.
3	Frank Gillard, interview with the author, 1996.
4	Ibid.
5–8	Chester Wilmot, *The Struggle for Europe*, p. 215.
9	Winston Churchill, *The Second World War*, vol. V, p. 514.
10	Frank Gillard, interview with the author, 1996.
11	Ibid.
12	Letter, Chester to Edith, June 1944. Wilmot Papers, series 3, folder 2.
13	Ibid.
14	Stephen Ambrose, *Pegasus Bridge*, pp. 51–52.
15	Ibid.
16	Letter, Chester to Edith, June 1944. Wilmot Papers, series 3, folder 2.
17	Desmond Hawkins (ed.), *War Report*, p. 14.
18	Frank Gillard, interview with the author, 1996.
19	Chester Wilmot, *The Struggle for Europe*, p. 234.
21–23	Wilmot Papers, series 3, folders 5–24.
24	Wilmot Papers, series 3, folder 1.
25	Chester Wilmot, *The Struggle for Europe*, p. 235.

18 Hello BBC! Hello BBC!

1	Chester Wilmot, *The Struggle for Europe*, p. 236.
2–4	Wilmot Papers, series 3, folders 5–24.
5	Chester Wilmot, *The Struggle for Europe*, p. 238.
6	Ibid.

7	Richard N Gale, *With the 6th Airborne Division in Normandy*, p. 76.
8	Chester Wilmot, *The Struggle for Europe*, p. 240.
9	Edith Wilmot, memoir, from notes of Alan Wood.
10	Wilmot Papers, series 3, folders 5–24.
11	Richard N Gale, *With the 6th Airborne Division in Normandy*, p. 87.
12	Wilmot Papers, series 3, folders 5–24.
13	Chester Wilmot, *The Struggle for Europe*, p. 241.
14	David Howarth, *Dawn of D-Day*, p. 61.
15	Wilmot Papers, series 3, folder 1.
16	Ibid.
17	Wilmot Papers, series 3, folders 5–24.
18–22	Wilmot Papers, series 3, folder 1.
23–25	Wilmot Papers, series 3, folders 5–24.
26	Wilmot Papers, series 3, folder 1.
27	Ibid.
28	Wilmot Papers, series 3, folders 5–24.
29–33	Howard Marshall to Malcolm Frost, BBC Written Archives.
34	Edith Wilmot, memoir.
35	Wilmot Papers, series 3, folder 1.
36	Ibid.
37	Wilmot Papers, series 3, folders 5–24.
38	Chester Wilmot, *The Struggle for Europe*, p. 393.
39	Max Hastings, *Overlord*, p. 132.
40	Max Hastings, *Overlord*, p. 134.
41	Papers of Reginald William Winchester ('Chester') Wilmot, Liddell Hart Centre for Military Archives.

19 Viva BBC!

1–3	Wilmot Papers, series 3, folders 5–24.
4	Wilmot Papers, series 3, folder 1.
5	Ibid.
6	Wilmot Papers, series 3, folders 5–24.
7	Ibid.
8	Frank Gillard, interview with the author, 1996.
9	Wilmot Papers, series 3, folder 1.
10	Ibid.
5	Brian Horrocks, *Corps Commander*, pp. 79–80.
6	Frank Gillard, interview with the author, 1996.
7	Robin Neillands, *The Battle for the Rhine*, p. 202.
8	Chester Wilmot, *The Struggle for Europe*, p. 498.
9	Desmond Hawkins (ed.), *War Report*, pp. 232–233.
10	Wilmot Papers, series 3, folder 1.
11	'Portrait of Chester Wilmot', BBC Home Service Basic, 9 February 1954, transcription, copy in Charles Moses, papers.
12	Frank Gillard, interview with the author, 1996.
13	Desmond Hawkins (ed.), *War Report*, pp. 247–251.

14	Desmond Hawkins (ed.), *War Report*, pp. 247–248, 251–252.
15	Wilmot Papers, series 3, folders 5–24.
16	Ibid.
17	Wilmot Papers, series 3, folder 1.
18	From Chester Wilmot's Memorial Programme, February 1954. Transcription, copy in Charles Moses, papers.
19	Wilmot Papers, series 3, folders 5–24.
20	Frank Gillard, interview with the author, 1996.
21	Desmond Hawkins (ed.), *War Report*, pp. 247–251.
22	Desmond Hawkins (ed.), *War Report*, pp. 247–248.
23	Desmond Hawkins (ed.), *War Report*, pp. 251–252.

20 Unhappy phrases

1–9	Wilmot Papers, series 3, folder 1. Regarding Parer's death, see also Neil McDonald, *Kokoda Front Line*, pp. 348–349.
10	Frank Gillard, interview with the author, 1996.
11	Antony Beevor, *Ardennes*, p. 170.
12	Nigel Hamilton, *Monty: The Field Marshal*, p. 213.
13	Ibid.
14	Wilmot Papers, series 3, folders 5–24.
15	Ibid.
16	Chester Wilmot, *The Struggle for Europe*, pp. 610–612.

21 So big was Wilmot's story ...

1	Chester Wilmot, *The Struggle for Europe*, p. 668.
2–6	Wilmot Papers, series 3, folders 5–24.
7	Desmond Hawkins (ed.), *War Report*, pp. 431–434.
8	Wilmot Papers, series 3, folders 5–24.
9	Ibid.
10	Wilmot Papers, series 3, folders 5–24; Desmond Hawkins (ed.), *War Report*, pp. 401–403.

22 A rather different spectacle

1	Wilmot Papers, series 3, folders 5–24.
2	Wilmot Papers, series 3, folders 5–24.
3	Revealed in BBC Retrospective programme.
4	BBC recording of the broadcast, transcription, copy in author's possession.
5	Edith Wilmot to her mother, copy in author's possession.
6	Memo, finance files, BBC Written Archives.
7–9	Wilmot Papers, series 3, folder 1a.
10	Edith Wilmot, memoir.
11	Jane Wilmot Crane, email to author.
12	Wilmot Papers, series 3, folders 5–24.
13	Telford Taylor, *The Anatomy of the Nuremberg Trials*, pp. 168, 171.
14	Ibid.
15	Wilmot Papers, series 3, folders 1a, 2.

16	Edith Wilmot, memoir.
17	Chester Wilmot, *The Struggle for Europe*, p. 17.

23 Passing to the other side

1	Basil H Liddell Hart, *The Strategy of Indirect Approach*, pp. 4–5.
2	Ibid.
3–5	Papers of Reginald William Winchester ('Chester') Wilmot, Liddell Hart Centre for Military Archives.
6	Edith Wilmot to her mother, copy in author's possession.
7	Papers of Reginald William Winchester ('Chester') Wilmot, Liddell Hart Centre for Military Archives.
8	Ibid.
9	Chester Wilmot to Liddell Hart, Liddell Hart Centre for Military Archives.
10	Chester Wilmot, *The Struggle for Europe*, p. 339.
11	Nigel Hamilton, *Monty: The Making of a General*, p. 472.
12	Ibid.
13	Edith Wilmot, memoir.
14	Wilmot Papers, series 4, folder 52a.
15	Wilmot Papers, series 2, folder 29c.
16	Papers of Reginald William Winchester ('Chester') Wilmot, Liddell Hart Centre for Military Archives.
17	Edith Wilmot, memoir.
18	Wilmot Papers, series 4, folder 52a.
19	Edith Wilmot, memoir.

LIST OF MAPS

The North African Coast	p. 104
Sidi Barrani – 9 December 1940	p. 112
Bardia – The Plan	p. 131
Tobruk – The Plan	p. 139
Greeece – The Withdrawal	p. 165
The Siege of Tobruk	p. 197
The Tobruk Salient	p. 213
Papua, New Guinea	p. 227
The Kokoda Track	p. 236
Operation Neptune: D-Day	p. 324
D-Day: The BBC Coverge	p. 335
Chester Wilmot: Dawn on D-Day	p. 344
Goodwood & Cobra: 25 July 1944	p. 363
Operation Market Garden	p. 381
The Ardennes – the site of the German's last offensive of the Second World War	p. 397

BIBLIOGRAPHY

Australian archives, Canberra and Sydney
Chester Wilmot's Australian dispatches and official correspondence with the ABC:
NAA: SP 300/9 (Sydney)
Blamey to Moses, SP/300/9

Australian War Memorial
AWM 67 Gavin Long, Papers of the Official Historian, 1939–1957
AWM 80 Department of Information, broadcast transcripts and press releases
Allen Papers, 3DRL2381
Blamey Papers, 3DRL6643; PR85/355
Morshead Papers, 3DRL2632
Rowell Papers, 3DRL6673

BBC written records, Reading, England
BBC 'War Report' Files
Files regarding Wilmot's possible disaccreditation
Administrative files regarding 'War Report'

Liddell Hart archive, King's College, London
15/151-163 Wilmot Papers

National Library Of Australia
Papers of Reginald William Winchester (Chester) Wilmot, MS 8436. This collection has some ABC dispatches, but mainly consists of his BBC broadcasts and private letters and correspondence.
Edith Wilmot Series, MS 8436/1-13
Alan and Mary Wood, original Wilmot biographers (work and biography not completed due to their passing), MS 8436/13/7-22.

Interviews
Aldridge, James, War Correspondent, Middle East 1941, interview with Neil McDonald and Peter Brune, London, 21 April, 2011.
Darling, Lieutenant-Colonel Gordon, ADC to General Rowell, July 2003.
Gillard, Frank, BBC Correspondent, Middle East and Europe, interview with the author, London, 17 July 1996.
Moses, Sir Charles, General Manager of the ABC, various interviews, Sydney, 1983–1986.

Bibliography

Santamaria, Bob, interview with the author, Melbourne, August 1996.
White, Osmar, interview with the author, March 1983.

Private papers
Edith Wilmot Memoir, copy in possession of the author.
Darling, Lieutenant-Colonel Gordon, ADC to General Rowell.

Books
Ambrose, Stephen. *Pegasus Bridge*, Simon & Schuster, New York, 1988
Aldridge, James. *Signed With Their Honour*, Michael Joseph, The Specialty Press, Melbourne, 1943
Barnett, Correlli. *The Desert Generals*, William Kimber and Co. Ltd, London, 1960
Beevor, Antony. *Berlin: The Downfall 1945*, Viking, London, 2002
———. *D-Day: The Battle for Normandy*, Viking 2009
———. *Ardennes 1944*, Viking, London, 2015
Belchem, Major-General David. *Victory in Normandy*, Chatto & Windus Ltd, London, 1980
Belfrage, Bruce. *One Man In His Time: An Autobiography*, Hodder and Stoughton, London, 1951
Bernage, Georges. *Red Devils in Normandy, 6th Airborne Division 5–6 June 1944*, Heimdal, Bayeux, 2002
Bond, Brian. *Liddell Hart: A Study of His Military Thought*, Cassell, London, 1977
Bradley, Omar N. *A Soldier's Story*, Rand McNally & Company, New York, 1951
Braga, Stuart. *Kokoda Commander: A Life of Major-General 'Tubby' Allen*, The Australian Army History Series, Oxford Univwersity Press, Melbourne, 2004
Breuer, William B. *Feuding Allies: The Private Wars of the High Command*, John Wiley & Sons Inc, USA and Canada, 1995
Briggs, Asa. *History of Broadcasting in the United Kingdom, Volume 2: The Golden Age of Wireless*, Oxford University Press, London, 1965
———. *History of Broadcasting in the United Kingdom, Volume 3: The War of Words*, Oxford University Press, London, 1995
Brune, Peter. *Those Ragged Bloody Heroes: From the Kokoda Trail to Gona Beach 1942*, Allen & Unwin, Sydney, 1991
———. *A Bastard of a Place: The Australians in Papua*, Allen & Unwin, Sydney, 2003
Buckley, John. *Monty's Men: The British Army and the Liberation of Europe*, Yale University Press, London, 2013
Churchill, Winston S. *The Second World War, Volume I, The Gathering Storm*, Cassell, London, 1948
———. *The Second World War, Volume II, Their Finest Hour*, Cassell, London, 1948
———. *The Second World War, Volume V, Closing The Ring*, Cassell, London, 1952
———. *The Second World War, Volume VI, Triumph and Tragedy*, Cassell, London, 1954
Coulthart, Ross. *Charles Bean: If People Really Knew: one man's struggle to report the Great War and tell the truth*, HarperCollins, Sydney, 2014
Danchev, Alex. *Alchemist of War: The Life of Basil Liddell Hart*, Phoenix Giant, London, 1998

Deighton, Len. *Battle of Britain*, Jonathon Cape Ltd, London, 1980

Delaforce, Patrick. *The Battle of the Bulge: Hitler's Final Gamble*, Pearson Education Ltd, Harlow, 2006

Dimbleby, Jonathon. *Richard Dimbleby*, Coronet Books, Hodder & Stoughton, London, 1977

Dimbleby, Richard. *The Frontiers are Green*, Hodder & Stoughton, London, 1943

Dixon, Jack. *Dowding & Churchill: The Dark Side of the Battle of Britain*, Pen & Sword Books Ltd, South Yorkshire, 2009

Doenitz, Admiral Karl. *Memoirs of Ten Years and Twenty Days*, Weidenfeld & Nicholson, London, 1958

Dunphie, Christopher. *The Pendulum of Battle: Operation Goodwood, July 1944*, Leo Cooper, Pen & Sword Books Ltd, South Yorkshire, 2004

Ebury, Sue. *Weary: The Life of Sir Edward Dunlop*, Viking, Melbourne, 1994

Edgar, Bill. *Warrior of Kokoda: A Biography of Brigadier Arnold Potts*, Army Military History Series, Allen & Unwin, Sydney, 1999

Eforgan, Estel. *Leslie Howard: The Lost Actor*, Vallentine Mitchell, Middlesex, Oregon, 2013

Eisenhower, General Dwight D. *Crusade in Europe*, William Heinemann Ltd, London, 1949

D'Este, Carlo. *Eisenhower: Allied Supreme Commander*, Weidenfeld & Nicholson, London, 2002

Gale, General Sir Richard. *Call to Arms: An Autobiography*, Hutchinson of London, 1968

———. *With the 6th Airborne Division in Normandy*, Sampson Low, London, 1948

Gedye, GER, *Fallen Bastions: The Central European Tragedy*, Victor Gollancz Ltd, London, 1942

Gibbon, Edward. *The History of the Decline and Fall of the Roman Empire, Vol. I*, Penguin Classics, London, 1994

De Guingand, Major-General Sir Francis. *Operation Victory*, Hodder & Stroughton, London, 1963

Gullett, H. B. *Not as a Duty Only: An Infantryman's War*, Melbourne University Press, Carlton, 1976

Hamilton, Nigel. *Monty: The Making of a General 1887–1942*, Hamish Hamilton Ltd, London, 1981

———. *Master of the Battlefield: Monty's War Years, 1942–1944*, McGraw-Hill Book Company, New York, 1983

———. *Monty: The Field Marshal 1944–1976*, Hamish Hamilton Ltd, London, 1986

Harclerode, Peter. *"Go To It!": The Illustrated History of the 6th Airborne Division*, Bloomsbury Publishing Ltd, London, 1990

Hastings, Max. *Overlord: D-Day and the Battle for Normandy 1944*, Michael Joseph Limited, London, 1984

Havers, Richard. *Here is the News: The BBC and the Second World War*, Sutton, London, 2007

Hawkins, Jack. *Anything For a Quiet Life*, Elm Tree Books, Hamish Hamilton, London, 1966

Hawkins, Desmond (ed). *War Report*, Oxford University Press, 1946

Hetherington, John. *Australians: Nine Profiles*, F. W. Cheshire, Melbourne, 1960

Bibliography

Hickman, Tom. *What did you do in the War, Auntie?*, BBC Books, London, 1995
Hitler, Adolf. *Mein Kampf*, Translation by Ralph Mannheim, Pimlico, London, 1969
Horne, Alister with David Montgomery, *The Lonely Leader: Monty 1944–1945*, Macmillan, London, 1994
Horner, David. *Blamey: The Commander-in-Chief*, Allen & Unwin, Sydney, 1998
———, *Crisis of Command: Australian Generalship and the Japanese Threat, 1941–1943*, Australian National University Press, Canberra, 1978
Horrocks, Brian. *Corps Commander*, Sidgwick & Jackson, London, 1977
Howard, John, & Bates, Penny. *The Pegasus Diaries: The Private Papers of Major John Howard DSO*, Pen & Sword Military, South Yorkshire, 2008
Howarth, David. *Dawn of D-Day*, Collins, London, 1959
Ingersoll, Ralph. *Top Secret*, Harcourt Brace and Company, New York, 1946
Innes, Arthur. *A History of England and the British Empire*, Macmillan, New York, 1913
Keegan, John. *Six Armies in Normandy: From D-Day to the Liberation of Paris*, Jonathan Cape, London, 1982
Knightly, Phillip. *The First Casualty: The War Correspondent as Hero, Propagandist, and Myth Maker, From the Crimea to Vietnam*, Andre Deutsch Ltd, London, 1975
Larrabee, Eric. *Commander in Chief, Franklin Delano Roosevelt, His Lieutenants & Their War*, Harper & Row, New York, 1987
Legg, Frank. *War Correspondent*, Rigby, Adelaide, 1964
Liddell Hart, BH (ed). *The Rommel Papers*, Collins, London, 1953
———. *The Memoirs: Vol. 1 & 2, Cassel & Company Ltd*, London, 1965
———. *History of the Second World War*, Pan Books, London, 1970
Liddell Hart, BH (ed). *Strategy*, First Meridian Printing, New York, 1991
———. *The Strategy of the Indirect Approach: The Decisive Wars of History,* Faber and Faber Ltd, London, 1941
Long, Gavin. *To Benghazi*, Australian War Memorial, Canberra, 1952
Longmate, Norman. *When We Won the War: The Story of Victory in Europe, 1945*, Hutchinson of London, 1977
Macintyre, Stuart. *A history for a nation: Ernest Scott and the making of Australian history*, Melbourne University Press, Carlton, Victoria, 1994
Macksey, Kenneth. *Beda Fomm, The Classic Victory*, Ballantine Books, New York, 1971
Maddox, Barbara. *The Tale of Two Bridges: Based on the diary of Colonel RG Pine-Coffin DSO, MC, The 7th (Light Infantry) Parachute Battalion*, Kerry Type Ltd, West Sussex, 2004
Margry, Karel (ed). *Operation Market Garden: Then and Now*, Vol. 1 & 2, Battle of Britain International Ltd, Essex, 2008
McDonald, Neil. *War Cameraman, The Story of Damien Parer*, Lothian, Melbourne, 1994
———. *Chester Wilmot Reports: Broadcasts That Shaped World War II*, ABC Books, Sydney, 2004
Merriam, Robert E. *Dark December: The Full Account of the Battle of the Bulge*, Westholme Publishing, Pennsylvania, 2011
Montgomery of Alamein KG, Field Marshal The Viscount. *The Memoirs*, Collins, London, 1958
Montgomery Hyde, H. *Norman Birkett: The Definitive Biography of the Legendary Barrister*, Penguin Books, London, 1964

Moorehead, Alan. *A Year of Battle*, Hamish Hamilton, London, 1943
_____. *Eclipse*, Hamish Hamilton, London, 1946
_____. *Mediterranean Front*, Hamish Hamilton, London, 1941
Moorehead, Alan. *Montgomery: The life story of one of the greatest leaders of our time*, Four Square Books, Landsborough Publications Ltd, London, 1958
Muggeridge, Malcolm (ed). *Ciano's Diary*, William Heinemann Ltd, Surrey, 1948
Neillands, Robin. *The Battle of Normandy 1944*, Cassell, London, 2002
_____. *The Battle for the Rhine 1944*, Weidenfeld & Nicolson London, 2005
Orange, Vincent. *Dowding of Fighter Command: Victor of the Battle of Britain*, Grub Street Publishing, London, 2008
Pitt, Barrie. *The Crucible of War: Western Desert 1941*, Book Club Associates, Jonathan Cape, London, 1980
Rees, Peter. *Bearing Witness, The remarkable life of Charles Bean, Australia's greatest war correspondent*, Allen & Unwin, Sydney, 2014
Reynolds, David. *In Command of History*, Penguin Books, London, 2005
Richardson, Charles. *Send for Freddie: The Story of Monty's Chief of Staff, Major-General Sir Francis de Guingand KBE, CB, DSO*, William Kimber & Co. Ltd, London, 1987
Roosevelt, Elliott. *As He Saw It*, Duell, Sloan and Pearce, New York, 1946
Rose, Jonathan. *The Literary Churchill: Author, Reader, Actor*, Yale University Press, New Haven, 2014
Rowell, Sydney F. *Full Circle*, Melbourne University Press, Melbourne, 1974
Ryan, Cornelius. *A Bridge Too Far*, Hamish Hamilton, London, 1974
_____. *The Longest Day: June 6, 1944*, Victor Gollancz, London, 1960
Semmler, Clement (ed). *The War Diaries of Kenneth Slessor*, University of Queensland Press, St Lucia, 1985
_____. *The War Despatches of Kenneth Slessor*, University of Queensland Press, St Lucia, 1987
Sereny, Gitta. *The German Trauma: Experiences and Reflections 1938–2000*, The Penguin Press, London, 2000
Slessor, Kenneth. *Selected Poems*, Angus & Robertson, Sydney 1993
Snagge, John, and Barsley, Michael. *Those Vintage Years of Radio*, Pitman Publishing, London, 1972
Speidel, Lieutenant-General Hans, (trans. by Ian Colvin). *We Defended Normandy*, Herbert Jenkins Ltd, London, 1951
Talbot, Godfrey. *Permission to Speak*, Hutchinson of London, 1976
Taylor, Telford. *The Anatomy of the Nuremberg Trials*, Bloomsbury Publishing Limited, London, 1993
Trevor-Roper, Hugh. *The Last Days of Hitler*, Papermac, London, 1995
Tully, Grace. *F.D.R. My Boss*, People's Book Club, Chicago, 1949
Tusa, Ann, and Tusa, John. *The Nuremberg Trial*, Macmillan, London, 1983
Various, *D-Day, The Normandy Invasion in Restrospect*, The University Press of Kansas, Lawrence, 1971
Vaughan-Thomas, Wynford. *Trust to Talk*, Hutchinson, London, 1980
Ward, Edward. *Number One Boy*, Joseph, London, 1969
Ward Price, G. *Year of Reckoning*, Cassell and Co. Ltd, London, 1939

Bibliography

Warner, Philip. *Horrocks: The General Who Led From The Front*, Pen & Sword Military, South Yorkshire, 2005
Wheeler-Bennett, John. *Munich: Prologue to Tragedy*, Macmillan, London, 1966
Weigley, Russell F. *Eisenhower's Lieutenants: The Campaigns of France and Germany, 1944–1945*, Indiana University Press, Bloomington, 1981
White, Osmar. *Green Armour*, Angus & Robertson, Sydney, 1945
Williams, Andrew. *D-Day to Berlin*, (by arrangement with the BBC, London), Hodder & Stroughton Ltd, London, 1996
Wilmot, Chester. *The Struggle for Europe*, Collins, London, 1952
_____. *Tobruk*, Angus and Robertson, Sydney, 1944
Wilmot, RWE. *Defending the Ashes, 1932–1933*, Robertson & Mullins, Melbourne, 1933
Woodhouse, Faye. *A Place Apart: A Study of Student Political Engagement at the University of Melbourne, 1930–1938*, (unpublished Doctoral thesis)
Wright, Stephen L. *The Last Drop: Operation Varsity, March 24–25, 1945*, Stackpole Books, Pennsylvania, 2008
Wykes, Alan. *The Nuremberg Rallies, Purnell's History of the Second World War, campaign book No. 8*, Hazell Watson & Viney Ltd, Aylesbury, 1969
Young, Desmond. *Rommel*, Collins, London, 1950

INDEX

ps indicates a photo or photos in the picture section.
CW = Chester Wilmot.

2nd Army *see* Second Army (British)
4th Indian Division 113, 116
6th Airborne Division 6–8, 324, 328–332, 336–337, 345, 348, 350, 356, 384, 387, 412
6th Division, AIF
   assault on Post 11: 125–133
   battle of Bardia 116–125
   command structure 97
   Diggers' ugly behaviour 99–100
   discipline 94–95, 98–99
   Operation Compass 105–115
21st Brigade 240, 245, 247, 260–261, 263
21st New Zealand Battalion 164, 166–167
39th Battalion 228–229, 235, 237, 244–245, 248, 250–251, 253, 256, 261–262, 266, 278–279, *ps*
53rd Battalion 228, 245, 260–262, 266

ABC (Australian Broadcasting Commission)
   CW accepts part-time job 27, 30
   CW joins Broadcast Unit 85–88
   and CW's dispute with Blamey 282–283, 290–291, 300–302, 304, 311, 314, 328
   see also Broadcast [Field] Unit; Moses, Charles
AIF *see* Second AIF
Airborne Division
   at Arnhem 387–389
   in Normandy 8, 324, 328, 330, 336–337, 348–349

Allen, A.S. ('Tubby') 97, 98, 116, 124–125, 137, 164, 167, 184, 192–193, 240, 285, *ps*
Amery, Leo 52–54
'And Our Troops were Forced to Withdraw' (Chester Wilmot) 250–260, 263, 267
Andrew, Basil John 192–193
Anschluss plebiscite 46–51
anti-Catholicism 15
appeasement
   Australian support for 77–78, 83
   CW's opposition to 42–44, 69, 75–77, 83–84
Ardennes offensive 396–398, 401–409
   see also Battle of the Bulge
Arnhem battles 384–389, 390
Auchinleck, Sir Claude 218, 452
Austen, Edwin 429
Australian and New Zealand Universities' Congress 27–28
Australian Broadcasting Commission. see ABC (Australian Broadcasting Commission)
Australian War Memorial 303–304, 307, 308
Austria 46–52
Auty, Bob 65

Bailey, Kenneth 17–18
Baldwin, Stanley 42
Balfe, John 210
Ball, Macmahon 17–18, 19–20, 77, 84
Banks, Terry 266
Bardia battle 116–125, 131(map)
Barrett, Sir James 39
Bartlett, Norman 130
Battle for Caen 354, 358, 367–368
Battle of Britain 446–448

Index

Battle of El Alamein 452–453
Battle of the Bulge 395–403, 397(map)
Bazley, Arthur 303–304, 308, 316
BBC (British Broadcasting Corporation)
   CW and 52–54, 311–315
   Reith legacy 317–318
   see also 'War Report'
Bean, CEW 85, 187, 274, 287, 301, 304, 308, *ps*
Bearup, TW 87, 222, 233, 282
Beasley, Jack 'Stabber' 292
Beda Fomm battle 144–149
Beecham, Sir Thomas 88–89
Belchem, David 448
Belsen 417–419
Benes, Edvard 65–66, 67–68, 71, 76, 77
Benjamin, Alan 22, 28–33, 35, 36, 38, 44–45, 49–52, 51–52, 79, *ps*
Bennett, John Wheeler 65
Berryman, Frank 97, 122, 130
Birkett, Sir Norman 441
Bissett, Harold 253
Blamey, Sir Thomas
   appointed to command AIF 85–86, 98
   attempts to ban Sons of the Anzacs 315–316
   censorship of CW's scripts 222–223, 284, 285
   charter from Australian Government 98–99
   corruption allegations 223, 234–235, 280–281, 283, 286, 289, 301, 312–313
   and decision to relieve Tobruk 215
   fitness as field commander 164, 166–169, 192, 285–286
   imposes reporting restrictions 273, 288, 293
   opposition to Greek campaign 150–151
   orders CW to record speech 121–122
   photo *ps*
   questionable personal behaviour 98, 169, 234–235, 283–284
   relations with CW 121, 190, 281–289, 301–303, 304, 311–312, 314–316
   relations with Lavarack 196–197, 287, 295
   relations with Rowell 99, 121, 192–193, 267–268, 270–274, 287
   relations with Wavell 99
   as 'The Sentinel' 78, 83, 121
   unpopularity among officers and troops 166–169, 287
Blamey, Tom 176
Bletcher, Neville 305
Boyd, Don 332
Boyle, Reg 87–88, 96–97, 102, 211, 216
Bradley, Omar 323, 354–355, 362, 398–399, 402, 455
Brewer, Sam 218
Bridgeford, William 192–193
'British', CW's use of word 99
broad front strategy 378, 395–396, 398, 400, 450
Broadcast [Field] Unit
   aims and objectives 96
   assault on Post 11: 125–130
   battle of Bardia 117–125
   Bethlehem Christmas programmes 101–102
   Boyle's intransigence 87–88, 96–97, 211
   broadcasting equipment and methods 88, 95, 96, 101–102, 120–121, 163, 169, 239
   Cecil as leader 86–88, 102, 151–152, 157, 169, 198–200, 222, 232–233
   censorship of material 140, 162, 183
   closure of New Guinea unit 293
   CW joins 85–88
   in Derna 141–144
   and Greek campaign 151–163, 169–175
   independence from AIF 152
   to Middle East 89–96
   restrictions on reporting in New Guinea 233, 273, 288, 293
   in Syria 198–200
   at Tobruk 133–141
   Townsville base 233, 238–239
Bruce, Stanley Melbourne 52
Brussels 373–374
Bryden, Bill 38
Burston, Samuel Roy 192
Butcher, Harry 450

Butler, Ewan 70–71
Byam, Guy 345, 352, 387–389

Caen 354, 358, 367–368
Cairo 103
Caro, Albert 255
Carrington, Peter 384, 386
Cattle, Peter 339, 340–341
Cecil, Lawrence H.
  and Boyle's intransigence 87–88, 96–97, 222
  CW and 86–87, 88, 90, 117, 122, 133, 140, 154, 198–199, 233
  as leader of Broadcast Unit 86–88, 102, 151–152, 157, 169, 198–200, 222, 232–233
  Sidon surrender 198–200
censorship 119–120, 140, 162, 183–184, 203, 208, 216, 222, 244, 283, 291
Chamberlain, Neville 42–44, 53–54, 83
Chapman, Ivan 178
Churchill, Randolph 44–45, 217–218
Churchill, Winston
  apprehension prior to D-Day 326
  and Battle of Britain 447–448
  complements CW on book 460–461
  and deployment of Australian troops 99, 230
  on fortification of Crete 189
  opposition to appeasement 42, 45, 69, 75, 78, 84
Clayton, Iltyd 187, 189
Clowes, Cyril 166–167, 192, 240, 267
Cohen, Morris 32
Collings, JS 304, 316
Cook, Betty 282–283
Cooperative Farm movement 71–72
Crete campaign
  German invasion 185–187
  lack of fortification 187, 189, 224
cricket commentaries
  Bung Wilmot 18–19
  Chester Wilmot 52, 54, 328
Crusader Offensive 216–220, 298
Cunningham, Sir Alan 216, 218
Curtin, John 271, 272, 274, 280, 302–303, 304, 311–312, 313, 328–329
Czechoslovakia
  demands of Sudeten Germans 57–58, 61, 64–69, 71, 76, 77
  Runciman mission 58, 66–67, 75–76
  war scare 57–58

D-Day
  BBC coverage 333–334, 335(map)
  planning for 323–326
Dalton, Hugh 54
de Valera, Eamon 55
Deamer, Syd 302
debates and debating
  at Melbourne Grammar 12
  at Melbourne University 17–18, 22, 28
  overseas inter-varsity contests 30–31, 35, 39–40, 43, 44–45
Decoy, HMS 200–203
Defence of the Ashes (RWE Wilmot) 19
Denny, Therese 456–458, *ps*
Department of External Affairs 29, 38
Department of Information (DOI)
  censorship by 291
  CW and 84–85
  hostility to *Sons of the Anzacs* project 307
  Overseas Broadcast Unit 84–85
  Parer and 232, 307, 309
  Photographic Unit 85, 123, 152
Derna 141–144
Dimbleby, Richard 140, 191, 215, 319, 410, 417–419, *ps*
Dorman-Smith, Eric 114, 144, 149, 452
Dowding, Hugh 447–448
Downs, Bill 385, 387
Dunlop, 'Weary' 17

Earl, 'Nobby' 256
Eather, Kenneth 269, 270, 272
Ector, Thierry and Viviane *ps*
Ector family 434
Eden, Anthony 44, 45
Edmondson, Jack 211–212
Eisenhower, Dwight D
  broad front strategy 378, 395–396, 398, 400, 450

Index

Montgomery's opinion of 378, 395–396, 398, 454–455
and Operation Overlord 323, 367
and Patton 433
plan for Rhineland campaign 405
and Stalin 419
and *The Struggle for Europe* 461
Elder, Ann 15, 18, 231
Eleusis 155
Elliott, Cyril 192
Eora Creek (Kokoda Track) 250, *ps*
Evans, A Perry 26–27
Evatt, HV 'Doc' 287

Fenton, George 121, 273–274, 281, 283, 296
Fighter Command 446–448
Fitchett, Ian 206
Flaherty, Robert 55–56
Foerste, Herbert 68–71
Franklin, RS 'Lofty' 12–13
free speech and freedom of the press 18, 25–26, 39, 81, 288–289
  see also censorship
Fried, Vilem 'Mickey' 65
Frost, Malcolm 328
Fu Teh-chen 33

Gale, Humphrey 455
Gale, Richard 313–314, 336, 344–345, 350, 412
Galloway, Alexander 99
Galloway, Leo 87
Gaza transmission mast 96, 102
Gedye, GER 50, 65
Geneva Convention violation 246
German Army surrender (4 May 1945) 420–425, *ps*
Gillard, Frank 320–322, 326, 333–334, 352, 360, 372, 387–388, 403
Gilliam, Laurence 332, 446
gliders
  D-Day 6–8, 330–331, 336–339, 340–342
  Operation Varsity 413–414
Godfrey, Arthur 130, 132–133
Goebbels, Joseph 71
Golden Stairs (Kokoda Track) 246–247

Gore, Syd 392
The Great Crusade (Chester Wilmot) 114–115, 441
The Greater Germany (film) 49
Greek campaign
  Blamey's anguish 176–177
  Blamey's fitness as field commander 164, 166–169, 192
  CW on 177–189, 297
  German air superiority 179, 181–182, 184–187
  initial decision to participate 150–151, 176
  threatened New Zealand withdrawal 164, 166–167
  withdrawal from Greece 165(map), 168, 170–175
Grenadier Guards 384–386
Griffith, Bill 331
Gullet, Henry 100–101
Gullett, HBS. 'Jo' 130

Halifax, Lord 42, 83
Hall, Ken G. 266, 313
Hawes, RE 303, 307
Hearman, Ben 255
Hearst, Randolph 40
Hele, Ivor 130, 177
Henderson, Sir Neville 51, 63
Herrin, Geoffrey 386–387, 429
Herring, Edmund 'Ned' 97, 106–107, 162, 184, 192, 281
Higgins, Arthur 305–306
Himmler, Heinrich 426–429
Hitler, Adolf 445
  at 1938 Nuremberg rally 62, 67–68
  appeasement policy towards 42–43
  death 420
  speech in Vienna 48–49
Hobson, Valerie 457
Hogan, Captain (doctor) 255
Holland, Allied invasion of 379–380, 381(map), 382–389
Hong Kong 31–33
Honner, Ralph 142, 248
Hornell, Sir William 31–32, 33

Horrocks, Sir Brian 371, 373, 377–378, 457–458
Humphrey, Hubert 39
Hurley, Frank 85, 86, 118, 123, 152, 206

'In a Dugout in Tobruk' (Chester Wilmot) 206–209, 298
indexes, Churchill's perusal of 461
indirect approach strategy 114–115, 378, 444–445, 455, 456, 461
Ingersoll, Ralph 449–450
inter-varsity debating contests 30–31, 35, 39–40, 44–45
Irwin, Edith *see* Wilmot, Edith
Irwin, Graham 458
Isurava battle 248–249, 253–255

Jackson, Robert H 439–440
Jacob, 'Tubby' 256
Japan
 aggression against China 32–33
 CW visits 34–38
 as perceived threat to Australia 226
Johnston, George 19, 233

Kelly, Jack 117
Kennehan, Marie 458
Key, Arthur 248–249, 258
Kienzle, Bert 237, 242, 262
Kindersley, Hugh 339, 350–351
Knox, Errol 300–302
Kokoda Front Line (film) 266–268
Kokoda Track
 aerial dropping of supplies 237–238, 242–243
 bombing of 7-mile aerodrome 244–245, 260
 construction of drop zone 237–238
 evacuation of the wounded 251–252
 map 235
 missing supplies 248
 photos *ps*
 withdrawal of troops down 250–260
Krcrouse, Frank 234–235, 280

Lacoste, Jerry 347

Lavarack, John 192–193, 196–197, 294–296
Legg, Frank 292, 294
Lehmann, Ludwig 60, 61
Leigh-Mallory, Trafford 323, 448
LHQ (Land Forces Headquarters) 276, 279
Liddell Hart, BH 114–115, 218, 443–446, 452, *ps*
Lloyd, Charles 'Gaffer' 291–292
Lohengrin (Wagner) 70
Long, Gavin 99, 190, 292
Longmore, Arthur 178
Luneburg Heath surrender (4 May 1945) 420–425, *ps*
Lustre Force 151
Lyons, Joe 29, 54, 83, 85

MacArthur, Douglas 233, 234
MacFarlane, Bill 87, 117, 140, 215, 238, 239
Mackay, Iven 97, 115, 123, 132, 134, 168, *ps*
Mackell, Austin 211, 213
Macksey, Kenneth 146
Macky, Neil 166
MacPherson, Stewart 372, 379–380, 410
Magarey, Rupert 258
Man of Aran (documentary film) 55–56
Mann, AE 78
Marie Walewska (film) 49
Maroubra Force 245, 248, 249, 260–263
Marshall, Howard 54, 328, 352, 356, 358–359, 372
mateship 209
Maxted, Stanley 379, 387–389, 410
McCall, Bob 300, 414
McGibbon, SJ 283
McGuinness, Frank 83
Melbourne Grammar 12–13, 20, 28, 153–154
Melbourne University 15–18, 36
Menzies, Robert Gordon 12, 83, 85, 151, 313
Merville battery 348–350
Middle East Command 97–98, 189–190, 224–225, 283
Milne Bay victory 267
Mission Ridge–Brigade-Hill battle 268–269
Molesworth, BH 292, 294

Index

Monson, Ron 170
Montgomery, Sir Bernard
  accepts German Army's surrender 421–425
  American criticisms of 378
  and Battle of El Alamein 452–453
  blocks Russian entry into Denmark 419–420
  meets CW's father 453
  on Normandy strategy 360–362, 367–368, 450–452, 454–455
  Operation Overlord and 323, 333–334
  Operation Varsity and 410–411, 412, 414–415
  opposes Eisenhower's broad front strategy 395–396, 398–403
  praises *The Struggle for Europe* 459
  supports BBC field broadcasting 320–322, 327
Moorehead, Alan 105, 147
Morgan, FE 323
Morris, Basil 229, 239–240, 287
Morshead, Leslie 97, 197, 203–204, 206, 216, 296–207
Moses, Charles
  as ABC General Manager 30, 53, 54, 87
  contributes to 'War Report' 409–410, 412
  photo *ps*
  support for CW in Blamey dispute 282, 289, 302, 304, 311, 314, 328
Mosley, Leonard 345, 351
motion picture contract 234–235, 280–281, 288–289, 301, 312–313
Munich Agreement 73–78, 83
Murdoch, Keith 83
Murdoch, Stanley 266
My Three Years with Eisenhower (Butcher) 450

Nagasaki 34
New Guinea campaign
  Blamey takes charge 270–274
  command crisis 270–274
  command structure 229, 239–240, 248, 269
  CW on 260–263, 275–280, 285

MacArthur's intervention 270, 271
  Port Moresby garrison 226, 228–229
  significance of Japanese landings 235, 240
  see also 21st Brigade; 39th Battalion; 53rd Battalion; Kokoda Track; Maroubra Force
Nibiewa assault 108
Nicholls, Alan 17
Nicholls, Kevin 22
Nicholson, Joy 382–384
Normandy campaign
  Caen operations 354, 358, 361–362, 364, 367–368
  capturing Orme bridgehead 343–348, 344(map)
  controversies about 367–368
  Operation Goodwood 357–358
  Operation Neptune 323–326, 324(map), 333–334
  Operation Overlord 323–326, 333–334
  Villers-Bocage engagement 364–365
Norris, Jack 347
North African campaigns
  Bardia 116–125
  Beda Fomm 144–149
  Derna 141–144
  Operation Compass 105–115
  Tobruk 133–141, 204–209, 215
NUAUS (National Union of Australian Students) 27–28, 79–81
Number One Boy (Ward) 140
Nuremberg (1945) 437
Nuremberg Rally (1934) 49, 59
Nuremberg Rally (1938) 49, 59–63, 67–68, 436–437
Nuremberg trial 438–441
Nye, Claude 253

'Observations on Operations of Maroubra Force' (Chester Wilmot) 260–263, 285
The Observer 462
O'Connor, Richard 114, 116–117, 144, 149, 195, 294, 297
Operation Cobra 362, 363(map), 364
Operation Compass 105–115

Operation Goodwood 361–362, 363(map)
Operation Market Garden 379–380, 381(map), 382–389
Operation Neptune 323–326, 324(map), 333–334
Operation Overlord 333–334
Operation Plunder 414
Operation Varsity 410–415
Otway, Nigel 349

Palmer, Nettie 38
Papua–New Guinea. see Kokoda Track; New Guinea campaign
Paraeus 179
Parer, Damien
  death 394
  and Department of Information 232, 307, 309
  film narrations 309–311
  filming in New Guinea 243, 244, 265–266, 282
  friendship with CW 152, 191, 209–210, 218–219, 306
  in Greece 152, 170
  Kokoda Front Line (film) 252, 267–268, 307, 309
  Kokoda march 245–248, 249
  in North Africa 137, 142, 209–210
  photo *ps*
  relationship with Rowell 241, 245
  return from Port Moresby 266
Patton, George 433
Pétain, Philippe 83–84, 198
Philippines 30–31
Photographic Unit (Department of Information) 85, 123, 152
Poett, Nigel 345
Port Moresby garrison 226, 228–229
Porter, Tom 269
Post 11 assault 125–133
Potts, Arnold 240, 245, 248, 260–261, 263, 269, 279
Pratt, Alec 32
Priestly, Raymond 24–28, 36, 37, 38–39
Prochazka, Vladimir 64

Rabia 113
RAF
  in Greek campaign 178–181, 183–184, 185–186
  see also Airborne Division; Operation Overlord
Ramsay, Sir Bertram 323
Rasmussen, GH 273, 296
Reith, Sir John 317–318
reserved occupations 81, 85
Rhineland campaign, Eisenhower's plan 405
Rhoden, Phil 255
Road to Kokoda (newsreel) 267
Robertson, Horace 116, 138, 222, 284, 287
Rommel, Erwin 195, 218, 297–298
Rommel, Manfred 446
Roosevelt and Hopkins (Sherwood) 455
Rowell, Sydney
  as Blamey's Chief of Staff 99, 121
  on Blamey's fitness at field commander 164, 166–169, 192–193
  CW's support of 285–286
  and New Guinea campaign 240–242, 244, 245–246, 248, 260, 263
  and New Guinea command crisis 266, 267–268, 270–274
  photo *ps*
  relations with CW 163, 192, 241, 245, 260, 263, 285–286, 314–315, 329, 453
  repute 241, 267–268
Runciman, Lord 58, 66–67, 75–76
Russo, Peter 35
Ryan, AP 390–391

Salient see Tobruk
Santamaria, BA 'Bob' 15, 18, 20, 22, 38, *ps*
Sarney, Harvey 422
Savige, Stan 97, 116, 130, 132
Scales, Mervyn 294
Scott, Ernest 17, 19–21, 433
Second AIF
  appointment of Blamey as commander 85–86, 98
  charter guaranteeing Australian command 98–99, 151
  see also Greek campaign; New Guinea

488

Index

campaign; North African campaigns
Second Army (British)
  advance into Holland 380, 382
  Battle of the Bulge 400–401
  drive to Belgian border 370–374
  drive towards Berlin 415
  Normandy strategy 451
  see also Operation Neptune; Operation Overlord
Shafto, Albert 223, 313
Shaw, AGL 13
Sherwood, Robert E. 455
Sidi Barrani 109, 111–112, 117
Sidon surrender 198–199
Siege of Tobruk *see* Tobruk
Silk, George 152, 170, 392
Slessor, Kenneth 150, 170, 176–177, 190, 312–313
Smibert, James 19, 77
Snagge, John 332–333, 424
Sofalia 113
A Soldier's Story (Bradley) 455
Sons of the Anzacs (documentary) 56–57, 303–304, 305–311, 315–316
South Tyrol Germans 71
Spanish Civil War 25–26, 27, 38
Spender, Percy 121–122, 283
Spry, Charles 164
Stack, Stephen 306
Stalag XIB and Stalag XXX 415–417
Star (Melbourne) 19, 24
Storey, George C. 56
'strategy of the indirect approach' 114–115, 378, 444–445, 455, 456, 461
The Struggle for Europe (Chester Wilmot)
  cited 6–8, 336, 345, 349, 405, 452
  contract for 395
  preparation and writing 114–115, 433, 441–442, 446, 452, 455–458
  reception and status 9, 298, 458–462
  and theory of indirect approach 377–378, 461
Sturdee, Vernon 228
Sublet, Frank 255, 259
Sudeten Germans 57–58, 61, 64–69, 71, 76, 77

Sun (Melbourne) 71
Sychrava, Dr (newspaper editor) 64–65
Syme, David 83
Syrian campaign 198–200

Thompson, William 42
Tobruk
  battle 133–141, 139(map)
  siege 195–197, 197(map), 204–213, 213(map), 215
Tobruk (Chester Wilmot)
  cited 122, 133, 137, 201–203, 204, 206, 211, 213, 217–219
  as classic 216, 298
  Curtin given copy 328–329
  CW's use of term 'British' 99
  sources for 293–298
Top Secret (Ingersoll) 450
Townsville 233, 238–239
Travers, 'Jika' 169
Treaty of Versailles 41–42
Treloar, John 294, 303
Trinity College 13, 17
Tripoli 297
Triumph of the Will (film) 49, 59
Tummar East 109–110

United States, CW's visit to 38–40
universities, CW's observations on 35, 39, 45
University Debating Society 17–18, 22
University of Melbourne 15–18, 36
Unknown Soldier's tomb 58

Vasey, George 195, 241
Vaughan-Thomas, Wynford 410
Villers-Bocage engagement 364–365
von Ribbentrop, Joachim 71
von Rundstedt, Gerd 404–405, 408, 445–446

Wallwork, Jim 330
Walton, Raymond 44–45
war correspondents, freedom of enquiry 288
'War Report' 8

appointment of CW to 314–315, 328
coverage of Operation Market Garden 379–380, 382–389
dedication of Tobruk War Cemetery 215
development 320
Dimbleby's Belsen report 417–419
dispatches on Arnhem battles 384–389
format and style 332–333
last MCN broadcast 429–430
leadership 328, 358–359, 372
liberation of Stalag XIB and Stalag XXX 415–417
Montgomery's cooperation 321–322, 327
and Operation Market Garden 379–380, 381(map), 382–389
procedures and equipment 321–322
recruitment of correspondents 327
Ward, Eddie 292
Ward, Edward 140–141, 182–183, 191, 213–215, 220
Ward Price, George 48
Wavell, Sir Archibald 98–99, 105, 149, 151, 188–190, 295–297
Weatley, Dennis 338–339
Western Desert campaigns. *see* North African campaigns
Westminster Abbey 58
What I Saw at Tobruk (Chester Wilmot) 134
White, Osmar 233, 242, 247, 251, 267, 301, *ps*
White, Sam 17–18
Williams, Edgar 'Bill' 374, 404
Williams, Ron Maslyn 152, 175, 307
Wilmot, Bung. see Wilmot, Reginald William Edward ('Bung') (CW's father)
Wilmot, Caroline (CW's daughter) *ps*
Wilmot, Chester (Reginald William Winchester)
   photos *frontispiece*, *ps*
  —*private life, opinions and character*
   birth and naming 9–10
   childhood and youth 10–12
   grief at sister's death 11

asthma illness 10–11
attends Melbourne Grammar 11–13
wins university scholarship 13
at Melbourne University 15, 17–22, 24–29
prowess as debater 12, 22, 30, 35, 39–40, 43
illnesses and asthma attacks 10–11, 113, 117, 144, 147, 149, 200, 234, 247, 369–70, 392, 411, 456
embraces student journalism 17, 19, 24
exhibits anti-Catholicism 15
romance with student 18–19
arguments with his mother 18–19
active in student politics 24, 25–28
relations with Vice Chancellor 26–29, 38–39
first meets Edith Irwin 79–81
graduation 27
unwillingness to practice law 27, 82, 430
meets ABC General Manager 30
visits Philippines, Hong Kong and Canton 30–33
visits Japan 34–38
has encounter with Japanese police 34–35
enjoys dancing 34, 62, 76
broadcasts from Tokyo to Australia 35
pro-China sympathies 36
reliance on primary sources 21, 433
dislike of Japanese militarism 36, 37–38
abandons academic plans 37
visits United States 38–40
admires Roosevelt and New Deal 40
in England and Ireland 42–45, 52–59
antipathy towards British upper class 43, 224–25
observations on universities 35, 39, 45
disdain for Chamberlain government and appeasement 42–44, 69, 73–77, 82–84
is 'ashamed to be an Englishman' 73
in Vienna 46–51

Index

witnesses Hitler's Anschluss speech 48–49
on freedom of speech 26–27
is regular movie goer 49, 55
questions authenticity of *Man of Aran* 55
broadcasts interviews with Amery and Dalton 52–54
broadcasts cricket commentaries 54, 52, 328
interviews de Valera 55
returns to Europe 59
visits Nuremberg 59–63
attends Nazi rally 62
experiences Nazi anti-Semitism 51–52
visits Prague 63–68
fears outbreak of war 63–66
visits Berlin 68–71
spots Joseph Goebbels 71
studies Danish Cooperative Farm movement 71–72
Stockholm romance 76
other romances and affairs 79–81, 76, 377, 456–58
returns to Australia 77
reports on his impressions of overseas universities 81
finds working at DOI disturbing 84–85
volunteers unsuccessfully for Second AIF 85
ill-health 10–11, 113, 117, 125, 144, 147, 149, 200, 234, 247, 369–70, 392, 411, 456
character 148–49, 190–91, 444
on value of mateship 209
on socialism 15, 40, 72, 225, 230, 432
interest in ancient Greece 153–54
marries Edith Irwin 230–32
birth of daughter 299–300
marriage relationship 299–300, 430–32, 433–35, 441, 457–58, 462
death of father 454
death 456–58

—*friendships and close relationships*
Allen 125, 137, 292
Ball 19–20, 77, 84
Benjamin 28–33, 35, 36, 38, 44–45, 49–52, 79
Cecil 86, 88, 154, 198–99, 233
Dalton 82
Foerste 82
Hurley 206, 209–10
Liddell-Hart 218, 443–46
Long 292
Montgomery 453
Parer 152, 191, 209–10, 218–19, 306
Priestly 26–29, 38–39
Rowell 163, 192, 241, 245, 260, 263, 285–86, 314–15, 329, 453
Santamaria 15
Scales 294
Smibert 19, 77
Ward (Edward) 182–83, 213–14, 220
Woodward 337–38

—*war correspondent: North Africa*
appointed ABC war correspondent 79, 84–85
leaves Melbourne for Perth 79
meets Broadcast Unit team 86–88
joins troopship in Fremantle 89–90
voyage to Middle East 91–96
designs Bethlehem Christmas programmes 101–2
covers first offensive in North Africa 105–15
asthma attacks 117, 125, 144, 147, 149, 200
records Blamey's Christmas message 117
tours Sidi Barrani battlefield 117
based at Sollum 118
has material censored 119–20, 162, 183–84, 203–4, 216, 222
ordered to record speeches by Blamey and Spender 121
misses first assaults on Bardia 121
takes revenge on Spender 122
covers Bardia action 122–25

Wilmot, Chester
—war correspondent: North Africa (cont.)
  has Christmas dinner with the Allens 125
  describes assault on Post 11: 125–30 and capture of Tobruk 133–39
  sends 'just in case' letter to his parents 134
  meets Damien Parer 137
  reports on fall of Derna 141–44
  gains Beda Fomm scoop 144–49
  amazed at ethics of British journalists 147–48
  aloofness from colleagues 148–49, 190–91
  arrival in Greece 151–56
  buys Greek primer 154
  observes action on Greek battlefront 155–62
  deals with Greek censorship 162
  trusted by senior officers 163, 184–85, 191–92
  escapes from Greece 169–75
  prepares critique of Greek and Crete campaigns 177–87
  discusses critique with Wavell 188–89
  enrages Blamey 190
  criticises Middle East Command 189–90, 224–25
  covers war in Syria 198–200
  sails for Tobruk 200–203
  relations with Morshead 203–4, 206
  covers siege of Tobruk 204–16, 218–20
  collaborates with Parer 209–10
  records Easter Battle story 210–13
  explores the Salient 213–15
  wounded by shrapnel 220
  writes on German tank tactics 220–22
  criticises Australian training methods 222–23
  returns to Australia 230
—war correspondent: New Guinea
  recommendations to ABC on war coverage 232
  covers MacArthur's first press conference 234
  warned off Blamey investigation 234–35
  records attack on Townsville 238–39
  posted to Port Moresby 238–40
  gains trust of senior officers 240, 241, 245, 260
  acts as unloader on 'biscuit bomber' 242–43
  reports on air power in New Guinea 242–43
  undertakes Kokoda march 246–60
  recounts fighting at Isurava 249, 253
  recounts and analyses Maroubra Force withdrawal 249–63
  presents case to prime minister 274, 280
  makes case against Blamey and LHQ 274–80
  on blunders of New Guinea campaign 275–80
  carpeted by Blamey 280
  Blamey withdraws CW's accreditation 281–82
  defends himself against Blamey's charges 283–89
  wins support of ABC general manager 282, 289
—war correspondent: Europe
  offered BBC Burma assignment 311–14
  Blamey's vendetta continues 314–16, 328, 352
  appointed to BBC's 'War Report' team 314–15, 328
  presented with Airborne Division beret 331–32
  anxious about D-Day mission 329–30
  on D-Day glider flight to France 330, 336–39, 340–42
  D-Day broadcasts and dispatches 336–39, 341–43, 347
  records capture of Merville battery 348–50
  covers Villers-Bocage operation 352–53

Index

methods as correspondent 353–54
covers American advances 354–56
threatened with second
  disaccreditation 356–60
exonerated by Montgomery 360–61
records launch of Operation
  Goodwood 357–58
on Caen 'breakthrough' 361–62,
  367–68
reports on tank engagements 365–66
covers Allied advance into Belgium
  370–74
dispatches from Brussels 374
intelligence contacts 374
opinion of Eisenhower 378
on invasion of Holland 380–81
Eindhoven scare 382–83
reports the taking of Nijmegen bridge
  384–87
briefs BBC Controller of News
  390–91
declines *News of the World* offer 391
covers attack on canal crossing
  392–94
dipatches on Ardennes offensive
  395–409
is propagandist for Allied unity
  406–9
coverage of Rhine crossing 410–15
describes Stalag camps 415–17
inspects Belsen 419
records German surrender at
  Luneburg Heath 421–25
reports Himmler's suicide 426–29
last MCN broadcast 429–30
tours American zone 432

attends Nuremberg trial 437–38,
  440–41
interviews Montgomery 454–55
lunches with Churchill 460–61
—publications (*see The Struggle for
  Europe; Tobruk*)
Wilmot, Edith (née Irwin; CW's wife) 22,
  79–80, 230–232, 299–300, 430–431,
  434–435, 441, 448, *ps*
  letters from CW 141–142, 153, 169–175,
  299, 330, 352, 353, 390–391
Wilmot, Geoffrey (CW's son) *ps*
Wilmot, Jane Morris (CW's daughter) 392,
  433–434, 435, *ps*
Wilmot, Janie (CW's mother) 18, 313, *ps*
Wilmot, Jean (CW's sister) 10, *ps*
Wilmot, Louise (CW's sister) 10, *ps*
Wilmot, Nancy (CW's sister) 10, *ps*
Wilmot, Reginald William Edward
  ('Bung'), (CW's father)
  death 454
  expulsion from Trinity College 13
  meeting with Montgomery 453
  photos *ps*
  political and religious views 14–15,
    77–78
  relations with Chester 14–15, 27, 36,
    77–78, 82, 282, 291, 301, 454
  as sporting journalist 10, 18–19
'The Wilmot Thesis' 367, 456
Wilson, Maitland 'Jumbo' 99, 190, 197
Woodward, David 337–338, 346, 347–348
'Wozzer' [Wazzir] incident 96
Wright, Basil 56

Youngman, Vin 17

493